STUDY GUIDE

Mark McNabb
The University of Texas at Dallas
Naveen Jindal School of Management

PEARSON

Boston Columbus Indianapolis New York San Francisco Upper Saddle River
Amsterdam Cape Town Dubai London Madrid Milan Munich Paris Montreal Toronto
Delhi Mexico Cit[y] ... Seoul Singapore Taipei Tokyo

Acquisitions Editor: Katie Rowland
Editorial Project Manager: Erin McDonagh
Project Manager: Karen Carter
Manufacturing Buyer: Carol Melville

---

1 2 3 4 5 6 7 8 9 10 OPM 16 15 14 13

www.pearsonhighered.com

PEARSON

ISBN-10: 0-13-344933-5
ISBN-13: 978-0-13-344933-4

Table of **Contents**

CHAPTER 1

Getting Started

Principles of Finance

Chapter Orientation

This book introduces finance as a means to make better business and personal decisions. Firms, nonprofit organizations, and individuals are faced with a multitude of decisions that affect their wealth at all times. The cost or benefit of a decision is scored in dollars or other unit of money. No matter what one chooses as their career and course of study, knowing sound practices in financial analysis can improve one's monetary and value outcomes.

Chapter Review: Terms and Concepts

1.1 **Finance** is the study of how businesses and individuals evaluate investments and raise capital to fund investments in their chosen alternatives.

Financial analysis of firm actions addresses three basic questions:

- **Capital budgeting** asks: what long-term investments should be pursued?
- **Capital structure** asks: how should the firm raise capital for those investments?
- **Working capital management** asks: how should the firm manage cash flows for the day-to-day operations of the firm.

Even if you do not plan to be a financial manager, many decisions faced by entrepreneurs, marketers, managers, and individuals require knowledge of the financial markets and the implications of financial actions. Even you plan to live on a trust and never work, there are many personal decisions than can be improved by applying sound financial practices to the decision process. Many of the same tools and processes used by corporations can improve your personal decisions on money, value, investment, and retirement.

1.2 There are three categories of legal forms of business organization: sole proprietorship, the partnership, and the corporation.

Sole proprietorship is a business owned by one individual; there is no legal separation between the business and its owner. The sole proprietor is held responsible for all the debts and actions of the business. Sole proprietors raise money, or capital, to invest in their business from personal funds, from family and friends, and from local banks that extend credit. The owner is personally liable for the business debts.

A **general partnership** is a business formed by two or more individuals sharing in the ownership and liability of the business as co-owners operating the business to make a profit. The partnership form allows for more owners and can raise capital more efficiently with more owners contributing for their share of **equity** (ownership). The owners are all liable for the debts and actions of the business just as a sole proprietor stands liable for his business. Income is taxed as personal income.

Limited partnership forms give some legal protection from creditors to limited junior partners who give up their management rights while retaining their ownership share. The **general partner** runs the business with full liability for the actions and debts of the business while the **limited partners** have liability for only the actual amount of their investment in the business.

Status as a **corporation** allows the business to operate as a separate entity from its owners which facilitates the raising of large sums of capital and executing business contracts.

Three advantages of corporate status:

- Liability of owners restricted to the amount of their investment in the business.
- Life of the business is not tied to the status of its investors: it has an independent legal life.
- Raising larger sums of capital is facilitated by limited liability, the ability to sell one's shares, and legal independence.

The owners, **shareholders**, elect a smaller executive group known as the **board of directors**, to appoint management and represent their best interests in the operation of the business. The largest drawback of the corporate form is the double taxation of corporate income paid out as dividends to shareholders. While proprietorships and partnerships pass income to owners without a tax at the organizational level, corporations have a separate identity which pays corporate income tax on profits and the shareholders will pay income tax on those profits distributed out of the corporation as dividends.

Entrepreneurs may not wish to raise capital in a corporate form due to the dilution of ownership created when shares are sold to outside investors. As a result, a hybrid form of organization, the **limited liability company** (LLC), combines the pass-through characterization of partnership income with the limited liability of a corporation to its owners, which may assist smaller businesses in their capital raising efforts. One drawback is that state law defines what constitutes a LLC, so some LLCs may be deemed corporations by different states.

Figure 1.1 lists the characteristics of the different business forms:

Figure 1.1
Characteristics of Different Forms of Business

Business Form	Number of Owners	Are Owners Liable for the Firm's Debts?	Do Owners Manage the Firm?	Does Ownership Change Dissolve the Firm?	Access to Capital	Taxation
Sole Proprietorship	One	Yes	Yes	Yes	Very limited	Personal Taxes
Partnership	Unlimited	Yes; each partner has unlimited liability	Yes	Yes	Very limited	Personal Taxes
Limited Partnership (with General Partners (GPs) and Limited Partners (LPs))	At least one GP, but no limit on LPs	GPs—unlimited liability LPs—limited liability	GPs—manages the firm LPs—no role in management	GPs—Yes LPs—No, can change[1]	Limited	Personal Taxes
Limited Liability Company	Unlimited	No	Yes	No	Dependent upon size	Personal Taxes

Figure 1.1 **(continued)**

Business Form	Number of Owners	Are Owners Liable for the Firm's Debts?	Do Owners Manage the Firm?	Does Ownership Change Dissolve the Firm?	Access to Capital	Taxation
Corporation	Unlimited	No	No –although managers generally have some ownership stake[2]	No	Very easy access	Double Taxation: Earnings taxed at corporate level Dividends taxed at personal level

[1]It is common for LLCs to require approval from the other partners before ownership can be transferred.
[2]Owners are not prohibited from managing the corporation.

How Does Finance Fit into the Firm's Organizational Structure?

The CFO manages the firm's overall financial affairs and usually supervises a treasurer and a controller. The treasurer manages issues affecting the capital structure and financing of the firm while the controller may deal with budgets, information processing, and producing financial statements.

Figure 1.2 shows the finance functions of a corporation and the roles of the Chief Financial Officer (CFO), the Treasurer, and the Controller.

Figure 1.2

How the Finance Area Fits into a Corporation
A firm's Vice President of Finance is many times called its Chief Financial Officer, or CFO. This person oversees all the firm's financial activities through the offices of the firm's Treasurer and Controller.

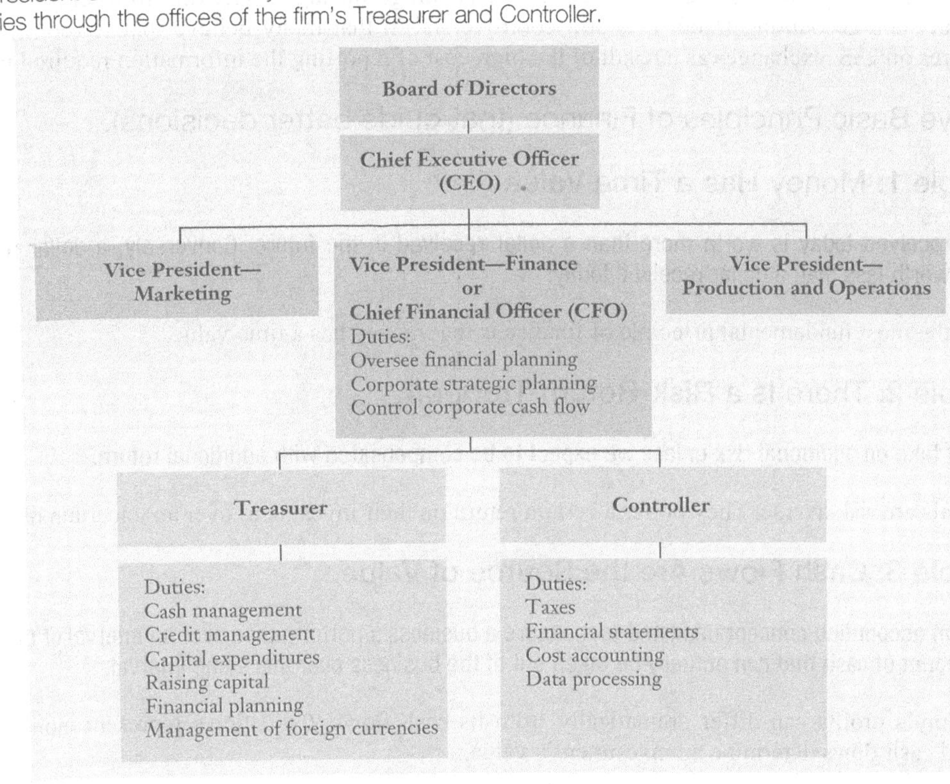

1.3 Financial managers work to improve the wealth of the firm's shareholders and must view their responsibility to improve operations for the benefit of the firm's owners.

Financial managers work in three major functions of the firm's operations:

- Making investment decisions (capital budgeting decisions).
- Making decisions on how to finance these investments (capital structure decisions).
- Managing funding for the company's day-to-day operations (working capital management).

In carrying out the above tasks, the financial managers must be aware that they are ultimately working for the firm's shareholders who are the owners of the firm.

Maximizing Shareholder Wealth

Maximizing shareholder wealth retains its place as the primary goal of any firm's management no matter how many goals are outlined in the corporate mission statement. Firms that practice good ethical behavior, good corporate ethics, will find that acting in a morally correct manner does benefit shareholders over the long term.

Ethical Considerations in Corporate Finance

Ethical behavior is necessary for long-term business and personal success.

Regulation Aimed at Making the Goal of the Firm Work: The Sarbanes-Oxley Act

The Sarbanes-Oxley Act was passed in 2002 to discourage managers at firms from engaging in financial misconduct and accounting fraud. It is still controversial in that many believe that fewer firms have listed their shares on U.S. exchanges as a result of the high cost of reporting the information required in the act.

1.4 The Five Basic Principles of Finance (that guide better decisions).

Principle 1: Money Has a Time Value.

A dollar received today is worth more than a dollar received in the future. Conversely, a dollar received in the future is worth less than a dollar received today.

Perhaps the most fundamental principle of finance is that money has a time value.

Principle 2: There Is a Risk-Return Tradeoff.

We won't take on additional risk unless we expect to be compensated with additional return.

Individuals are risk-averse. They prefer a certain return on their investment over an uncertain return.

Principle 3: Cash Flows Are the Source of Value.

Profit is an accounting concept designed to measure a business's performance over an interval of time. Cash flow is the amount of cash that can actually be taken out of the business over this same interval.

A company's profits can differ dramatically from its cash flows. Cash flows represent money that can be spent and cash flows determine an investment's value.

Principle 4: Market Prices Reflect Information.

Investors respond to new information by buying and selling their investments. The speed with which investors act and the way that prices respond to the information determines the efficiency of the market.

The prices of financial claims traded in the public financial markets respond rapidly to the release of new information.

Principle 5: Individuals Respond to Incentives.

The agency problem in finance refers to aligning the interests of managers to do what is best for shareholders. Compensation plans, the board of directors, financial markets, and the takeover market work to see that managers work for the benefit of owners.

The **agency problem** challenges those who employ managers because managers may make decisions that benefit the personal interests of management rather than the interests of owners. Compensation contracts tied to shareholder wealth will align the interests of management to maximize shareholder wealth and reduce spending on perquisites. Compensation may reduce the reluctance to issue debt when raising capital. Board of directors, auditors, bankers, credit rating agencies, and security analysts monitor the actions of management. Financial markets impound the information gathered on firm actions and results and assign a value to the firm's stock and bonds accordingly.

Answers to **Concept Checks**

Concept Check **1.1**

1. What are the three basic types of issues that arise in business and that are addressed by the study of business finance?
2. List three non-finance careers to which the study of finance applies.

Answer 1: The three basic issues addressed in finance are: working capital management, capital structure, and capital budgeting.

Answer 2: Three non-finance careers that rely on finance are accounting, marketing, and information management; but, almost every type of business and legal activity requires an understanding of financial concepts.

Concept Check **1.2**

1. What are the primary differences between a sole proprietorship, a partnership, and a corporation?
2. Explain why large and growing firms tend to choose the corporate form of organization.
3. What are the duties of a corporate treasurer?
4. What are the duties of a corporate controller?

Answer 1: A sole proprietorship and a partnership differ by the number of owners; both sets of owners bear full risk for the debts and actions of their business. The income of proprietors and partners is not taxed at the organizational level but passed through. A corporation may have a management team separate from owners and owners enjoy limited liability for the actions and debts of the corporation. Corporations suffer double taxation by paying corporate income taxes and then distributing dividends to the owners which are taxed.

Answer 2: Large and growing corporations prefer the corporate form because the limited liability status allows them to raise large sums of capital necessary to conduct operations.

Answer 3: A corporate treasurer has duties that may include cash management, credit management, capital spending analysis, capital raising responsibilities, financial planning, and currency risk management.

Answer 4: A controller has duties that may include tax compliance, financial statement preparation, cost accounting, and data processing.

Concept Check 1.3

1. What is the goal of the firm?
2. Why is ethics relevant to the financial management of the firm?
3. What was the Sarbanes-Oxley Act of 2002? What did it accomplish?

Answer 1: The primary goal of the firm is to maximize shareholder wealth.

Answer 2: Good ethical practices are consistent with shareholder wealth maximization.

Answer 3: Sarbanes-Oxley Act of 2002 attempts to regulate the business practices of management to better align them with shareholders. Sarbanes-Oxley safeguards the interests of shareholders by reducing agency costs; however, some suggest it has a great cost relative to its benefits.

Concept Check 1.4

1. What are the five principles of finance?
2. A fundamental guiding principle of investing is that higher risks require higher rewards or returns. Give two examples of the risk-return relationship.
3. What do we mean when we say that market prices reflect information?

Answer 1: The five principles of finance are: Money has a time value; there is a risk-return tradeoff; cash flows are the source of value; market prices reflect information; and individuals respond to incentives.

Answer 2: Two examples of the risk-return tradeoff are: investors require a positive expected return before they part with their cash to invest and bond investors facing more risk usually receive higher interest payments as compensation for the higher risk.

Answer 3: Market prices should immediately adjust higher on good information that was not expected by the market and adjust downward on negative information surprises.

Multiple Choice Quiz

1. Debt is
   a. the ownership interest in a corporation.
   b. an asset of the business.
   c. money that has been borrowed and must be repaid.
   d. the means to profit by the business.

2. Equity is
   a. the ownership interest in a corporation.
   b. an asset of the business.
   c. money that has been borrowed and must be repaid.
   d. the means to profit by the business.

3. Capital structure refers to
    a. the investment in current assets by the firm.
    b. the mix of long-term sources of funds after capital raising by the firm.
    c. the mix of investments picked by the firm.
    d. the shape of the firm's headquarters.

4. A general partner
    a. is the only owner of the business.
    b. has limited liability for the firm's debts.
    c. does not run the business but receives income from it.
    d. operates the business and is liable for its debts.

5. A limited partner
    a. has limited liability for the firm's debts beyond the amount invested.
    b. has limited liability for the firm's debts up to the amount invested.
    c. does not run the business and receives no income from it.
    d. operates the business but is not liable for its debts.

6. A shareholder
    a. owns bonds of a corporation.
    b. is an equity owner of a partnership.
    c. owns shares of a corporation.
    d. is fully liable for the debts of a corporation.

7. Opportunity cost
    a. is the value of an investment.
    b. is the cost to undertake the current investment by a business.
    c. is the value of the next best alternative forgone due to a business decision.
    d. is the benefit from not making an investment.

8. Which of the following is NOT a duty of the Chief Financial Officer:
    a. oversee the management team.
    b. oversee financial planning.
    c. contribute to strategic planning.
    d. control corporate cash flow.

9. A limited liability company (LLC)
    a. combines the debt liability of a partnership with the ownership of a proprietor.
    b. combines the tax liability of a corporation with the ownership of a proprietor.
    c. combines the limited liability of a partnership with the ownership of a proprietor.
    d. combines the limited liability of a corporation with the ownership of a proprietor.

10. Corporations have
    a. a limited life.
    b. a limited legal status that does not equal an individual entity.
    c. a hybrid status between owner and investor with no separate legal rights.
    d. a fully separate legal status from its owners.

Answers to **Multiple Choice Questions**

1. C
2. A
3. B
4. D
5. B
6. C
7. C
8. A
9. D
10. D

Self Test with **Solutions**

Picture the Problem

Decide on Solution Strategy

Solve

Analyze

Self Test 1

You are starting a business that will only require your services as its only employee. Friends and family have said they would give you money to start your business. What business form are you likely to use and how would you characterize their investments.

Step 1: Picture the Problem

You are starting a business that only needs a little capital and an informal structure.

Step 2: Decide on a Solution Strategy

Looking at your options of proprietorship, partnership, and corporation – you will start out as a sole proprietorship. The investments by others should be considered loans if you wish to control the fate of your business and its ownership.

Step 3: Solve

Offer to take the investments as debt and repay your investors over time with interest so you may retain full control of the business. If you need to raise more capital, then you may consider making the investors limited partners for a small percentage of ownership. The costs of incorporation will make that form of organization unnecessary.

Step 4: Analyze

Retaining full ownership keeps you motivated to improve your wealth and work harder for the success of the business. If the gains in the business were to accumulate mostly to your investors, then you are running a charity and most would choose another line of business.

CHAPTER 2

Firms and the Financial Market

Chapter **Orientation**

This chapter covers the characteristics of financial markets and the role these markets play in our lives. The material describes the role of commercial banks in our financial markets and presents the principles of risk-return tradeoffs and markets pricing information. The chapter also delineates debt and equity financial markets.

Chapter Review: **Terms and Concepts**

2.1 **The Basic Structure of U.S. Financial Markets**: where money and credit are exchanged have many participants.

There are three primary market participants:

- **Borrowers:** are businesses and individuals who need money.
- **Savers (Investors):** are individuals and businesses that have money to invest.
- **Financial Institutions (intermediaries):** bring savers and borrowers together.

2.2 **The Financial Marketplace: Financial Institutions** facilitate the movement of money from savers (individuals) to borrowers (businesses).

Borrowers must pay savers a return on their money (capital). Institutions that perform this function of raising money are called **financial intermediaries. Money markets** deal in short-term debt securities that mature in less than one year while **capital markets** deal in equity or debt securities for the long term. The financial markets work across national boundaries for individuals and firms seeking to invest or borrow.

Commercial banks, acting as intermediaries, collect the savings of individuals and established businesses and lend them out to borrowers.

Non-bank financial intermediaries providing services to businesses include:

- Financial services corporations
- Insurance companies
- Investment banks
- Investment companies (mutual funds, hedge funds, and private equity firms)

Figure 2.1

Financial Markets, Institutions, and the Circle of Money

Financial markets consist of institutions that facilitate the transfer of savings from individuals and firms with excess cash to borrowers who have less cash than they need.

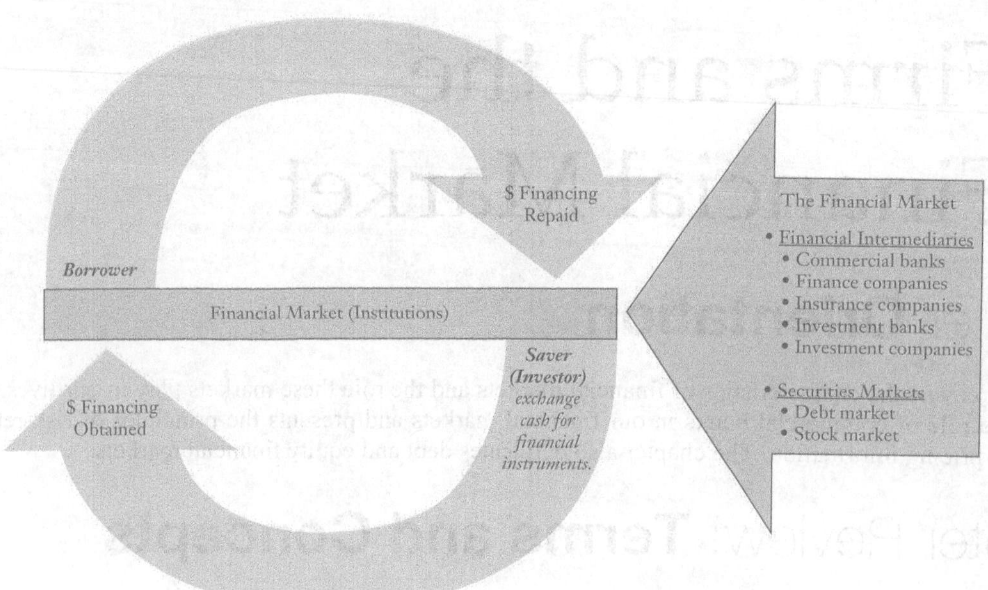

Financial services companies provide lending or leasing programs to firms and individuals. **Insurance companies** collect premiums to protect customers from specific losses to person or property. **Investment banks** provide capital raising and advisory services to business and governments. **Investment (fund) companies** pool savings of individuals and invest the proceeds into securities issued by firms and governments.

Mutual fund companies collect money directly from individuals and sell them units of various funds at their net asset value (NAV), which is a value determined usually at the end of the day depending on the value of the fund holdings. Mutual funds can be a **load fund** (with a sales charge to a broker) or **no-load fund** (with no charges and an internal sales staff). An **ETF**, or **exchange-traded fund**, is similar to a passive mutual fund traded on an exchange like a stock. ETFs and mutual funds are an inexpensive means for investors to diversify across many securities with a purchase of one fund.

Hedge funds are offered to wealthier and more financially savvy **accredited investors**, who can withstand the higher risk and illiquidity of their investments. These funds typically charge 2 and 20, 2 percent of assets and 20 percent of profits, much more than the 1 percent of assets fee of mutual funds and ETFs. **Private equity firms** are specialized investment funds. Some PE firms invest in venture capital startups; two-thirds of private equity funds are invested in leveraged buyouts of poorly performing firms in order to restructure them.

2.3 The Financial Marketplace: Securities Markets

Financial securities represent either an ownership or debt claim on firms that issue them.

Public companies have securities traded in the public financial markets. A **primary market** is where new securities are sold from the firm to an individual or institution for the first time. A primary issue raises new capital for the firm. A **secondary market** allows traders to exchange or trade previously issued securities and no new money is raised for the firm that had issued those securities.

Figure 2.2

Security Markets Provide a Link between the Corporation and Investors

Step 1: Initially, the corporation raises funds in the financial markets by selling securities (a primary market transaction). Step 2: The corporation then invests this cash in return-generating assets—new projects. Step 3: The cash flow from those assets is either reinvested in the corporation, given back to the investors, or paid to the government in the form of taxes. Step 4: Immediately after the securities have been issued, they are traded among investors in the secondary market, thereby setting their market price.

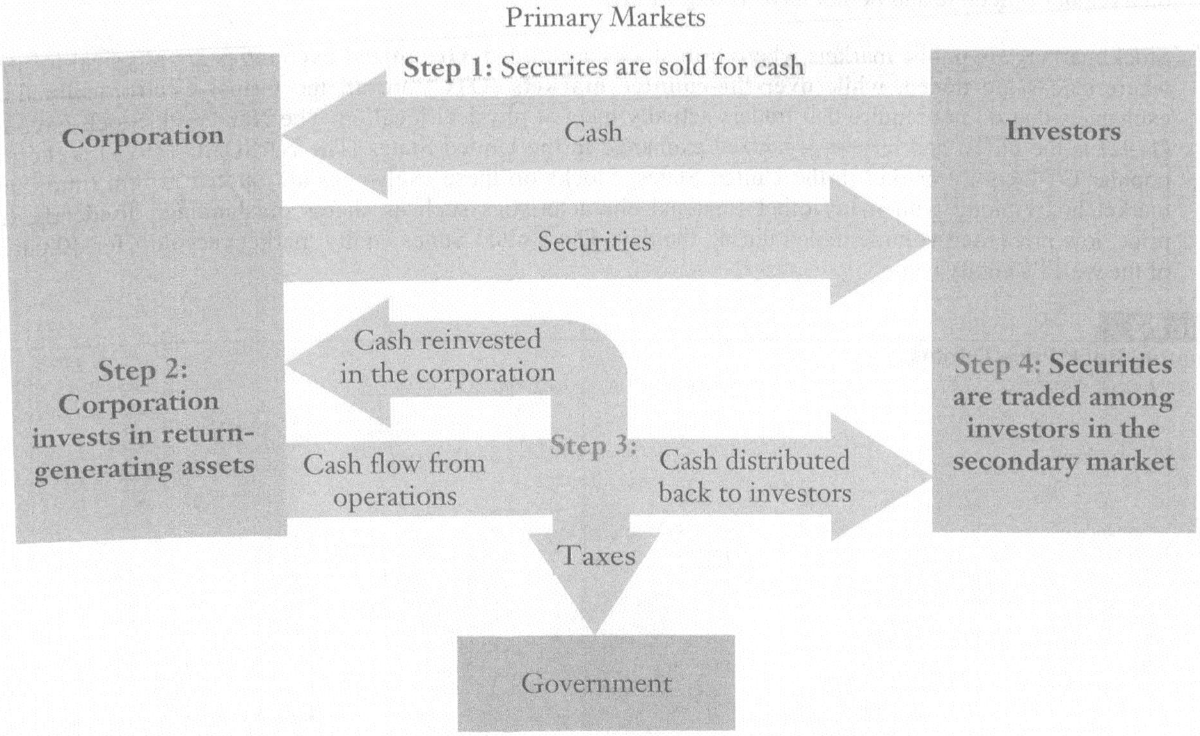

How Securities Markets Bring Corporations and Investors Together

The text lists four steps in the capital raising process in the securities markets:

Step 1: The firm sells securities to investors. Corporations raise money in the securities markets by selling either debt or equity. When the firm initially sells the securities to the public it is considered to take place in the primary markets. This is the only time the firm receives money in return for its securities.

Step 2: The firm invests the funds it raises in its business. Next, the corporation invests the cash raised in the security market in hopes that it will generate cash flows — for example, they may invest in a new restaurant, a new hotel, a factory expansion, or a new product line.

Step 3: The firm distributes the cash earned from its investments. The cash flow from the firm's investments is reinvested in the corporation, paid to the government in taxes, or distributed to the investors who own the securities issued in Step 1. In the latter case, the cash is distributed to the investors that loaned the firm money (that is, bought the firm's debt securities) through the payment of interest and principal. Cash is paid to the investors that bought equity (stock) through the payment of cash dividends or the repurchase of the shares of the firm's previously issued stock.

Step 4: Security trading in the secondary market. Immediately after the securities are sold to the public, the investors who purchase them are free to resell them to other investors. These subsequent transactions take place in the secondary market.

There are two major types of financial securities: **debt** and **equity**. Debt can have a maturity or life of a year or less and these securities are known as financial **notes,** which are sold in the money markets. Longer term maturity debts are known as **bonds** and are sold in the capital markets.

Equity securities represent ownership of the firm that issues stock. **Common stock** grants owners a residual interest in the firm, allows owners to vote on major corporate decisions and entitles owners to receive dividends. **Preferred stock** gives an owner priority on dividends and assets over the common shareholders and is a hybrid of stock and bond features. Preferred shares have some features like a common stock in that they have no maturity date, the dividends are not tax deductible for the firm, and non-payment of dividends does not cause bankruptcy. Preferred shares also are similar to bonds in that they usually pay a fixed amount on a regular timetable and do not have voting rights.

Stock markets are public markets where firm stocks are traded. **Organized exchanges** are physical locations where stocks are traded, while **over-the-counter markets** (OTC) are all the virtual electronically linked exchanges that do not require that traders actually meet at physical location. The New York Stock Exchange (1792) is the oldest and largest organized exchange in the United States. The NASDAQ (1971) is the most popular OTC equity market in the United States. Stocks on these exchanges are quoted in real time during market hours along with many other financial characteristics such as shares outstanding, dividends, high price, low price, and volume traded during the day. The United States equity markets account for 40 percent of the world's equity value.

Figure 2.3

Common Stock Price Quotes

The following is typical of what you would see if you looked at www.google.com/finance

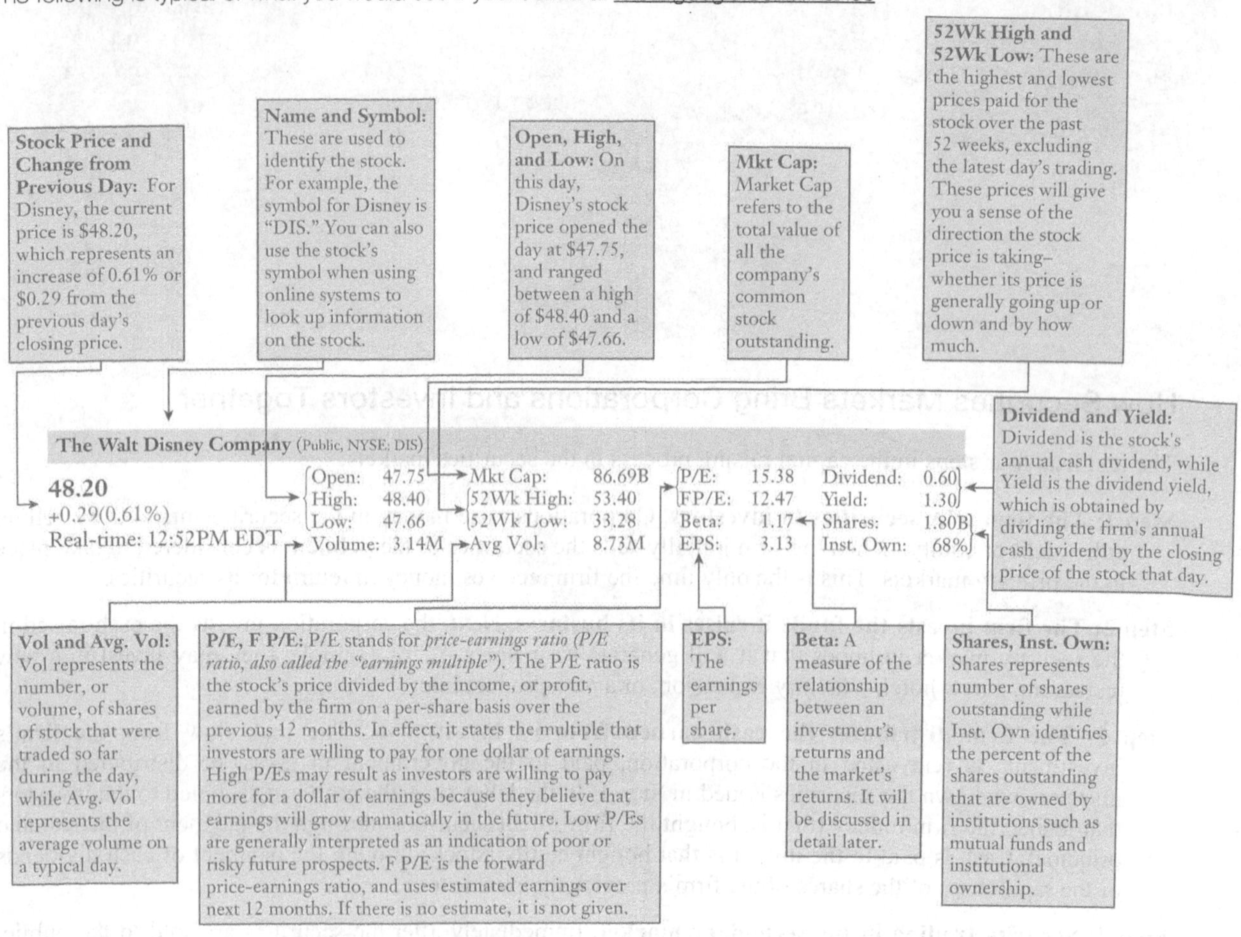

Table 2.2 lists many different financial securities and their characteristics:

Table 2.2

Characteristics of Different Financial Instruments

Money Market Debt

For the Borrower:

- Good way of inexpensively raising money for short periods of time
- Short-term rates tend to be lower than long-term rates
- Can borrow money to match short term needs
- If interest rates rise, the cost of borrowing will immediately rise accordingly

For the Investor:

- Very Liquid — you have access to your money when you need it
- Safe — generally invested in high quality investments for brief periods
- Low Returns — rates tend to be close to the rate of inflation

Instrument	Market	Major Participants	Riskiness	Original Maturity	Interest Rates*
U.S. Treasury bills	Money—Debt	Issued by U.S. Treasury	Default-free	4 weeks to 1 year	0.09% to 0.14%
Bankers' acceptances	Money—Debt	A firm's promise to pay, guaranteed by a bank	Low risk of default, dependent on the risk of the guaranteeing bank	Up to 180 days	0.23% to 0.38%
Commercial paper	Money—Debt	Issued by financially secure firms to fund operating expenses or current assets (e.g., inventories and receivables)	Low default risk	Up to 270 days	0.14% to 0.25%
Negotiable certificates of deposit (CDs)	Money—Debt	Issued by major money-center commercial banks with a denomination of at least $100,000 to large investors	Default risk depends on the strength of the issuing bank	2 weeks to 1 year	National average 0.30%
Money market mutual funds	Money—Debt	Issued by mutual funds and invested in debt obligations like Treasury bills, CDs and commercial paper, held by individuals and businesses	Low degree of risk	No specific maturity date (can be redeemed any time)	0.02% to 0.19%
Consumer credit, including credit card debt	Money—Debt	Non-mortgage consumer debt issued by banks/credit unions/ finance companies	Risk is variable	Varies	Variable depending upon the risk level

Table 2.2 (continued)

Long-Term Debt and Fixed Income Securities Market

For the Borrower:

- Interest rates are locked in over the entire life of the debt
- Has a tax advantage over common stock in that interest payments are tax deductible while dividend payments are not

For the Investor:

- Can be used to generate dependable current income
- Some bonds produce tax-free income
- Long-term debt tends to produce higher returns than short-term debt
- Less risky than common stock
- Investor can lock in an interest rate and know the future returns (assuming the issuer does not default on its payments)

Instrument	Market	Major Participants	Riskiness	Original Maturity	Interest Rates*
U.S. Treasury notes and bonds	Capital—Debt	Issued by the U.S. government to mutual funds, businesses, individuals, and foreign countries	No default risk but price will decline if interest rates rise	Notes have original maturities of 2, 5, and 10 years; bonds have original maturities greater than 10 years	0.17% to 2.31%
Federal agency debt	Capital—Debt	Issued by federal agencies (Fannie Mae, Ginnie Mae, and others) to businesses, individuals and foreign countries	Close to Treasury debt, but not obligations of the federal government, still very low risk	Up to 30 years	0.14% to 2.74%
Mortgages	Capital—Debt	Borrowings from commercial banks and savings and loan banks (S&Ls) by individuals	Risk is variable, with subprime mortgages having a good deal of risk	Up to 30 years	2.83% (15-year fixed) to 3.41% (30-year fixed)
Municipal bonds (state and local government bonds)	Capital—Debt	Issued by state and local governments to individuals, institutional investors, and foreign countries	Riskier than U.S government securities with the level of risk dependent upon the issuer, but exempt from most taxes	Up to 30 years	3.41% (30-year, AAA-rated bonds)
Corporate bonds	Capital—Debt	Issued by corporations to individuals and institutional investors	Risk is dependent upon the financial strength of the issuer, riskier than U.S. government securities but less risky than preferred and common stocks.	In general up to 40 years, however Walt Disney and Coca-Cola have issued 100-year bonds	2.11% (10-year, AAA bonds), 3.85% (20-year AAA bonds)

Table 2.2 (continued)

Preferred Stock

For the Issuer:

- Dividends can be omitted without the risk of bankruptcy
- Has the disadvantage that dividends are not tax deductible for the issuer, whereas interest payments from debt are tax deductible

For the Investor:

- To corporate investors, it has a tax advantage since at minimum, 70 percent of dividends received are tax free

Instrument	Market	Major Participants	Riskiness	Original Maturity	Interest Rates*
Preferred stocks	Capital—Equity (Preferred Stock)	Issued by corporations to individuals, other corporations, and institutional investors	Riskier than corporate bonds, less risky than common stock	No maturity date	Dependent upon risk, generally ranging from 4.03% to 8.47%

Common Stock

For the Issuer:

- The issuing firm is not legally obligated to make payments
- Does not have a maturity date
- Issuance of common stock increases creditworthiness because the firm has more investor money to cushion the firm in the case of a loss
- Has a tax disadvantage relative to debt, while interest payments are deductible for tax purposes, common stock dividends are not

For the Investor:

- Over the long run, common stock has outperformed debt-based financial assets
- Along with the increased expected return comes increased risk

Instrument	Market	Major Participants	Riskiness	Original Maturity	Interest Rates
Common stocks	Capital—Equity (Common Stock)	Issued by corporations to individuals, other corporations, and institutional investors	Risky, with dividends only paid when they are declared	No maturity date	Do not pay interest

* The yields were taken from http://online.wsj.com, http://www.bloomberg.com, http://research.stlouisfed.org, http://finance.yahoo.com, and http://www.bankrate.com, retrieved November 21, 2012.

Financial Markets and the Financial Crisis

Beginning in 2007, the United States experienced its worst banking and financial crisis since the Great Depression of the 1930s. When real estate values dropped, as our economy slowed, and highly leveraged home owners defaulted, the value of MBS (mortgage-backed securities) and the financial institutions that operated in these markets plunged. This occurred globally and shows the importance of Principle 5: Individuals Respond to Incentives. Since the banks who originated the underlying loans intended to sell the loan to a mortgage pool to be repackaged into MBS, they did not have a strong incentive to determine if the original loan was sound. The result of the financial crisis was to end the independence of major investment banks and was a catalyst to pass the Dodd-Frank Act in 2010. Dodd-Frank intends to restrict banks from repeating the mistakes that led to the financial crisis but many believe that it adds very costly bureaucracy to the finance industry.

Answers to **Concept Checks**

Concept Check **2.2**

1. Explain how individuals and firms use financial intermediaries to raise money in the financial markets.
2. How do commercial banks differ from other non-bank financial intermediaries?
3. What are examples of investment companies?
4. What is a hedge fund and how does it differ from a mutual fund?
5. What are the two principal types of private equity firms?

Answer 1: The intermediaries such as commercial bankers and funds connect savers (investors) with borrowers (users of capital, usually firms and governments).

Answer 2: Commercial banks are the first financial intermediary for most individuals and businesses. They take deposits and lend the funds out, charging interest on the loans. Unlike investment funds, commercial banks cannot own equity in companies.

Answer 3: Investment companies are mutual funds, hedge funds, and private equity firms. These are non-bank financial institutions which also include financial services companies, insurance companies, and investment banks.

Answer 4: A hedge fund has wealthy accredited investors, who are considered to be savvy, and has more regulations to satisfy when attracting clients. It may invest in a broader range of securities and bet that values fall, which is not permitted at many mutual funds. Managers of hedge funds charge higher fees.

Answer 5: The two types of private equity firms are leverage buyout funds and venture capital funds.

Concept Check **2.3**

1. What are debt and equity securities and how do they differ?
2. How is a primary market different from a secondary market?
3. How does common stock differ from preferred stock?

Answer 1: Debt securities are the liabilities of a firm and have a finite life with no voting rights. Equity securities are ownership interests of a firm, pay dividends, have voting rights in the case of common stock, and do not trigger financial default if dividends are not paid.

Answer 2: A primary market is where a firm sells newly issued securities to the public for the first time to raise capital. A secondary market trades the previously issued securities of a firm and no capital is raised for the firm's use but is exchanged between traders.

Answer 3: A common stock has voting rights and participates fully in the performance of the firm. Preferred stocks have priority over common stock in the receipt of dividends and assets and usually receive a fixed dividend payment no matter how well the firm does.

Multiple Choice **Quiz**

1. How does common stock differ from a bond?
   a. It is a liability of a corporation.
   b. It is an asset of the business.
   c. It represents money that has been borrowed and must be repaid.
   d. It is an ownership interest in the firm.

2. Credit default swaps are
   a. an ownership interest in a corporation.
   b. an asset of the business.
   c. a contract that pays off if a firm defaults or files for bankruptcy.
   d. a contract that pays off when a firm issues debt.

3. How does an ETF differ from a mutual fund?
   a. An ETF does not pay dividends.
   b. An ETF is a security.
   c. An ETF allows investors to diversify.
   d. An ETF trades on an exchange like a stock.

4. Leveraged buyout funds are operated by
   a. mutual fund companies.
   b. ETF companies.
   c. private equity firms.
   d. commercial banks.

5. A load fund
   a. gives the investor the highest returns.
   b. does not have a sales commission.
   c. pays a sales commission to brokers.
   d. pays a sales commission to the exchange.

6. Notes
   a. are the press releases by the firm's CFO.
   b. are long-term borrowings of the firm.
   c. are debts sold in the money markets.
   d. are equity securities that pay dividends.

7. Preferred stock is a hybrid security because
   a. it receives interest like a bond and is taxable like a stock.
   b. it does not have voting rights and does not have a finite life.
   c. it is paid from the same accounts as the firm's bonds and common stock.
   d. it shares in the upside of the firm's performance and paid first in default.

8. The purpose of a financial market is:
   a. to issue debt.
   b. to match those who need capital with those who have capital.
   c. to provide a physical place to trade.
   d. to issue equity.

9. A primary market
   a. allows traders to trade previously issued securities.
   b. allows banks to sell notes to their best clients.
   c. allows businesses to raise capital from the public for the first time.
   d. allows the public to borrow at near money market rates.

10. Commercial banks
    a. are often the first financial institution used by individuals and businesses.
    b. are the largest owners of american companies.
    c. lend only to businesses.
    d. perform many of the same functions as investment banks.

Answers to **Multiple Choice Questions**

1. D
2. C
3. D
4. C
5. C
6. C
7. B
8. B
9. C
10. A

Self Test **with Solutions**

Picture the Problem

Decide on Solution Strategy

Solve

Analyze

Self Test 1

An investor is seeking a safe investment that lowers the tax exposure of his investment portfolio. What securities type would accomplish that goal? If the goal was to invest with the minimum default risk, which securities type would the investor hold? What type of securities would the investor hold to profit from a business recovery?

Step 1: Picture the Problem

You are allocating investments across the many investment security types available.

Step 2: Decide on a Solution Strategy

Looking at the table on securities and their characteristics, you will find some with the desired characteristics.

Step 3: Solve

Municipal bonds pay interest that is exempt from federal income tax, which is the larger tax for many investors. The securities issued and backed by our federal government have no default risk as the US Treasury can print money to pay the claims (however, this cannot be abused). The best means to capture the gains from a recovering economy require the ownership of common stocks which lie at the most risky end of the spectrum.

Step 4: Analyze

Different investors will seek out characteristics in investment alternatives that correlate best to the risks and returns that they seek. Financial intermediaries through our financial markets supply many different securities as a result of the various demands of investors.

CHAPTER 3

Understanding Financial Statements, Taxes, and Cash Flows

Chapter Orientation

This chapter presents the characteristics of financial statements issued by firms and how to understand these disclosures. A key part of analyzing firm performance, generating a cash flow forecast, derives from information found in the firm's financial statements. This chapter explains differences between the financial information that is relevant to a financial analyst and the financial statement information presented by accountants. Cash flow as a source of corporate value is stressed in the chapter.

Chapter Review: Terms and Concepts

3.1 **Financial statements** contain important accounting information used by financial analysts and by the managers of the firm.

There are four basic financial statements:

- **Income Statement:** totals revenue, expenses, and profit over a recent quarter or year.
- **Balance Sheet:** values assets, liabilities, and owner's equity at a specific point in time.
- **Statement of Cash Flows:** reports cash inflows/outflows over a recent period.
- **Statement of Shareholders' Equity:** reports changes in common stock, preferred stock account, and the owners' retained earnings accounts.

Why Study Financial Statements?

Assess current performance—view financial condition from outside investor perspective

Monitor and control operations—analyze accounting measures and performance for executive compensation, credit and cost pricing decisions

Forecast future performance—use current financials as a baseline for forecasting

Earnings and cash flows are not the same and one can be positive while the other is negative.

What Are the Accounting Principles Used to Prepare Financial Statements?

Revenue Recognition Principle—Revenue that should be reported for a certain period should result from when (1) the firm's goods and services were exchanged for cash or accounts receivable or (2) the firm has completed the sale and is entitled to the cash. The general rule counts a sale when the goods sold leave the firm's premises.

Matching Principle—Costs that should be reported are those costs associated when the product of the work is sold.

Historical Cost Principle—Most assets and liabilities are reported on the balance sheet at their historical cost, not their market value.

3.2 The Income Statement

An income statement measures the amount of profit earned, usually in a quarter or year.

Revenues (or Sales) – Expenses = Profits

This financial statement follows the principles of revenue recognition and expense matching. Table 3.1 presents the income statement of H. J. Boswell and is described below.

Reading and Interpreting Boswell's Income Statement

Recall from Equation (3–1) that the income statement contains three basic elements: revenues, expenses, and profits. We will use these elements to analyze each of the components of the income statement found in Table 3.1:

1. Revenues. Sales totaled $2,700 million for the 12-month period ended December 31, 2013.
2. Cost of Goods Sold. Next we see that the firm spent $2,025 million on **cost of goods sold,** the cost of producing or acquiring the products or services that the firm sold during the period.
3. Gross Profit. Subtracting cost of goods sold from revenues produces a gross profit of $675 million.
4. Operating Expenses. Operating expenses include salaries paid to the firm's administrative staff, the firm's electric bills, and so forth. One operating expense is depreciation expense ($135 million for Boswell in 2013). **Depreciation expense** is the expensing or allocation of the cost of the firm's long-lived assets (like its plant and equipment) over the useful lives of the assets.
5. Net operating Income. After deducting $292.50 million in operating expenses, Boswell's *net operating income* is $382.50 million. The firm's **net operating income** shows us profits from its ongoing operations—before it makes interest payments and pays its taxes. For our purposes net operating income will be synonymous with **earnings before interest and taxes** or **EBIT**.
6. Interest Expense. Financing costs is the interest paid on money the firm borrowed. In this instance Boswell incurred interest expense equal to $67.50 million during 2013.
7. Earnings before Taxes. Subtract Boswell's interest expense of $67.50 million from its operating income of $382.50 million to determine its earnings before taxes of $315 million.
8. Income Taxes. Next, we determine the firm's income tax obligation of $110.25 million.
9. Net Income. The income statement's bottom line is **net income**. By subtracting the tax liability of $110.25 million from earnings before taxes of $315 million leaves net income of $204.75 million.

Table 3.1 **H. J. Boswell, Inc.**

Income Statement (expressed in millions, except per share data) for the Year Ended December 31, 2013

Sales		$ 2,700.00
Cost of goods sold		(2,025.00)
Gross profits		$ 675.00
Operating expenses:		
Selling expenses	$ (90.00)	
General and administrative expense	(67.50)	
Depreciation and amortization expense	(135.00)	
Total operating expense		(292.50)
Operating income (EBIT or earnings before interest and taxes)		$ 382.50
Interest expense		(67.50)
Earnings before taxes		$ 315.00
Income taxes		(110.25)
Net income		$ 204.75
Additional information:		
Dividends paid to stockholders during 2013		$ 45.00
Number of common shares outstanding		90.00
Earnings per share (EPS)		$ 2.28
Dividends per share		$ 0.50

Income from operating activities

Cost of debt financing

Cost of corporate income taxes

Net Income Income resulting from operating and financing

Evaluating Boswell's per Share Earnings and Dividends

We calculate earnings per share by dividing net income by outstanding shares and dividends per share by total dividends by outstanding shares.

Connecting the Income Statement and Balance Sheet

The remaining part of earnings that were not paid out in dividends, retained earnings, flow to the retained earnings account on the balance sheet.

Interpreting Firm Profitability Using the Income Statement

To assess the financial performance in terms of profitability, divide gross profit, operating income, and net income by sales to find profit margins useful in historical or peer comparisons.

Gross profit margin is 25 percent ($675 million of gross profits ÷ $2,700 million of sales = 25%). Since the gross profit equals revenues minus the firm's cost of goods sold, the **gross profit margin** indicates the firm's "mark-up" on its cost of goods sold per dollar of sales. Note that the percent mark-up is generally expressed as a percentage of the firm's cost of goods sold. That is, the mark-up percentage equals gross profit divided by cost of goods sold or $675 million $2,025 million = 33.3%.

Operating profit margin is only 14.2 percent ($382.5 million of net operating income ÷ $2,700 million of sales = 14.2%). The **operating profit margin** is equal to the ratio of net operating income or **earnings before interest and taxes (EBIT)** divided by firm sales.

Net profit margin is only 7.6 percent of firm revenues (7.6% = $204.75 million of net profits ÷ $2,700 million of sales). The **net profit margin** captures the effects of all the firm's expenses and indicates the percentage of revenues left over after interest and taxes have been considered.

GAAP and Earnings Management

While firms comply with generally accepted accounting practices, firms do smooth earnings between years to influence investor and creditor opinion as well as compensation. Because of Principle 5: Individuals Respond to Incentives, owners require audited financial statements to see that corporate performance is reported accurately. The audit opinion follows GAAP to provide reasonable assurance that the financial statements are presented fairly, in all material respects, and/or give a true and fair view in accordance with the financial reporting framework.

3.3 Corporate Taxes

Taxes are a critical factor when determining cash flow.

Computing Taxable Income

Taxes are computed on earnings before taxes, which comes after interest expense on the income statement. Tax liability is the product of a tax rate multiplied by taxable income. The federal income tax is the larger income tax but firms also may pay state and local income taxes.

Federal Income Tax Rates for Corporate Income

For 2013 the corporate income tax rates in the United States were as follows:

Taxable Income	Marginal Tax Rate
$0–$50,000	15%
$50,001–$75,000	25%
$75,001–$100,000	34%
$100,001–$335,000	39%
$335,001–$10,000,000	34%
$10,000,001–$15,000,000	35%
$15,000,001–$18,333,333	38%
Over $18,333,333	35%

Marginal and Average Tax Rates

Firms should consider the tax paid on each additional dollar earned, the marginal tax rate. The average rate equals the total taxes paid divided by total earnings before tax. Most analyses assume 35 percent is the typical corporate tax rate.

Dividend Exclusion for Corporate Shareholders

To avoid double taxation (which is detrimental to investment in the corporate sector), Congress allows corporations to exclude 70 percent to 100 percent of the dividends they receive from taxation depending on how much of the dividend paying firm's stock is owned by the receiver.

A firm pays income tax on dividends according to the following chart:

Ownership Interest	Dividend Exclusion	Dividend Income	Taxable Income
< 20%	70%	$100,000	$30,000
20% to 79%	75%	$100,000	$25,000
80% or more	100%	$100,000	$0

3.4 The Balance Sheet

A balance sheet is a snapshot of a firm's financial position on a specific date.

A balance sheet is defined by the following equation:

Total Assets = Total Liabilities + Total Shareholders' Equity

Total liabilities equal total money owed to creditors. Total shareholders' equity is the difference between total assets and total liabilities and also is known as **book value**.

Assets are usually reported on the balance sheet at **historical cost**, the amount spent to acquire the asset. Cash and marketable securities are reported at the lower amount of historical cost or at **market value**, the value it would sell for in a competitive market. Net **property, plant, and equipment** is the historical cost less accumulated depreciation (a charge against the value of a fixed asset).

The balance sheet totals the book value of the assets which is rarely the same as market value.

Table 3.2 presents the balance sheet of H. J. Boswell.

Table 3.2 **H. J. Boswell, Inc.**

Balance Sheet ($ millions)
December 31, 2012 and 2013

Assets	2012	2013	Liabilities and Owners' Equity	2012	2013
Cash	$ 94.50	$ 90.00	Accounts payable	$ 184.50	$ 189.00
Accounts receivable	139.50	162.00	Accrued expenses	45.00	45.00
Inventory	229.50	378.00	Short-term notes	63.00	54.00
Other current assets	13.50	13.50	Total current liabilities	$ 292.50	$ 288.00
Total current assets	$ 477.00	$ 643.50	Long-term debt	720.00	771.75
Gross plant and equipment	1,669.50	1,845.00	Total liabilities	$1,012.50	$1,059.75
Less accumulated depreciation	(382.50)	(517.50)	Common stockholders' equity		
Net plant and equipment	$1,287.00	$1,327.50	Common stock–par value	45.00	45.00
Total assets	$1,764.00	$1,971.00	Paid-in capital	324.00	324.00
			Retained earnings	382.50	542.25
			Total common stockholders' equity	$ 751.50	$ 911.25
			Total liabilities and stockholders' equity	$1,764.00	$1,971.00

Legend:

Assets: The Left-Hand Side of the Balance Sheet

Current Assets. Assets that the firm expects to convert into cash in 12 months or less. Examples include cash, accounts receivable, inventories, and other current assets.

- **Cash.** Every firm must have some cash on hand at all times because cash expenditures can sometimes exceed cash receipts.
- **Accounts receivable.** The amounts owed to the firm by its customers who purchased on credit.
- **Inventory.** Raw materials that the firm utilizes to build its products, partially completed items or work in process, and finished goods held by the firm for eventual sale.
- **Other current assets.** All current assets that do not fall into one of the named categories (cash, accounts receivable, and so forth). Prepaid expenses (prepayments for insurance premiums, for example) are a common example of an asset in this catch-all category.

Gross Plant and Equipment. The sum of the original acquisition prices of plant and equipment still owned by the firm.

Accumulated Depreciation. The sum of all the depreciation expenses charged against the prior year's revenues for fixed assets that the firm still owns.

Net Plant and Equipment. The undepreciated value of the firm's plant and equipment.

Liabilities and Stockholders' Equity: The Right-Hand Side of the Balance Sheet

Current Liabilities. Liabilities that are due and payable within a period of 12 months or less. Examples include the firm's accounts payable, accrued expenses, and short-term notes.

- **Accounts payable.** The credit suppliers extended to the firm when it purchased items for its inventories.
- **Accrued expenses.** Liabilities that were incurred in the firm's operations but not yet paid. For example, the company's employees might have done work for which they will not be paid until the following week or month. The wages owed by the firm to its employees are recorded as accrued wages.
- **Short-term notes.** Debts created by borrowing from a bank or other lending source that must be repaid in 12 months or less.

Long-Term Debt. All firm debts that are due and payable more than 12 months in the future. A 25-year mortgage loan used to purchase land or buildings is an example of long-term liability. If the firm has issued bonds, the portion of those bonds that is not due and payable in the coming 12 months is also included in long-term debt.

Common Stockholders' Equity. Common stockholders are the residual owners of a business. They receive whatever income is left over after the firm has paid all of its expenses. In the event the firm is liquidated, the common stockholders receive only what is left over—but never lose more than they invested— after the firm's other financial obligations have been paid.

The Balance Sheet of H. J. Boswell

At the end of 2013, Boswell owned $1,971 million in total assets, had debts totaling $1,059.75 million, and had total common shareholders' equity of $911.25 million.

Assets: The Left-Hand Side of the Balance Sheet

Current Assets

Current assets consist of the firm's cash plus other assets the firm expects to convert to cash within 12 months or less. Boswell had current assets of $643.5 million at the end of 2010, comprised principally of its **inventories** of $378 million, which include raw materials used to make the firm's products, goods in process and finished goods that are ready for sale, and its accounts receivable of $162 million which reflects the value of prior credit sales that have not been collected.

Fixed Assets

Fixed assets are assets that the firm does not expect to sell within one year. These include plant and equipment, land and other investments that are expected to be held for an extended period of time and frequently cannot be easily converted to cash. Boswell has **gross plant and equipment** totaling $1,845 million at the end of 2013. This total represents the combined historical dollar amounts the firm has paid to acquire fixed assets. **Net plant and equipment** is equal to gross plant and equipment less **accumulated depreciation** expense. The latter is the sum of all depreciation expenses deducted in the firm's income statement in previous periods for the plant and equipment.

Liabilities and Stockholders' Equity: The Right-Hand Side of the Balance Sheet

H. J. Boswell Inc. has borrowed a total of $1,059.75 million and raised $911.25 million in equity to finance its total investment in firm assets.

Current Liabilities

Boswell's **current liabilities** represent the amount that the firm owes to creditors that must be repaid within a period of 12 months or less. Typically a firm's current liabilities will include **accounts payable** which is what the firm owes its suppliers for items purchased for its inventories and **notes payable** which are short-term loans to banks and other creditors. Current liabilities totaled $288 million at the end of 2013.

Long-Term Debt

The firm also owed $771.75 million in **long-term debt** like loans from banks and other lenders that have maturities longer than one year. This also includes bonds sold by the firm in the public markets.

Shareholders' Equity

The stockholders' equity account is broken down into the following components:

Par value is the value of a share before it is sold to the public, usually a nominal amount ($1).

Paid in capital is the amount paid above the par value or $324 million over the $45 million par value for Boswell.

Retained earnings are the portion of net income retained and not paid out as dividends. Boswell has retained a total of $542.25 million over the course of its existence.

Stockholders' equity is the sum of the par value of stock plus paid in capital plus retained earnings.

$$\begin{matrix}\text{Stockholders'} \\ \text{Equity}\end{matrix} = \begin{matrix}\text{Par Value of} \\ \text{Common Stock}\end{matrix} + \begin{matrix}\text{Paid in} \\ \text{Capital}\end{matrix} + \begin{matrix}\text{Retained} \\ \text{Earnings}\end{matrix} \tag{3–3}$$

Shareholders' equity can be thought of as the difference between total assets and total liabilities.

$$\begin{pmatrix}\text{Stockholders'}\\ \text{Equity}\end{pmatrix} = \begin{pmatrix}\text{Total}\\ \text{Assets}\end{pmatrix} - \begin{pmatrix}\text{Total}\\ \text{Liabilities}\end{pmatrix} \tag{3–4}$$

Firm Liquidity and Net Working Capital

Firm liquidity refers to its ability to convert assets into cash. Liquidity considers both the speed that an asset is converted and the loss in value due to conversion. Highly liquid assets convert to cash quickly at their full value. The firm's overall liquidity can be described by its **net working capital** condition, current assets minus current liabilities seen in Figure 3.1.

$$\begin{matrix}\text{Net Working}\\ \text{Capital}\end{matrix} = \begin{pmatrix}\text{Current}\\ \text{Assets}\end{pmatrix} - \begin{pmatrix}\text{Current}\\ \text{Liabilities}\end{pmatrix} \tag{3–5}$$

Figure 3.1

The Balance Sheet

The balance sheet represents a snapshot of the firm. Specifically, it lists the assets the firm has acquired, classified as current and long-term (or fixed) assets, as well as the sources of financing the firm has used to finance the acquisition of its assets. Net working capital is an important measure of a firm's ability to pay its bills on time and is equal to the difference in the dollar amount of current assets (assets the firm expects to convert to cash within the year) and current liabilities (debts the firm must repay within the year). Stockholders' equity is the total investment of the firm's owners in the firm and is equal to the difference in total assets and total liabilities.

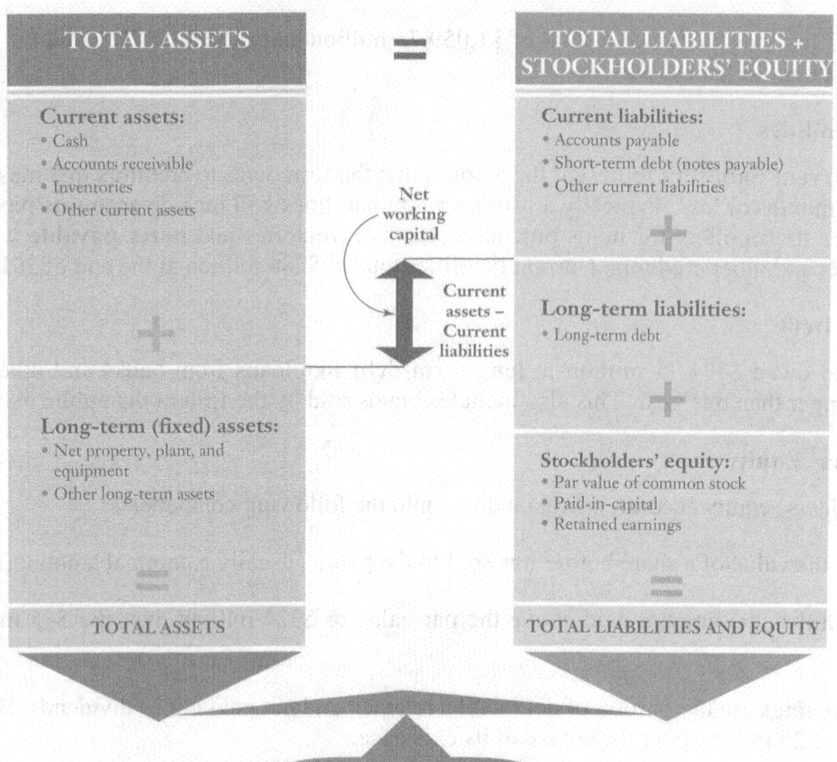

Debt and Equity Financing

The right hand side of the balance sheet shows sources of financing used in the business on the left hand side. Debts are borrowings and equity equals the money the owners provided by purchasing stock in the firm plus the retained earnings of the firm. Equity owners have a residual claim on the firm's income while debt owners have a priority over equity owners in the case of a bankruptcy.

Book Values, Historical Costs, and Market Values

Book values differ from market values for two reasons: inflation and asset depreciation. Book values can have little in common with the actual market value of the firm.

3.5 The Cash Flow Statement

The cash flow statement reports inflows and outflows of cash (sources and uses) during a period usually a quarter or a year to explain the change in cash.

$$\text{Change in Cash Balance} = \text{Ending Cash Balance} - \text{Beginning Cash Balance} \quad (3\text{–}6)$$

Sources and Uses of Cash

A source of cash brings cash into the firm and a use of cash causes cash to leave the firm. Increases in assets use cash while increases in liabilities and equity financing are sources of cash. Profits are sources while dividends are a use of cash.

We can summarize all the sources and uses of cash for Boswell in 2013 using the following criteria for identifying sources and uses of cash:

Sources of Cash	Uses of Cash
Decrease in an asset account	Increase in an asset account
Increase in a liability account	Decrease in a liability account
Increase in an owners' equity account	Decrease in an owners' equity account

For Boswell, we summarize sources and uses of cash for 2013 as follows ($ millions):

Sources of Cash:

Increase in accounts payable	$ 4.50	
Increase in long-term debt	51.75	
Increase in retained earnings	159.75	
Total Sources of Cash		$ 216.00

Uses of Cash

Increase in accounts receivable	$ 22.50	
Increase in inventory	148.50	
Increase in net plant and equipment	40.50	
Decrease in short-term notes	9.00	
Total Uses of Cash		$ 220.50

Change in Cash Balance = Sources of Cash – Uses of Cash = $216.00 – 220.50 =$ (4.50)

H. J. Boswell's Cash Flow Statement

Sources and uses of cash are classified into three broad categories:

Operating Activities—the core business activities of the firm

Investment Activities—the purchase or sale of long-term assets (PP&E).

Financing Activities—sources/uses from debt and equity changes including dividends.

The basic format of the statement is the following:

Beginning Cash Balance

Plus: Cash Flow from Operating Activities

Plus: Cash Flow from Investing Activities

Plus: Cash Flow from Financing Activities

Equals: Ending Cash Balance

The key learning point is that the cash flow statement provides a detailed account of the major decisions that the firm's management made during the period that had an effect on the firm's sources and uses of cash. Analysts can look at the operating activities to see whether the firm's operations are generating cash or review the firm's investing activities for clues as to whether the firm is still growing by increasing its expenditures for new capital equipment. Analysts can use the financing activities section to analyze how the firm finances its operations.

Quality of Earnings—Evaluating Cash Flow from Operations

By comparing cash flow growth to earnings growth, we can gain a better understanding of the firm's performance.

$$\text{Quality of Earnings} = \frac{\text{Cash Flow from Operations}}{\text{Net Income}}$$

Sustainable Capital Expenditures—Evaluating Investment Activities

By comparing cash generated by the business to cash needed to invest in capital expenditures (usually a three-year average), analysts can judge if the firm is dependent upon financial markets for its investments.

$$\text{Capital Acquisitions Ratio} = \frac{\text{Cash Flow from Operations}}{\text{Cash Paid for Capital Expenditures (CAPEX)}}$$

Table 3.4 **H. J. Boswell, Inc.**

Statement of Cash Flow for the Year Ending December 31, 2013

($ millions)

Ending cash balance for 2012 (beginning balance for 2013)			**$94.50**
Operating Activities			
Net income	$204.75		
Increase in accounts receivable	(22.50)		
No change in other current assets			
Depreciation expense	135.00		
Increase in accounts payable	4.50		
No change in accrued expenses			
Cash flow from operating activities		*$ 173.25*	
Investing activities			
Purchases of plant and equipment	(175.50)		
Cash flow from investing activities		*(175.50)*	
Financing activities			
Decrease in short-term notes	(9.00)		
Increase in long-term debt	51.75		
Cash dividends paid to shareholders	$ (45.00)		
Cash flow from financing activities		*(2.25)*	
Increase (decrease) in cash during the year			*$ (4.50)*
Ending cash balance for 2013			**$90.00**

Applying the Principles of Finance to Chapter 3:

Principle 1: Money has a time value. A firm's financial statements do not reflect the time value of money.

Principle 3: Cash flows are the source of value. Accounting statements can be used to develop current cash flow estimates and to determine the potential of the firm to generate future cash flows.

Principle 4: Market Prices Reflect Information. Investors and values of firms react to new information on the firm by the buying and selling of securities. The efficiency of the market is determined by the speed of and the reactions to value changes.

Principle 5: Individuals Respond to Incentives. Managers respond to incentives. Shareholders want managers to make decisions that increase shareholder value.

Answers to **Concept Checks**

Concept Check **3.1**

1. Name the four basic financial statements that make up the published financial reports of a firm and describe the basic function of each.
2. What are the three uses of a firm's financial statements for the firm's management?
3. Describe the revenue recognition, matching, and historical cost principles as they are applied in the construction of a firm's financial statements.

Answer 1: The income statement presents the revenues and expenses of the firm for a period, usually a quarter or a year. The balance sheet describes the assets, liabilities, and shareholders' equity of the firm at a specific point in time. The statement of cash flows shows the inflows and outflows of money over a period, usually a quarter or a year. The statement of shareholders' equity shows the changes in common stock, preferred stock, and retained earnings over a period of time.

Answer 2: Management use financial statements to monitor and control operations such as compensation, credit, and cost pricing to assess current financial performance, and to forecast future performance.

Answer 3: Revenue recognition principles report revenue in the period that the good or service is considered to be sold and the firm is entitled to the cash. Matching principle will have firms report costs that are associated with the product or service sold during the period. The historical cost principle report most assets and liabilities at historical costs, not market value.

Concept Check **3.2**

1. What information can we derive from a firm's income statement?
2. List the entries in the income statement.
3. What does the acronym GAAP stand for?

Answer 1: The income statement contains three elements: revenues, expenses, and profits over a period, usually a quarter or a year.

Answer 2: The entries in an income statement are:

	Revenues (Sales)	
-	Cost of Goods Sold (CGS)	
	=	Gross Profit
-	Operating Expenses	
	=	Net Operating Income
-	Interest Expense	
	=	Earnings Before Taxes
-	Income Taxes	
	=	Net Income

Answer 3: GAAP is generally accepted accounting principles, which are accounting principles that represent industry and government conventions on accounting practices.

Concept Check **3.3**

1. What is the difference between the average and marginal tax rates?
2. What is the marginal tax rate for a firm that currently earns $75,000 in earnings before taxes and expects to earn $80,000 next year?
3. How are dividends received by corporations taxed?

Answer 1: Average tax rates are the percentage of tax paid on all income while marginal tax rates are the percentage of tax paid on one additional dollar of earnings.

Answer 2: For a company that earns $80,000, or $5,000 above the $75,000 tax bracket, the tax rate on every dollar will be 34 percent on the earnings over $75,000.

Answer 3: Dividends are partially taxed if received by corporations. For firms that own up to 20 percent of the dividend paying firm, they may exclude 70 percent of the dividend income. For firms that own between 20 percent and 79 percent, they may exclude 75 percent of the dividend income. For firms that own 80 percent of the dividend paying firm, they may exclude all of the dividend income.

Concept Check **3.4**

1. Describe the basic categories of assets and liabilities reported in a firm's balance sheet.
2. What does the term *net working capital* mean and how is it computed?

Answer 1: The basic categories of assets and liabilities on a balance sheet are current assets, fixed or long-term assets, current liabilities, long-term debt, and shareholders' equity.

Answer 2: Net working capital is equal to current assets less current liabilities. It is the net amount of capital generated or used by the operations of the firm and is a liquidity measure.

Concept Check **3.5**

1. Describe the content and purpose of the cash flow statement.
2. Is an increase in accounts receivable a source of cash or a use of cash? Explain.
3. Is a decrease in accounts payable a source or use of cash? Explain.
4. When an asset balance increases this indicates that the firm has more of that asset, so why is this a use of cash?

Answer 1: The cash flow statement describes management decisions affecting the sources and uses of cash to explain the change in cash on a balance sheet during a period, usually a quarter or a year. The statement of cash flow answers questions about the firm's actions over a period.

Answer 2: An increase in accounts receivable is a use of cash. Increases in assets require the firm to spend its cash to grow the asset. The firm is using its own cash to lend to customers.

Answer 3: The decrease in accounts payables is a use of cash as decreases in liabilities remove funds from the firm.

Answer 4: To increase the amount of assets, a firm must spend cash to buy them. An increase in asset balances is a use of cash.

Multiple Choice **Quiz**

1. Accounts receivable are
   a. credit supplied but not yet sold.
   b. credit sold but not yet extended.
   c. credit extended to the firm.
   d. credit sales that have not yet been collected.

2. Paid in capital is the
   a. difference between assets and liabilities.
   b. sum of par value and retained earnings.
   c. amount collected for stock sold above par value.
   d. nominal value placed on common stock.

3. Marginal tax rates are
   a. always lower than the average tax rate.
   b. the rate paid on one more dollar of earnings.
   c. the rate paid on total dollar earnings.
   d. always equal to the corporate average tax rate.

4. Net operating income is
   a. the bottom line income in an income statement.
   b. the pretax earnings number, EBT.
   c. Sales – CGS – Operating Expenses or EBIT.
   d. Gross Profit –Interest.

5. A liquid asset can be sold
   a. quickly at or near market value.
   b. quickly at or near historical cost.
   c. at a profit in a matter of weeks.
   d. in a reasonable time for a reasonable amount.

6. Net plant and equipment is the sum of equipment
   a. bought at market value.
   b. bought at historical cost less accumulated depreciation.
   c. bought at market value less accumulated depreciation.
   d. bought at historical cost less annual depreciation.

7. Retained earnings are the sum of
   a. previous years' earnings less dividends.
   b. previous years' earnings that were not retained.
   c. previous dividends paid.
   d. historical cost of earnings.

8. A statement of cash flows has which three parts?
   a. operating, investing, and equity.
   b. operating, liability, and equity.
   c. operating, investing, and financing.
   d. assets, Liabilities, and Equity.

9. Net working capital equals
   a. Assets – Liabilities.
   b. Current Assets –Current Liabilities.
   c. PPE – Inventory.
   d. Paid in capital –Par.

10. Corporations consider dividend income different from interest income because they may
    a. exclude some or all dividends from tax based on ownership.
    b. exclude all interest from tax.
    c. pay a lower rate on dividends.
    d. exempt dividends from state income tax.

Answers to **Multiple Choice Questions**

1. D
2. C
3. B
4. C
5. A
6. B
7. A
8. C
9. B
10. A

Self Test **with Solutions**

Picture the Problem

Decide on Solution Strategy

Solve

Analyze

Self Test 1: Financial Statements

Construct an Income Statement and a Balance Sheet from the following accounts; use Long Term Debt to make the Balance Sheet total correctly.

Accounts Payable	10,000
Accounts Receivable	15,000
Accrued Expenses	30,000
Accumulated Depreciation	80,000
Cash	25,000
Common Equity	100,000
Cost of Goods Sold	50,000
Gross Profit	220,000
Income Taxes 35%	______
Interest Expense	40,000
Inventories	40,000
Long-Term Debt	______
Net PPE	200,000
Operating Expenses	80,000
PPE	280,000
Revenues	270,000
Short-Term Notes	60,000

Step 1: Picture the Problem

The balance sheet is comprised of two basic components: the firm's investments in assets (the left column) and the sources of financing for those assets (the right column):

Current assets Cash Accounts receivable Inventories Other current assets Total current assets	**Current liabilities** Accounts payable Short-term debt (notes payable) Other current liabilities Total current liabilities
	Long-term liabilities Long-term debt
Long-term (fixed) assets Gross property, plant and equipment Less: Accumulated depreciation Net property, plant and equipment Other long-term assets Total long-term assets	**Owners' equity** Par value of common stock Paid in capital Retained earnings Total equity
Total assets	**Total liabilities and owners' equity**

Whereas the balance sheet represents a picture of the firm's assets and sources of financing at a point in time, the income statement in contrast measures the flow of revenues or sales into the firm and expenses incurred in generating those revenues out of the firm over a range of time. The standard form of the income statement can be envisioned as follows:

Revenues recognized as having been earned during the period
Less: Cost of the goods and services sold
Equals: Gross Profit
Less: Operating Expenses (including depreciation, sales and administrative expenses
Equals: Net Operating Income (Profit)
Less: Interest Expense
Equals: Earnings before Taxes
Less: Income Taxes
Equals: Net Income

Step 2: Decide on a Solution Strategy

The income statement is defined in Equation (3-1) as follows:

$$\text{Revenues} - \text{Expenses} = \text{Profits}$$

The balance sheet is defined in Equation (3-2) as follows:

$$\text{Total Shareholders' Equity} + \text{Total Liabilities} = \text{Total Assets}$$

Identifying the various entries by category we can construct the two statements.

Step 3: Solve

a. The income statement follows:

Revenues	270,000
CGS	50,000
Gross Profit	220,000
Operating Expenses	80,000
Net Operating Income	140,000
Interest Expense	40,000
Earnings Before Tax	100,000
Income Tax	35,000
Net Income	65,000

b. The balance sheet follows:

Cash	25,000	Accounts Payable	10,000
Accounts Receivable	15,000	Short-term Notes	60,000
Inventories	40,000	Accrued Expenses	30,000
Current Assets	80,000	Current Liabilities	100,000
PPE	280,000	Long Term Debt	80,000
Accumulated Depreciation	80,000	Common Equity	100,000
Net PPE	200,000		
Total Assets	280,000	Total Liabilities and Equity	280,000

Step 4: Analyze

To balance the liabilities and owners equity with total assets, long-term debt must be $80,000.

Self Test 2: Statement of Cash Flow

Construct a Statement of Cash Flows from the following and find cash from operating activities, investments, financing activities, and total change in cash.

Capital Expenditures	90,000
Changes in Working Capital	–30,000
Debt Issuance	70,000
Depreciation Expense	50,000
Dividends Paid	15,000
Net Income	65,000
Stock Retirement	20,000

Solution:

Step 1: Picture the Problem

The statement of cash flow combines information from the income statement and balance sheet to identify from where the firm received cash and how it was spent during the period. The sources and uses of cash are categorized into one of three categories: operating activities, investing activities, and financing activities. Adding sources and subtracting sources of cash from the beginning cash balance explains the firm's ending cash balance as follows:

Beginning Cash Balance

Plus: Cash flow from operating activities

Plus: Cash flow from investing activities

Plus: Cash flow from financing activities

Equals: Ending Cash Balance

Step 2: Decide on a Solution Strategy

The firm's cash flow statement provides a rich source of information that can be used to discover what the firm has done that required the expenditure of cash or gave rise to an inflow of cash. To analyze the firm's sources and uses of cash we can focus on each of the major segments of the statement: cash flows from operations, cash flows from investing activities, and cash flows from financing activities.

Steps 3 and 4: Solve and Analyze

Statement of Cash Flows	
Net Income	65,000
Depreciation	50,000
Changes in Net Working Capital	-30,000
Changes in Operating Activities	85,000
Capital Expenditures	-90,000
Changes in Investing Activities	-90,000
Dividends	-15,000
Debt Issuance	70,000
Stock Retirement	-20,000
Changes in Financing Activities	35,000
Total Change in Cash	30,000

a. Operating cash flow and financing cash flow is sufficient to pay for capital spending (CAPEX).

b. Debt issues are a source of funds and stock retirements are a usage of cash.

CHAPTER 4

Financial Analysis
Sizing Up Firm Performance

Chapter **Orientation**

This chapter covers the process of extracting information from the firm's financial statements. The financial analysis process allows analysts to gather information about a firm's financial condition, which is important to the valuation of the firm. Financial analysis uses past financial performance to predict future performance and gives information about the firm's risks.

Chapter Review: **Terms and Concepts**

4.1 Why Do We Analyze Financial Statements?

There are several reasons an internal financial analysis might be done:

- To evaluate the performance of employees and determine their pay raises and bonuses.
- To compare the financial performance of the firm's different divisions.
- To prepare financial projections, such as those associated with the launch of a new product.
- To evaluate the firm's financial performance in light of its competitors and determine how the firm might improve its own operations.

A variety of firms and individuals that have an economic interest in a firm's financial performance might undertake an external financial analysis:

- Banks and other lenders deciding whether to loan money to the firm.
- Suppliers who are considering whether to grant credit to the firm.
- Credit-rating agencies trying to determine the firm's creditworthiness.
- Professional analysts who work for investment companies considering investing in the firm or advising others about investing.
- Individual investors deciding whether to invest in the firm.

4.2 Common-Size Statements: Standardizing Financial Information

A common size financial statement is a standardized version of a financial statement in which all entries are presented in percentages. To create a common size income statement we simply divide each entry in the income statement by the company's sales. For a common size balance sheet, we divide each entry in the balance sheet by the firm's total assets. Once these entries are converted to percentages, we can compare them with other firms that may have higher or lower sales and assets.

The common size income statement allows us to quickly identify Boswell's largest expenses. For example, the firm's cost of goods sold make up 75percent of the firm's sales. By contrast, the firm's operating expenses make up only 10.8 percent of its sales. Finally, the company's net income constitutes 7.6 percent of each dollar of sales. The decline in gross profits to net income as a percent of sales is to be expected because as we move down the income statement, we deduct more types of expenses.

Table 4.1 H. J. Boswell, Inc.

Common-Size Income Statement for the Year Ending December 31, 2013

Sales		100.0%
Cost of goods sold		–75.0%
Gross profits		25.0%
Operating expenses:		
Selling expenses	–3.3%	
General and administrative expense	–2.5%	
Depreciation and amortization expense	–5.0%	
Total operating expense		–10.8%
Operating income (EBIT, or earnings before interest and taxes)		14.2%
Interest expense		–2.5%
Earnings before taxes		11.7%
Income taxes		–4.1%
Net income		7.6%

The common size balance sheets for both 2012 and 2013 makes it relatively easy to analyze what changed during the year. For example, you can tell that the firm increased its investment in current assets by 5.6 percent of its total assets (due to the sizeable increase in its inventories by 6.2 percent). Meanwhile, the firm's investment in its fixed assets actually declined. The firm's current liabilities fell by 2 percent of its total assets, and its long-term debt decreased by 1.7 percent of its total assets.

Table 4.2 **H. J. Boswell, Inc.**

Common-Size Balance Sheets for the Years Ending December 31, 2012 and 2013

	2012	2013	Change
Cash	5.4%	4.6%	–0.8%
Accounts receivable	7.9%	8.2%	0.3%
Inventory	13.0%	19.2%	6.2%
Other current assets	0.8%	0.7%	–0.1%
Total current assets	27.0%	32.6%	5.6%
Gross plant and equipment	94.6%	93.6%	–1.0%
Less accumulated depreciation	–21.7%	–26.3%	–4.6%
Net plant and equipment	73.0%	67.4%	–5.6%
Total assets	100.0%	100.0%	0.0%
	2012	**2013**	**Change**
Accounts payable	10.5%	9.6%	–0.9%
Accrued expenses	2.6%	2.3%	–0.3%
Short-term notes	3.6%	2.7%	–0.8%
Total current liabilities	16.6%	14.6%	–2.0%
Long-term debt	40.8%	39.2%	–1.7%
Total debt	57.4%	53.8%	–3.6%
Common stockholders' equity			
Common stock—par value	2.6%	2.3%	–0.3%
Paid in capital	18.4%	16.4%	–1.9%
Retained earnings	21.7%	27.5%	5.8%
Total common stockholders' equity	42.6%	46.2%	3.6%
Total liabilities and equity	100.0%	100.0%	0.0%

4.3 Using Financial Ratios

Financial ratios allow analysts to standardize the financial information in the income statement and balance sheet. Ratios may answer the following questions about the firm's financial performance:

Question	Category of Ratios Used to Address the Question
1. How liquid is the firm? Will it be able to pay its bills as they come due?	Liquidity ratios
2. How has the firm financed the purchase of its assets?	Capital structure ratios
3. How efficient has the firm's management been in utilizing its assets to generate sales?	Asset management efficiency ratios
4. Has the firm earned adequate returns on its investments?	Profitability ratios
5. Are the firm's managers creating value for shareholders?	Market value ratios

There are financial ratios for each category of analysis. We can compare the firm's current financial ratios to historical levels to find changes over time. Also, we can compare the firm's ratios to the ratios of its competitors, or peer firms. The ratio comparisons are a starting point in the financial analysis of a firm.

Liquidity Ratios

Liquidity ratios indicate the ability of a firm to meet short-term obligations and bills. Analysts look at the overall liquidity of the firm as well as the liquidity of specific current accounts.

- Analyzing overall liquidity—current assets versus current liabilities ratio, by examining this ratio, we can compare a firm's ratio with its peer ratios.
- Analyzing the liquidity of accounts receivable and inventories—by measuring the timeliness these accounts are converted into cash, we can measure a firm's liquidity.

Overall Liquidity Measures

Current Ratio—the most commonly used measure of liquidity.

$$\text{Current Ratio} = \frac{\text{Current Assets}}{\text{Current Liabilities}} \tag{4–1}$$

Acid Test (Quick) Ratio—a liquidity measure that excludes inventory (it may not be liquid).

$$\text{Acid-Test (or Quick) Ratio} = \frac{\text{Current Assets} - \text{Inventory}}{\text{Current Liabilities}} \tag{4–2}$$

Measuring the Liquidity of Individual Asset Categories

Average Collection Period—measures the number of days it takes to collect on receivables.

$$\begin{matrix}\text{Average Collection} \\ \text{Period}\end{matrix} = \frac{\text{Accounts Receivable}}{\text{Annual Credit Sales/365 days}} = \frac{\text{Accounts Receivable}}{\text{Daily Credit Sales}} \tag{4–3}$$

Accounts Receivable Turnover Ratio—measures the number of times in a year receivables are collected.

$$\begin{matrix}\text{Accounts Receivable} \\ \text{Turnover}\end{matrix} = \frac{\text{Annual Credit Sales}}{\text{Accounts Receivable}} \tag{4–4}$$

How Long Does It Take to Turn the Firm's Inventory into Cash?

Inventory Turnover Ratio—measures the number of times in a year the inventory is sold.

$$\text{Inventory Turnover} = \frac{\text{Cost of Goods Sold}}{\text{Inventories}} \quad (4\text{–}5)$$

Days Sales in Inventory—measures in days how long it takes to sell inventory.

$$\text{Days Sales in Inventory} = 365 \div \frac{\text{Cost of Goods Sold}}{\text{Inventories}}$$

Capital Structure Ratios—measure the mix of debt and equity used to finance the firm.

Debt Ratio—measures the percentage of the firm's assets financed by total debt.

$$\text{Debt Ratio} = \frac{\text{Total Liabilities}}{\text{Total Assets}} \quad (4\text{–}6)$$

Times Interest Earned Ratio—measures the abilities to pay interest on the firm's debts.

$$\text{Times Interest Earned} = \frac{\text{Operating Income or EBIT}}{\text{Interest Expense}} \quad (4\text{–}7)$$

Asset Management Efficiency Ratios—show the efficiency of converting assets into sales.

Analysts may examine the turnover ratios for a number of asset categories to gain a better understanding of the firm's performance.

Total Asset Turnover Ratio (TATO)—measures sales per dollar of assets invested.

$$\text{Total Asset Turnover} = \frac{\text{Sales}}{\text{Total Assets}} \quad (4\text{–}8)$$

Fixed Asset Turnover Ratio—measures sales per dollar of property, plant, and equipment (PPE) assets invested.

$$\text{Fixed Asset Turnover} = \frac{\text{Sales}}{\text{Net Plant and Equipment}} \quad (4\text{–}9)$$

Peer Comparison of Asset Utilization Ratios (for performance evaluation)

Asset Utilization Efficiency	Boswell	Peer Group	Assessment
Total Asset Turnover	1.37	1.15	Good
Fixed Asset Turnover	2.03	1.75	Good
Receivables Turnover	16.67	14.60	Good
Inventory Turnover	5.36	7.0	Poor

Profitability Ratios—answers whether the firm earns an adequate return relative to sales.

Determinants of Firm Profitability and Return on Investment

- **Cost Control**—how well firm keeps expenses under revenues.
- **Efficiency of Asset Utilization**—how well firm uses assets to generate sales.

Cost Control: Is the Firm Earning Reasonable Profit Margins?

Gross Profit Margin—gross profits divided by sales.

$$\text{Gross Profit Margin} = \frac{\text{Gross Profits}}{\text{Sales}} \tag{4–10}$$

Operating Profit Margin—net operating income divided by sales, how well does a firm control cost of goods sold and operating expenses.

$$\text{Operating Profit Margin (OPM)} = \frac{\text{Net Operating Income or EBIT}}{\text{Sales}} \tag{4–11}$$

Net Profit Margin—net income divided by sales.

$$\text{Net Profit Margin} = \frac{\text{Net Income}}{\text{Sales}} \tag{4–12}$$

Return on Invested Capital—links profitability to asset efficiency.

Operating Return on Assets Ratio (OROA)—EBIT divided by total assets. A low OROA depicts higher expense relative to sales.

$$\begin{array}{c}\text{Operating Return}\\ \text{on Assets (OROA)}\end{array} = \frac{\text{Net Operating Income or EBIT}}{\text{Total Assets}} \tag{4–13}$$

Decomposing the Operating Return on Assets Ratio—analysts can separate OROA into a cost control and an asset utilization ratio.

$$\begin{array}{c}\text{Operating Return}\\ \text{on Assets}\end{array} = \overset{\textbf{Cost Control}}{\left(\begin{array}{c}\text{Operating Profit}\\ \text{Margin (OPM)}\end{array}\right)} \times \overset{\textbf{Asset Utilization}}{\left(\begin{array}{c}\text{Total Asset}\\ \text{Turnover (TATO)}\end{array}\right)} \tag{4–13a}$$

We calculate this as follows:

$$\begin{array}{c}\text{Operating Return}\\ \text{on Assets}\end{array} = \left(\frac{\text{Net Operating Income (EBIT)}}{\text{Sales}}\right) \times \left(\frac{\text{Sales}}{\text{Total Assets}}\right)$$

$$= \left(\frac{\text{Net Operating Income (EBIT)}}{\text{Total Assets}}\right) \tag{4–13b}$$

By looking at a variety of profitability and asset efficiency ratios, analysts can examine deviations from historical and peer norms that may suggest areas in cost control and utilization that require more effort and attention.

Is the Firm Providing a Reasonable Return on the Owners' Investment?

Return on Equity—net income divided by common equity, shows return to common stockholders' investment.

$$\text{Return on Equity} = \frac{\text{Net Income}}{\text{Common Equity}} \qquad (4\text{–}14)$$

DuPont Method—decomposes ROE into three parts: profitability, asset utilization, and leverage. Financial leverage is termed the effect of debt upon ROE.

$$\text{Return on Equity} = \text{Profitability} \times \text{Efficiency} \times \text{Equity Multiplier}$$

$$\text{Return on Equity} = \text{Net Profit Margin} \times \text{Total Asset Turnover} \times \frac{1}{1 - \text{Debt Ratio}}$$

$$\text{Return on Equity} = \frac{\text{Net Income}}{\text{Sales}} \times \frac{\text{Sales}}{\text{Total Assets}} \times \frac{1}{1 - \text{Debt Ratio}} \qquad (4\text{–}14a)$$

Market Value Ratios—indicate how the market values the firm's shares.

Price-Earnings Ratio—The most popular valuation ratio shows how much investors will pay for $1 of earnings. PE ratios are usually higher for firms with higher growth.

$$\text{Price-Earnings Ratio} = \frac{\text{Market Price per Share}}{\text{Earnings per Share}} \qquad (4\text{–}15)$$

Market-to-Book Ratio—compares the market value to the accounting equity value of the firm. Book value per share is the equity accounting value divided by shares outstanding.

$$\text{Market-to-Book Ratio} = \frac{\text{Market Price per Share}}{\text{Book Value per Share}} = \frac{\text{Market Price per Share}}{\text{Common Shareholders' Equity} \big/ \text{Common Shares Outstanding}} \qquad (4\text{–}16)$$

A market to book value ratio greater than 1 indicates the market value is above the lifetime historical cost of equity. Value investors look for stocks with low market to book ratios.

4.4 Selecting a Performance Benchmark

Benchmarks—two types.

- **Trend Analysis**—comparison to historic trends
- **Peer Group Comparisons**—comparison to competitors

Trend Analysis

This examines performance to see if ratios are improving or deteriorating over time.

Peer Group Analysis

This analysis examines performance of firms in the same industry. This information is available from Standard and Poor's and on the Internet from sites such as Google's and Yahoo!'s finance pages.

4.5 The Limitations of Ratio Analysis

Problems When Using Ratios

- Industry benchmark choice can be difficult since a firm may belong to many industries.
- Industry peer benchmarks may not be representative.
- Industry average ratio may not be desirable.
- Firm accounting practices may vary widely.
- Firms may have seasonal changes to ratios.
- It can be difficult to understand whether the differences in ratios are meaningful.
- Quality of the ratio analysis is no better than the quality of the financial statements.

Answers to **Concept Checks**

Concept Check **4.1**

1. What are some common reasons for analyzing a firm's financial statements?
2. What are some of the firms that engage in external financial statement analysis and what are their motives?

Answer 1: The primary reasons to analyze financial statements are to set compensation, to forecast future financial performance, and to compare with competitors.

Answer 2: Banks, creditors, suppliers, and credit analysts evaluate financial statements to determine credit worthiness. Investment banks have analysts that evaluate the market value of a firm's securities.

Concept Check **4.2**

1. What is the reason for converting financial statements to common size statements?
2. How are the common size income statement and balance sheet constructed?

Answer 1: Common size statements allow analysts to compare financials to prior firm historical performance and to competitors.

Answer 2: The common size income statement finds the percentage value of each account in the income statement relative to sales. The common size balance sheet determines the percentage value of each account in the balance sheet relative to total assets.

Concept Check **4.3**

1. Why are ratios helpful in financial statement analysis?
2. What are the five basic questions that we address with financial statement analysis?
3. What is the DuPont system of financial analysis, and why is it a useful tool for analyzing financial performance?

Answer 1: Financial ratios allow analysts to standardize the financial information in the income statement and balance sheet.

Answer 2: The five basic questions are:

1. How liquid is the firm? Will it be able to pay its bills as they come due?
2. How has the firm financed the purchase of its assets?
3. How efficient has the firm's management been in utilizing its assets to generate sales?
4. Has the firm earned adequate returns on its investments?
5. Are the firm's managers creating value for shareholders?

Answer 3: DuPont Analysis decomposes a firm's ROE into profitability, asset efficiency, and leverage components. By separating firm performance into three components, managers can identify areas of underperformance relative to their industry peers.

Concept Check **4.4**

1. Describe how time series comparisons of a firm's ratios provide a benchmark for performing financial statement analysis.
2. Why is the selection of a proper set of peer firms so important when using them as a benchmark of performance?

Answer 1: Time series of historical performance display trends in a ratio's timeline.

Answer 2: Finding firms that closely match the subject firm provides representative ratios.

Concept Check **4.5**

1. Why is picking a peer group a limitation of financial ratio analysis?
2. How are financial ratio comparisons like clues in solving a puzzle?

Answer 1: The limitations of using peer group ratios are:

- Industry benchmark choice can be difficult since a firm may belong to many industries.
- Industry peer benchmarks may not be representative.
- Industry average ratio may not be desirable.
- Firm accounting practices may vary widely.
- Firms may have seasonal changes to ratios.
- It can be difficult to understand whether the differences in ratios are meaningful.
- Quality of the ratio analysis is no better than the quality of the financial statements.

Answer 2: Financial ratios provide clues for future analysis by showing discrepancies and deviations from historical and peer company norms.

Multiple Choice **Quiz**

1. The acid test (quick) ratio has current liabilities as a denominator and
   a. current assets as a numerator.
   b. current assets and fixed assets as a numerator.
   c. current assets less inventory as a numerator.
   d. current assets less cash as a numerator.

2. Capital structure refers to the
   a. liquidity of firm assets.
   b. types of debt securities owned by the firm.
   c. fixed assets of the firm.
   d. mix of debt and equity securities used to finance the firm's assets.

3. Financial leverage is the magnifying effect of
   a. equity on owner's returns.
   b. debt on ROE.
   c. debt on ROA.
   d. equity on ROA.

4. DuPont analysis relates ROE to
   a. profitability, equity, and debt.
   b. profitability, equity, and leverage.
   c. profitability, asset efficiency, and leverage.
   d. profitability, operating efficiency, and leverage.

5. Market-to-book ratios are the ratio of
   a. market value of equity to the accounting value of equity.
   b. market value of debt to the accounting value of debt.
   c. market value of equity to the appraised value of equity.
   d. market value of equity to the appraised value of debt.

6. Notes payable are
   a. borrowed money for the long-term that is owed to the firm.
   b. borrowed money for the long-term that the firm owes.
   c. borrowed money for a period of a year or less the firm owes.
   d. borrowed money for a period of a year or less that is owed to the firm.

7. A firm with 18.25 days sales' in inventory has an inventory turnover ratio of
   a. 4.
   b. 10.
   c. 18.25.
   d. 20.

8. The determinants of firm profitability and returns on investment are
   a. sales and leverage.
   b. profitability and cost control.
   c. cost control and asset efficiency.
   d. sales and asset efficiency.

9. Times interest earned is a measure of
   a. the time between interest payments.
   b. the ability to pay interest from operating income.
   c. the ability to pay interest from net income.
   d. the ability to pay interest from net earnings.

10. The inventory turnover ratio is
    a. CGS divided by inventory.
    b. inventory divided by sales.
    c. inventory divided by 365.
    d. CGS divided by 365.

Answers to **Multiple Choice Questions**

1. C
2. D
3. B
4. C
5. A
6. C
7. D
8. C
9. B
10. A

Self Test **with Solutions**

Picture the Problem

Decide on Solution Strategy

Solve

Analyze

Self Test 1: Ratio analysis

Hawaiian Ice Company had the following results for 2012. Prepare a ratio analysis for the firm for profitability, asset efficiency, leverage, and market valuation compared to industry averages.

Hawaiian Ice Company Income Statement	**2012**	
Revenue	40,000	(Annual credit sales $20,000)
CGS	25,000	
Gross Profit	15,000	
Depreciation	5,000	
Earnings before Interest and Tax	10,000	
Interest	1,000	
Earnings Before Tax	9,000	
Taxes 35%	3,150	
Net Income	5,850	

Hawaiian Ice Company Balance Sheet	**2012**	
Cash	5,000	
Accounts Receivable	0	
Inventory	10,000	
Current Assets	15,000	
PPE	80,000	
Total Assets	95,000	
Accounts Payable	5,000	
Short-term Notes	40,000	
Current Liabilities	45,000	
Long-term Debt	0	
Common Equity	50,000	(Outstanding shares 2,500, Price $90 each)
Total Liabilities and Equity	95,000	

a. Based on the preceding statements, complete the following table:

	Industry Averages	**HI Actual 2012**
Current ratio	1.80	
Acid-test ratio	0.70	
Average collection period	37.00	
Inventory turnover	2.50	
Debt ratio	58.0%	
Times interest earned	3.80	
Operating profit margin	10.0%	
Total asset turnover	1.14	
Fixed asset turnover	1.40	
Operating return on assets	11.4%	
Return on equity	9.5%	
Price to earnings	25X	
Market to book	5X	

b. Evaluate the firm's financial position at the end of 2010 in terms of its liquidity, profitability, and capital structure.

c. Evaluate the firm in terms of its market valuation.

Step 1: Picture the Problem

By comparing financial ratios to an industry benchmark, analysts can determine the performance of the firm. Analysts also can compare the firm to its historical ratios to find deviations in performance. Firms aim to have good growth with reasonable leverage and good profitability and asset efficiency.

Step 2: Decide on a Solution Strategy

By organizing the ratio analysis into the areas of profitability, asset efficiency, leverage, and market valuation, analysts can make informed decisions on the firm's performance. Comparing these ratios against an industry average may indicate a problem or just a difference in management policy, so interpretation comes with greater understanding of industry practices and the business environment.

Profitability and Investment Return Ratios

Gross Profit Margin—gross profits divided by sales.

$$\text{Gross Profit Margin} = \frac{\text{Gross Profits}}{\text{Sales}} = \frac{15,000}{40,000} = 38\% \qquad (4\text{–}10)$$

Operating Profit Margin—net operating income divided by sales, how well does a firm control cost of goods sold and operating expenses.

$$\text{Operating Profit Margin (OPM)} = \frac{\text{EBIT}}{\text{Sales}} = \frac{10,000}{40,000} = 25\% \qquad (4\text{–}11)$$

Net Profit Margin—net income divided by sales.

$$\text{Net Profit Margin} = \frac{\text{Net Income}}{\text{Sales}} = \frac{5,850}{40,000} = 14.6\% \qquad (4\text{–}12)$$

Return on Equity—net income divided by common equity, return to common stockholders' investment.

$$\text{Return on Equity} = \frac{\text{Net Income}}{\text{Common Equity}} = \frac{5,850}{50,000} = 11.7\% \qquad (4\text{–}14)$$

Liquidity ratios

Current Ratio—the most commonly used measure of liquidity.

$$\text{Current Ratio} = \frac{\text{Current Assets}}{\text{Current Liabilities}} = \frac{15,000}{45,000} = 33.3\% \qquad (4\text{–}1)$$

Acid-Test (Quick) Ratio—a liquidity measure that excludes inventory (it may not be liquid).

$$\text{Acid-Test (or Quick) Ratio} = \frac{\text{Current Assets} - \text{Inventory}}{\text{Current Liabilities}} = \frac{5,000}{45,000} = 11.1\% \qquad (4\text{–}2)$$

Individual Asset Category Measures of Liquidity

Average Collection Period—measures the number of days it takes to collect on receivables.

$$\text{Average Collection Period} = \frac{\text{Accounts Receivable}}{\text{Annual Credit Sales/365 days}} = \frac{0}{20,000/365 = 0\%} \qquad (4\text{–}3)$$

Accounts Receivable Turnover Ratio—the number of times in a year receivables are collected.

$$\text{Accounts Receivable Turnover} = \frac{\text{Annual Credit Sales}}{\text{Accounts Receivable}} = \frac{20,000}{0} = \text{NA} \qquad (4\text{–}4)$$

Asset Efficiency ratios

Operating Return on Assets Ratio (OROA)—EBIT divided by total assets. A low OROA depicts higher expense relative to sales.

$$\text{Operating Return on Assets (OROA)} = \frac{\text{EBIT}}{\text{Total Assets}} = \frac{10,000}{95,000} = .105\% \qquad (4\text{–}13)$$

Inventory Turnover Ratio—measures the number of times in a year the inventory is sold.

$$\text{Inventory Turnover} = \frac{\text{CGS}}{\text{Inventories}} = \frac{25,000}{10,000} = 2.5 \text{ times} \qquad (4\text{–}5)$$

Total Asset Turnover Ratio (TATO)—measures sales per dollar of assets invested.

$$\text{Total Asset Turnover} = \frac{\text{Sales}}{\text{Total Assets}} = \frac{40,000}{95,000} = .421 \text{ times} \qquad (4\text{–}8)$$

Fixed Asset Turnover Ratio—measures sales per dollar of PPE assets invested.

$$\text{Fixed Asset Turnover} = \frac{\text{Sales}}{\text{Net PPE}} = \frac{40,000}{80,000} = .50 \text{ times} \qquad (4\text{–}9)$$

Leverage Ratios

Debt Ratio—measures the percentage of the firm's assets financed by total debt.

$$\text{Debt Ratio} = \frac{\text{Total Liabilities}}{\text{Total Assets}} = \frac{45,000}{95,000} = 47.4\% \qquad (4\text{–}6)$$

Times Interest Earned Ratio—measures the abilities to pay interest on the firm's debts.

$$\text{Times Interest Earned} = \frac{\text{Operating Income or EBIT}}{\text{Interest Expense}} = \frac{10,000}{1,000} = 10\text{X} \qquad (4\text{–}7)$$

Market Valuation Ratios

Price-Earnings Ratio —The most popular valuation ratio shows how much investors will pay for $1 of earnings. PE ratios are usually higher for firms with higher growth.

$$\text{Price-Earnings Ratio} = \frac{\text{Market Price per Share}}{\text{Earnings per Share}} = \frac{90}{2.34} = \frac{\text{Market Value}}{\text{Net Income}} = \frac{225,000}{5,850} = 38\text{X} \qquad (4\text{–}15)$$

Price-to-Sales Ratio—The next most popular valuation ratio shows how much investors will pay for $1 of sales. P/S ratios are usually higher for firms with higher growth.

$$\text{Price-to-Sales Ratio} = \frac{\text{Market Price per Share}}{\text{Revenues per Share}} = \frac{90}{16} = \frac{\text{Market Value}}{\text{Sales}} = \frac{225,000}{40,000} = 5.6\text{X}$$

Market-to-Book Ratio—compares the market value to the accounting equity value of the firm. Book value per share is the equity accounting value divided by shares outstanding.

$$\text{Market-to-Book Ratio} = \frac{\text{Market Price per Share}}{\text{Book Value per Share}} = \frac{\text{Market Price per Share}}{\text{Common Shareholders' Equity} \big/ \text{Common Shares Outstanding}} \quad (4\text{–}16)$$

On a total item basis,

$$\text{Market-to-Book Ratio} = \frac{\text{Market Value of Equity}}{\text{Accounting Equity}} = \frac{90\text{X}2{,}500}{50{,}000} = 4.5\text{X}$$

Step 3: Solve

a. Financial ratio analysis for Hawaiian Ice:

	Industry Averages	**Actual 2012**
Profitability Ratios		
Gross profit margin	N/A	38%
Operating profit margin	10%	25%
Net profit margin	N/A	15%
Return on equity	9.5%	12%
Liquidity Ratios		
Current ratio	1.80	.33
Acid-test ratio	0.70	.11
Average collection period	37.00	N/A
Accounts receivable turnover	N/A	N/A
Asset Efficiency Ratios		
Inventory turnover	2.50	2.50
Total asset turnover	1.14	.42
Fixed asset turnover	1.40	.50
Operating return on assets	11.4%	10.5%
Leverage Ratios		
Debt ratio	58%	47%
Times interest earned	3.8	10
Market Valuation Ratios and EPS		
P/E ratio	15X	38X
P/S ratio	N/A	5.6X
Market-to-book ratio	5X	4.5X
EPS	N/A	$2.34

b. Hawaiian Ice Company has very good profit margins. However, its use of fixed assets is subpar. It has below normal debt ratio with no long-term debt but a weaker liquidity position than industry norms because it is very dependent upon short-term debt and accounts payable (supplier financing) for its liquidity to meet obligations.

c. Hawaiian Ice has $2.34 per share in earnings and $16 per share in sales with a stock price of $90 per share. It has a market to book ratio that is lower (better) than industry norms and a P/E ratio that is 38X compared with 15X for the industry.

Step 4: Analyze

Hawaiian Ice is a profitable firm with assets that are not producing as efficiently as the industry average. This may warrant further investigation to see if some assets can be sold or improved to increase the sales-per-asset ratio. The firm's reliance on short-term financing may not be a problem at present, but in times when banks are not lending, it could be a source of risk to the firm and its owners. The market valuation ratios show the firm has an attractive price to sales ratio but the P/E seems high.

Self Test 2: Common Size Statements

Prepare common size financial statements for Hawaiian Ice Company and analyze how the firm has increased revenue and profits from 2010 to 2012.

Income Statement	**2010**	**2011**	**2012**
Revenue	40,000	50,000	75,000
CGS	25,000	32,000	45,000
Gross Profit	15,000	18,000	30,000
Interest	1,000	5,000	10,000
Depreciation	5,000	6,000	6,000
Earnings Before Tax	9,000	7,000	14,000
Taxes 35%	3,150	2,450	4,900
Net Income	5,850	4,550	9,100

Balance Sheet	**2010**	**2011**	**2012**
Cash	5,000	6,000	7,000
Accounts Receivable	0	5,000	10,000
Inventory	10,000	12,400	19,000
Current Assets	15,000	23,400	36,000
PPE	80,000	85,000	85,000
Total Assets	95,000	108,400	121,000
Accounts Payable	5,000	6,000	10,000
Short-term Notes	40,000	48,400	49,000
Current Liabilities	45,000	54,400	59,000
Long-term Debt	0	0	0
Common Equity	50,000	54,000	62,000
Total Liabilities and Equity	95,000	108,400	121,000

Steps 1 and 2: Picture the Problem and Decide on a Solution Strategy

To construct a common size statement, divide income statement items by total sales. For the balance sheet, divide by total assets.

Step 3: Solve

Income Statement	**2010**	**2011**	**2012**
Revenue	100%	100%	100%
CGS	63%	64%	60%
Gross Profit	37%	36%	40%
Interest	3%	10%	13%
Depreciation	13%	12%	8%
Earnings Before Tax	23%	14%	19%
Taxes 35%	8%	5%	7%
Net Income	15%	9%	12%
Balance Sheet			
Cash	5%	6%	6%
Accounts Receivable	0%	5%	8%
Inventory	11%	11%	16%
Current Assets	16%	22%	30%
PPE	84%	78%	70%
Total Assets	100%	100%	100%
Accounts Payable	5%	6%	8%
Short-term Notes	42%	45%	40%
Current Liabilities	47%	50%	49%
Long-term Debt	0%	0%	0%
Common Equity	53%	50%	51%
Total Liabilities and Equity	100%	100%	100%

Step 4: Analyze

Common size statement analysis finds that Hawaiian Ice Company has grown sales without having to grow PPE significantly. While operating income has improved due to lower cost of goods, net profit margin has declined due to rising interest costs. Since sales have grown at a faster rate than PPE, depreciation expense has declined as a percentage of sales. Increases in sales efficiency have benefited the firm.

Total assets have grown more due to the increase in inventories than PPE, a potential problem if the trend continues. Part of the growth in sales has resulted from the growth in credit sales lending and rising accounts receivable. The firm does not rely on long-term debt financing and should consider the risk of relying solely on short-term financing and accounts payable.

CHAPTER 5

Time Value of Money

The Basics

Chapter **Orientation**

This chapter introduces the Valuation of Financial Assets section and presents the time value of money concept. Money has a value that differs at different points in time. The sooner you receive cash, the more value it has to you. The formulas in this chapter can determine the value of money through time. This chapter and the next present the evaluation tools and solution methods that can be used on a variety of problems and in many finance classes.

Chapter Review: **Terms and Concepts**

5.1 Using Timelines to Visualize Cash Flows

Timelines depict a linear representation of cash flows through time, showing inflows, outflows, and the applicable interest rate.

5.2 Compounding and Future Value

Compounding is the process that determines what an amount today will be worth after a period of growth. Compounding includes interest earned on earlier interest payments, thus longer compounding periods will grow money dramatically. **Compound interest** is the interest earned on interest. **Simple interest** only calculates interest on principal. **Present value** is the cash flow value today and **future value** is what the cash flow is worth in the future. The **interest rate** is the growth rate in value per period. The **Future Value Interest Factor** $(1 + i)^n$ is a multiplier to find the future value of a present amount.

To move money through time, you may –

Do the math

Use a financial calculator

Use a spreadsheet on a personal computer.

To compound over shorter periods of time than one year, interest rates must be converted from annual (i) to the desired period (i / m) to find days, weeks, months, quarters, etc. and the number of time periods must be adjusted from years to the number of periods (m* *Years*) to find the number of periods in days, weeks, months, quarters, etc.

5.3 Discounting and Present Value

Discounting is the opposite process from compounding: it finds today's value of a future amount by applying a **discount rate**. The inverse of the Future Value Interest Factor is the **Present Value Interest Factor** and is used to find today's value of a future amount. In addition to finding the value of money, it is possible to solve for the amount of time or the interest rate needed to accomplish a monetary goal.

In addition to solving for the present or future value of cash flows, you may solve for (*N*) the number of periods needed or (*i*) the rate needed to equate a present value to its future value. **The Rule of 72** is a quick approximation to find how long in years that it takes a value to double by dividing 72 by an annual interest rate. These formulas also can be used to solve population growth and other non-monetary questions.

5.4 Making Interest Rates Comparable

The **annual percentage rate (APR)** is the simple rate or the rate of interest paid without compounding (m * rate per period). APR also is known as the **stated** or **nominal rate**. The compounded rate of interest is called the **effective annual rate (EAR)**. By using a future value formula, you can calculate the EAR by compounding a periodic rate over one year.

Continuous compounding finds the ultimate limit for the EAR through compounding by raising e (2.71828) to the annual interest rate.

To find the value of cash flows, this book suggests a 4 step process:

Picture the Problem (by using timelines of cash flows)

Decide on the Solution Strategy

Solve

Analyze

To solve time value of money problems, the simplest can be solved with these formulas:

Future Value (for compounding 1 amount):

$$\text{Future Value in year } n\ (FV_n) = \text{Present Value } (PV)\left(1+\text{Annual Interest Rate } (i)\right)^{\text{Number of Years } (n)}$$

Present Value (for discounting 1 amount):

$$\text{Present Value } (PV) = \text{Future Value in year } n\ (FV_n)\left[\frac{1}{\left(1+\text{Annual Interest Rate } (i)\right)^{\text{Number of Years } (n)}}\right]$$

Future Value (for compounding 1 amount with periods other than one year):

$$\text{Future Value in year } n\ (FV_n) = \text{Present Value } (PV)\left(1+\frac{\text{Annual Interest Rate } (i)}{\text{Compounding Periods per Year } (m)}\right)^{m\times(\text{Number of Years } (n))}$$

Present Value (for discounting 1 amount with periods other than one year):

$$\text{Present Value } (PV) = \text{Future Value in year } n \ (FV_n) \left[\frac{1}{\left(1+\dfrac{\text{Annual Interest Rate } (i)}{\text{Compounding Periods per Year } (m)}\right)^{m\times(\text{Number of Years } (n))}} \right]$$

Annual Percentage Rate (APR used by banks):

$$\text{Present Value } (PV) = \text{Future Value in year } n \ (FV_n) \left[\frac{1}{\left(1+\dfrac{\text{Annual Interest Rate } (i)}{\text{Compounding Periods per Year } (m)}\right)^{m\times(\text{Number of Years } (n))}} \right]$$

Effective Annual Rate (EAR compounds periodic rates into a nominal annual rate):

$$\text{Effective Annual Rate (EAR)} = \left(1+\frac{\text{Quoted Annual Rate}}{\text{Compounding Periods per year } (m)}\right)^{m} - 1$$

In addition to the formulas, the chapter covers the steps to find solutions on a financial calculator and an Excel spreadsheet.

Answers to **Concept Checks**

Concept Check **5.1**

1. What is a timeline, and how does it help you solve time value of money problems?
2. Does Year 5 represent the end of the fifth year, the beginning of the sixth year, or both?

Answer 1: A timeline is a linear representation of the timing of cash flows. A timeline identifies the timing and amount of a stream of payments – both cash received and cash spent – along with the interest rate it earns.

Answer 2: Year 5 represents the end of Year 5 and the beginning of Year 6.

Concept Check **5.2**

1. What is compound interest, and how is it calculated?
2. Describe the three basic approaches that can be used to move money through time.
3. How does increasing the number of compounding periods affect the future value of a cash sum?

Answer 1: Compounded interest is interest earned on both the initial principal and interest reinvested on prior periods. The formula for finding the compounded future value compounded over any subperiod is:

$$\begin{matrix}\text{Future Value} \\ \text{in year } n \\ (FV_n)\end{matrix} = \begin{matrix}\text{Present} \\ \text{Value } (PV)\end{matrix}\left(1+\frac{\begin{matrix}\text{Annual} \\ \text{Interest Rate } (i)\end{matrix}}{\begin{matrix}\text{Compounding} \\ \text{Periods per} \\ \text{Year } (m)\end{matrix}}\right)^{m\times(\text{Number of Years } (n))}$$

Answer 2: The three approaches are:

Do the math (work the formulas)

Use a financial calculator

Use a spreadsheet

Answer 3: Earning interest more frequently increases future values.

Concept Check **5.3**

1. What does the term *discounting* mean with respect to the time value of money?
2. How is discounting related to compounding?

Answer 1: Discounting finds the value today of an amount paid in the future.

Answer 2: Discounting is the inverse of compounding.

Concept Check **5.4**

1. How does an EAR differ from an APR?
2. What is the effect of having multiple compounding periods within a year on future values?

Answer 1: APR is a simple or nominal rate earned on a cash flow while EAR reflects the value of compounding.

Answer 2: Earning interest more frequently increases future values.

Multiple Choice **Quiz**

1. Compounding is the process of
   a. finding the future value in simple interest.
   b. finding the present value in simple interest.
   c. finding the future value of payments using interest-on-interest.
   d. finding the present value of payments using interest-on-interest.

2. Discounting is the process of
   a. finding the future value in simple interest.
   b. finding the present value in simple interest.
   c. finding the future value of payments using interest-on-interest.
   d. finding the present value of payments using interest-on-interest.

3. Compound interest is
   a. the simple rate.
   b. the period rate.
   c. the interest earned on principal.
   d. the interest earned on interest.

4. Simple interest is
   a. the simple rate.
   b. the period rate.
   c. the interest earned on principal.
   d. the interest earned on interest.

5. Annual Percentage Rate (APR) is
   a. a simple rate.
   b. a compounded rate.
   c. an effective rate.
   d. a rate on interest multiplied by the number of periods.

6. If $m > 1$, Effective Annual Rate (EAR) is
   a. higher than the nominal rate.
   b. lower than the nominal rate.
   c. can be higher or lower than the nominal rate.
   d. equal to the stated rate.

7. Future value is
   a. equal to an amount you would have to invest to reach a target value.
   b. equal to what a cash flow is worth today
   c. equal to what a cash flow is worth in the future
   d. equal to interest earned on a future payment

8. Present value is
   a. equal to an amount you would have to invest to reach a target value.
   b. equal to what a cash flow is worth today.
   c. equal to what a cash flow is worth in the future.
   d. equal to interest earned on a future payment.

9. If an investor invests $100 at an annual rate of 6 percent for one year and the money was compounded semiannually, how much will the investor have at the end of the year?
   a. $103
   b. $106.09
   c. $106.36
   d. $112

10. If an investor invests $100 at an annual rate of 6 percent for two years and earns simple interest, how much will the investor have at the end of two years?
   a. $106.36
   b. $112
   c. $112.36
   d. $112.72

Answers to **Multiple Choice Questions**

1. C
2. D
3. D
4. C
5. A
6. A
7. C
8. B
9. B
10. B

Self Test **with Solutions**

Picture the Problem

Decide on Solution Strategy

Solve

Analyze

Self Test 1

You invest $1,000 in an oil trust. Your account earns 8 percent annually but funds are compounding value weekly. How much will you have in the account in 40 years?

Step 1: Picture the Problem

You are investing today and you want to know the value in 40 years (2,080 weeks).

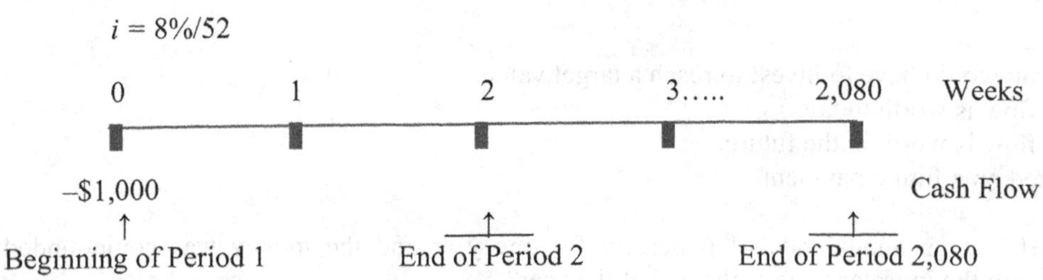

Step 2: Decide on a Solution Strategy

This is a future value problem with compounding periods other than one year.

$$\text{Future Value in year } n \ (FV_n) = \text{Present Value } (PV) \left(1 + \frac{\text{Annual Interest Rate } (i)}{\text{Compounding Periods per Year } (m)}\right)^{m \times (\text{Number of Years } (n))}$$

Step 3: Solve

FV = 1,000 (FV factor) for a weekly rate of 0.08 / 52 for 2,080 weeks.

$$FV = 1000\left(1+\frac{0.08}{52}\right)^{52\times 40} = \$24,472.28$$

Using a Financial Calculator.

Enter	2,080	8.0/52	-1,000	0	
	N	I/Y	PV	PMT	FV
Solve for					$24,472.28

Using an Excel Spreadsheet.

=FV(rate,nper,pmt,pv) or with values entered =FV(0.08/52,2080,0,-1000) equals $24,472.28

Step 4: Analyze

A $1,000 investment will be worth $24,472. If you wish to retire, you will have to invest more.

Self Test 2

You buy a bond that only pays you $10,000 in ten years. Investors in that bond expect to earn 5 percent annually with semiannual compounding. What is today's fair value of that bond?

Step 1: Picture the Problem

You are valuing today a $10,000 amount that will be paid to you in ten years (which is 20 periods with semi-annual compounding).

$i = 6\%/2$

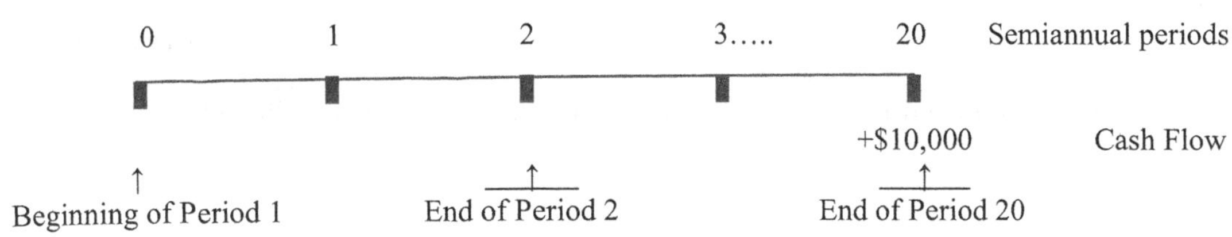

Step 2: Decide on a Solution Strategy

This is a present value problem with compounding periods other than one year.

$$\begin{matrix}\text{Future Value}\\ \text{in year } n\\ (FV_n)\end{matrix} = \begin{matrix}\text{Present}\\ \text{Value } (PV)\end{matrix}\left(1+\frac{\begin{matrix}\text{Annual}\\ \text{Interest Rate } (i)\end{matrix}}{\begin{matrix}\text{Compounding}\\ \text{Periods per}\\ \text{Year } (m)\end{matrix}}\right)^{m\times(\text{Number of Years } (n))}$$

Step 3: Solve

PV = FV / (PV factor) for a semiannual rate of 0.06 / 2 for 20 semiannual periods.

= $5,536.76

Using a Financial Calculator.

Enter	20	6.0/2	0	+10000	
	N	I/Y	PMT	FV	PV
Solve for					$5,536.76

Using an Excel Spreadsheet

=PV(rate,nper,pmt,fv) or with values entered = FV(0.06/2,20,0,+10000) equals $5,536,76

Step 4: Analyze

A $10,000 payoff in ten years is worth $5,537 today. To earn your return, do not pay more.

Self Test 3

You are comparing bank CDs: one bank promises to pay 4.14 percent annual rate compounded quarterly while the other bank offers you 4.14 percent rate annually compounded monthly. Which bank CD should you buy?

Step 1: Picture the Problem

You are investing today and you want to know the value in one year as an effective annual rate.

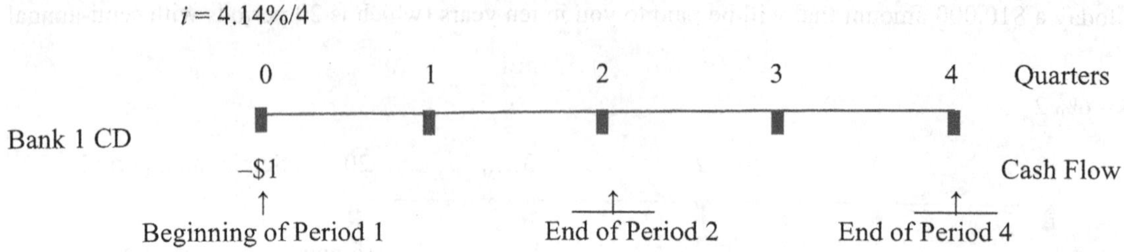

Vs.

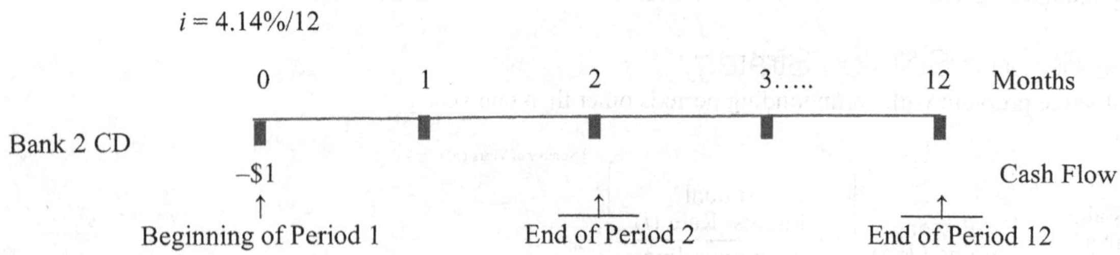

Step 2: Decide on a Solution Strategy

This is an effective annual rate problem with compounding periods other than one year. One approach would be to find the future value of $1 in each CD using the FV formula.

$$\begin{matrix}\text{Future Value}\\ \text{in year } n\\ (FV_n)\end{matrix} = \begin{matrix}\text{Present}\\ \text{Value } (PV)\end{matrix}\left(1+\frac{\begin{matrix}\text{Annual}\\ \text{Interest Rate } (i)\end{matrix}}{\begin{matrix}\text{Compounding}\\ \text{Periods per}\\ \text{Year } (m)\end{matrix}}\right)^{m\times(\text{Number of Years } (n))}$$

Another approach would be to find the Effective Annual Rate of each CD.

$$\begin{matrix}\text{Effective}\\ \text{Annual Rate}\\ \text{(EAR)}\end{matrix} = \left(1+\frac{\begin{matrix}\text{Quoted}\\ \text{Annual Rate}\end{matrix}}{\begin{matrix}\text{Compounding Periods}\\ \text{per year } (m)\end{matrix}}\right)^{m} - 1$$

Step 3: Solve

Bank 1 EAR = (FV factor) for a quarterly rate of 0.0414 / 4 for 4 quarters.

$$EAR = \left(1+\frac{0.0414}{4}\right)^{4} - 1 = 0.04204 = 4.204\%$$

Bank 2 EAR = (FV factor) for a monthly rate of 0.04 / 12 for 12 months.

$$EAR = \left(1+\frac{0.0414}{12}\right)^{12} - 1 = 0.04219 = 4.219\%$$

Using a Financial Calculator. Bank 1

Enter	4	4.14/4	-1	0	
	N	I/Y	PV	PMT	FV
Solve for					1.04204 (then –1)

Using a Financial Calculator. Bank 2

Enter	12	4.14/12	-1	0	
	N	I/Y	PV	PMT	FV
Solve for					1.04219 (then –1)

Using an Excel Spreadsheet.

=FV(rate, nper, pmt, pv) or with values entered =FV(0.0414/4,4,0,-1) equals 1.04204 then subtract 1

=FV(rate, nper, pmt, pv) or with values entered =FV(0.0414/12,12,0,-1) equals 1.04219 then subtract 1

Step 4: Analyze

Choose the CD from Bank 2; it earns a higher effective annual yield (EAR).

Self Test 4

Your credit card company informs you that your card will carry an APR of 14 percent compounded continuously. What is your effective annual rate (EAR)?

Step 1: Picture the Problem

You want to know the maximum effective annual rate with compounding every instant.

Step 2: Decide on a Solution Strategy

This is an effective annual rate problem with compounding periods described by the continuous time formula for future value.

$$EAR = e^{+\text{quoted annual rate}}$$

Step 3: Solve

Notice that this is solved with a financial calculator or with a spreadsheet.

Using a Financial Calculator. Credit Card Rate of 14 percent

Enter	.14	
	EXP or e	
Solve for		1.15027 (then –1)

Using an Excel Spreadsheet.

=EXP(rate) or with value entered =EXP(.14) equals 1.15027 then subtract 1

Step 4: Analyze

The continuous annual effective annual yield (EAR) is 1.15027 – 1 = 15.027%.

Self Test 5

The cost of medical care in the United States is expected to grow at a rate of 8 percent annually from today's value of $2B. How many years will it take for medical care to double?

Step 1: Picture the Problem

You want to know the number of years needed to double health care from 2 to 4 billion. You know the present value is 2 and the future value is 4, linked by a growth rate of 8 percent per year.

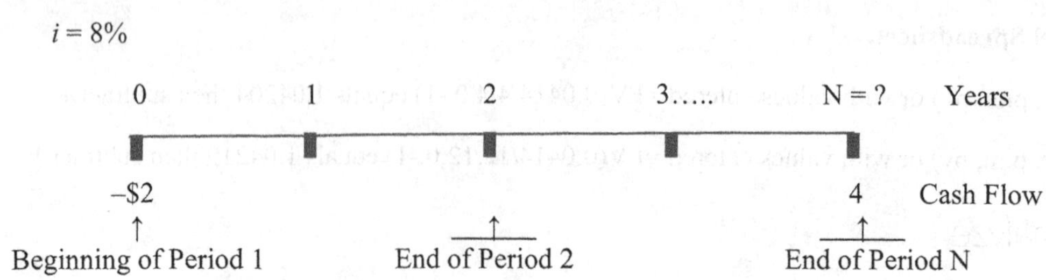

Step 2: Decide on Solution Strategy

This is a future value problem with annual compounding periods (m = 1 per year) that solves for 'N' or the number of periods.

$$\text{Future Value in year } n\ (FV_n) = \text{Present Value } (PV)\left(1+\frac{\text{Annual Interest Rate } (i)}{\text{Compounding Periods per Year } (m)}\right)^{m\times(\text{Number of Years } (n))}$$

Step 3: Solve

Notice that this is best solved with a financial calculator or with a spreadsheet since guessing which 'N' requires lots of time and repetition.

$FV = 2(1+.08)^N = 4$ Note for ease of calculation the billions were omitted.

Using a Financial Calculator.

Enter	4	8.0	-2	0	
	FV	I/Y	PV	PMT	N
Solve for					9.006 Years

Using an Excel Spreadsheet.

=NPER(rate, pmt, pv, fv) or with values entered =FV(0.08 ,-2,4) equals 9.006 Years

Step 4: Analyze

At a rate of 8 percent growth, health care costs will double in nine years. Some calculators may round significantly to the nearest whole number.

Self Test 6

Your financial goal is to take \$50,000 and grow it to \$500,000 in 45 years for your retirement. What rate would you need to earn in order to accomplish your goal?

Step 1: Picture the Problem

You want to know the rate needed to earn \$500,000 in 45 years on an initial investment of \$50,000. You know the present value of your investment today is \$50,000 and the future value is \$500,000, and that the two values are linked by an unknown growth rate over 45 years.

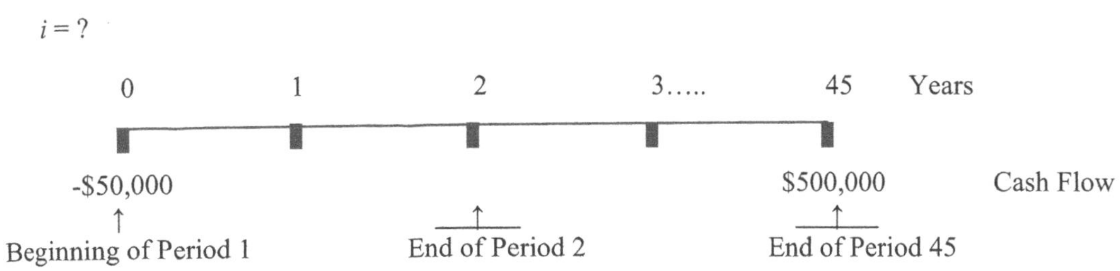

Step 2: Decide on a Solution Strategy

This is a future value problem with annual compounding periods (m = 1 per year) for 45 years that solves for 'i' or rate.

$$\text{Future Value in year } n\ (FV_n) = \text{Present Value } (PV)\left(1+\frac{\text{Annual Interest Rate } (i)}{\text{Compounding Periods per Year } (m)}\right)^{m\times(\text{Number of Years } (n))}$$

Step 3: Solve

Notice that this is best solved with a financial calculator or with a spreadsheet since guessing the correct 'i' requires lots of time and repetition.

$$FV = 50{,}000(1+i)^{45} = 500{,}000$$

Using a Financial Calculator.

Enter	45	-50,000	0	500,000	
	N	PV	PMT	FV	I/Y
Solve for					5.25% per year

Using an Excel Spreadsheet.

=Rate(nper, pmt, pv, fv) or with values entered =FV(45,0,-50000,500000) equals 5.25 percent per year

Step 4: Analyze

At a rate of 5.25 percent growth, your account will grow to $500,000. If you start with only half of your investment or $25,000 it only takes a rate of 6.88 percent to compound it to $500,000. In the later years, compound interest becomes very large.

CHAPTER 6

The Time Value of Money

Annuities and Other Topics

Chapter **Orientation**

This chapter covers the valuation of cash flows that repeat over time: annuities and perpetuities. These financial analysis tools can value many different types of bonds and stocks. The skills in this chapter solve many common personal finance questions such as finding the amount owed on monthly car and home loans or determining how much needs to be saved for retirement.

Chapter Review: **Terms and Concepts**

6.1 Annuities

Ordinary Annuities

An annuity is a series of periodic equal dollar payments over a span of time. The most common annuity is one with payments made at the end of each period, an ordinary annuity. The characteristics of an ordinary annuity are that:

- Payments are made at the end of the period.
- Payments are equal periods apart.
- Payments are made for a finite span of time.

The Future Value of an Ordinary Annuity

A timeline is useful for visualizing the cash flows of an annuity. The cash flows along a timeline can be solved as individual problems and summed up by repeating the valuation for each cash flow. The future value formula is:

$$FV_n = PV(1 + i)^n \qquad (5\text{–}1a)$$

This is good for finding the value of one amount in the future, but to quickly find the value of a series of payments over time requires a future value annuity formula with the following definitions:

$$FV_n = PMT\left[\frac{(1+i)^n - 1}{i}\right] \qquad (6\text{–}1c)$$

Important Definitions and Concepts

- FV_n is the future value of the annuity at the end of the *n*th period. Thus, if periods were measured in years, the future value at the end of the third year would be FV_3.
- *PMT* is the annuity payment deposited or received at the end of each period.
- *i* is the interest (or compound) rate per period. Thus, if the periods were measured in years, it would be the annual interest rate.
- *n* is the number of periods for which the annuity will last.

A financial calculator or a spreadsheet can quickly solve annuity problems.

Using a Financial Calculator for five payments, one a year for five years, of $5,000 at a rate of 6 percent.

Enter	5	6.0	0	-5,000	
	N	I/Y	PV	PMT	FV
Solve for					28,185.46

Using an Excel Spreadsheet: =*FV*(rate,nper,pmt,pv) or with values entered =FV(.06,5,-5000,0)

By using the formulas, calculators, or spreadsheets, analysts can solve for any of the parts of the equation: number of periods, interest rate, payments, future value, or present value.

Suppose that you would like to have $50,000 saved 10 years from now to finance your goal of getting an MBA. If you are going to make equal annual end-of-year payments to an investment account that pays 8 percent, how big do these annual payments need to be? We know that $n = 10$, $i = 8$, and $FV_{10} = \$50,000$ in Equation 6–1c, and what we do not know is the value of *PMT*. Substituting into equation 6–1c we get,

$$FV_n = PMT\left[\frac{(1+i)^n - 1}{i}\right] \qquad (6\text{–}1c)$$

$$\$50,000 = PMT\left[\frac{(1+0.08)^{10} - 1}{0.08}\right]$$

$$\$50,000 = PMT(14.4866)$$

$$\frac{\$50,000}{14.4866} = PMT = \$3,451$$

Solving for interest rate or number of periods is efficiently done by calculator or spreadsheet.

Interest rate example: In 15 years you hope to have $30,000 saved to buy a sports car. You are able to save $1,022 at the end of each year for the next 15 years. What rate of return must you earn on your investments in order to achieve your goal?

It is easy to solve this problem with a financial calculator or with Excel, but as we describe below, solving it with the mathematical formula can be somewhat difficult.

Using the Mathematical Formula. Substituting the numbers into Equation 6–1c we get,

$$FV_n = PMT\left[\frac{(1+i)^n - 1}{i}\right] \qquad (6\text{–}1c)$$

$$\$30{,}000 = \$1{,}022\left[\frac{(1+i)^{15} - 1}{i}\right]$$

$$\frac{\$30{,}000}{\$1{,}022} = \left[\frac{(1+i)^{15} - 1}{i}\right]$$

$$29.354 = \left[\frac{(1+i)^{15} - 1}{i}\right]$$

The only way to solve for the interest rate at this point is by trial and error. We substitute different numbers for i until we find the value of i that makes the right side of the expression equal to 29.354.

Using a Financial Calculator. We can use a financial calculator to solve for i directly as follows:

Enter	15		0	-1,022	30,000
	N	I/Y	PV	PMT	FV
Solve for		9.0			

Using an Excel Spreadsheet: =RATE(nper,pmt,pv,fv) or with values entered =RATE(15,-1022,0,30000).

Number of periods example: Suppose you are investing \$5,000 at the end of each year in an account that pays 7 percent. How long before your account is worth \$51,300?

Using a Financial Calculator. We can use a financial calculator to solve for i directly as follows:

Enter		7.0	0	-5,000	51,300
	N	I/Y	PV	PMT	FV
Solve for	8.0				

Thus it will take 8 years for end of year deposits of \$5,000 every year to grow to \$51,300

Using an Excel Spreadsheet: =NPER(rate,pmt,pv,fv) or with values entered =NPER(7%,-5000,0,51300).

The Present Value of An Annuity

Solving present value of annuity problems can be solved by separating the cash flows along a timeline into individual problems and summing, but it is quicker to use an annuity formula. Similar to the future value of annuity problems, doing the math with a formula, a calculator, or a spreadsheet can be used to solve for either the present value, the number of periods, the interest rate, or the payment of an annuity. The present value of annuity formula and the accompanying definitions are:

$$\text{Present Value} = PMT\left[\frac{1 - \frac{1}{(1+i)^n}}{i}\right] \qquad (6\text{–}2b)$$

Important Definitions and Concepts

- *PV* is the present value of the annuity.
- *PMT* is the annuity payment deposited or received at the end of each period.
- *i* is the discount (or interest) rate on a per-period basis. For example, if annuity payments were received annually, *i* would be expressed as an annual rate; if the payments were received monthly, it would be the monthly rate.
- *n* is the number of periods for which the annuity will last. If the annuity payments were received annually, *n* would be the number of years; if the payments were received monthly, it would be the number of months.

Amortized Loans

Amortized loans, or installment loans, are paid off in equal payments as an annuity. The payments include both principal and interest. Home mortgages and car loans are common amortized loans.

Example amortized loan: Suppose you plan to get a $6,000 car loan at 15 percent annual interest with annual payments that you will pay off over four years. What will your annual payments be on this loan? Let's solve this using a financial calculator.

Enter	4	15.0	6,000		0
	N	I/Y	PV	PMT	FV
Solve for				-2,101.59	

Example loan amortization schedule:

Table 6.1 The Loan Amortization Schedule for a $6,000 Loan at 15% to Be Repaid in Four Years

Year	Amount Owed on the Principal at the Beginning of the Year (1)	Annuity Payment (2)	Interest Portion of the Annuity = (1) × 15% =(3)	Repayment of the Principal Portion of the Annuity = (2) − (3) = (4)	Outstanding Loan Balance at Year End, after the Annuity Payment = (1) − (4) = (5)
1	$6,000.00	$2,101.59	$900.00	$1,201.59	$4,798.41
2	4,798.41	2,101.59	719.76	1,381.83	3,416.58
3	3,416.58	2,101.59	512.49	1,589.10	1,827.48
4	1,827.48	2,101.59	274.12	1,827.48	0.00

Amortized Loans with Monthly Payments

To adjust annuities from yearly to monthly payments, you must adjust periods using *m*, the number of compounding periods, by multiplying years by 12 and adjust the interest rate by dividing the annual rate by 12. For daily payments, *m* equals 365 and for weekly, *m* equals 52.

To find the outstanding balance on the loan, solve for the present value of the loan with the number of periods remaining on the loan.

Home mortgage example: To buy a house you'll need to take out a $150,000, 30-year mortgage at an annual rate of 6 percent. What will your monthly mortgage payments be?

Mathematical Formulas. As we saw in the previous chapter in equation (5–1b), in order to determine *n*, the number of periods, we multiply the number of years by *m*, where m is the number of times compounding occurs each year. To determine the interest rate per period, we divide the annual interest rate by *m*, where *m* is the number of times compounding occurs per year. Modifying equation (6–2b) for non-annual compounding, we find

$$PV = PMT\left[\frac{1-\dfrac{1}{\left(1+\text{annual interest rate}/m\right)^{\text{numberof of years}\bullet m}}}{\text{annual interest rate}/m}\right] \quad (6\text{–}2c)$$

Substituting *annual interest rate* = .06, *number of years* = 30, *m* = 12, and PV = \$150,000 into Equation (6–2c), we get,

$$\$150{,}000 = PMT\left[\frac{1-\dfrac{1}{\left(1+0.06/12\right)^{30\times 12}}}{0.06/12}\right]$$

Notice that when you convert the annual rate of 6% to a monthly rate (by dividing it by 12), the monthly rate drops to 0.005 or 0.5%.

$$\$150{,}000 = PMT\left[\frac{1-\dfrac{1}{(1+0.005)^{360}}}{0.005}\right]$$

$$\$150{,}000 = PMT\,(166.7916144)$$

$$PMT = \$150{,}000 \,/\, 166.7916144 = \$899.33$$

Using a Financial Calculator. Because there are 360 monthly periods in 30 years, 360 is entered for [N], and [I/Y] becomes 0.5 (annual interest rate of 6% divided by *m* which is 12).

Enter	360	0.5	150,000		0
	[N]	[I/Y]	[PV]	[PMT]	[FV]
Solve for				-899.33	

Using an Excel Spreadsheet: =PMT(rate,nper,pv,fv) or with values entered =PMT(0.005,360,150000,0)

Annuities Due

An annuity is a series of periodic equal dollar payments over a span of time. An annuity due is one with payments made at the beginning of each period, so for future values it compounds interest for one more period than an ordinary annuity. Some typical annuity due problems solve values from lottery payouts and savings for retirement. The characteristics of an annuity due are that:

- Payments are made at the beginning of the period.
- Payments are equal periods apart.
- Payments are made for a finite span of time.

The Future Value of an Annuity Due

The future value of an annuity due is:

$$FV_n(\text{annuity due}) = \text{PMT}\left[\frac{(1+i)^n - 1}{i}\right](1 + i) \qquad (6\text{–}3)$$

Example annuity due: Recall that earlier we calculated the future value of a five-year ordinary annuity of \$5,000 earning 6% interest to be \$28,185.46. If we now assume this is a five-year annuity due, its future value increases from \$28,185.46 to \$29,876.59.

$$= \$5{,}000\left[\frac{(1+0.06)^5 - 1}{0.06}\right](1 + 0.06) = \$28{,}185.46(1 + 0.06) = \$29{,}876.59$$

6.2 Perpetuities

A perpetuity is a series of payments that continue forever. Perpetuities can be level or equal every period or growing at the same rate every period. Preferred stocks are presumed to pay dividends forever as corporations have no finite life.

Calculating the Present Value of a Level Perpetuity

This formula divides cash flow by a discount rate:

$$PV = \frac{PMT}{i} \qquad (6\text{–}5)$$

Important Definitions and Concepts

- PV = the present value of a level perpetuity
- PMT = the constant dollar amount provided by the perpetuity
- i = the interest (or discount) rate per period

Calculating the Present Value of a Growing Perpetuity

This formula divides cash flow by a discount rate:

$$PV = \frac{PMT}{(r-g)} \qquad (6\text{–}6)$$

Important Definitions and Concepts

- PV = the present value of a growing perpetuity.
- $PMT_{\text{period 1}}$ = the amount of the payment made at the end of the first period (e.g., this was \$100 in the example used above).
- i = the rate of interest used to discount the growing perpetuity's cash flows.
- g = the rate of growth in the payment cash flows from period to period.

Example level and growing perpetuity: Suppose you receive \$100 a year forever and your discount rate is 10 percent. What is the value of those cash flows? What if the cash flows grew at an annual rate of 5 percent? What is the value of those cash flows?

In the first problem, it is a level perpetuity of \$100 discounted at 10 percent forever, \$100/0.10 = \$1,000.

In the second problem, it is a growing perpetuity of \$100, growing at 5 percent, discounted at 10 percent forever, \$100 / (0.10 – 0.05) = \$2,000.

6.3 Complex Cash Flow Streams

Timelines and diagrams can be helpful when trying to visualize complex cash flows that are a mix of annuities, perpetuities, and single cash flows.

Example Complex Cash Flow: Consider the cash flows below with a 10 percent interest rate and find the present value today.

i = 10%

0	1	2	3	4	5	6	7	8	9	10 Years
	\$400	\$400	\$400	\$400	–\$200	\$500	\$500	\$500	\$500	\$500 Cash Flow

\$1,052.68 *PV* today Year 5 to 10 cash flows \$1,695.35 *PV* at Year 5 of Year 5 to 10 cash flows

\$1,267.95 *PV* today Year 1 to Year 4 cash flows

\$2,320.65 Sum of the *PVs*

This is a four-year annuity of \$400 at 10 percent, a negative cash flow of –\$200 in Year 5, and another annuity of five years of \$500 at 10 percent. The solution could separate the problem into ten present value problems or into two annuities and a single cash flow. Standing at the end of Year 5 there is a –\$200 payment and an annuity of \$500 for five years.

- Year 5 = –200 + *PV* Annuity of \$500 for five years at 10 percent
- *PV* Annuity in a calculator is Solve *PV* (N = 5, I = 10%, PMT = –500, FV = 0) = \$1,895.35
- Less \$200 at the end of Year 5 equals the *PV* of all cash flows from Year 5 to Year 10 = \$1,695.35
- *PV* that Year 5 amount to Year 0 is one cash flow of \$1695.35 for five years at 10% = \$1,052.68
- For the \$400 cash flows in Year 1 to Year 4, *PV* Annuity of \$400 for four years at 10 percent
- *PV* Annuity in a calculator is Solve *PV* (N = 4, I = 10%, PMT = –400, FV = 0) = \$1,267.95
- So the four-year annuity is today's value of \$1,267.95.
- The five-year annuity plus the –\$200 is discounted twice to a value of \$1,052.68 today.
- The total value today of all the cash flows is the sum of \$1,267.95 plus \$1,052.68 = \$2,320.65

Answers to **Concept Checks**

Concept Check **6.1**

1. Define the term *annuity* as it relates to cash flows.
2. Distinguish between an ordinary annuity and an annuity due.
3. Describe the adjustments necessary when annuity payments occur on a monthly basis.

4. How would you determine how much you currently owe on an outstanding loan?

Answer 1: An annuity is a series of periodic equal dollar payments over a span of time.

Answer 2: An ordinary annuity pays cash flows at the end of a period while an annuity due pays cash flows at the beginning of a period.

Answer 3: For monthly payment cycles, *m* equals 12, years are multiplied by 12 and interest rates are divided by 12.

Answer 4: To find the remaining outstanding balance of a loan, find the present value for the number of periods remaining.

Concept Check 6.2

1. Define the term *perpetuity* as it relates to cash flows.
2. What is a growing perpetuity, and how is it calculated?

Answer 1: A perpetuity pays periodic equal cash flows forever.

Answer 2: A growing perpetuity grows cash flows at the same rate forever. This formula has cash flow in the numerator and interest rate less growth rate in the denominator.

Concept Check 6.3

1. When are cash flows comparable—that is, when can they be added together or subtracted from each other?
2. Why would you want to be able to compare cash flows that occur in different time periods with each other?

Answer 1: Cash flows are comparable when they are valued in the same time period.

Answer 2: Real world investments have irregular cash flow patterns and in order to value any project, analysts would need to state cash flows in the same time period to make them comparable.

Multiple Choice Quiz

1. An amortized loan has
   a. smaller payments at the beginning of the loan.
   b. larger payments at the beginning of the loan.
   c. payments that vary with interest rates.
   d. equal payments consisting of principle and interest.

2. An ordinary annuity has
   a. payments at the end of the period.
   b. payments at the beginning of the period.
   c. growing payments across the period.
   d. payments forever.

3. An annuity due has
   a. payments at the end of the period.
   b. payments at the beginning of the period.
   c. growing payments across the period.
   d. payments forever.

4. A level perpetuity has
   a. payments at the end of the period.
   b. payments at the beginning of the period.
   c. growing payments at a level growth rate forever.
   d. payments forever.

5. A growing perpetuity has
   a. payments at the end of the period.
   b. payments at the beginning of the period.
   c. growing payments at a level growth rate forever.
   d. payments forever.

6. To find the outstanding balance on a loan,
   a. multiply the payments remaining times the number of periods.
   b. subtract the total of the past payments from the original loan value.
   c. find the future value of the remaining payments.
   d. find the present value of the remaining payments.

7. To value a quarterly cash flow, you must adjust
   a. payments and years by multiplying by 3.
   b. years by multiplying by 4.
   c. interest and years by dividing by 4.
   d. interest by dividing by 4 and periods by multiplying years by 4.

8. To value a growing perpetuity, divide the cash flow by
   a. interest rates.
   b. growth rates.
   c. interest rates less growth rates.
   d. growth rates less interest rates.

9. The proper formula to find the value of annuity today is
   a. cash flow divided by interest rate.
   b. $\text{Present Value} = PMT\left[\dfrac{1-\dfrac{1}{(1+i)^n}}{i}\right]$.
   c. cash flow divided by growth rate.
   d. $FV_n = PMT\left[\dfrac{(1+i)^n - 1}{i}\right]$.

10. To adjust the future value of an ordinary annuity formula to an annuity due,
    a. multiply by (1 + rate).
    b. divide by (1 + rate).
    c. multiply by *PMT*.
    d. divide by *PMT*.

Answers to **Multiple Choice Questions**

1. D
2. A
3. B
4. D
5. C
6. D
7. D
8. C
9. B
10. A

Self Test **with Solutions**

Picture the Problem

Decide on Solution Strategy

Solve

Analyze

Self Test 1: Ordinary Annuity

Consider the problem faced by an investor who wishes to retire in 40 years. The investor will earn 10 percent per year and invest $3,000 per year at the end of the year. How much will the investor have in 40 years?

Step 1: Picture the Problem

The problem calculates the future value of a $3,000 annuity for 40 years at a rate of 10 percent.

Step 2: Decide on a Solution Strategy

To solve, use the future value of an ordinary annuity formula (payments occur at the end of the period).

Step 3: Solve

To solve for the future value of $3,000 in 40 years, use a future value of an annuity formula.

$$FV_n = PMT\left[\frac{(1+i)^n - 1}{i}\right]$$

$$FV_n = 3000\left[\frac{(1+.1)^{40} - 1}{.1}\right] = \$1,327,777.67$$

Using a financial calculator

Solve FV (N = 40, PMT = -3000, i = .10, PV=0) = 1,327,777.67

Using a spreadsheet

=FV(rate, nper, pmt, pv) with values entered =FV(.10,40,-3000,0)

Step 4: Analyze

By investing $3,000 a year at 10 percent annually, the investor will have $1.327 million for retirement. If the investor earns a lower rate of return or invests less each year, the amount available for retirement will be less.

Self Test 2: Annuity Due

In Self Test 1, the investor would have $1,327,777.67 for retirement by investing $3,000 at the end of each year for 40 years. If the investor wanted to invest his annual funds at the beginning of each period to reach the same value in 40 years, how much should he invest?

Step 1: Picture the Problem

The problem calculates the payments starting at the beginning of the year that grow to equal $1,327,777.67 in 40 years. This requires the use of an annuity due formula.

Step 2: Decide on a Solution Strategy

To solve, we used the future value of an ordinary annuity formula since payments occur at the end of the period.

To solve this part, we will use the future value of an annuity due formula because payments will occur at the beginning of the period.

Step 3: Solve

To solve for the future value of $3,000 in 40 years, use a future value of an annuity formula.

$$FV_n(\text{annuity due}) = \text{PMT}\left[\frac{(1+i)^n-1}{i}\right](1+i) \quad 1327777.67 = \text{PMT}\left[\frac{(1.1)^{40}-1}{.1}\right] \tag{1–1}$$

Using a financial calculator set for annuity due

Solve PMT (N = 40, PMT = -3000, i = .10, PV=0, FV=1327777.67, AD=1) = 2,727.27

Using a spreadsheet

=PMT(rate, nper, pv, fv, ad) with values entered =PMT(.10,40,0,1327777.67,1)

Step 4: Analyze

By investing $2,727.27 at the beginning of the year at 10 percent annually, the investor will have $1.327 million for retirement in 40 years. By moving payments ahead one year, the investor makes a smaller payment.

Self Test 3: Outstanding Balance on a Loan

You financed $40,000 at 6 percent for 60 months to buy a car and two years later you decide to trade it for a new model. If the dealer offers you $25,000 for your old car, will you have enough to pay off the first loan?

Step 1: Picture the Problem

This problem is solved in three steps: find the payments of the first loan, find the outstanding balance for the remaining three years of the first loan, and compare the outstanding balance to the $25,000 offered for the used car. This requires the use of the present value of an ordinary annuity formula.

Step 2: Decide on a Solution Strategy

To solve the first step, we will use the present value of an ordinary annuity formula to find the amount of the payments since payments occur at the end of the period. Adjust i and N by $m = 12$.

To solve the second part, we will use the present value of an ordinary annuity formula for the value of those payments over the remaining 36 months (60 – 24) of the loan. This is the outstanding balance.

In the third step, we compare the outstanding balance to $25,000 to see if the trade-in value pays for the first loan.

Step 3: Solve

To solve for the payments that pay off a present value of $40,000 at 6% annual rate (i = .06/12 =.005) in five years (N = 60 months), use a present value of an annuity formula.

$$\text{Present Value} = PMT\left[\frac{1-\frac{1}{(1+\mathrm{i})^{\mathrm{n}}}}{\mathrm{i}}\right], \quad 40000 = PMT\left[\frac{1-\frac{1}{(1.005)^{60}}}{.005}\right]$$

Using a financial calculator set for ordinary annuity

Solve PMT (N = 60, i = .005, PV=40000, FV=0) = 773.31

Using a spreadsheet

=*PMT*(rate, nper, pv, fv) with values entered =*PMT*(.005,36,40000,0)

Next, solve for the value of those loan payments with 36 months left on the loan.

$$\text{Present Value} = PMT\left[\frac{1-\frac{1}{(1+i)^{n}}}{i}\right] \quad \text{Present Value} = 773.71\left[\frac{1-\frac{1}{(1.005)^{36}}}{.005}\right] = 25419.55$$

Compare the $25,000 offered for the trade with the loan payoff of $25,419.55.

Step 4: Analyze

The dealer is offering $25,000 or $419.55 less than the outstanding balance of the loan, so you will have to pay the extra to pay off the first loan.

Self Test 4: Level Perpetuity

You are the beneficiary of your rich uncle's trust that makes a payment from his corporation once a year forever. Your accountant tells you that the $60,000 annual payment makes you a virtual millionaire using an interest rate of 6 percent to value the payments. Is your accountant right?

Step 1: Picture the Problem

The problem calculates the value of payments of $60,000 every year forever at a rate of 6 percent. This requires the use of a perpetuity formula.

Step 2: Decide on a Solution Strategy

To solve the problem, use a perpetuity formula.

Step 3: Solve

To solve for the present value of $60,000, use a perpetuity formula.

$$PV = \frac{PMT}{i} = \frac{60000}{0.06}$$

$$= \$1,000,000$$

Using a financial calculator is trivial

Solve 60,000/0.06 equals 1,000,000

Using a spreadsheet

=60,000/0.06 equals 1,000,000

Step 4: Analyze

You are a millionaire using your accountant's discount rate. However, if you use a rate of 10 percent, you are worth only $600,000, about half.

Self Test 5: Growing Perpetuity

A real estate trust pays, for every unit you own, $2 in dividends next year and forecasts that dividend will grow at 5 percent indefinitely. What would be the value of one unit of that real estate trust, if investors use an interest or discount rate of 10 percent?

Step 1: Picture the Problem

The problem calculates the value of growing payments of $2 every year forever, growing at a rate of 5 percent, and discounted at 10 percent. This requires the use of a growing perpetuity formula.

Step 2: Decide on a Solution Strategy

To solve the problem, use a growing perpetuity formula.

Step 3: Solve

To solve for the present value of $60,000, use a perpetuity formula.

$$PV = \frac{PMT}{(r-g)} = \frac{2}{(0.10-0.05)} = \$40$$

Using a financial calculator is trivial

Solve 2/0.05 equals 40

Using a spreadsheet

=2/(0.10 – 0.05) equals 40

Step 4: Analyze

Each unit of the trust is worth $40. If the discount rate or the growth rate changes, then the value will change. High growth rates increase value while higher discount rates reduce value.

CHAPTER 7

An Introduction to Risk and Return

History of Financial Market Returns

Chapter **Orientation**

This chapter covers risk and return: its qualitative and quantitative aspects. This chapter presents the volatile nature of markets and the history of risk and returns. This chapter relies on basic statistics to describe uncertainty as many in finance know it. Another issue presented by the chapter is what returns investors should expect in the future. Finally, the concept of an efficient market and its implications for individuals and firms also is discussed.

Chapter Review: **Terms and Concepts**

7.1 Realized and Expected Rates of Return and Risk

Calculating the Realized Return from an Investment

The **cash return** is the gain or loss on an investment.

$$\text{Cash Return} = \text{Ending Price} + \text{Cash Distribution (Dividend)} - \text{Beginning Price} \qquad (7\text{–}1)$$

The **realized rate of return** is the actual rate of return actually experienced after a stock is traded during a period. If we express the rate of return on an investment as a percentage, it is called the **holding period return**.

$$\text{Rate of Return} = \frac{\text{Cash Return}}{\text{Beginning Price}} = \frac{\text{Ending Price} + \text{Cash Distribution (Dividend)} - \text{Beginning Price}}{\text{Beginning Price}} \qquad (7\text{–}2)$$

Note that realized returns may be positive or negative but we expect returns for risky assets to be positive (or else we would not invest). Investors trade between wanting more return and wanting less risk and as a result of these decisions, assets change values. A table of realized returns follows:

Table 7.1 Measuring an Investor's Realized Rate of Return from Investing in Common Stock

	Stock Prices		Cash Distribution (Dividend)	Return	
	Beginning (Oct 8, 2008)	Ending (Oct 9, 2009)		Dollar	Rate
Company	A	B	C	D = C + B − A	E = D/A
Dick's Sporting Goods (DKS)	$15.32	$22.69	$0.00	$7.37	45.0%
Duke Energy (DUK)	16.38	15.82	1.16	$0.60	1.8%
Emerson Electric (EMR)	32.73	37.75	1.32	$6.34	19.4%
Sears Holdings (SHLD)	57.74	67.86	0.00	$10.12	17.5%
Walmart (WMT)	55.81	49.68	1.06	(5.07)	−9.1%

Legend:
We formalize the return calculations found in Columns D and E using Equations (7–1) and (7–2):

Column D (Cash or Dollar Return)

$$\begin{matrix}\text{Cash}\\\text{Return}\end{matrix} = \begin{matrix}\text{Ending}\\\text{Price}\end{matrix} + \begin{matrix}\text{Cash Distribution}\\\text{(Dividend)}\end{matrix} - \begin{matrix}\text{Beginning}\\\text{Price}\end{matrix} = P_{End} + Div - P_{Beginning} \quad (7\text{–}1)$$

Column E (Rate of Return)

$$\begin{matrix}\text{Rate of}\\\text{Return, } r\end{matrix} = \frac{\text{Cash Return}}{\text{Beginning Price}} = \frac{P_{End} + Div - P_{Beginning}}{P_{Beginning}} \quad (7\text{–}2)$$

Calculating the Expected Return from an Investment

Investors make the risk-return tradeoff based on the **expected rate of return**, not realized. The expected rate of return represents the average of a possible set of returns or outcomes. By multiplying each return outcome by its probability and then summing the weighted returns, you will find the average rate of return, the expected rate of return. The right column of the following table shows the weighted probabilities and their sum.

Column G of Table 7.2 contains the products of the probability of each state of the economy (recession, moderate, or strong growth) found in Column B and the rate of return earned if that state occurs (Column F). By adding up these probability-weighted rates of return for the three states of the economy, we calculate an expected rate of return for the investment of 12.6 percent.

Equation (7–3) summarizes the calculation in Column G of Table 7.2 where there are three possible outcomes.

$$\begin{matrix}\text{Expected Rate}\\\text{of Return}\\{[E(r)]}\end{matrix} = \begin{pmatrix}\text{Rate of} & \text{Probability}\\\text{Return 1} \times & \text{of Return 1}\\(r_1) & (Pb_1)\end{pmatrix} + \begin{pmatrix}\text{Rate of} & \text{Probability}\\\text{Return 2} \times & \text{of Return 2}\\(r_2) & (Pb_2)\end{pmatrix} + \ldots + \begin{pmatrix}\text{Rate of} & \text{Probability}\\\text{Return } n \times & \text{of Return } n\\(r_n) & (Pb_n)\end{pmatrix} \quad (7\text{–}3)$$

We can use Equation (7–3) to calculate the expected rate of return for the investment in Table 7.2 where there are three possible outcomes as follows:

$$E(r) = (-10\% \times 0.2) + (12\% \times 0.3) + (22\% \times 0.5) = 12.6\%$$

Table 7.2 Calculating the Expected Rate of Return for an Investment in Common Stock

State of the Economy	Probabiliy of the State of the Economy[a] (Pb_i)	End-of-Year Selling Price for the Stock	Beginning Price of the Stock	Cash Return from Your Investment	Percentage Rate of Return = Cash Return/Beginning Price of the Stock	Product = Rate of Return x Probability of State of the Economy
Column A	Column B	Column C	Column D	Column E= C − D	Column F = E ÷ D	Column G = B × F
Recession	20%	$9,000	$10,000	–$1,000	–10% = –$1,000 ÷ $10,000	–2.0%
Moderate growth	30%	11,200	10,000	1,200	12% = $1,200 ÷ $10,000	3.6%
Strong growth	50%	12,200	10,000	2,200	22% = $2,200 ÷ $10,000	11%
Sum	100%					12.6%

[a]The probabilities assigned to the three possible economic conditions have to be determined subjectively, which requires management to have a thorough understanding of both the investment cash flows and the general economy.

Measuring Risk

Analysts need to estimate risk or return variability. Two popular measures, variance and standard deviation, measure deviation from expected return. The steps to measuring expected return and standard deviation follow:

Example

A stock with 10 percent probability of a 10 percent loss, 20 percent probability of a 5 percent gain, 40 percent probability of a 15 percent gain, 20 percent probability of a 25 percent gain, and a 10 percent probability of a 40 percent gain has an expected return of 15 percent.

$$E(r) = (0.10)(-10\%) + (0.20)(5\%) + (0.40)(15\%) + (0.20)(25\%) + (0.10)(40\%) = 15\%$$

The variance, or average of the squared deviations, is calculated too.

Specifically, the formula for the return variance of an investment with many possible future returns can be calculated using Equation (7-4) as follows:

$$\begin{matrix}\text{Variance in}\\ \text{Rates of Return}\\ (\sigma^2)\end{matrix} = \left[\left(\begin{matrix}\text{Rate of Return}\\ \text{for State 1}\\ (r_1)\end{matrix} - \begin{matrix}\text{Expected Rate}\\ \text{of Return}\\ E(r)\end{matrix}\right)^2 \times \begin{matrix}\text{Probability}\\ \text{of State 1}\\ (Pb_1)\end{matrix}\right] + \ldots + \left[\left(\begin{matrix}\text{Rate of Return}\\ \text{for State } n\\ (r_n)\end{matrix} - \begin{matrix}\text{Expected Rate}\\ \text{of Return}\\ E(r)\end{matrix}\right)^2 \times \begin{matrix}\text{Probability}\\ \text{of State } n\\ (Pb_n)\end{matrix}\right] \quad (7\text{–}4)$$

Note that the variance is measured using squared deviations of each possible return from the mean or expected return. This means that the variance is a measure of the average "squared" deviation around the mean. For this reason it is customary to measure risk as the square root of the variance which we learned in our statistics class was called the standard deviation.

For the publishing company's common stock, we calculate the variance and standard deviation using the following five-step procedure:

Step 1: Calculate the expected rate of return using Equation (7–3). This was calculated above to be 15 percent.

Step 2: Subtract the expected rate of return of 15 percent from each of the possible rates of return and square the difference.

Step 3: Multiply the squared differences calculated in Step 2 by the probability that those outcomes will occur.

Step 4: Sum all the values calculated in Step 3 together. The sum is the variance of the distribution of possible rates of return. Note that the variance is actually the *average squared difference between the possible rates of return and the expected rate of return.*

Step 5: Take the square root of the variance calculated in Step 4 to calculate the standard deviation of the distribution of possible rates of return. Note that the standard deviation (unlike the variance) is measured in rates of return.

Another way to view the dispersion of returns is by charting the outcomes. The following chart compares a Treasury Bill to a stock's dispersion.

Figure 7.1

Probability Distribution of Returns for a Treasury Bill and the Common Stock of the Ace Publishing Company

A probability distribution provides a tool for describing the possible outcomes or rates of return from an investment and the associated probabilities for each possible outcome. Technically, the following probability distribution is a discrete distribution since there are only five possible returns that the Ace Publishing Company stock can earn. The Treasury Bill investment offers only one possible rate of return (5%) since this investment is risk-free.

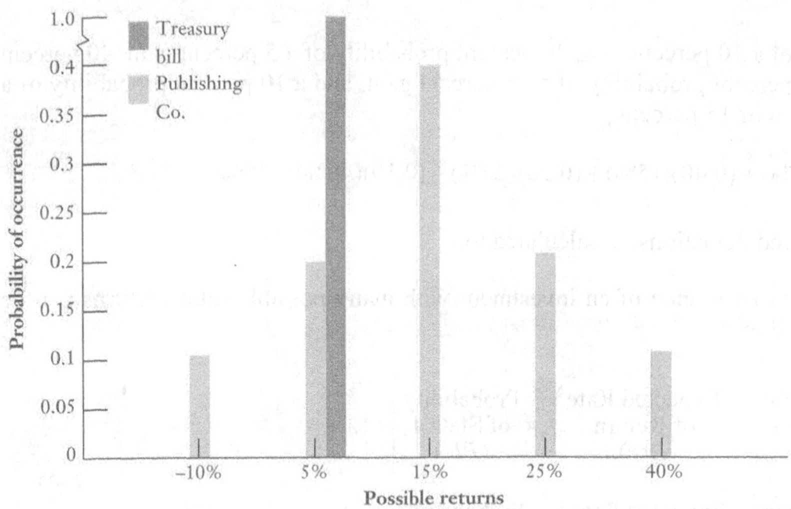

Chance or Probability of Occurrence	Rate of Return on Investment
1 chance in 10 (10%)	−10%
2 chances in 10 (20%)	5%
4 chances in 10 (40%)	15%
2 chances in 10 (20%)	25%
1 chance in 10 (10%)	40%

Table 7.3 **Measuring the Variance and Standard Deviation of an Investment in Ace Publishing's Common Stock**

Computing the variance and standard deviation in the rate of return earned from a stock investment can be carried out using the following five-step process:

Step 1: Calculate the expected rate of return.

Step 2: Subtract the expected rate of return from each of the possible rates of return and square the difference.

Step 3: Multiply the squared differences calculated in Step 2 by the probability that those outcomes will occur.

Step 4: Sum all the values calculated in Step 3 together to calculate the variance of the possible rates of return.

Step 5: Take the square root of the variance calculated in Step 4 to calculate the standard deviation of the distribution of possible rates of return.

State of the World	Rate of Return	Chance or Probability		Step 2	Step 3
a	b	c	d = b × c	e = [b − E(r)]²	f = e × c
1	−0.10	0.10	−0.01	0.0625	0.00625
3	0.05	0.20	0.01	0.0100	0.00200
4	0.15	0.40	0.06	0.0000	0.00000
4	0.25	0.20	0.05	0.0100	0.00200
5	0.40	0.10	0.04	0.0625	0.00625

Step 1: Expected Return (E(r)) = → 0.15
Step 4: Variance = → 0.0165
Step 5: Standard Deviation = → 0.1285

The five-step procedure above for the calculation of the standard deviation follows:

$$\text{Standard Deviation}, \sigma = \sqrt{\text{Variance}, \sigma^2}$$

$$\sigma = \sqrt{\left([r_1 - E(r)]^2 Pb_1\right) + \left([r_2 - E(r)]^2 Pb_2\right) + \ldots + \left([r_n - E(r)]^2 Pb_n\right)} \quad (7\text{–}5)$$

Where,
σ = standard deviation
r_i = possible return i
$E(r)$ = the expected return
Pb_i = the probability of return i occurring.

Using Equation (7–5) to calculate the standard deviation we find:

$$\sigma = \begin{bmatrix} \left((-0.10-0.15)^2 \times 0.10\right) + \left((0.05-15)^2 \times 0.20\right) \\ +\left((0.15-0.15)^2 \times 0.40\right) + \left((0.25-0.15)^2 \times 0.20\right) \\ +\left((0.40-0.15)^2 \times 0.10\right) \end{bmatrix}^{1/2} = \sqrt{0.0165} = 0.1285 \text{ or } 12.85\%$$

7.2 A Brief History of Financial Market Returns

U.S. Financial Markets: Domestic Investment Returns

Investors expect to earn a return on their investments with the riskier ones that are more likely to disappoint offering a higher return for that risk. How does an investment offer a higher return? Its price has to come down to make the future cash flows worth more.

From higher to lower risk (from the risk-return figure below):

- Small Stocks—as measured by the value of their equity (shares × price)
- Larger Stocks—S&P500 is a popular large stock index
- Government Bonds—default free long-term debt of a country
- Treasury Bills—less than one year maturity government debt (very safe)

Figure 7.2

Historical Rates of Return for U.S. Financial Securities: 1926–2011

The following graph provides historical insight into the performance characteristics of various asset classes over an 86-year period of time. This graph illustrates the hypothetical growth of inflation and a $1 investment in four traditional asset classes over the time period January 1, 1926, through December 31, 2011.

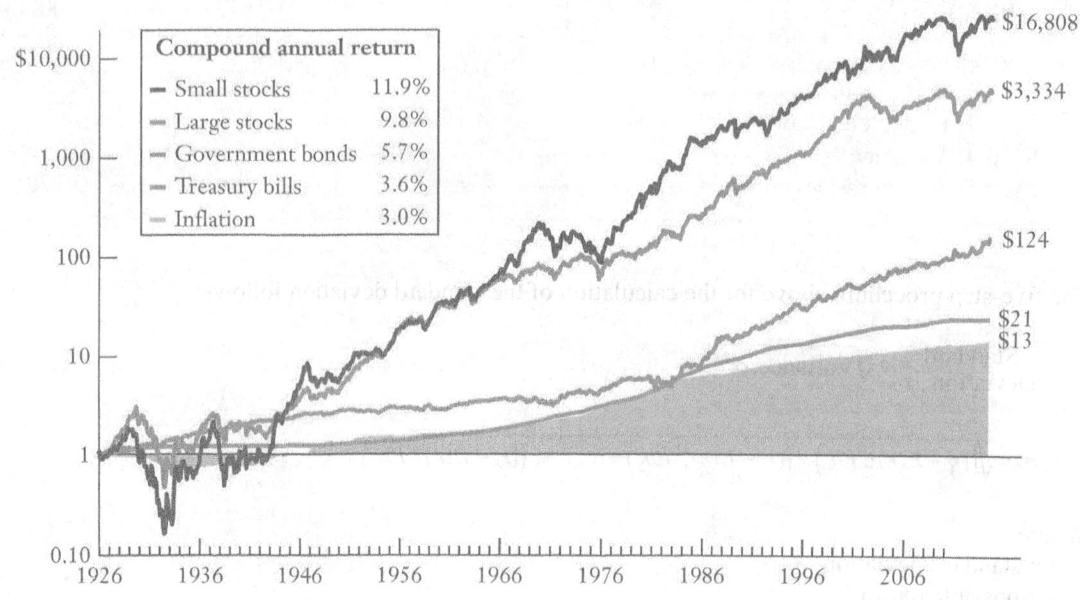

Legend:

Small stocks in this example are represented by the fifth capitalization quintile of stocks on the NYSE for 1926–1981 and the performance of the Dimensional Fund Advisors, Inc. (DFA) U.S. Micro Cap Portfolio thereafter. Large stocks are represented by the Standard & Poor's 90 index from 1926 through February 1957 and the S&P 500® index thereafter, which is an unmanaged group of securities and considered to be representative of the U.S. stock market in general. Government bonds are represented by the 20-year U.S. government bond, Treasury bills by the 30-day U.S. Treasury bill, and inflation by the Consumer Price Index. Underlying data is from the *Stocks, Bonds, Bills, and Inflation® (SBBI®) Yearbook*, by Roger G. Ibbotson and Rex Sinquefield, updated annually. An investment cannot be made directly in an index.

Source: © 2012 Morningstar. All rights reserved. Used with permission.

	Small Stocks	Large Stocks	Government Bonds	Treasury Bills
Compound annual return	11.9%	9.8%	5.7%	3.6%
Standard deviation	32.8%	20.5%	9.6%	3.1%

Another chart of returns with real estate and commodities:

Figure 7.3

Stocks, Bonds, Commodities, and Real Estate

This image illustrates the hypothetical growth of a $1 investment in domestic stocks, international stocks, commodities such as copper, REITs (real estate investment trusts that invest in commercial real estate and real estate mortgage loans), and commodities over the time period January 1, 1980, to December 31, 2011.

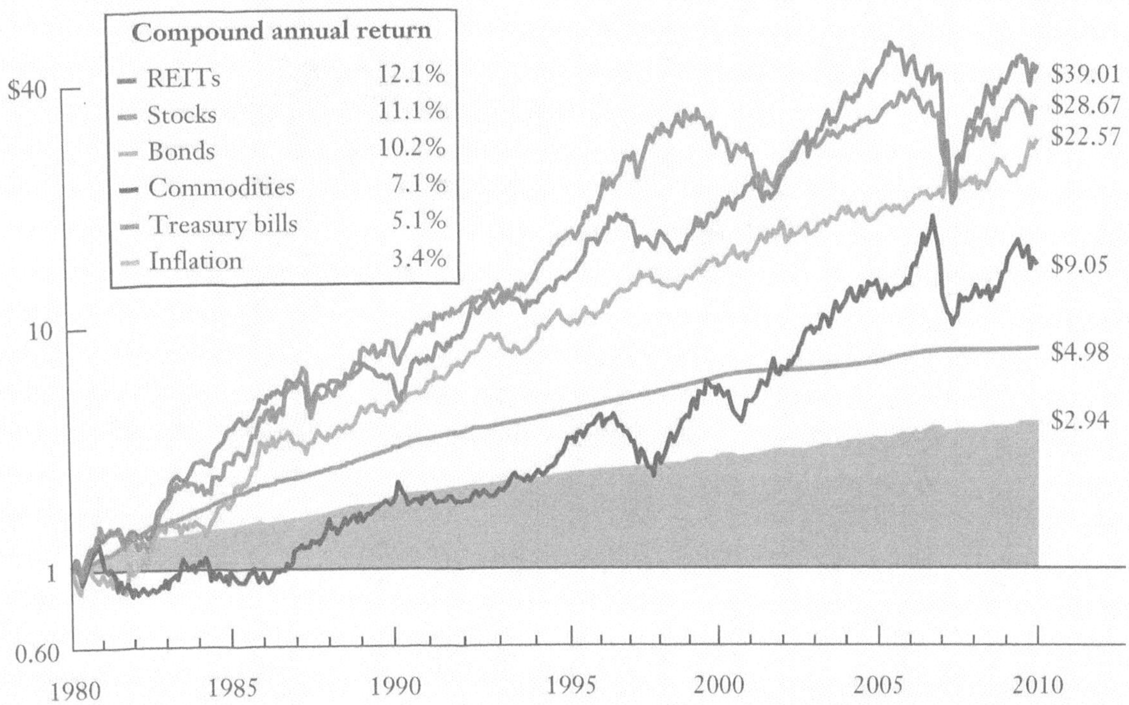

Legend:

Stocks in this example are represented by the Standard & Poor's 500®, which is an unmanaged group of securities and considered to be representative of the U.S. stock market in general. Bonds in this example are represented by the 20-year U.S. government bond, Treasury bills by the 30-day U.S. Treasury bill, and inflation by the Consumer Price Index. Commodities are represented by the Morningstar Long-Only Commodity Index and REITs by the FTSE NAREIT All Equity REITs Index®. An investment cannot be made directly in an index.

Source: © 2012 Morningstar. All rights reserved. Used with permission.

Lessons Learned:

#1: Riskier investments have historically realized higher returns. Equities earn more than bonds which earn more than Treasury Bills. The difference between the equity return and the government debt return is the equity risk premium.

#2: Riskier investments have greater standard deviations.

Global Financial Markets: International Investing

Developed country markets tend to have lower returns and less risk (standard deviation or **volatility**) compared to emerging markets. An emerging market is located in an economy in the middle to lower tier of economic development as measured by per capita income. Developed countries are sometimes called industrialized nations (G7 nations).

The figures below show the returns and risks in global and emerging markets:

Figure 7.4

Historical Rates of Return in Global Markets: 1970–2011

This figure reports the ranges of annual returns for domestic and international composites, as well as the Europe and Pacific regional composites, over the period 1970 through 2011.

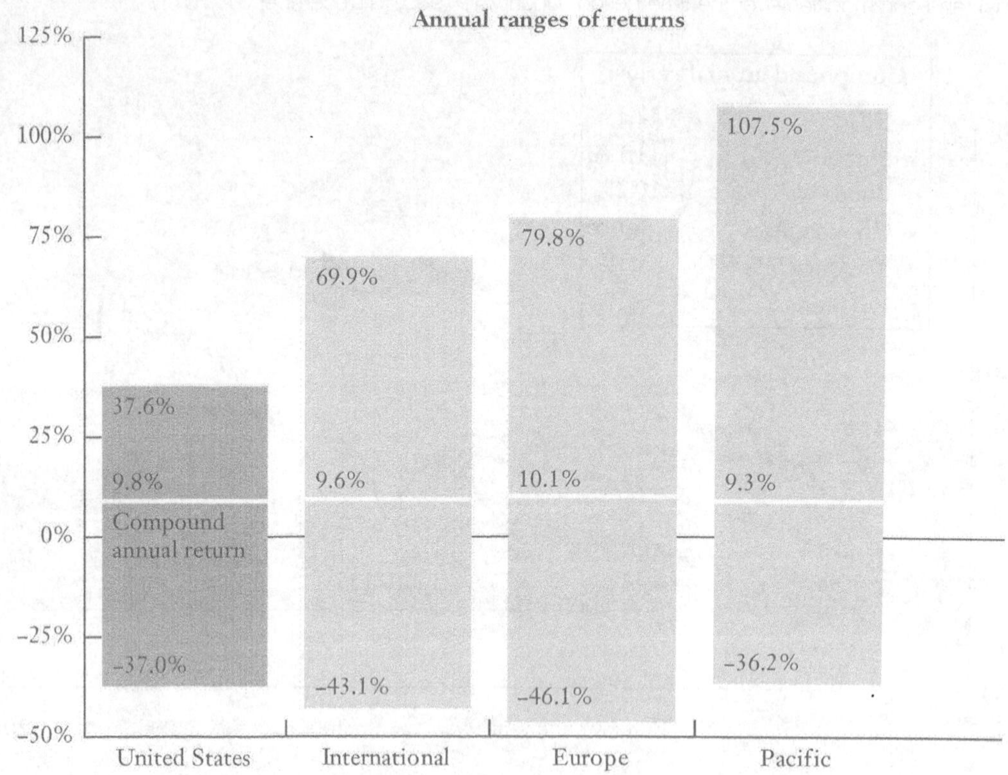

Legend:

U.S. stocks in this example are represented by the Standard & Poor's 500® index, which is an unmanaged group of securities and considered to be representative of the U.S. stock market in general. International stocks are represented by the Morgan Stanley Capital International Europe, Australasia, and Far East (EAFE®) Index, European stocks by the Morgan Stanley Capital International Europe Index, and Pacific stocks by the Morgan Stanley Capital International Pacific Index. An investment cannot be made directly in an index. The data assumes reinvestment of income and does not account for taxes or transaction costs.

Source: © 2012 Morningstar. All rights reserved. Used with permission.

Figure 7.5

Investing in Emerging Markets: 1988–2011

The following graph illustrates the range of returns as well as the compound annual return of selected developed and emerging countries. Although both sets experienced growth, emerging markets experienced a much greater upside and often deeper downside.

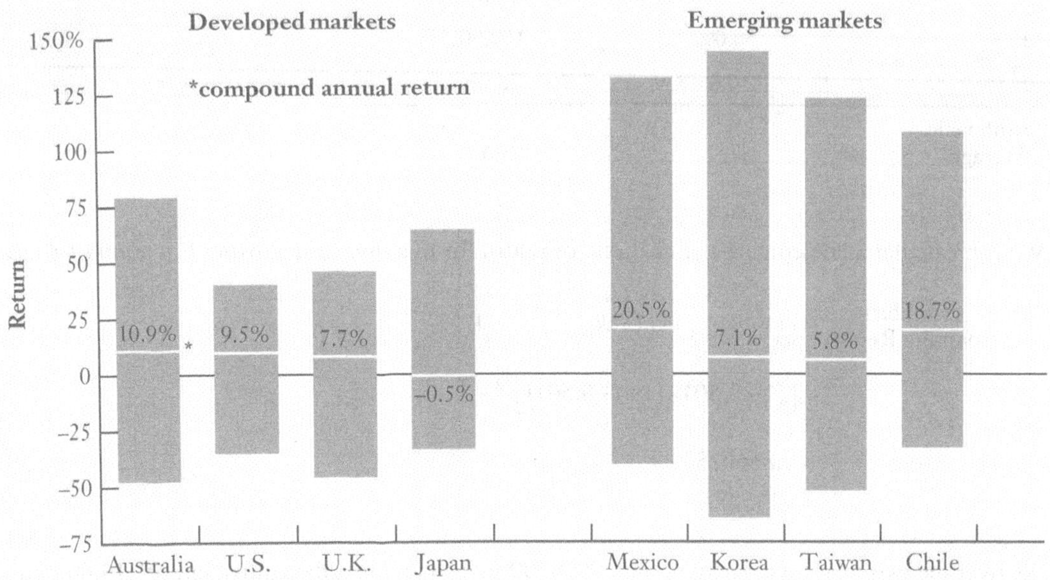

Legend:

Equities for the U.K., Australia, Japan, Taiwan, and Mexico are represented by the Morgan Stanley Capital International country indexes. Equities for Korea and Chile are represented by the Morgan Stanley Capital International Emerging Market country indexes. United States equities are represented by the Standard & Poor's 500®, which is an unmanaged group of securities and considered to be representative of the U.S. stock market in general. An investment cannot be made directly in an index. Keep in mind that the countries illustrated do not represent investment advice. The developed countries illustrated are a common range of investment options. Emerging-market countries were chosen based on availability of historical data; those with the longest stream of data were selected.

*Compounded annual return

Source: © 2012 Morningstar. All rights reserved. Used with permission.

7.3 Geometric vs. Arithmetic Average Rates of Return

The simple average of several years of returns is the arithmetic average and will be a little less than the compounded return, the geometric average, over the period. Looking ahead only one year we should expect to earn the average return on an asset. Looking ahead more than one year, we should expect to earn the geometric return. The geometric average return finds the growth rate of an investment. Use the formula below to compute a geometric average return:

$$\text{Geometric Average Return} = \left[\begin{array}{l}\left(1+\begin{array}{c}\text{Rate of Return}\\ \text{for Year 1, } r_{Year1}\end{array}\right)\times\left(1+\begin{array}{c}\text{Rate of Return}\\ \text{for Year 2, } r_{Year2}\end{array}\right)\\ \times\ldots\times\left(1+\begin{array}{c}\text{Rate of Return}\\ \text{for Year } n\text{, } r_{Year\,n}\end{array}\right)\end{array}\right]^{1/n} - 1 \qquad (7\text{–}6)$$

An example of the two types of return averages follows for a stock that grew by 50 percent and fell by 50 percent across a two year span and had a –13.4 percent geometric return and a 0 percent arithmetic:

Year	Annual Rate of Return	Value of the Stock
0		$100.00
1	50.0%	150.00
2	–50.0%	75.00
Arithmetic Average		0.00%

We can calculate the geometric annual rate of return for this investment using Equation (7-6) as follows:

$$\begin{aligned}\text{Geometric Average Return} &= \left[(1+R_{Year1})\times(1+R_{Year2})\right]^{1/2}-1\\ &= \left[(1+0.50)\times(1+(-0.50))\right]^{1/2}-1\\ &= 0.866025^{\frac{1}{2}}-1\\ &= -13.40\%\end{aligned}$$

So, over the two-year investment period, the $100 investment lost the equivalent of –13.40 percent per year.

Choosing the Right "Average"

Question being addressed:	Appropriate Average Calculation:
What annual rate of return can we expect for next year?	The arithmetic average rate of return calculated using annual rates of return.
What annual rate of return can we expect over a multiyear horizon?	The geometric average rate of return calculated over a similar past period.

7.4 What Determines Stock Prices?

It is easy to think that by analyzing public news that you can beat the market. However, the markets constantly frustrate investors who do this. Why? The *efficient markets hypothesis* suggests that additional analysis of already public information will not yield improved results over the assessment made by others in the market. In a market where information is priced efficiently, the way to increase return requires investors to take more risk as there are no shortcuts to higher returns. This efficient markets frustration is the basis for modern finance and market analysis by investors.

The Efficient Markets Hypothesis

The **efficient markets hypothesis** states that securities prices reflect future expected cash flows based on all information available to investors. An **efficient market** is one in which all available information is fully incorporated into securities' prices and returns on investments are not predictable. There are three types of market efficiency:

- Weak form—price and volume information is in the price of securities.
- Semi-strong form—all publicly available information is in the price of securities.
- Strong form—all public and private informatiion is in the price of securities.

Do We Expect Financial Markets to be Perfectly Efficient?

If a security is underpriced, investors will bid for its shares until it is no longer underpriced. Since this process is always present, it is unlikely investors will easily find strategies that beat the market as others would trade away the profits. Private information can beat the market in limited cases. There is no free lunch as research and data collection are costs to the investor, thus the market is just inefficient enough to compensate researchers for their costs but does not offer easy profits.

The Behavioral View

Another view of markets does not assume that investors are rational. Behavioral Finance believes that prices may not reflect all publicly available information because investors do not rationally process the information. Investors can underreact and overreact to news.

Market Efficiency: What Does the Evidence Show?

Market inefficiencies exist in a few subtle ways (value, momentum, over and under-reaction). The challenge for investors is that these effects diminish as they become widely known, which is what an efficient market would do. The chart below shows the major types of anomalies:

Table 7.4 Summarizing the Evidence of Anomalies to the Efficient Market Hypothesis

Anomaly	Description
#1. Value stocks outperform growth stocks	*Value stocks, which are stocks with tangible assets that generate current earnings, have tended to outperform growth stocks, which are stocks with low current earnings that are expected to grow in the future.* More specifically, stocks with low price-earnings ratios, low price-to-cash flow, and low price-to-book value ratios tend to outperform the market.
#2. Momentum in stock returns	Stocks that have performed well in the past 6 to 12 months tend to continue to outperform other stocks.
#3. Over- and under-reaction to corporate announcements	*The market has tended to underreact to many corporate events.* For example, stock prices react favorably on dates when firms announce favorable earnings news, which is exactly what we would expect in an efficient market. However, on the days after favorable earnings news, stock returns continue to be positive on average. This is known as post-earnings announcement drift. Similarly, there is evidence of some degree of predictability in stock returns following other major announcements, like the issuance of stock or bonds.

Answers to **Concept Checks**

Concept Check **7.1**

1. If you invested $100 one year ago that is worth $110 today, what rate of return did you earn on your investment?
2. What is the expected rate of return and how is it different than the realized rate of return?
3. What is the variance in the rate of return of an investment?
4. Why is variance used to measure risk?

Answer 1: Rate of return = 110 / 100 – 1 = 10%.

Answer 2: The expected rate of return is the promised return at the beginning of the investment while the realized rate of return is the return actually earned in the financial markets based on the actual prices of the investment.

Answer 3: Variance or standard deviation represents the uncertainty of the outcomes around the expected return and is the quantitative measure of risk. Variance is the averaged squared difference between the realized returns and the expected return. Variance is stated in squared values while standard deviation is stated in return measured.

Answer 4: Variance or standard deviation represents the uncertainty of the outcomes around the mean return and is the quantitative measure of risk. Variance and its square root, standard deviation, allows analysts to develop confidence intervals and quantify risk to assess the costs and benefits of investment decisions.

Concept Check **7.2**

1. How well does the risk-return principle hold up in light of historical rates of return? Explain.
2. What is the equity risk premium and how is it measured?
3. Does the historical evidence suggest that investing in emerging markets is more or less risky than investing in developed markets?

Answer 1: In general, higher risk assets such as equity has returned more than lower risk assets such as government debt.

Answer 2: The equity risk premium is the difference between equity returns and government bond returns and represents the compensation to investors for equity risk.

Answer 3: Emerging markets have higher returns and standard deviations than developed markets and are more risky.

Concept Check **7.3**

1. How is a simple arithmetic average computed? For example, what is the arithmetic average of the following annual rates of return: 10 percent, −10 percent, and 5 percent?
2. How is a geometric average rate of return computed? For example, what is the geometric average of the following annual rates of return: 10 percent, −10 percent, and 5 percent?
3. Why is the geometric average different from the arithmetic average?

Answer 1: The simple arithmetic average divided the sum of the returns by the number of outcomes. Arithmetic return = (10% + –10% + 5%) / 3 = 1.66%

Answer 2: The geometric return is the *Nth* root of the compounded return using the number of outcomes. Geometric return = (1.10 × 0.90 × 1.05) raised to 1/3 power less 1 = 1.3%

Answer 3: The simple average shows the average return for one year but the geometric return shows the growth of an investment through the time period.

Concept Check **7.4**

1. What is an "efficient market"?

2. What are the three categories of information that are commonly used to categorize tests of the efficient market hypothesis?

3. How do behavioral biases affect the efficiency of market prices?

Answer 1: An efficient market is one in which all available information is fully incorporated into securities' prices and returns on investments are not predictable.

Answer 2: The three types of market efficiency are:

Weak form: prices reflect price and volume history of asset prices.

Semi-strong form: prices reflect public information.

Strong form: prices reflect public and private information.

Answer 3: Behavioral biases can cause investors to over and under-react to information and make mistakes when processing public information.

Multiple Choice **Quiz**

1. The arithmetic return is
   a. the sum of returns divided by their number.
   b. the compounded return.
   c. the expected return over the risk-free rate.
   d. the deviation around an expected return.

2. The geometric return is
   a. the sum of returns divided by their number.
   b. the compounded return.
   c. the expected return over the risk-free rate.
   d. the deviation around an expected return.

3. An emerging country is
   a. an industrialized nation with lower returns and risk.
   b. a country with below average per capita income.
   c. a country with dramatically increasing exports.
   d. an industrialized nation with higher returns and risk.

4. A developed country is
   a. an industrialized nation with lower returns and risk.
   b. a country with below average per capita income.
   c. a country with dramatically increasing exports.
   d. an industrialized nation with higher returns and risk.

5. An efficient market is a financial market with
   a. rational and irrational investors.
   b. securities that accurately reflect information.
   c. rational investors that process public information slowly.
   d. securities that allow investors using analysis to beat the market.

6. The equity market risk premium is
   a. the return over the corporate debt rate.
   b. the risk as measured by standard deviation.
   c. the risk as measured by volatility.
   d. the return of equities over government debt.

7. The expected rate of return is
   a. the return forecasted to occur in the future.
   b. the actual return calculated on the investment.
   c. the geometric average return.
   d. the return above the risk-free rate.

8. The realized rate of return is
   a. the return forecasted to occur in the future.
   b. the actual return calculated on the investment.
   c. the geometric average return.
   d. the return above the risk-free rate.

9. The three types of market efficiency are
   a. weak, developed, and emerging.
   b. behavioral, efficient, and inefficient.
   c. weak, semi-strong, and strong.
   d. inefficient, semi-strong, and efficient.

10. Semi-strong markets allow
    a. analysts using charts to beat the market.
    b. analysts using public information to beat the market.
    c. analysts using private information to beat the market.
    d. no analysts to beat the market.

Answers to **Multiple Choice Questions**

1. A
2. B
3. B
4. A
5. B
6. D
7. A
8. B
9. C
10. C

Self Test **with Solutions**

Picture the Problem

Decide on Solution Strategy

Solve

Analyze

Self Test 1: Returns and Risk

You are an analyst for an economic forecasting service and your staff has come up with a table of likely market outcomes for the next four years. What is the average return, geometric return, the variance and standard deviation of the return series?

Year 1:	10%
Year 2:	14%
Year 3:	20%
Year 4:	–20%

Step 1: Picture the Problem

The problem asks for the risk and return of a series of returns.

Step 2: Decide on a Solution Strategy

To solve, we will use the formulas for arithmetic return, geometric return, and variance.

Step 3: Solve

To solve for the arithmetic return, take the average of the returns.

$$\text{Average Return}_n = \sum \text{Returns} / N = \frac{0.10 + 0.14 + 0.20 - 0.20}{4} = 6\%$$

The average return to be expected in any one year is 6 percent.

To solve for the geometric return, use the following formula:

$$\text{Geometric Return} = [\,(1 + r_1) \times (1 + r_2) \times (1 + r_3) \times (1 + r_4)\,]^{1/n} - 1$$

$$\text{Geometric Return} = [\,1.10 \times 1.14 \times 1.20 \times .80\,]^{1/4} - 1 = 4.75\%$$

The geometric return was 4.75 percent as a growth rate over four periods.

To solve for the variance and the standard deviation, use the following formula:

$$\text{Standev} = \text{SQRT}\ (r_1 - E(r)]^2 \times Pb_1 + [\,r_2 - E(r)\,]^2 \times Pb_2 + [\,r_3 - E(r)\,]^2 \times Pb_3 + [\,r_4 - E(r)\,]^2 \times Pb_4$$

$$\sigma = \sqrt{[r_1 - E(r)]2 \times .25 + [r_2 - E(r)]2 \times .25 + [r_3 - E(r)]2 \times .25 + [r_4 - E(r)]2 \times .25}$$

Pb are equally likely so for $N = 4$, $Pb = 0.25$.

$$\sigma = \sqrt{[0.10 - 0.06]2 \times 0.25 + [0.14 - 0.06]2 \times 0.25 + [0.20 - 0.06]2 \times 0.25 + [-0.20 - 0.06]2 \times 0.25}$$

$$\sigma = \sqrt{[0.04]2 \times 0.25 + [0.08]2 \times 0.25 + [0.14]2 \times 0.25 + [-0.26]2 \times 0.25}$$

$$\sigma = \sqrt{[0.0016] \times 0.25 + [0.0064] \times 0.25 + [0.0196] \times 0.25 + [0.0676] \times 0.25}$$

$$\sigma = \sqrt{[0.0004] + [0.0016] + [0.0049] + [0.0169]} = \sqrt{0.0238} = 0.154$$

The variance is 0.0238 and the standard deviation is 0.154.

Step 4: Analyze

If you wanted to state the expected return for next year in the market, use the mean return of 6 percent. If you wanted to consider how your investment would grow over the next four years, use the geometric return of 4.75 percent. The standard deviation of 15.4 percent +/– 2X will give you a confidence interval to show the riskiness of the investment (–24 percent to +36 percent CI suggests a wide dispersion around the 6 percent mean).

CHAPTER 8

Risk and Return

Capital Market Theory

Chapter **Orientation**

This chapter covers risk and return for a single security and for a portfolio of securities. The chapter introduces the basics of modern portfolio theory and systemic risk. Another major topic is the Capital Asset Pricing Model role as the standard model for finding the required rate of return on an investment. How to calculate the beta risk measure for an investment or a portfolio is presented. To beat the market, in standard portfolio theory, requires the investor to take more risk and usually more leverage which can lead to significant losses similar to those experienced in mortgage backed securities in the capital market disruption of 2008. Diversification is one of the significant implications from modern portfolio theory for every investor and institution.

Chapter Review: **Terms and Concepts**

8.1 Portfolio Returns and Portfolio Risk

Diversification lowers the risk of a portfolio. To diversify, add assets that are not identical to your holdings.

Calculating the Expected Return of a Portfolio

Expected Rate of Return = weighted average of the asset returns for a portfolio

For N assets the formula is:

$$\begin{aligned}\text{Expected Portfolio Return} &= \left(\begin{array}{c}\text{Fraction of Portfolio}\\\text{Invested in Asset 1}\end{array}\times\begin{array}{c}\text{Expected Rate of}\\\text{Return on Asset 1}\end{array}\right)\\ &+\left(\begin{array}{c}\text{Fraction of Portfolio}\\\text{Invested in Asset 2}\end{array}\times\begin{array}{c}\text{Expected Rate of}\\\text{Return on Asset 2}\end{array}\right)\\ &+\left(\begin{array}{c}\text{Fraction of Portfolio}\\\text{Invested in Asset 3}\end{array}\times\begin{array}{c}\text{Expected Rate of}\\\text{Return on Asset 3}\end{array}\right)\\ &+\cdots+\left(\begin{array}{c}\text{Fraction of Portfolio}\\\text{Invested in Asset } n\end{array}\times\begin{array}{c}\text{Expected Rate of}\\\text{Return on Asset } n\end{array}\right)\end{aligned}$$

Portfolio Expected Rate of Return

$$E = [W_1 \times E(r_1)] + [W_2 \times E(r_{2]})] + [W_3 \times E(r_3)] + \cdots + [W_n \times E(r_n)] \qquad (8\text{–}1)$$

Important Definitions and Concepts

- $E(r_{portfolio})$ = the expected rate of return on a portfolio of n assets (three in this case)

- W_i = the portfolio weight for asset *i*.
- $E(r_i)$ = the expected rate of return earned by asset *i*. Recall from Chapter 7 that we can estimate the expected rate of return for a risky asset using Equation (7–3). In this chapter we will assume that this calculation has already been made and the expected rate of return for risky assets is known.
- $[W_1 \times E(r_1)]$ = the contribution of asset 1 to the portfolio expected return.
- Note that the expected rate of return on a portfolio of *n* assets is simply a weighted average of the expected rates of return on each of the *n* assets.

Evaluating Portfolio Risk

Standard deviation is the primary risk measure of a portfolio.

Portfolio Diversification

Diversification lowers risks (usually) as more assets are added to a portfolio. The portfolio risk will be lower than a simple average of the asset risks. This results from the assets having different correlations. If the assets moved identically—had **perfect correlation** of +1.00 or 100 percent—there would be no benefit to adding more assets.

The **correlation coefficient** measures the degree that assets move in the same direction. It may vary from –1 (perfect negative correlation) to +1 (perfect positive correlation). A zero correlation means the two assets have no return relationship while perfectly negative correlated assets move in opposite directions at the same time. The great benefit in diversifying portfolio risk is that to lower the risk of a portfolio, the asset correlation need only be less than +1 to lower risk which allows an investor to make many choices.

Diversification Lessons

1st: A portfolio can be less risky than the average risk of its individual investments.

2nd: Key to reducing risk is to find assets that are not perfectly positively correlated.

Calculating the Standard Deviation of a Portfolio's Returns

Standard deviation is the primary measure of an asset's risk and an important part of a portfolio's risk. Portfolio risk will be lower than the simple average of the asset risks. The lower the correlation coefficient, the greater will be the benefit from diversification. To see the impact of correlation on a portfolio, look at the calculation of a portfolio's standard deviation. The standard deviation of two assets in a two-asset portfolio is calculated by the following formula:

$$\sigma_{portfolio} = \sqrt{W_1^2\sigma_1^2 + W_2^2\sigma_2^2 + 2W_1W_2\rho_{1,2}\sigma_1\sigma_2} \qquad (8\text{–}2)$$

Important Definitions and Concepts

- $\sigma_{portfolio}$ = the standard deviation in portfolio returns.
- W_i = the proportion of the portfolio that is invested in asset *i*,
- σ_i = the standard deviation in the rate of return earned by asset *i*, and
- $\rho_{i,j}$ = the correlation coefficient between the rate of return earned by assets *i* and *j*. The symbol $\rho_{i,j}$ (pronounced "rho") represents the correlation coefficient between the rates of return for asset 1 and asset 2.

Correlation impacts the third term in the equation of a portfolio's risk. If correlation is zero or negative, it is easy to see that the third term removes risk from the calculation of standard deviation. While it may not be obvious, even having assets with .99 correlation in a portfolio have less risk than the average of the asset risks.

In this example, the average of the asset standard deviations is 0.20 and if correlation is 0.75, the portfolio standard deviation drops to 0.187 (about 6.5 percent lower).

$$\sigma_{portfolio} = \sqrt{W^2_{Apple}\sigma^2_{Apple} + W^2_{Coke}\sigma^2_{Coke} + 2W_{Apple}W_{Coke}\rho_{Apple,Coke}\sigma_{Apple}\sigma_{Coke}}$$
$$= \sqrt{(0.5^2 \times 0.20^2) + (0.5^2 \times 0.20^2) + (2 \times 0.5 \times 0.5 \times 0.75 \times 0.20 \times 0.20)}$$
$$= \sqrt{0.035} = 0.187$$

Correlation coefficient of +0.75 indicates the stock returns of the two firms move together but not in perfect unison.

In this example, the average of the asset standard deviations is .20 and if correlation is 1.00, the portfolio standard deviation stays at .20.

$$\sigma_{portfolio} = \sqrt{W^2_{Apple}\sigma^2_{Apple} + W^2_{Coke}\sigma^2_{Coke} + 2W_{Apple}W_{Coke}\rho_{Apple,Coke}\sigma_{Apple}\sigma_{Coke}}$$
$$= \sqrt{(0.5^2 \times 0.20^2) + (0.5^2 \times 0.20^2) + (2 \times 0.5 \times 0.5 \times 1.00 \times 0.20 \times 0}$$
$$= \sqrt{0.040} = 0.20$$

Correlation coefficient of +1.0 indicates the stock returns of the two firms move in exact unison.

This figure shows the relationship between correlation and the risk of a portfolio.

Figure 8.1

Diversification and the Correlation Coefficient—Apple and Coca-Cola

The effects of diversification on the risk of the portfolio are contingent on the degree of correlation between the assets included in the portfolio. If the correlation is +1 (meaning the two assets are perfectly correlated and move together in lockstep as was the case with sunglasses and suntan lotion), then there is no benefit to diversification. However, where the correlation is -1 (meaning the two assets move in lockstep in opposite directions as was the case with sunglasses and umbrellas), it will be possible to construct a portfolio that completely eliminates risk.

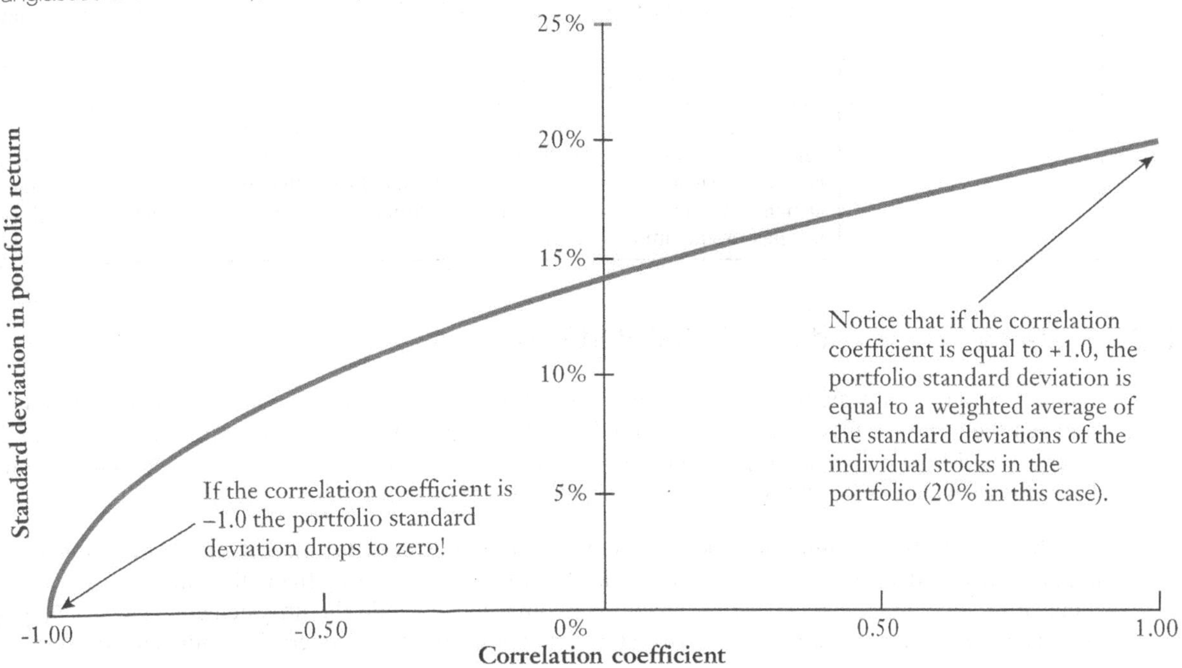

Legend:

Correlation	E(Return)	Standard Deviation
−1.00	0.14	0%
−0.80	0.14	6%
−0.60	0.14	9%
−0.40	0.14	11%
−0.20	0.14	13%
0.0	0.14	14%
0.20	0.14	15%
0.40	0.14	17%
0.60	0.14	18%
0.80	0.14	19%
1.00	0.14	20%

All portfolios are comprised of equal investments in Apple and Coca-Cola shares.

This table summarizes the relationship between correlation and diversification.

Correlation Between Investment Returns	Diversification Benefits
+1	None. No risk has been eliminated because there is no diversification by combining the investments since they are identical. This is exactly the case we saw earlier in this chapter when we combined the sunglasses product line with the sunscreen lotion—no elimination of risk.
0.0	There is substantial value to diversification.
−1	Diversification is extremely effective in reducing portfolio risk. In fact, it is possible to select the portfolio weights for two investments whose returns are perfectly negatively correlated, such that all variability is eliminated from the portfolio return and the portfolio standard deviation is zero. Earlier, we encountered this correlation when we considered the sunglasses and umbrella example.

8.2 Systematic Risk and the Market Portfolio

While correlation is a significant factor in a portfolio's risk, it is impractical to compute the correlations between thousands of investments. The Capital Asset Pricing Model simplifies things greatly by finding that investors will hold a diversified portfolio that includes all risky investments known as the **market portfolio**. Then, the relevant risk becomes an asset's correlation to the market portfolio.

Risk has two parts: a **systematic risk** that is correlated to the risk of the market and an **unsystematic risk** or unique part that does not contribute to the risk of the market and only affects the unique security. You may think of the systematic part as the big macro-economic factor while the unsystematic risk is a firm-specific risk. The important risk for diversified investors (the ones following Modern Portfolio Theory and CAPM) is the systematic risk of an investment.

$$\text{Total risk} = \text{Systematic risk} + \text{Unsystematic risk} \qquad (8\text{–}3)$$

Diversification and Unsystematic Risk

Systematic risk also is called **non-diversifiable risk** since all assets in the economy face this risk and react to changes in that risk. Unsystematic risk is **diversifiable risk** as the impact of a unique risk is diminished to have no effect on a diversified portfolio with many assets. Usually it takes about 50 stocks from different industries to create a well diversified portfolio with almost no unsystematic risk and only systematic risk.

Diversification and Systematic Risk

Systematic risk will exist in a portfolio after all the unique risk has been diversified away. Some systematic risk factors are believed to be interest rates, wars, inflation, and other large macro-economic factors.

Figure 8.2

Portfolio Risk and the Number of Investments in the Portfolio

Adding more investments to a portfolio that are not highly correlated with the other assets in the portfolio can dramatically reduce the risk of the portfolio. In fact, for randomly selected shares of common stock, the benefits of diversification can be virtually fully achieved with a portfolio of less than 50 stocks (assuming equal investment in each stock).

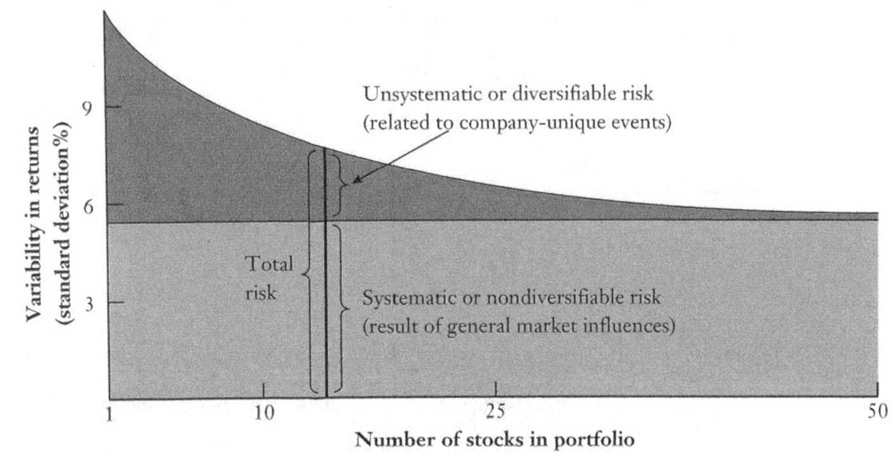

Systematic Risk and Beta

Systematic risk is measured by an asset's correlation with the return on the market portfolio. The quantitative measure of systematic risk is the **beta coefficient** of an asset. Beta measures the amplitude and the direction of an asset's correlation with the market return. Beta is the slope of the risk-return line and measures the amount of compensation for a unit of market risk. The market beta is 1.00 and an asset may have a positive or negative value which represents the percentage of market risk that asset possesses. A risk-free bond doesn't vary with the market return (on a portfolio of risky assets) so it has a beta of zero. Betas are relatively easy to calculate if you have the data, but you may choose to use one of the many data sources on financial websites that calculate betas on stocks.

Figure 8.3

Estimating Home Depot's Beta Coefficient

A firm's beta coefficient is the slope of a straight line that fits the relationship between the firm's stock returns and those of a broad market index. In the graph below the market index used is the Standard and Poor's (S&P) 500 Index.

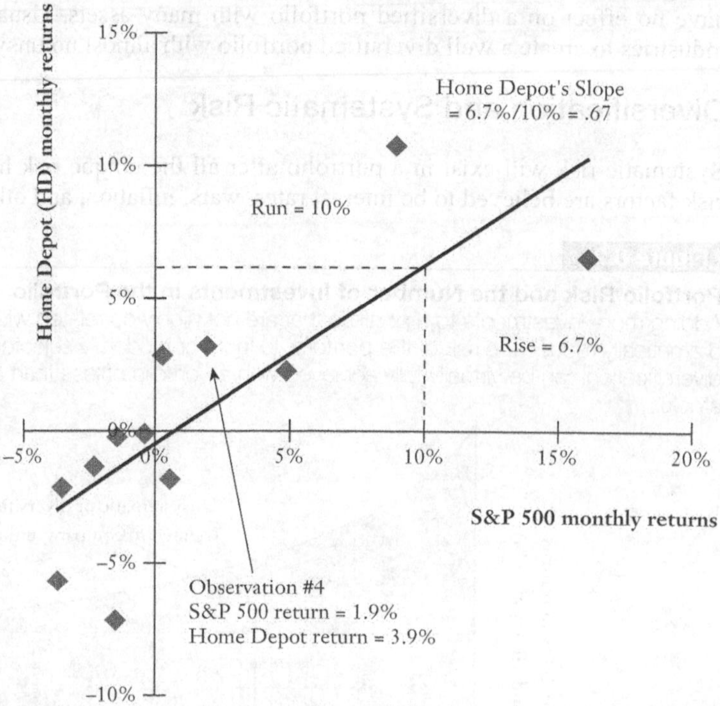

Calculating beta:

1. Visual—the slope of a straight line can be estimated visually by drawing a straight line that best "fits" the scatter of Home Depot's stock returns and those of the market index. The beta coefficient then is the "rise over the run." The blue dots on the graph correspond to values indicated on the chart.
2. Financial calculator—financial calculators have built-in functions for computing the beta coefficient. However, because the procedure varies from one calculator to another we do not present it here.
3. Excel—Excel's Slope function can be used to calculate the slope as follows: =slope(C2:C12,B2:B12)
4. Internet—there are a number of resources that can be used to obtain beta estimates on the Internet, including Yahoo! Finance and Google finance. The estimates can differ depending on the time period used to make the estimate.

Observation	Date	S&P 500 Returns	Home Depot Stock Returns
1	Nov-10	–0.23%	–1.47%
2	Dec-10	6.53%	16.05%
3	Jan-11	2.26%	4.88%
4	Feb-11	3.90%	1.90%
5	Mar-11	–0.10%	–0.43%
6	Apr-11	2.85%	0.24%
7	May-12	–1.35%	–2.34%
8	Jun-12	–1.83%	0.52%
9	Jul-12	–2.15%	–3.56%
10	Aug-12	–5.68%	–3.72%
11	Sep-12	–7.18%	–1.53%
12	Oct-12	10.77%	8.91%

Calculating Portfolio Beta

Systematic risk of a portfolio is measured by the **portfolio beta**. It is a simple weighted average of the individual asset betas. To calculate beta from several assets, use the following formula:

Portfolio Beta

$$\text{Portfolio Beta} = \begin{pmatrix} \text{Proportion of} & \text{Beta for} \\ \text{Portfolio Invested} \times & \text{Asset 1} \\ \text{in Asset 1 } (W_1) & (\beta_1) \end{pmatrix} + \begin{pmatrix} \text{Proportion of} & \text{Beta for} \\ \text{Portfolio Invested} \times & \text{Asset 2} \\ \text{in Asset 2 } (W_2) & (\beta_2) \end{pmatrix} + \ldots + \begin{pmatrix} \text{Proportion of} & \text{Beta for} \\ \text{Portfolio Invested} \times & \text{Asset } n \\ \text{in Asset } n \ (W_n) & (\beta_n) \end{pmatrix} \quad (8\text{–}4)$$

Or, written using symbols the beta for a portfolio is simply the weighted average of the individual assets' betas that are held in the portfolio, i.e.,

$$\beta_{\text{portfolio}} = W_1\beta_1 + W_2\beta_2 + \ \ldots \ + W_n\beta_n$$

Important Definitions and Concepts

- W_i = the proportion of the portfolio that is invested in the Asset i.
- β_i = the beta coefficient for Asset i, and
- $\beta_{portfolio}$ = the portfolio beta which is a weighted average of the betas for the individual assets contained in the portfolio

For example, consider the following portfolio that is comprised of three investments with betas equal to 1.20, .70, and .25. If half the portfolio is invested in the first investment and one-fourth in each of the remaining investments, we can calculate the portfolio beta using Equation (8–4) as follows:

$$\begin{aligned} \beta_{\text{portfolio}} &= W_1\beta_1 + W_2\beta_2 + W_3\beta_3 \\ &= (0.50 \times 1.20) + (0.25 \times 0.70) + (0.25 \times 0.25) = 0.8375 \end{aligned}$$

The beta for the three-investment portfolio is therefore .8375.

8.3 The Security Market Line and the CAPM

The key insight of the CAPM is that investments with the same beta have the same expected rate of return and that investors will require a higher rate of return on investments that have higher betas. The slope of the line mapped out by changing beta and graphing the expected return is the **security market line** (SML). The SML is known as the reward to risk level and is the graphical representation of the compensation per unit of beta or market risk. The security market line, or CAPM pricing equation, uses the following formula to find expected returns:

The CAPM pricing equation:

$$\begin{matrix}\text{Expected Return on} \\ \text{Risky Asset } j\end{matrix} = \begin{matrix}\text{Risk-free} \\ \text{Rate of Return}\end{matrix} + \begin{matrix}\text{Beta for} \\ \text{Asset } j\end{matrix} \times \begin{pmatrix}\begin{matrix}\text{Expected Return} \\ \text{on the} \\ \text{Market Portfolio}\end{matrix} - \begin{matrix}\text{Risk-free} \\ \text{Rate of Return}\end{matrix}\end{pmatrix}$$

$$E\left(r_{Asset\ j}\right) = r_f + \beta_{Asset\ j}\left[E\left(r_{\text{market}}\right) - r_f\right] \quad (8\text{–}6)$$

Low beta portfolios are similar to portfolios holding risk-free investments, Treasury bonds. High beta portfolios have all or more of their investment allocated to the market (risky asset) portfolio. Higher beta portfolios have greater systematic risk and will react dramatically if the macro-economic factors that influence undiversifiable risk change.

Using the CAPM to Estimate Required Rates of Return

The CAPM explains how risk and return are traded off in the capital markets. The beta factor is applied to the **market risk premium** (the amount that the expected market return exceeds the risk-free return). To repeat, the CAPM beta is used to find the SML and the risk-return payoff:

$$E\left(r_{Asset\,j}\right) = r_f + \beta_{Asset\,j}\left[E\left(r_{\text{market}}\right) - r_f\right] \quad (8\text{–}6)$$

All assets are priced by this equation and should fall on the security market line. If they fall above, the assets are underpriced and investors will buy them until the expected return falls back on to the SML. Overpriced assets that fall below the SML are sold until there's no profit in trading (fair value or on the SML). CAPM provides the discount rate for all the cash flows in an economy and a reason for arbitrage if prices are not correct.

Answers to **Concept Checks**

Concept Check **8.1**

1. How is the expected rate of return on a portfolio related to the expected rates of return of the individual assets contained in the portfolio?
2. When the returns of two risky investments are perfectly negatively correlated, how does combining them in a portfolio affect the overall riskiness of the portfolio?
3. When the returns of two risky investments are perfectly positively correlated, how does combining them in a portfolio affect the overall riskiness of the portfolio?

Answer 1: The expected rate of return on a portfolio is a simple weighted average of the individual asset returns.

Answer 2: Portfolio risk will decline when two negatively correlated assets are combined. With perfectly negatively correlated assets, the asset holdings can be weighted in a manner to eliminate systematic risk completely.

Answer 3: There is no risk reduction in a portfolio from diversification if all the assets are perfectly positively correlated. Portfolio risk is a weighted average of the asset risks.

Concept Check **8.2**

1. What are some factors that influence the returns of a company like Home Depot that would constitute a source of systematic risk? Unsystematic risk?
2. How many different shares of stock are required to essentially diversify away unsystematic risk?

Answer 1: Systematic risk includes interest rates, inflation, and large macro-economic factors. Unsystematic risks include firm specific events such as management or labor issues, sales lost to weather, and a supply disruption unique to Home Depot.

Answer 2: A portfolio of 50 non-identical stocks has mostly systematic risk.

Concept Check **8.3**

1. Who are Harry Markowitz and William Sharpe, and what did they do that was so important in finance?
2. How is the portfolio beta related to the betas of the individual investments in the portfolio?
3. Explain the concept of the security market line.
4. What is the market risk premium and how is it related to the Capital Asset Pricing Model?

Answer 1: Markowitz and Sharpe are winners of the Nobel Prize in Economics for their work on portfolio diversification and the Capital Asset Pricing Model.

Answer 2: The portfolio beta is a simple weighted average of the individual asset betas.

Answer 3: The security market line maps out the expected rate of return for a given level of risk or beta. If assets do not fall on the SML, traders would either buy or sell the assets until the resulting price changes moved the assets back on to the SML.

Answer 4: The market risk premium is the excess return of the market return over the risk-free asset return. CAPM finds that beta is the measure of risk in terms of the market unit of risk, the excess return. Multiplying beta times the market risk premium determines the amount of excess return an asset should have based on its systematic (beta) risk.

Multiple Choice **Quiz**

1. The risk of a portfolio is best described as
   a. the excess return of the market portfolio over the risk-free return.
   b. the standard deviation of the expected portfolio returns.
   c. the slope of the risk-return line, the CAPM risk measure.
   d. the line that maps out the expected return-beta relationship.

2. The security market line is
   a. the line that represents the excess return-risk relationship.
   b. the standard deviation of the returns.
   c. the slope of the risk-return line, the CAPM risk measure.
   d. the line that maps out the expected return-beta relationship.

3. The beta of a portfolio is
   a. the excess return of the market portfolio over the risk-free return.
   b. the standard deviation of the returns.
   c. the slope of the risk-return line, the CAPM risk measure.
   d. the line that maps out the expected return-beta relationship.

4. The market risk premium is
   a. the excess return of the market portfolio over the risk-free return.
   b. the standard deviation of the returns.
   c. the slope of the risk-return line.
   d. the line that maps out the expected return-beta relationship.

5. Firm-specific risk is
   a. the excess return of the market portfolio over the risk-free return.
   b. the diversifiable risk of an asset.
   c. the non-diversifiable risk of an asset.
   d. the weighted average return of all possible outcomes.

6. Systematic risk is
   a. the excess return of the market portfolio over the risk-free return.
   b. the diversifiable risk of an asset.
   c. the non-diversifiable risk of an asset.
   d. the weighted average return of all possible outcomes.

7. Diversification is
   a. the return from beta.
   b. the benefit of holding only unique risks.
   c. the cost of owning diversifiable risks.
   d. the reduction in risk from owning less than perfectly correlated assets.

8. The correlation coefficient is
   a. a measure of amplitude of changes in asset returns.
   b. a measure of total variation for an asset.
   c. a measure of the relationship of an asset's return to all risky returns.
   d. a measure of the degree of variation between asset returns.

9. The CAPM is
   a. a model of the excess return due to total variation.
   b. a model of non-diversifiable risk of a security relative to all risky returns.
   c. a model of diversifiable risk of a security relative to all risky returns.
   d. a model of correlations and total variation in a portfolio.

10. The beta coefficient is
   a. a measure of the relatedness of asset returns to market returns.
   b. a measure of amplitude of changes in asset returns.
   c. a measure of total variation for an asset.
   d. a measure of the relationship of an asset's return to all risky returns.

Answers to **Multiple Choice Questions**

1. B
2. D
3. C
4. A
5. B
6. C
7. D
8. D
9. B
10. A

Self Test with **Solutions**

Picture the Problem

Decide on Solution Strategy

Solve

Analyze

Self Test 1: Portfolio Returns and Risk

You are a portfolio consultant for an institution that intends to own a two-asset portfolio. The institution has one of the choices below.

a. What is the expected return, the standard deviation, and the beta of each choice.
b. If the market return is 10 percent and the risk-free rate is 5 percent, what is the CAPM predicted return of your choices?
c. Are there overvalued or undervalued portfolios according to CAPM?

Choices Faced by the Institution:

Portfolio 1: 60 percent bonds and 40 percent US stocks

Portfolio 2: 60 percent bonds and 40 percent Emerging Market stocks

Portfolio 3: 60 percent US stocks and 40 percent Emerging Market stocks

Returns, Standard Deviations, Correlations, and Beta of the Asset Choices:

	$E(r)$	Standev	Correlation	Beta
Bonds:	6%	0.10	US = 0.5, EM = 0.4	0
US Stocks:	10%	0.20	Bond = 0.5, EM = 0.2	1
EM Stocks	12%	0.30	Bond = 0.4, US = 0.2	1.4

Step 1: Picture the Problem

The problem asks for the risk and return of a portfolio measured by expected return, standard deviation, and beta.

Step 2: Decide on a Solution Strategy

To solve, we will use the formulas for expected return of a portfolio, the standard deviation of a portfolio, the beta of a portfolio, and the CAPM expected return.

Step 3: Solve

To solve for the expected portfolio return, take the weighted average of the asset returns.

$$E(r_{\text{portfolio}}) = W_a E(r_a) + W_b E(r_b)$$

$$\text{Portfolio 1} = (0.60 \times 0.06) + (0.40 \times 0.10) = 0.076 \text{ or } 7.6\%$$

$$\text{Portfolio 2} = (0.60 \times 0.06) + (0.40 \times 0.12) = 0.084 \text{ or } 8.4\%$$

$$\text{Portfolio 3} = (0.60 \times 0.10) + (0.40 \times 0.12) = 0.108 \text{ or } 10.8\%$$

To solve for the portfolio beta, take the weighted average of the asset betas.

$$\beta_{\text{portfolio}} = W_a\beta_a + W_b\beta_b$$

$$\text{Portfolio 1} = (0.60 \times 0) + (0.40 \times 1.0) = 0.40$$

$$\text{Portfolio 2} = (0.60 \times 0) + (0.40 \times 1.4) = 0.56$$

$$\text{Portfolio 3} = (0.60 \times 1) + (0.40 \times 1.4) = 1.16$$

To solve for the portfolio standard deviation, use the following formula:

$$\sigma_{\text{portfolio}} = \sqrt{W_1^2\sigma_1^2 + W_2^2\sigma_2^2 + 2W_1W_2\rho_{1,2}\sigma_1\sigma_2}$$

$$\sigma_{\text{Portfolio 1}} = \sqrt{(6^2 \times 0.10^2) + (0.4^2 \times 0.20^2) + (2 \times 0.6 \times 0.4 \times 0.50 \times 0.10 \times 0.20)} = .122$$

$$\sigma_{\text{Portfolio 2}} = \sqrt{(6^2 \times 0.10^2) + (0.4^2 \times 0.30^2) + (2 \times 0.6 \times 0.4 \times 0.40 \times 0.10 \times 0.30)} = .154$$

$$\sigma_{\text{Portfolio 3}} = \sqrt{(6^2 \times 0.20^2) + (0.4^2 \times 0.30^2) + (2 \times 0.6 \times 0.4 \times 0.20 \times 0.20 \times 0.30)} = .186$$

The portfolio expected returns and standard deviations are:

Portfolio 1	$sd = 0.122$	$E(r) = 7.6\%$	$E(r)/sd = 0.62$
Portfolio 2	$sd = 0.154$	$E(r) = 8.4\%$	$E(r)/sd = 0.55$
Portfolio 3	$sd = 0.186$	$E(r) = 10.8\%$	$E(r)/sd = 0.58$

To solve for the CAPM expected return, use the following formula:

CAPM: $E(r) = rf + Beta\,X\,(Rm - rf)$

Portfolio 1 Expected Return = 0.05 + 0.4 (0.10 – 0.05) = 7.0%

Portfolio 2 Expected Return = 0.05 + 0.56 (0.10 – 0.05) = 7.8%

Portfolio 3 Expected Return = 0.05 + 1.16 (0.10 – 0.05) = 10.8%

Step 4: Analyze

Two of the three portfolios have different expected returns from their CAPM expected return. In an efficiently priced market, this should not occur. Investors will sell the overvalued portfolio and buy the undervalued portfolio. Portfolio 3 has an expected return of 10.8 percent in either case and is fairly valued. The two portfolios containing bonds have CAPM expected returns lower than the expected returns that are offered in the market. Since the U.S. equity and the EM equity are priced correctly using CAPM, bonds must be mispriced.

Given that CAPM is our model of the economic universe, we should buy the assets that are undervalued in the market. Those assets offer a return greater than what CAPM requires. Bonds are mispriced since a beta of 0 would have an expected return of 5 percent, not 6 percent. The market has priced bonds too low (thus the higher return), so investors would prefer either portfolio with bonds as one component. The CAPM returns difference is 0.6 percent for either Portfolio 1 or 2, so buying either would be preferred to Portfolio 3. Evaluating their Sharpe ratios, Portfolio 1 has less standard deviation risk per unit of return, so fund managers may prefer it to Portfolio 2.

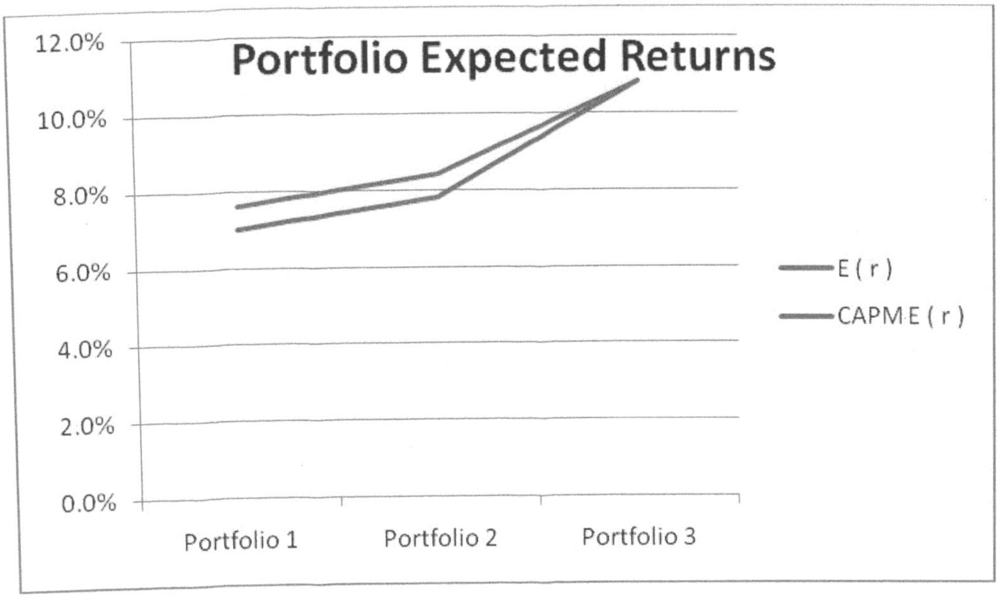

CHAPTER 9

Debt Valuation and Interest Rates

Chapter **Orientation**

This chapter covers debt and the characteristics of government and corporate fixed income securities. Businesses are regular users of debt financing for operations. The chapter describes the difference between public and private debt markets that issuers use to raise capital. The chapter also presents the formula to calculate the value and yield to maturity of a bond. Bonds can have low or high risk depending on the source of their cash flows and other factors. The chapter ends with the impact of inflation on debt securities and on the yield curve.

Chapter Review: **Terms and Concepts**

9.1 Overview of Corporate Debt

A firm can choose to raise debt capital by taking a loan from a financial institution directly or by selling bonds in the financial markets. Bonds are public debts because they are traded in the markets. Since issuing a bond is expensive, smaller companies usually borrow from banks. Bonds are preferred for long-term needs while loans are better for short-term needs. A bond with a long maturity allows the firm to lock in a borrowing rate for a long time.

Borrowing Money in the Private Financial Market

Firms borrow from banks by taking out a loan in a private market transaction between the borrower and the bank directly. When bonds are issued in the public markets, anyone can buy the debt.

Floating Rate Loans

Loans in the private market are typically floating rate loans that reset monthly or quarterly. The interest on a floater may change at the reset date to reflect changes in the market for loans or in the firm's performance. These loans reset to track changes in LIBOR (London Interbank Offered Rate) an index of overnight daily interest borrowing rates traded in the short-term money markets. Some loans may be fixed-rate loans.

A floating rate loan will specify the following terms:

- The spread over LIBOR in basis points (100 = 1%).
- The loan's maximum and minimum annual rate: the ceiling and floor.
- The maturity date or when the loan is to be repaid.
- The collateral that the lender may take if the loan is not repaid.

A transaction loan is used for a purchase of an asset. The following chart describes different types of bank loans and assets pledged as collateral:

Table 9.1 Types of Bank Debt

Bank loans are typically classified in one of two ways: (i) by the intended use of the loan, e.g., working capital or transaction loans, and (ii) by whether the loan is secured by collateral or not.

(Panel A) Types of Bank Loans—Classified by Intended Use

Working capital loans	Typically, these loans set up a line of credit based on an open-ended credit agreement whereby the firm has prior approval to borrow up to a set limit. This type of credit agreement is similar to that of a personal credit card that provides a line of credit up to an agreed-upon limit. The credit is then used to provide cash needed to support the firm's day-to-day business needs.
Transaction loans	Firms use this type of loan to finance a specific asset. These loans typically call for installment payments designed to repay the principal amount of the loan, plus interest, with fixed monthly or annual payments. Home mortgage and automobile loans are examples of transaction loans that require installment payments.

(Panel B) Types of Bank Loans—Classified by the Collateral Used to Secure the Loan

Secured debt	This type of debt acts as a promise to pay that is backed by granting the lender an interest in a specific piece of property, known as collateral. The property used to secure the loan can include virtually any tangible business asset and could include accounts receivable, inventory, plant and equipment, and real estate.
Unsecured debt	A promise to pay that is not supported by collateral so that the lender relies upon the creditworthiness and reputation of the borrower to repay the debt when due.

Borrowing Money in the Public Financial Market

Firms may sell bonds in the financial markets to individuals, mutual funds, and other institutions. **Corporate bonds** are securities sold by a corporation with a promise to make future payments at regular intervals through a maturity date. Stocks may pay dividends when the firm chooses to pay them. If a firm fails to make payments on its debt, a bond trustee may declare the firm insolvent and force it into bankruptcy.

Basic Bond Features

The **bond indenture** is the legal agreement between the firm issuing bonds and the bond trustee who represents the bond owners. This document lists the rights and obligations of the firm and for bondholders. If the firm cannot repay its debt, the bondholder may execute claims **on assets and income** with priority before paying the shareholders. The value that must be repaid to the bondholder at the maturity date is the **par** or **face value** of the bond.

The promised payment of the bond is stated as the **coupon interest rate** and it is the percentage of the par value of the bond that is paid annually as interest (even though many bonds pay semiannual interest). The **current yield** is the promised payment divided by the current price of the bond. **Floating rate bonds** have payments that vary with the rate traded in the market at later dates.

The **maturity** of the bond is the length of time until the bond repays its full par value or redeems. Bonds may have call provisions that allow the issuer to retire the bond in order to issue new debt at a lower interest rate due to changes in market conditions. A call protection period will prevent rapid recalls of bonds which investors do not like. The **conversion feature** on some bonds allows the bond to convert into a number of shares in the firm's stock.

Bond Ratings and Default Risk

Moody's, Standard and Poor's, and Fitch are the three major bond rating agencies. The amount of return the firm has to offer is tied to its **bond rating**, its credit quality as a borrower. Rating agencies consider a number of qualitative and quantitative factors to judge default risk, or how likely repayment will be timely, when assigning bond ratings. The following table summarizes:

Table 9.2 Bond Terminology

Indenture	The legal agreement between the firm issuing the bonds and the bond trustee who represents the bondholders. It lists the specific terms of the loan agreement, including a description of the bonds, the rights of the bondholders, the rights of the issuing firm, and the responsibilities of the trustee.
Priority of claim on assets and income	In the case of insolvency, claims of debt in general, including bonds, are honored before those of both common stock and preferred stock. In addition, interest payments hold priority over dividend payments for common and preferred stock.
Par value	The par value of a bond, also known as its face value, is the principal that must be repaid to the bondholder at maturity. In general, corporate bonds are issued with par values in increments of \$1,000. Also, when bond prices are quoted in the financial press, prices are generally expressed as a percentage of the bond's par value.
Maturity and repayment of principal	The maturity date refers to the date on which the bond issuer must repay the principal or par value to the bondholder.
Coupon interest rate	The coupon rate on a bond indicates the percentage of the par value of the bond that will be paid out annually in the form of interest.
Current yield	The current yield on a bond refers to the ratio of the annual interest payment to the bond's current market price. If, for example, we have a bond with an 8 percent coupon interest rate, a par value of \$1,000, and a market price of \$700, it would have a current yield of 11.4 percent calculated as follows: $\text{Current Yield} = \frac{\text{Annual Interest Payment}}{\text{Current Market Price of the Bond}} = \frac{0.08 \times \$1000}{\$700} = \frac{\$80}{\$700} = 0.114 \text{ or } 11.4\%$ (9–1)
Call provision	The call provision provides the issuer of the bond with the right to redeem or retire a bond before it matures.
Conversion feature	In addition, some bonds have a **conversion feature** that allows bondholders to convert their bonds into a set number of shares of common stock.

Table 9.3 Interpreting Bond Ratings

Ratings are intended to reflect the likelihood of default by the issuing firm in the future.

Bond Rating Category	Standard & Poor's	Moody's	Description
Investment Grade:			
Prime or Highest Strong	AAA	Aaa	Highest quality, extremely strong capacity to pay.
High Quality	AA	Aa	Very strong capacity to pay.
Upper Medium	A	A-1, A	Upper medium quality. Strong capacity to pay.
Medium	BBB	Baa-1, Baa	Lower medium quality; changing circumstances could impact the firm's ability to pay.
Not Investment Grade:			
Speculative	BB	Ba,	Speculative elements; faces uncertainties.
Highly speculative	B, CCC,CC	B, Caa, Ca	Extremely speculative and highly vulnerable to nonpayment.
Default	D	C	Income bond; doesn't pay interest.

9.2 Valuing Corporate Debt

The value of corporate debt equals the present value of the promised cash flows discounted at the market's required yield (rate of return).

$$\text{Bond Value} = \left(\begin{array}{c}\text{Present Value of the}\\ \text{Bond's Coupon Interest}\\ \text{Payments}\end{array}\right) + \left(\begin{array}{c}\text{Present Value of the}\\ \text{Principal Amount (par value)}\\ \text{of the Bond Issue}\end{array}\right) \quad (9\text{–}2)$$

Step-by-Step: Valuing Bonds by Discounting Future Cash Flows

We can calculate the value of a bond using a simple three-step valuation procedure:

Step 1. Determine bondholder cash flows, which are the amount and timing of the bond's promised interest and principal payments to the bondholders.

Step 2. Estimate the appropriate discount rate on a similar risk bond, where the discount rate is the return the bond will yield if it is held to maturity and all bond payments are made. We can either calculate the discount rate ourselves or use market data for bonds of a similar default risk.

Step 3. Calculate the present value of the bond's interest and principal payments from Step 1 using the discount rate estimated in Step 2.

Step 1: Determine Bondholder Cash Flows

For example, examining a bond indenture for Ford Motor Company (F), issued on September 5, 2007, shows us that the bond had a $1,000 par value, paid a coupon rate of 6.5 percent per year with interest paid semiannually, and matured in 2018. This means that Ford must pay .065 x $1,000/2 = $32.50 per bond every six months until 2018, at which time the $1,000 principal will be due.

Step 2: Estimate the Appropriate Discount Rate

We find the present value of the bond's contractual interest and principal payments by using the semiannual *yield to maturity* as our discount rate. The **yield to maturity** (YTM) on a bond is the discount rate that equates the present value of the bond's contractual cash flows (interest and principal at maturity) with the current market price of the bond. *This also is the return the investor will earn on the bond if the investor is paid everything that is contractually promised by the issuing firm and the bond is held until maturity.*

Calculating a Bond's Yield to Maturity

We calculate the yield to maturity (*YTM*) for a bond by solving one of the following equations.

For annual interest payments:

$$\text{Bond Price} = \frac{\text{Interest}_{\text{year 1}}}{(1+YTM)^1} + \frac{\text{Interest}_{\text{year 2}}}{(1+YTM)^2} + \frac{\text{Interest}_{\text{year 3}}}{(1+YTM)^3} + \cdots + \frac{\text{Interest}_{\text{year } n}}{(1+YTM)^n} + \frac{\text{Principal}}{(1+YTM)^n} \quad (9\text{–}2a)$$

For semiannual interest payments:

$$\begin{array}{c}\text{Beta Value}\\ \text{(semi-annual payments)}\end{array} = (\text{Interest}/2)\left[\frac{1-\dfrac{1}{\left(1+\dfrac{YTM_{\text{Market}}}{2}\right)^{2n}}}{\dfrac{YTM_{\text{Market}}}{2}}\right] + \text{Principal}\left[\frac{1}{\left(1+\dfrac{YTM_{\text{Market}}}{2}\right)^{2n}}\right] \quad (9\text{–}2c)$$

Using Market Data for Yield to Maturity

Several data sources supply bond yield data in the form of a **credit spread over Treasury Bonds**. A bond with an 'AA' rating with a maturity of 10 years that has a credit spread of 80 basis points. To find the appropriate rate, take the 10 year Treasury bond rate and add .8 percent to it. One online source of spread data is Bonds Online, www.bondsonline.com/Todays_Market/Corporate_Bond_Spreads.php .

Promised Returns vs. Expected Yield to Maturity

The YTM of a bond is its promised return assuming everything that is owed is actually paid. However, bonds selling at extreme discounts may be expected to earn back only a part of the proceeds. So a bond with a 37 percent yield to maturity may only expect to earn a more bond-like 12 percent in the high yield markets when the firm only returns part of the principle owed.

Example Promised vs. Expected Returns

A bond that matures in one year selling for $800 that promises to pay $100 in interest and $1,000 in principal would have a *YTM* of 37.5 percent. However, if traders only expect to recover 70 percent of the principal and interest owed with a 50 percent probability of default, the bond would have an expected return of 16.9 percent (50 percent of 37.5 percent and 50 percent of -3.75 percent).

Assuming the bond pays as promised (No default):

$$\text{Bond Price (for a bond with one year to maturity)} = \frac{\text{Interest}_{\text{year 1}} + \text{Principal}}{(1 + YTM)}$$

or

$$YTM_{Default} = \frac{(\text{Interest}_{\text{year 1}} + \text{Principal}) \times .70}{\text{Bond Price}} - 1 = \frac{\$70 + \$700}{\$800} - 1 = -0.0375 \text{ or } -3.75\%$$

Assuming a default probability of 50 percent and a 70 percent recovery rate:

$$YTM_{Default} = \frac{(\text{Interest}_{\text{year 1}} + \text{Principal}) \times .70}{\text{Bond Price}} - 1 = \frac{\$70 + \$700}{\$800} - 1 = -0.0375 \text{ or } -3.75\%$$

The expected *YTM* is a weighted average of the *YTM* calculated in the default outcome and in the no-default outcome:

$$E(YTM) = YTM_{No\ Default} \times (1 - \text{Probability of Default}) + YTM_{Default} \times (\text{Probability of Default})$$

$$= \left[37.5\% \times (1 - .50)\right] + \left[-3.75\% \times (1 - .50)\right] = 16.9\% \qquad (9\text{–}3)$$

Quoted Yields to Maturity for Corporate Bonds

The financial press quotes yield to maturity as the promised rate, so remember that the expected return could be lower when comparing bonds. The valuation of bonds using YTM also is called discounted cash flow valuation. This is the approach we use in the third step to bond valuation.

Step 3: Use Discounted Cash Flow to Value Corporate Bonds

The valuation of a bond takes into account the time value of money by discounting the contractual or promised interest and principal payments back to the present. Since the bond interest payments are a level annuity payment stream that stretches over the next *n* years, we can apply the level annuity discounting factor to calculate its present value. This allows the use of the PMT function on a calculator.

For annual payments:

$$\begin{aligned}\text{Present Value of Interest Payments} &= \frac{\text{Interest}}{(1 + YTM_{\text{Market}})^1} + \frac{\text{Interest}}{(1 + YTM_{\text{Market}})^2} + \cdots + \frac{\text{Interest}}{(1 + YTM_{\text{Market}})^n} \\ &= \text{Interest}\left[\frac{1 - \dfrac{1}{(1 + YTM_{\text{Market}})^n}}{YTM_{\text{Market}}}\right]\end{aligned}$$

The present value of the principal payment (par value) received at the maturity of the bond (corresponding to FV on your financial calculator) is calculated as follows:

$$\text{Present Value of Principal} = \text{Principal}\left[\frac{1}{(1 + YTM_{\text{Market}})^n}\right]$$

Thus, Equation (9-2) can be restated as follows:

$$\text{Bond Value} = \text{Interest}\left[\frac{1 - \dfrac{1}{(1 + YTM_{\text{Market}})^n}}{YTM_{\text{Market}}}\right] + \text{Principal}\left[\frac{1}{(1 + YTM_{\text{Market}})^n}\right] \tag{9-2b}$$

For semiannual payments:

$$\text{Bond Value (semiannual payments)} = (\text{Interest}/2)\left[\frac{1 - \dfrac{1}{\left(1 + \dfrac{YTM_{\text{Market}}}{2}\right)^{2n}}}{\dfrac{YTM_{\text{Market}}}{2}}\right] + \text{Principal}\left[\frac{1}{\left(1 + \dfrac{YTM_{\text{Market}}}{2}\right)^{2n}}\right] \tag{9-2c}$$

N= Years X 2 and I = *YTM* / 2

Coupon interest = Annual interest / 2 or Coupon rate × Par / 2

9.3 Bond Valuation: Four Key Relationships

To find the value of the bond using the discounted cash flow method, we need the bond's interest payments, par value, the term to maturity, and the appropriate discount rate. The four relationships are:

First Relationship

The value of a bond is inversely related to changes in the market's required yield to maturity.

Figure 9.1 shows this inverse relationship between required yields and the value of a bond.

Figure 9.1

Bond Value and Yields to Maturity (5-Year Bond, 12 percent Coupon Rate)

Bond prices and yields to maturity vary inversely. Since principal and interest payments are fixed, the price of the bond must adjust such that the bond yields the market's current yield to maturity. For example, if the market yield to maturity were to increase from 12 percent to 15 percent, the price of the bond would have to fall from $1,000 to $899 in order for an investor who bought the bond today to earn 15 percent.

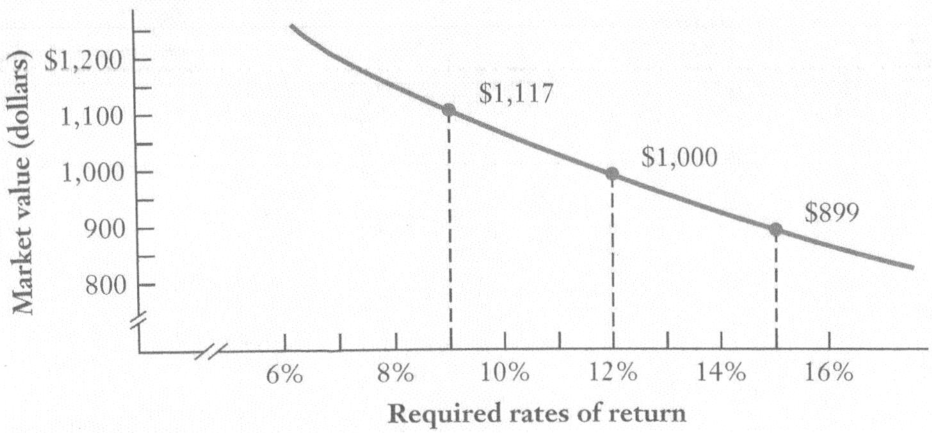

The risk to an investor that the value of his or her investment will change is known as **interest-rate risk.**

Second Relationship

The market value of a bond will be less than the par value if the yield to maturity is above the coupon interest rate and will be valued above par value if the yield to maturity is below the coupon interest rate.

A bond that is bought at a less than its par value is called a **discount bond** and a **premium bond** sells at a higher price than the bond's par value.

Third Relationship

As the maturity date approaches, the market value of a bond approaches its par value.

Whether a bond is at a premium or discount, its price will approach its par value as the bond nears maturity.

The table and figure below show how time to maturity affects bond values.

Table 9.5 Bond Prices Relative to Maturity Date

Regardless of whether a bond is selling at a premium or discount, its price will approach its par value as the bond nears maturity. Bond prices are calculated for a $1,000 par value bond that pays a 12 percent coupon that spans the five years up to the time the bond matures. Three interest rate or yield scenarios are considered: a par scenario in which the market's required yield to maturity and coupon rate of the bond are equal, a discount bond scenario in which the market's required yield to maturity is 15 percent but the bond pays a coupon of only 12 percent, and, finally, a premium bond scenario in which the market's required yield to maturity is only 9 percent but the bond pays a coupon of 12 percent.

		Years to Maturity					
	12% Coupon Bond	**5**	**4**	**3**	**2**	**1**	**0**
	12% Yield Scenario	$1,000.00	$1,000.00	$1,000.00	$1,000.00	$1,000.00	$1,000.00
Discount Bond	15% Yield Scenario	$899.44	$914.35	$931.50	$951.23	$973.91	$1,000.00
Premium Bond	9% Yield Scenario	$1,116.69	$1,097.19	$1,075.94	$1,052.77	$1,027.52	$1,000.00

Figure 9.2

Value of a 12 Percent Coupon Bond during the Life of the Bond

As a bond approaches its maturity, the price of the bond approaches the principal or par value of the bond.

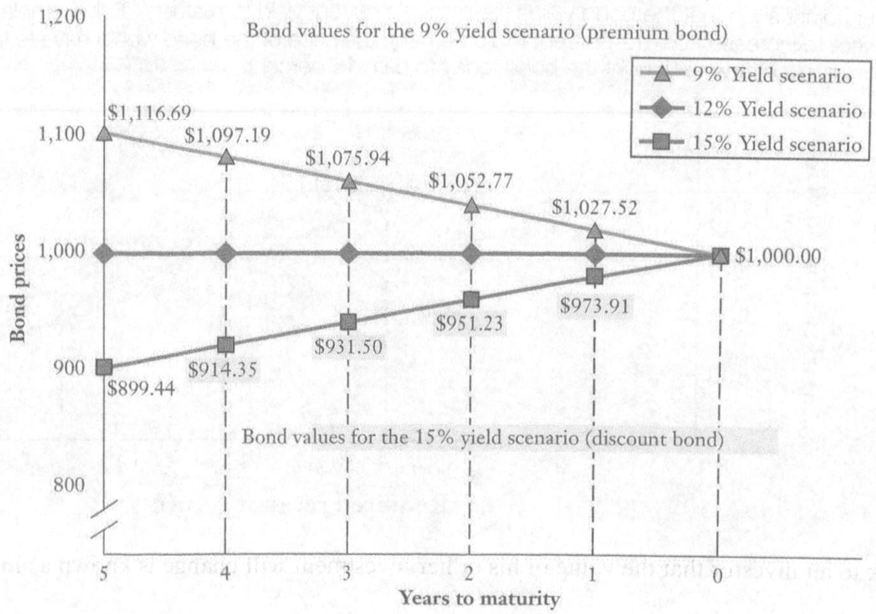

Fourth Relationship

Long-term bonds have greater interest rate risk than short-term bonds.

Longer maturity bonds experience greater price changes in response to interest rate changes than do shorter-term bonds because values of distant cash flows vary more with rate changes.

The table below shows this effect:

Table 9.6 **Bond Price Fluctuations for Bonds with Different Maturities**

The longer the term to maturity, the greater will be the changes in bond prices in response to a given change in the market rate of interest.

	Years to Maturity					
	5	**10**	**15**	**20**	**25**	**30**
15% (Increased Yield)	$899.44	$849.44	$824.58	$812.22	$806.08	$803.02
% Price Decrease	−10.1%	−15.1%	−17.5%	−18.8%	−19.4%	−19.7%
12% (Base Case)	**$1,000.00**	**$1,000.00**	**$1,000.00**	**$1,000.00**	**$1,000.00**	**$1,000.00**
% Price Increase	11.7%	19.3%	24.2%	27.4%	29.5%	30.8%
9% (Decreased Yield)	$1,116.69	$1,192.53	$1,241.82	$1,273.86	$1,294.68	$1,308.21

9.4 Types of Bonds

Major bond types vary by these attributes:

- Secured versus unsecured
- Priority of claim
- Initial offering market
- Abnormal risk
- Coupon level
- Amortizing or non-amortizing
- Convertibility

Secured versus Unsecured

A basic distinction between types of bonds is whether the bond issue is secured by collateral or not. A **secured bond** has specific assets pledged to support repayment of the bond. The term **debenture** applies to any unsecured long-term debt whereas a **mortgage bond** is a bond secured by a lien on real property.

Priority of Claims

The priority of claim refers to the place in line where the bondholders stand in securing repayment out of the dissolution of the firm's assets. **Subordinated debentures** have a lower priority than secured debt and **unsubordinated debentures.** Because of this increased risk, the interest rate paid on them is more than on secured debt.

Initial Offering Market

Bonds also are classified by where they were originally issued (in the domestic bond market or not). For example, **Eurobonds** are bonds issued in a country different from the one in which the currency of the bond is denominated.

Abnormal Risk

Junk, or high-yield, bonds have a below-investment grade bond rating. **Fallen angels** are firms with sound financial histories that face severe financial problems and now have poor credit ratings.

Coupon Level

Bonds with a zero or very low coupon are called **zero coupon bonds** and their return results from the appreciation of the bonds.

Amortizing or Non-Amortizing

The payments from **amortizing bonds**, like a home mortgage loan, include both the interest and a principal. On the other hand, the payments to the bondholder from a **non-amortizing bond** only include interest (principal is repaid on the maturity date).

Convertibility

Convertible bonds are debt securities that can be converted into a firm's stock at a pre-specified price or conversion ratio of shares.

The following table lists different types of bonds:

Table 9.7 Types of Corporate Bonds

Corporations issue a variety of types of bonds that differ with respect to how principal and interest are to be repaid, where the bonds were initially issued or sold and the type of collateral that is used to secure the bond.

Debentures	Any form of unsecured long-term debt. Because they are unsecured, the earning ability of the issuing corporation is of great concern to the bondholder. They are riskier than secured bonds and as a result must provide investors with a higher yield than secured bonds provide. Often, the issuing firm attempts to provide some protection to the holder of the bond by prohibiting the firm from issuing more secured long-term debt that would further tie up the firm's assets and leave the bondholders less protected. To the issuing firm, the major advantage of debentures is that no property has to be secured by them. This allows the firm to issue debt and still preserve some future borrowing power.
Subordinated debentures	The claims of the subordinated debentures are honored only after the claims of secured debt and unsubordinated debentures have been satisfied.
Mortgage bonds	Bonds secured by a lien on real property. Typically, the value of the real property is greater than the amount of the bonds issued. This provides the mortgage bondholders with a margin of safety in the event the market value of the secured property declines. In the case of foreclosure, the bondholders get the proceeds from the sale of the secured property. If the proceeds from this sale do not cover the bonds, the bondholders become general creditors, similar to debenture bondholders, for the unpaid portion of the debt.
Eurobonds	Bonds issued in a country different from the one in whose currency the bond is denominated. For example, a bond that is issued in Europe or in Asia by an American company and that pays interest and principal to the lender in U.S. dollars would be considered a Eurobond. Thus, even if the bond is not issued in Europe, it merely needs to be sold in a country different from the one in whose currency it is denominated to be considered a Eurobond.
Zero coupon and very-low coupon bonds	These bonds require either no coupon interest payments (these are called *zeroes*) or very low interest payments. Consequently, the bondholder receives all or most of their return at maturity. Since these bonds pay little or no interest they must sell at a deep discount. For the investor, a zero coupon bond is like a US savings bond. The obvious appeal of zero coupon bonds is to those investors who need a lump sum of money at some future date but don't want to be concerned about reinvesting interest payments. Today, zero coupon bonds are not often issued by corporations. The dominant player in this market is the US government, with the government's zero coupon bonds called STRIPS.
Junk (high-yield) bonds	High-risk debt that has a below investment-grade bond rating (see the discussion of bond ratings that follows). Junk bonds are also called high-yield bonds because they pay interest rates that are 3 to 5 percent higher than those of the highest rated bonds.
Floating-rate bonds	A floating- or variable-rate bond is simply one in which the coupon rate fluctuates according to the level of current market interest rates. These bonds are quite popular with municipalities and foreign governments, but are far less common among corporations.
Convertible bonds	Convertible bonds are debt securities that can be converted into a firm's stock at a pre-specified price.

9.5 Determinants of Interest Rates

Interest rates vary due to several factors.

Real Rate of Interest and the Inflation Premium

The rate quoted is known as the nominal rate and has several components: the real rate, the credit premium, the maturity premium, and the inflation premium. The Fisher Effect shows how the nominal rate is a combination of real rates and inflation premiums.

$$\text{Nominal Rate of Interest} = \text{Real Rate of Interest, } r_{real} + \text{Inflation Premium} + \text{Default Premium} + \text{Maturity Premium} \quad (9\text{–}3)$$

Important Definitions and Concepts

- **Nominal rate of interest or Yield to maturity** = the rate of interest that will be earned from holding a bond until maturity where the bond pays the holder the promised interest and principal in accordance with what is promised. This rate is NOT adjusted for the loss of purchasing power resulting from inflation.
- **Real rate of interest** = the rate of increase in purchasing power experienced over time. This rate of interest is the nominal rate of interest after adjusting for the effects of inflation.
- **Inflation premium** = a premium for the expected rate of increase in prices of goods and services in the economy over the term of the bond or note.
- **Default premium** = a premium to reflect the risk of default by the borrower.
- **Maturity premium** = a premium that reflects the term structure of interest rates. In general, longer maturity debt has a higher rate, but this is not always the case, (see Bond pricing relationship #4 discussed earlier).

Fisher Effect

The relationship between the nominal rate of interest, r_{nominal}, the anticipated rate of inflation, r_{infation}, and the real rate of interest, r_{real}, is known as the **Fisher effect**. It is captured in the Equation (9-4) below:

$$(1 + r_{nominal}) = (1 + r_{real})(1 + r_{inflation}) \tag{9–4}$$

or, rearranging the terms of the equation we can solve for the nominal rate of interest, , as follows:

$$\begin{aligned} r_{nominal} &= (1 + r_{real})(1 + r_{inflation}) - 1 \\ &= r_{real} + r_{inflation} + (r_{real} \times r_{inflation}) \end{aligned} \tag{9–4a}$$

Important Definitions and Concepts

- $r_{nominal}$ = the nominal or observed rate of interest which has not been adjusted for the effects of inflation.
- r_{real} = the rate of increase in purchasing power from an investment which is calculated by netting out the anticipated increase in the price of goods and services (inflation) from the nominal rate of interest on the investment.
- $r_{inflation}$ = the rate of inflation in the economy which reflects the anticipated rate at which the general level of prices for goods and services will rise annually.

In the chapter's example, the nominal rate of interest is 13.4 percent and the anticipated rate of inflation is 5 percent. We can solve for the real rate of interest using Equation (9-4b):

$$r_{real} = \frac{(1 + r_{nominal})}{(1 + r_{inflation})} - 1 \tag{9–4b}$$

Substituting into Equation (9-4b) we calculate the real rate of interest to be 8 percent, as shown below:

$$r_{real} = \frac{(1 + .134)}{(1 + .05)} - 1 = .08 \text{ or } 8\%$$

Therefore, the nominal rate of interest is equal to the sum of the real rate of interest (r_{real}), the expected rate of inflation, $r_{\text{inflation}}$, and the product of the real rate and the rate of inflation.

Note that if the expected rate of inflation is low, then the cross product ($r_{real} \times r_{inflation}$) will be very small. It is customary to ignore this cross product term and estimate the real rate of interest simply by subtracting the anticipated rate of inflation from the nominal rate of interest.

Real rate of interest ≈ Nominal interest rate – Inflation premium

Default Premium

In addition to accounting for the time value of money and inflation, a firm's bonds must pay a rate that accounts for the risk of default. The risk of default is the possibility that the bond issuer (the borrower) will fail to repay principal and interest in a timely manner. For any given maturity, bonds with higher probabilities of default will require a higher promised yield.

Maturity Premium: The Term Structure of Interest Rates

The longer the bond's maturity, the more the bond price fluctuates when interest rates change. Thus, long-term bonds have greater interest rate risk than do short-term bonds. The compensation that investors demand for bearing interest rate risk on longer-term bonds is known as the **maturity premium**.

The relationship between interest rates and time to maturity with risk held constant is known as the **term structure of interest rates** or **the yield curve.** Figure 9.3 illustrates a hypothetical term structure of US Treasury Bonds. Generally, the yield curve rises for longer maturities although there are times when it is flat, hump-shaped and even negative in slope. The yield curve can shift up or down and slope upward and downward based on changes in inflation, maturity premiums, and real rates.

The two figures below demonstrate this:

Figure 9.3

The Term Structure of Interest Rates or Yield Curve

The yield curve shows the relationship between yield to maturity and maturity dates for a set of similar bonds (typically U.S. Government or Treasury securities). In this example the 20-year bond has a yield to maturity of 13 percent while the 5-year security yields only 11.5 percent. Thus, the yield curve is said to be upward sloping. The upward sloping yield curve is the most typical; however flat and inverted (downward sloping) yield curves are sometimes observed.

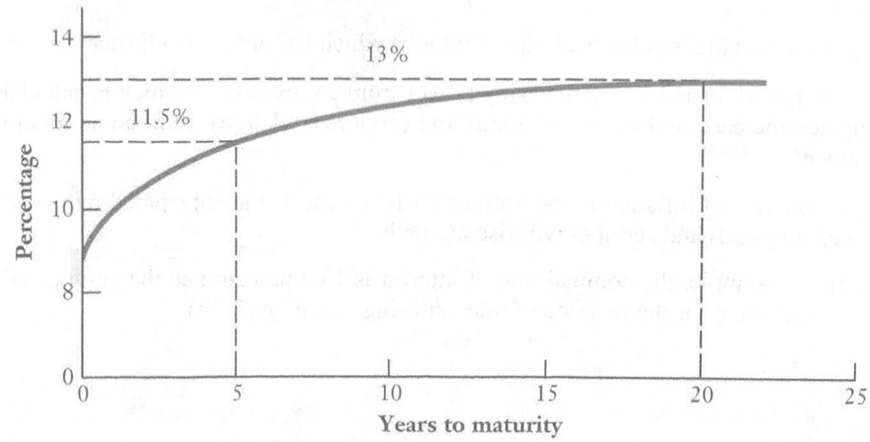

Figure 9.7

Historical Term Structure of Interest Rates for Government Securities

The term structure of interest rates is not fixed and can change dramatically in a brief period of time in response to changing expectations and economic conditions. The three term structures plotted here capture upward-sloping, flat, and downward-sloping (inverted) term structures observed within a span of only 13 months.

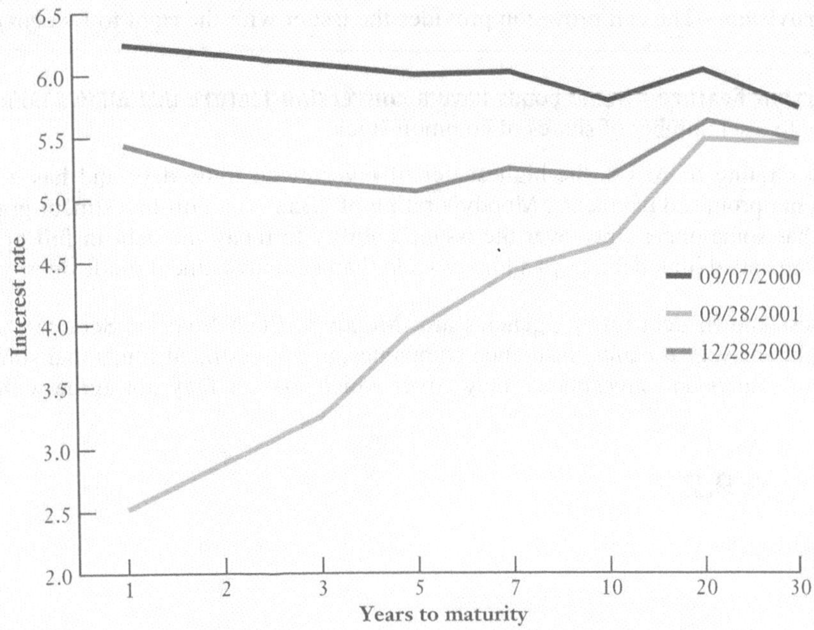

Answers to **Concept Checks**

Concept Check **9.1**

1. What is a bond indenture?
2. What are the key features of a bond? Which of these features determines the cash flows paid to the bondholder?
3. What is the difference between an Aaa and a Ba bond in terms of risks to the bondholder? What are the principal bond rating agencies?

Answer 1: A bond indenture is the legal document (between the trustee and the firm) governing the rights and obligations of the bond issuer and investors.

Answer 2: Key features of a bond are:

- **Priority of Claim on Assets and Income** —During insolvency, the claims of debt are honored before those of both common and preferred stock. Also, interest payments hold priority over dividend payments for common and preferred stock.
- **Par Value**—The par value of a bond, also known as its face value, is the principal that must be repaid to the bondholder at maturity. In general, corporate bonds are issued with par values in increments of $1,000.
- **Maturity and Repayment of Principal**—The maturity date refers to the date on which the bond issuer must repay the principal or par value to the bondholder.

- **Coupon Interest Rate**—The coupon rate on a bond indicates the percentage of the par value of the bond that will be paid out annually in the form of interest.
- **Current Yield**—The current yield is the ratio of the annual interest payment to the bond's current market price.
- **Call Provision**—The call provision provides the issuer with the right to redeem or retire a bond before it matures.
- **Conversion Feature**—Some bonds have a **conversion feature** that allows bondholders to convert their bonds into a set number of shares of common stock.

Answer 3: Moody's rating of Aaa is the highest tier of investment grade debt and has a very low probability of defaulting or delaying promised payments. Moody's rating of "Baa" is a non-investment grade debt or a speculative grade debt which has some uncertainty over the issuer's ability to repay the debt in full or on time. Speculative or high yield debt, often called junk debt, pays a higher yield than safe investment grade debt.

The largest and best known debt rating agencies are: Moody's, Fitch Investor Services, and Standard & Poor's. There are many debt analysts at banks, insurance companies, and investment funds that sometimes issue reports on the credit quality of issuers and investments they cover which may or may not agree with the three firm's credit ratings.

Concept Check 9.2

1. How do you calculate the value of a bond?
2. How do you estimate the appropriate discount rate?
3. Why might the expected returns be different from the yield to maturity?
4. How do semiannual interest payments affect the asset valuation equation?

Answer 1: The value of a bond is the sum of the present value of a bond's interest payments and principal payment.

Answer 2: The appropriate discount rate can be calculated from the prices of other bonds or found online in terms of a credit spread over the Treasury Bond.

Answer 3: The bond's quoted yield is the promised yield of the bond as if the bond's interest and principal is fully repaid. The expected return of a bond reflects the possibility of partial repayment and is relevant to investors in high yielding bonds of poor credit quality.

Answer 4: Semiannual interest payments change the bond valuation equation by doubling the number of periods, reducing the discount rate by half, and finding the cash flow for six months of interest (C X par / 2).

Concept Check 9.3

1. Explain the relationship between bond value and the bond's yield to maturity.
2. As interest rates increase, why does the price of a long-term bond decrease more than the price of a short-term bond?
3. Why does a bond sell at a premium when the coupon rate is higher than the market's yield to maturity on a similar bond and vice versa?
4. As the maturity date of a bond approaches, what happens to the price of a discount bond? Is the result the same if the bond is a premium bond?

Answer 1: Bond values decline as YTM rises – it is a discount rate for the bond's cash flows.

Answer 2: As rates rise, the distant cash flows of a bond fall more than the near cash flows according to the present value formula.

Answer 3: Bonds sell at a premium when the promise to pay (coupon) exceeds the required rate of return (YTM) by the market. Bonds sell at a discount when the promise to pay is less than the market's required return.

Answer 4: For both discount and premium bonds, the price of the bond moves toward par value as the maturity date nears.

Concept Check **9.4**

1. What is the difference between debentures, subordinated debentures, and mortgage bonds?
2. How does an investor receive a return from a zero- or very-low-coupon bond?
3. What are junk bonds, and why do they typically have a higher interest rate than other types of bonds?

Answer 1: Mortgage bonds have property as collateral, debentures are senior claims on the assets and cash flow of the firm (junior to mortgage holders), and subordinated owners are junior debt owners with priority over the equity owners.

Answer 2: A zero coupon bond rewards an investor with capital appreciation as the price of the bond moves toward the par value over time.

Answer 3: Junk bonds are bonds with lower credit ratings and higher default risk so investors require a greater rate of return.

Concept Check **9.5**

1. What is the yield curve?
2. What is the typical shape of the yield curve for U.S. Treasury securities?

Answer 1: The yield curve or term structure plots the YTM of bonds by maturity.

Answer 2: Due to the maturity premium and inflation, the slopes is upward usually.

Multiple Choice **Quiz**

1. The yield to maturity
   a. is the return expected by investors assuming a default.
   b. is the annual rate of interest paid.
   c. is the graph that plots interest rates and maturity.
   d. is the return expected by investors assuming all promised cash flows are paid.

2. Unsubordinated debentures are
   a. debts with real property as collateral.
   b. debts that have no principle payments prior to maturity.
   c. debts senior to equity and other unsecured debts.
   d. debts senior to equity and junior to unsecured debts.

3. The nominal rate of a bond is
   a. the quoted rate that is not adjusted for inflation.
   b. the inflation premium of a bond.
   c. the inflation-adjusted quoted rate.
   d. the expected return of the bond in case of default.

4. Non-amortizing bonds are
   a. debts with real property as collateral.
   b. debts that have no principle payments prior to maturity.
   c. debts senior to equity and other unsecured debts.
   d. debts senior to equity and junior to unsecured debts.

5. Mortgage bonds are
   a. debts with real property as collateral.
   b. debts that have no principle payments prior to maturity.
   c. debts senior to equity and other unsecured debts.
   d. debts senior to equity and junior to unsecured debts.

6. Interest rate risk is
   a. the risk that the coupon rate changes.
   b. the risk that the credit quality goes up.
   c. the risk that the payments are late or not paid.
   d. the risk that the market risk premium changes.

7. Default risk is
   a. the risk that the coupon rate changes.
   b. the risk that the credit quality goes up.
   c. the risk that the payments are late or not paid.
   d. the risk that the returns required by the market change.

8. The current yield is
   a. the yield expected by investors assuming default.
   b. the yield based on today's bond price and the annual coupon.
   c. the yield promised on a fixed rate bond.
   d. the yield promised on a floating rate bond.

9. The coupon rate is
   a. the return expected by investors assuming default.
   b. the annual rate of interest paid.
   c. the graph that plots of interest rates and maturities.
   d. the return expected by investors assuming all promised cash flows are paid.

10. The bond indenture contains
    a. par value, coupon rate, current yield, conversion feature.
    b. par value, coupon rate, conversion feature, inflation premium.
    c. par value, conversion feature, term structure, coupon rate.
    d. par value, conversion feature, call provision, coupon rate.

Answers to **Multiple Choice Questions**

1. D
2. C
3. A
4. B
5. A
6. D
7. C
8. B
9. B
10. D

Self Test with **Solutions**

Picture the Problem

Decide on Solution Strategy

Solve

Analyze

Self Test 1: Determining Yield to Maturity

You are a portfolio manager for Vanguard's high yield corporate bond fund and have found a bond issued by a home builder, Centex, that is priced at $920. The Centex bond pays a semiannual coupon at rate of 8 percent and matures in three years.

a. What is the yield to maturity of the Centex bond?

b. If the market assesses a 10 percent probability of default and a 20 percent loss on principal and interest over the four years, what is the expected yield if you pay $920 today?

c. If you were buying the bond, which of the two yields should you rely upon for your decision?

Step 1: Picture the Problem

The problem requires the manager to determine the YTM and then the expected yield by using the bond valuation equation.

Step 2: Decide on a Solution Strategy

To solve, we will use the bond valuation equation first to solve for YTM and then rework it to solve for the expected rate of return after adjusting for default and then averaging the default and no default rates to approximate the rate of return expected by the market.

Step 3: Solve

To solve for the *YTM*, use the bond valuation equation for a three year, 8 percent coupon, semiannual paying bond that has a par or face value of $1,000.

$$\text{Bond Value} = \left(\text{Interest}/2\right)\left[\frac{1-\dfrac{1}{\left(1+\dfrac{YTM}{2}\right)^{2n}}}{\dfrac{YTM}{2}}\right] + \text{Principal}\left[\frac{1}{\left(1+\dfrac{YTM}{2}\right)^{2n}}\right]$$

Coupon (Annual) = 8 percent of $1,000 par = $80, Semiannual interest = $40

Periods = Years X 2 = 3 X 2 = 6

Rate = semiannual rate, solve for *I* and *YTM* = 2 X *i*

Par value = $1,000 (the future value paid at the end)

Today's present value is the traded price of the bond = $920

To see the inputs in the equation,

$$\$920 = 40\times\left[\frac{1-\dfrac{1}{\left(1+\dfrac{YTM}{2}\right)^{6}}}{\dfrac{YTM}{2}}\right] + \$1000\times\left[\frac{1}{\left(1+\dfrac{YTM}{2}\right)^{6}}\right]$$

Solving the formula requires guessing the semiannual rate, but we can take the inputs of the bond valuation formula to our calculator or spreadsheet.

Enter	**6**	**?**	**-920**	**40**	**1,000**
	N	I/Y	PV	PMT	FV
Solve for		**5.61%= semiannual rate, thus *YTM* = 2 × 5.61%**			

Using an Excel spreadsheet,

=Rate(nper ,pmt,pv,fv) or with values entered =Rate(6,40,-920,1000) equals .05607

Doubling the semiannual rate equals the promised rate, *YTM* = 11.21%

To solve for the expected yield, use the bond valuation equation for a three-year, 8 percent coupon, semiannual paying bond that has a par or face value of $1,000 but include the loss expectation in the credit premium which was 20 percent loss of coupons and principal. Then plug the lower cash flows into the bond valuation equation.

$$\text{Bond Value} = \left(\text{Interest}/2\right)\left[\frac{1-\dfrac{1}{\left(1+\dfrac{YTM}{2}\right)^{2n}}}{\dfrac{YTM}{2}}\right] + \text{Principal}\left[\frac{1}{\left(1+\dfrac{YTM}{2}\right)^{2n}}\right]$$

Coupon (Annual) = 8 percent of $1,000 par = $80 less $16 loss, Semiannual interest = $40 less $8

Periods = Years X 2 = 3 X 2 = 6

Rate = semiannual rate, solve for I and $YTM = 2 \text{ X } i$

Par value = $1,000 (the future value paid at the end) less $200 = $800

Today's present value is the traded price of the bond = $920

To see the inputs in the equation,

$$\$920 = 32\times\left[\frac{1-\dfrac{1}{\left(1+\dfrac{YTM}{2}\right)^{6}}}{\dfrac{YTM}{2}}\right] + \$800\times\left[\frac{1}{\left(1+\dfrac{YTM}{2}\right)^{6}}\right]$$

Solving the formula requires guessing the semiannual rate, but we can take the inputs of the bond valuation formula to our calculator or spreadsheet.

Enter	**6**	**?**	**-920**	**32**	**800**
	N	I/Y	PV	PMT	FV
Solve for		**1.38%= semiannual rate, thus *YTM* = 2 × 1.38%**			

Using an Excel spreadsheet,

=Rate(nper ,pmt,pv,fv) or with values entered =Rate(6,40,-920,1000) equals .0138

Doubling the semiannual rate equals the promised rate, YTM = 2.76%

The expected return is the weighted average of the no default and the default return.

Expected return = No Default return × No Default probability + Default return × Default Probability

$= 11.21\% \times 90\% + 10\% \times 2.76\% = 10.37\%$

Step 4: Analyze

This discount bond has a YTM, promised yield, of 11.21 percent which is greater than the coupon rate. Because it has a low default probability and loss ratio, the expected return of 10.37 percent is only slightly less than the YTM. As long as similar corporate bonds have returns of 10.37 percent or less, the bond is attractive as an investment as the promised return is not the relevant yield to investors, expected return is the correct yield for decisions on investments.

Self Test 2: Bond Valuation

You are a portfolio manager for Vanguard's high yield corporate bond fund and have found a bond issued by a home builder, Centex, that is priced at $920. The Centex bond pays a semiannual coupon at an annual rate of 8 percent and matures in three years. You have determined that it is a A- rated security when the similar maturity Treasury Bond yields 5.5 percent.

From Bonds Online, you found the following credit spreads:

Maturity	1yr	2yr	3yr	5yr	10yr
T-Bond	2%	4%	5.5%	6%	5%
AAA	10bp	20bp	40bp	30bp	30bp
AA	15bp	30bp	50bp	35bp	40bp
A	25bp	37bp	65bp	80bp	100bp
A- /BBB	40bp	76bp	90bp	80bp	95bp

a. What is your value for the Centex bond using a corporate spread over T-Bonds?
b. Compared to the price in the market should you buy the bond?

Step 1: Picture the Problem

The problem requires the manager to value the bond using the discounted cash flow method and the bond valuation equation.

Step 2: Decide on a Solution Strategy

To solve, we will use the bond valuation equation with a semiannual YTM that reflects the credit spread approach.

Step 3: Solve

To solve for the value, use the bond valuation equation for a three-year, 8 percent coupon, semiannual paying bond that has a par or face value of $1,000.

For the *YTM*, find the required rate by adding a credit spread to the Treasury Bond yield for a three-year bond. The three-year Treasury has a *YTM* of 5.5 percent and the appropriate credit spread for an A- rated bond is 90 basis points. $YTM = TB + CS$ = 5.5 percent + .9 percent = 6.4 percent. The semiannual rate equals 3.2 percent.

$$\text{Bond Value} = \left(\text{Interest}/2\right)\left[\frac{1-\dfrac{1}{\left(1+\dfrac{YTM}{2}\right)^{2n}}}{\dfrac{YTM}{2}}\right] + \text{Principal}\left[\frac{1}{\left(1+\dfrac{YTM}{2}\right)^{2n}}\right]$$

Coupon (Annual) = 8 percent of $1,000 par = $80, Semiannual interest = $40

Periods = Years X 2 = 3 X 2 = 6

Rate = semiannual rate, Treasury 5.5% + 90bps = 6.4% annual, 3.2% s.a.

Par value = $1,000 (the future value paid at the end)

Solve for today's present value

To see the inputs in the equation,

$$\text{Value} = 40 \times \left[\frac{1-\dfrac{1}{\left(1+\dfrac{.064}{2}\right)^{6}}}{\dfrac{.064}{2}}\right] + \$1000 \times \left[\frac{1}{\left(1+\dfrac{.064}{2}\right)^{6}}\right]$$

Solving for present value can be done working the formula, but we can take the inputs of the bond valuation formula to our calculator or spreadsheet, too.

Enter	**6**	**3.2**	**?**	**40**	**1,000**
	N	**I/Y**	**PV**	**PMT**	**FV**
Solve for			**$1,043.05**		

Using an Excel spreadsheet,

=PV(rate,nper ,pmt ,fv) or with values entered =PV(.032,6,40,1000) equals 1,043.05

Step 4: Analyze

This discount bond has a *YTM*, promised yield, of 11.21 percent at the discount price of $920. The value of the bond under the credit spread approach uses a *YTM* of 6.4 percent and finds a much higher value of $1,043.05.

Given the OTC market for bonds is both illiquid and not as efficient as an actively traded securities market, it is possible the bond is undervalued by the market (assuming the expected return hasn't changed). Buy the bond. As funds look to buy this bond, it is likely that holders of the bonds will reassess their valuation and the price will correct toward its intrinsic value of $1,043.05. The wide spread in values could motivate more research into the bond's features to see if it is callable or if there is some other risk depressing the price and raising the *YTM*.

CHAPTER 10

Stock Valuation

Chapter **Orientation**

This chapter details the characteristics and valuation of stock. Firms have two basic choices when raising external capital for expansion: sell bonds or sell stock. By understanding the factors that move stock prices, you can make more informed choices for your own investments. Analysts and company managers are very interested in these factors as they separate the good firms from the bad, the good investments from the poor ones, and the smart decisions from the dumb ones. This chapter also covers stock market characteristics and a senior form of equity known as preferred stock.

Chapter Review: **Terms and Concepts**

10.1 Common Stock

Common stock represents the ownership interest, a residual claim after debt is paid. Common shareholders elect a board of directors to represent their interests. The board hires and fires the management team.

Characteristics of Common Stock

Common stock does not have a maturity date, but exists as long as the firm does. Equity has the most junior claim— the firm's debt and preferred stock are paid first.

Claims on Income

The common shareholders have the right to the firm's income that remains after bondholders and preferred stockholders have been paid. The common shareholders either receive cash payments in the form of dividends or capital gains from stock.

The main advantage of owning stock is that it has a potentially unlimited upside. The disadvantage is that debt and preferred stock are paid first so there may be little left for common owners.

Claims on Assets

Common has a residual claim on assets. In many bankruptcies, the common stock receives nothing. As a result of the higher risk of common stock, shareholders typically earn more than the other two classes of investors (bondholders and preferred shareholders). Common has earned about 9.6 percent annually in the last century as a result of carrying risk.

Voting Rights

Common shareholders usually are the only voting class of investors. Some stocks with two classes of stock have a voting and a non-voting class. Most stocks have only one class due to the Public Utility Holding Company Act of 1935 and the NYSE's opposition to dual class stocks. Google is a modern example of a firm with two classes of common with one giving control to its executive management team who founded the firm.

Common shareholders must approve changes in the firm's charter which usually includes decisions to merge or issue stock. A **proxy** gives a party other than the shareholder the right to vote in the firm's next annual meeting on corporate affairs.

If shareholders disagree with managers, a proxy fight over a corporate proposal at the annual meeting may occur. Provisions may be voted on individually, known as **majority voting**, or as a group, known as **cumulative voting**, depending on the firm's rules for proxy votes. A simple majority of the board is all that is necessary to approve corporate actions.

Agency Costs and Common Stock

In the real world, the management team may pick the board and control many of the proxy votes. The effect is to create an agency problem between the owners and the management team when the managers make choices for their benefit and not the shareholders. Managers may turn down good investments, or take bad ones, if their choices are biased by short-term considerations on compensation and job security.

Valuing Common Stock Using the Discounted Dividend Model

The value of a stock equals the sum of the present value of its cash flows. This task is more difficult as stocks don't have finite terms or exact promises of cash flow payments or dividends. The dividend is based on the profitability of the firm and management's decision to pay a dividend. Dividends are lower in emerging firms and higher in mature firms with little need to invest in new projects in their industry.

Equity value is based on the expected value of dividends over the infinite life of the firm. The dividend stream is discounted by an appropriate expected rate of return that reflects the risk of owning stock in the firm (or a firm of equal risk). This is the investor's required rate of return. The steps for valuing stock are below.

Three-Step Procedure for Valuing Common Stock

To value common stock, we will use the same three-step procedure we used to value bonds.

Step 1: Estimate the amount and timing of the receipt of the future cash flows the common stock is *expected* to provide.

Step 2: Evaluate the riskiness of the common stock's future dividends, and determine the rate of return an investor might expect to receive from a comparable risk investment, which becomes the investor's required rate of return.

Step 3: Calculate the present value of the expected dividends by discounting them back to the present at the investor's required rate of return.

The value of a common stock is equal to the present value of all future dividends.

Basic Concept of the Stock Valuation Model

The valuation equation for \$1.75 dividend and \$50 selling price in one year, 15 percent IRR:

$$\begin{array}{c}\text{Value of Common}\\ \text{Stock Today}\end{array} = \frac{\$1.75 + 50.00}{(1+.15)^1} = \$45.00$$

If the sale of the stock takes place a nearly infinite time away, then the value of the stock is the present value of the dividends. However, by using the equation below, the analyst has to forecast dividends from now to infinity. You could say this is challenging.

$$\text{Value of Common Stock} = \frac{\text{Dividend for Year 1}}{\left(1 + \text{Stockholder's Required Rate of Return}\right)^1} + \frac{\text{Dividend for Year 2}}{\left(1 + \text{Stockholder's Required Rate of Return}\right)^2}$$
$$+ \frac{\text{Dividend for Year 3}}{\left(1 + \text{Stockholder's Required Rate of Return}\right)^3} + \cdots + \frac{\text{Dividend for Year } \infty}{\left(1 + \text{Stockholder's Required Rate of Return}\right)^\infty}$$

The great simplification is when we assume the present dividends grow at a constant rate forever. The valuation equation becomes the constant dividend growth model:

The Constant Dividend Growth Rate Model

$$\text{Value of Common Stock in Year 0} = \frac{\text{Dividend Paid in Year 0}\left(1 + \text{Dividend Growth Rate}\right)^1}{\left(1 + \text{Stockholder's Required Rate of Return}\right)^1} + \frac{\text{Dividend Paid in Year 0}\left(1 + \text{Dividend Growth Rate}\right)^2}{\left(1 + \text{Stockholder's Required Rate of Return}\right)^2}$$
$$+ \frac{\text{Dividend Paid in Year 0}\left(1 + \text{Dividend Growth Rate}\right)^3}{\left(1 + \text{Stockholder's Required Rate of Return}\right)^3} + \cdots + \frac{\text{Dividend Paid in Year 0}\left(1 + \text{Dividend Growth Rate}\right)^\infty}{\left(1 + \text{Stockholder's Required Rate of Return}\right)^\infty} \quad (10\text{–}1)$$

This **constant dividend growth rate model** of common stock valuation is defined as follows:

$$V_{cs} = \frac{\text{Dividend in Year 0}\left(1 + \text{Dividend Growth Rate}\right)}{\text{Stockholder's Required Rate of Return} - \text{Dividend Growth Rate}} = \frac{\text{Dividend in Year 1}}{\text{Stockholder's Required Rate of Return} - \text{Dividend Growth Rate}} \quad (10\text{–}2)$$

Figure 10.1

A Quick Reference Guide for the Constant Dividend Growth Rate Valuation Model

If the rate of growth in common stock dividends is expected to be constant into the indefinite future and this rate of growth is less than the common stockholders' required rate of return, the discounted cash flow valuation model for common stock reduces to the following simple formula:

$$V_{cs} = \frac{D_0(1+g)}{r_{cs} - g} = \frac{D_1}{r_{cs} - g} \quad (10\text{–}2)$$

Definitions and Assumptions:

- V_{cs} = the value of a share of common stock which is equal to the present value of all future expected dividends.
- D_0 = the most recent annual cash dividend received by the common stockholder which was paid in the year the valuation is being done (year 0).
- g = the annual rate of growth in the cash dividend payment which is assumed to be constant forever.
- $D_1 = D_0(1+g)$ =the expected dividend for the end of year 1.
- r_{cs} = the common stockholder's required rate of return for the shares of common stock. Note that this is not a market yield or promised rate of return but is the rate of return the investor expects to earn from investing in the firm's stock. This expected rate of return reflects the riskiness of the stock's future dividends.

What Causes Stock Prices to Go Up and Down?

We can use the constant dividend growth rate model of stock valuation in Equation (10–2) to develop a better understanding of what causes stock prices to move up and down.

$$V_{cs} = \frac{D_0(1+g)}{r_{cs} - g} = \frac{\text{Dividend in Year 1}}{\text{Stockholder's Required Rate of Return} - \text{Growth Rate}} \qquad (10\text{–}2)$$

There are changes in three variables that affect share value: next year's dividend, the investor's required rate of return, and the expected rate of growth.

Determinants of the Investor's Required Rate of Return

The investor's rate of return is determined by two key factors: the level of interest rates and the risk of the stock according to CAPM.

$$\text{Expected Rate of Return} = \text{Risk-Free Rate of Interest} + \text{Common Stock Beta Coefficient}\left(\text{Expected Rate of Return on the Market Portfolio} - \text{Risk-Free Rate of Interest}\right) \qquad (8\text{–}6)$$

Figure 10.2 contains a quick reference guide to the CAPM including definitions.

Figure 10.2

A Quick Reference Guide for the Capital Asset Pricing Model

The Capital Asset Pricing Model, CAPM, is deceptively simple. It states that the expected rate of return on any risky investment can be thought of as the sum of the risk free rate of interest and a risk premium. The risk premium, in turn, is determined by the market risk premium for the market portfolio and the beta coefficient for the investment.

$$r_{cs} = r_f + \beta_{cs}\left[E(r_m) - r_f\right] \qquad (8\text{–}6)$$

Important Definitions and Concepts

- r_{cs} = the investor's required rate of return on a firm's common stock.
- r_f = the risk-free rate of interest.
- β_{cs} = the beta of the stock.
- $E(r_m) - r_f$ = the market risk premium or the difference in the expected rate of return on the market portfolio, $E(r_m)$, and the risk-free rate of interest, r_f.

If the risk-free rate rises or the systematic risk of a stock increases, then the investor's required rate of return will rise accordingly, and the share price will fall.

Determinants of the Growth Rate of Future Dividends

The growth rate of expected future dividends also can change and lead to a change in the stock price. The key determinants of a firm's growth opportunities relate to the rates of return the firm expects to earn when they reinvest earnings (the return on equity or ROE), and the proportion of firm's earnings that they reinvest (retain or do not pay out in cash dividends), which is known as the retention ratio, *b*. The growth rate in the firm's dividends, *g*, can be thought of simply as the product of the firm's ROE and the ratio of the earnings it retains (the retention ratio, *b*).

$$\text{Rate of Growth in Dividends } (g) = \text{Retention Ratio } (b) \times \text{Rate of Return on Equity } (ROE)$$

where the retention ratio, *b*, is equal to one minus the dividend payout ratio (D_1/E_1)

$$\text{Rate of Growth in Dividends } (g) = \left(1 - \text{Dividend Payout Ratio}\right) \times \text{Rate of Return on Equity } (ROE) \qquad (10\text{–}3)$$

Figure 10.3

A Quick Reference Guide for the Growth Rate in Earnings and Dividends

The rate of growth a firm can expect in its future dividends is a function of how much of the firm's earnings are reinvested in the firm (i.e., the dividend retention ratio, *b*), and the rate of return the firm is expected to earn on the reinvested earnings *(ROE)*.

$$g = (1 - D_1 / E_1) \times ROE \qquad (10\text{–}3)$$

Definitions and Important Concepts

- g = the expected rate of growth in dividends.
- D_1/E_1 = the dividend payout ratio reflecting the ratio of cash dividends to be paid next period divided by the firm's earnings.
- $b = (1 - D_1/E_1)$ which is the proportion of firm earnings that are retained and reinvested in the firm.
- ROE = the return on equity earned when the firm reinvests a portion of its earnings back into the firm.
- Equation (10–3) requires that the retention ratio, b, and ROE remain constant for all future periods.

10.2 The Comparables Approach to Valuing Common Stock

The discounted dividend valuation model is a good representation of what drives stock prices even if it doesn't always give the correct stock price when compared to the stock market. The inputs – growth, dividend, expected required return – make sense. Because these inputs are difficult to estimate to infinity, analysts often turn to the comparable multiples approach to valuation. By looking at various valuation ratios of similar firms, analysts can infer the value of a stock. This is relative valuation rather than absolute.

Defining the P/E Ratio Valuation Model

The P/E ratio or multiple shows the amount the market is willing to pay for $1 dollar of earnings and is the most popular multiple for valuation. The multiple is based on trailing earnings (last four quarters of earnings) or forward earnings (the next four quarters of estimates):

$$\begin{matrix}\text{Value of}\\ \text{Common Stock,}\\ V_{cs}\end{matrix} = \left(\begin{matrix}\text{Appropriate}\\ \text{Price Earnings Ratio}\end{matrix}\right) \times \left(\begin{matrix}\text{Estimated Earnings}\\ \text{Per Share for Year 1}\end{matrix}\right) = \frac{P}{E_1} \times E_1 \qquad (10\text{–}4)$$

Figure 10.4

A Quick Reference Guide for the Price-Earnings Stock Valuation Model

The price/earnings stock valuation model is sometimes referred to as a relative valuation model that is based on comparable firm valuations. This reflects the fact that the price-earnings ratio used to value the stock measures value relative to firm earnings and is chosen by looking at comparable firms.

$$V_{cs} = \frac{P}{E_1} \times E_1 \qquad (10\text{–}4)$$

Important Definitions and Concepts

- V_{CS} = the value of the common stock of the firm.
- P/E_1 = the price earnings ratio for the firm based on the current price per share divided by earnings for the end of year 1.[1]
- E_1 = estimated earnings per share of common stock for the end of year 1.

---

[1] Technically this definition of the P/E ratio is the "forward P/E" ratio since it used predicted earnings one year hence. However, for our purposes we will follow the convention of using the end-of-period earnings figure.

What Determines the P/E Ratio for a Stock?

First, look at similar stocks. Look at the market and at the industry to decide how to adjust the multiple for the firm's stock. Expectations for growth rates, risk, inflation, interest rates, leverage, and profitability may influence the multiple. By expanding the dividend valuation equation, we find that dividend and reinvestment policies of the firm affect growth rates and that risk impacts the multiple, too.

To open our discussion of the determinants of a firm's P/E ratio, let's first review the constant dividend growth model of stock value presented earlier in Equation (10–2), i.e.,

$$V_{cs} = \frac{D_0(1+g)}{r_{cs} - g} = \frac{\text{Dividend in Year 1}}{\text{Stockholder's Required Rate of Return} - \text{Growth Rate}} \qquad (10\text{–}2)$$

Recall that D_1 is the dividend expected at the end of the year, r_{cs} is the investor's required rate of return and g is the expected rate of growth in dividends. If we assume that the current market price of the firm's shares (P) is equal to the value of the firm's shares, V_{cs}, (i.e., the present value of expected future dividends) we can rewrite Equation (10–2) as follows:

$$\frac{P}{E_1} = \frac{D_1/E_1}{r_{cs} - g} = \frac{D_1/E_1}{r_{cs} - [(1 - D_1/E_1) \times ROE]} \qquad (10\text{–}5a)$$

Now we are ready to investigate the determinants of the P/E ratio. Specifically, looking at Equation (10–5) and (10–5a) we see that there are two fundamental determinants of a firm's P/E ratio:

1. Growth rate in dividends—the rate of growth in firm dividends is determined by how much of the firm's earnings are retained and reinvested (i.e., $1 - D_1E_1$) and the rate of return the firm earns when it reinvests those funds *(ROE)*.
2. Investor-required rates of return—the rate of return the firm's stockholders require that the firm earn on their investment in the firm's stock, *rcs*.

Looking at the P/E equation, we can make some quick observations about the mechanical or mathematical relationships between the above variables and the P/E ratio:

- First, the higher the rate of growth in dividends, the higher the P/E ratio will be.
- Second, the higher the investor's required rate of return is, other things being the same, the smaller the P/E ratio will be. The required rate of return, r_{cs}, is in the denominator.

But what causes the growth rate in dividends (and earnings) and the investor's required rate of return to go up and down? These are the real determinants of the P/E ratio.

- **Firm factors impacting the investor's required rate of return, r_{cs}:** The higher the investor's required rate of return, the lower the P/E ratio. If the firm becomes more risky, r_{cs} will rise, and as a result, the P/E ratio will fall.
- **Economic or macro factors impacting the investor's required rate of return, r_{cs}:** Higher interest rates and greater uncertainty will increase investor's required rate of return, while lower interest rates and less uncertainty will lower investor's required rate of return. As a result, when interest rates and uncertainty declines, P/E ratios on all stocks rise.
- ***Firm factors impacting the growth rate:*** The growth rate in firm dividends is itself determined by two variables—dividend policy and the profitability of the firm's investment opportunities.
    - ***Dividend policy***—firms that retain and reinvest their earnings might grow whereas firms that pay out all their earnings in dividends cannot grow.

- *Firm investment opportunities*—firm earnings and future dividends can only grow the ROE exceeds the investor's required rate of return, r_{cs}, if that's the case, the higher the return on new investments (ROE), the higher the growth rate.

An Aside on Managing for Shareholder Value

ROE has to exceed the required rate of return for projects to add value to the firm and its stock. New investments must meet that goal or the firm will not be profitable or successful in the future.

A Word of Caution about P/E Ratios

Firms do not compute earnings the same way. Analysts may choose a different version of earnings for their multiples. For example, operating earnings may give a better view of the earnings potential of the firm before any charges.

10.3 Preferred Stock

Features of Preferred Stock

Preferred dividends are **fixed**, shareholders do not share in firm's upside.

Preferred may have **multiple classes**, some may be convertible.

Preferred has a **priority claim on assets and income** over common in bankruptcy.

Cumulative preferred dividends require their dividends are paid before common.

Preferred is safer than common, riskier than debt, a **hybrid security**.

Like common, preferred has no maturity date, dividend payments are not tax deductible, and non-payment of dividends does not trigger a default. Like debt it has fixed payments and doesn't share in firm's upside.

Valuing Preferred Stock

Value of preferred is the present value of the dividend stream, a fixed perpetuity usually.

$$\text{Value of Preferred Stock} = \frac{\text{Annual Preferred Stock Dividend}}{\text{Market's Required Yield on Preferred Stock}} \tag{10–6}$$

Figure 10.5

Quick Reference Guide for the Preferred Stock Valuation Model

The value of a share of preferred stock, like any security, is defined by the present value of the cash flows it is expected to produce to the owner of the stock. Since the preferred shares typically pay a fixed dividend, this cash flow stream is a level perpetuity, which, as we saw in equation (6-5), makes discounting the future dividends simple. We divide the dividend by the required rate of return on the preferred stock:

$$\text{Value of Preferred Stock } (V_{ps}) = \frac{\text{Annual Preferred Stock Dividend}}{\text{Market's Required Yield on Preferred Stock}} = \frac{D_{ps}}{r_{ps}} \tag{10–6}$$

Important Definitions and Concepts:

- V_{ps} = the value of a share of preferred stock.
- D_{ps} = the annual preferred stock dividend. This dividend is the contractually *promised* dividend. Remember that preferred dividends are only paid if the firm has the cash to pay them, and they must be

paid *before* common stockholders get any dividends. The critical point here is that the preferred stock dividend may be skipped in some years if the company is unable to pay it such that the annual dividend is a *promised* dividend (not the expected dividend). The amount of the dividend is computed as the product of the promised dividend rate and the par or face value of the preferred stock and is prescribed in the security contract.

- r_{ps} = the *market yield* or rate of return on the preferred stock's contractually promised dividend. This market yield is analogous to the yield to maturity on a bond discussed in Chapter 9. Note that since this market yield is based on the promised dividend we also can think of it as a *promised rate of return* to the preferred stock investor that will be realized only if preferred stock dividends are always paid in a timely manner.

- $\frac{D_{ps}}{r_{ps}}$ = the present value of a level perpetuity, which equals the promised dividend on preferred stock discounted using the market yield or promised rate of return to the preferred stockholders (recall that we defined this useful present value equation in Chapter 6).

Dealing with Reality: Promised versus Expected Return for Preferred Stock

Just as in the case of bonds the expected return (after considering all the risks) could be lower than the promised return which is the mathematical, dividend / price. When valuing, we use the market yield for similar stocks. Preferred valuation is a promised payment stream discounted by a promised rate of return.

Estimating the Market Yield. The market yield is found either buy dividing the dividend by the price of a similar preferred issued by the firm or its peers.

Example for a preferred with a \$1.52 dividend and a price of \$25.46 equals *r* of 5.97 percent.

$$V_{ps} = \frac{D_{ps}}{r_{ps}}$$

$$r_{ps} = \frac{D_{ps}}{V_{ps}} = \frac{\$1.52}{\$25.46} = .0597 \text{ or } 5.97\%$$

In summary, the value of a preferred stock is the present value of all future dividends. Because most preferred stocks are perpetuities and non-maturing with the dividends continuing to infinity, we simply use our formula for the present value of a perpetuity.

A Quick Review: Valuing Bonds, Preferred Stock, and Common Stock

We use the same discounted cash flow procedure to value both preferred and common stock. However, there is a subtle difference between how bonds and preferred stock are valued and how common stock is valued. Bonds and preferred stock are valued using *promised yields* and *promised cash flows*. However, common stock valuation estimates the expected dividends for each future period and discounts these *expected dividends* using an *expected rate of return*. Table 10.2 summarizes the application of discounted cash flow in valuing all three types of securities.

Table 10.2 **Summary of Discounted Cash Flow Valuation of Bonds, Preferred Stock, and Common Stock**

Bonds and preferred stock state a promised cash payment to the security holder. In the case of a bond, interest and principal must be paid in accordance with the terms of the bond contract (indenture). Preferred shares have stated dividend yields, which when multiplied by the face or par value of the preferred stock, equal the promised preferred dividend. Both bonds and preferred stock are valued by discounting these promised cash flows back to the present. However, since these are promised (and not expected) cash flows, we discount the cash flows using promised yields as reflected in current market prices of similar securities. Common stock, on the other hand, does not have a contractual promised dividend payment, so we apply the discounted cash flow model in this instance by estimating expected future dividends and then discounting them back to the present using the expected rate of return that an investor would require if investing in a stock with the risk attributes of the shares being valued.

Type of Security	Cash Flow	Discount Rate	Valuation Model
Bond	**Promised interest and principal payments**. These payments are set forth in the contract between the bond issuing company and the owner of the bond.	**Market or promised yield to maturity (YTM)**. Typically the YTM on a similar bond is used to value a bond. This YTM is the realized rate of return to the bondholder *only* if all promised payments are made on time. Consequently, the yield to maturity calculated for a bond is a promised yield not the expected yield.	$\text{Bond Value} = \text{Interest}\left[\frac{1 - \frac{1}{(1 + YTM\ \text{market})^n}}{YTM\ \text{market}}\right] + \text{Principal}\left[\frac{1}{(1 + YTM)^n}\right]$
Preferred Stock	**Promised dividends.** Dividends are defined using a contractually set dividend yield that is multiplied by the par or face value of the preferred stock to get the preferred stock dividend.	**Market or promised yield on preferred stock**. We typically calculate this yield using market prices and promised dividends for similar shares of preferred. This yield is a promised yield that will only be earned if the preferred stock dividends are fully paid every period as promised.	$\text{Value of Preferred Stock } (V_{ps}) = \frac{\text{Annual Preferred Stock Dividend}}{\text{Market's Required Yield on Preferred Stock}} = \frac{D_{ps}}{r_{ps}}$
Common Stock	**Expected future dividends.** No dividend is prescribed for common stock. Instead dividends must be estimated so we value common stock using expected rather than promised future cash flows. In the constant dividend growth rate model dividends are estimated using a constant rate of growth from year to year.	**Investor's expected rate of return which is the investor's required rate of return**. Since common stock dividends are risky we used expected future dividends and discount them using a risk-adjusted or expected rate of return for investing in shares of stock of firms with similar risk to the common stock being valued. We can estimate this expected rate of return using the CAPM.	$\text{Value of Common Stock } (V_{cs}) = \frac{D_0(1 + g)}{r_{cs} - g}$

10.4 The Stock Market

The stock market is the secondary market where shares are traded and where Initial Public Offerings of new stock (IPOs) are traded after they come to the primary market (between issuer and investors). Organized exchanges trade at a location and over-the-counter markets trade through networks virtually.

Organized Exchanges

The New York Stock Exchange (NYSE), also called the "Big Board," is the oldest of all the organized exchanges and has more than 80 percent of the typical trading volume. It began in 1792 when 24 traders signed the Buttonwood Agreement, a pact named after the tree under which traders gathered, obligating them to "give preference" to each other in security trading. When winter came, the 24 traders moved to the back of Wall Street's Tontine Coffee House, leaving the other traders out in the cold.

While the NYSE is considered an organized exchange because of its physical location, the majority of its trades are done electronically without a face-to-face meeting of traders. To be listed on the NYSE, a firm must meet strict requirements dealing with profitability and market value, and be widely owned. If a listed company fails to meet the requirements, the exchange will delist it and it will no longer be traded on the NYSE.

Much of the trading on the NYSE is made up of block trades. A **block trade** is transaction involving 10,000 shares or more by one holder. In a similar vein, a **block holding** is a block of 10,000 shares or more held by a single individual or institution. In recent years, block trades have accounted for between a quarter and a third of the reported Big Board volume. This tells us that large, institutional investors play a major role in the workings of the NYSE.

The **American Stock Exchange (AMEX)** is the nation's second largest, floor-based exchange. Its listings generally include firms somewhat smaller than those listed on the NYSE. In addition to common stocks, the American Stock Exchange also has a significant presence in ETFs and options. The AMEX merged with Nasdaq in 1998, but it operates as a separate entity.

Over-the-Counter (OTC) Market

The **over-the-counter (OTC) market** is a network of dealers that has no listing or membership requirements (although there are listing requirements on Nasdaq). It draws its name from the fact that historically banks acted as the primary dealer and they sold smaller securities and bonds right "over the counter" from inventory they kept on hand. Today, the OTC market is electronic rather than personal. It also is the primary market for bond trading.

OTC listings usually are companies too new or too small to be eligible for listing on a major exchange. These companies also often have fewer shares available. As a result, small amounts of buying or selling may have a significant impact on the price of those OTC-listed stocks.

Nasdaq handles the OTC stocks that are traded more frequently. Nasdaq, known more formally as the National Association of Security Dealers Automated Quotations system, debuted in 1971 and was the world's first electronic stock market. It was set up to allow dealers to post bid and ask prices, as well as how many shares the dealers were willing to trade. While Nasdaq lists more companies than the NYSE, they tend to be smaller companies.

The Nasdaq stock market has two tiers of listed companies: Nasdaq National Markets, made up of around 4,000 companies like Dell (D), Microsoft (MSFT), eBay (EBAY), Intel (INTC), and Oracle (ORCL), and the Nasdaq SmallCap Market, which includes more than 1,000 smaller emerging growth companies. There are about 1,000 market participants, in general trading firms that are linked electronically, with trading information broadcast to over 350,000 terminals worldwide.

Answers to **Concept Checks**

Concept Check **10.1**

1. What are the attributes of common stock that distinguish it from bonds and preferred stock?
2. What does agency cost mean with respect to the owners of a firm's common stock?
3. Describe the three-step process for valuing common stock using the discounted dividend model.

Answer 1: Common stock is a residual owner of the firm with voting rights. Bonds and preferred stock have fixed payments and do not share in the firm's upside.

Answer 2: Common shareholders hire a board to represent them and to hire a good management team. However, managers with little stock may choose to invest or not to invest and run operations to their benefit and job security rather than maximize value for the shareholders.

Answer 3: The three step process:

Three-Step Procedure for Valuing Common Stock

To value common stock, we will use the same three-step procedure we used to value bonds.

Step 1: Estimate the amount and timing of the receipt of the future cash flows the common stock is *expected* to provide.

Step 2: Evaluate the riskiness of the common stock's future dividends, and determine the rate of return an investor might expect to receive from a comparable risk investment, which becomes the investor's required rate of return.

Step 3: Calculate the present value of the expected dividends by discounting them back to the present at the investor's required rate of return.

The value of a common stock is equal to the present value of all future dividends.

Concept Check **10.2**

1. If a corporation decides to retain its earnings and reinvest them in the firm, does the market value of the firm's shares always increase? Why or why not?
2. What is the price/earnings model of equity valuation?
3. How does a firm's dividend policy affect the firm's P/E ratio?

Answer 1: No, it depends on whether the earnings are reinvested in projects with a return that exceeds the required rate of return by investors in the firm.

Answer 2: P/E ratios rely on relative valuation methods to find the value of stock by multiplying the Price to Earnings multiple times an earnings number or earnings estimate to find the value of equity.

Answer 3: The dividend policy can impact the amount of earnings that is reinvested in the firm. Lower reinvestment can lead to lower firm growth from new projects and lower stock value.

Concept Check **10.3**

1. What are three common features of preferred stock?
2. What is the market's required yield on a preferred stock?
3. Explain the meaning of the following statement: The market yield is a promised rate of return rather than an expected rate of return.

Answer 1: Preferred stock has an infinite life but fixed dividends and a priority between debt and common stock.

Preferred dividends are **fixed**, shareholders do not share in firm's upside.

Preferred may have **multiple classes**, some may be convertible.

Preferred has a **priority claim on assets and income** over common in bankruptcy.

Cumulative preferred dividends require their dividends are paid before common.

Preferred is safer than common, riskier than debt, a **hybrid security**.

Answer 2: The market's required yield is the required rate of return on a similar preferred issued by the firm or its peers and it is the discount rate for preferred dividends to value preferred stock.

Answer 3: The market yield is the promised rate of return that discounts promised cash flows that the preferred stock will receive. The rate assumes all payments will be made and links the present price of the stock to its dividend.

Concept Check **10.4**

1. What are the largest organized exchanges on which shares of common stock are bought and sold?
2. What is the difference between an organized exchange and the over-the-counter market?

Answer 1: The NYSE has 80 percent of the trading volume and the AMEX has 3 percent.

Answer 2: An organized exchange has a physical location while the OTC market is virtual and linked by networks.

Multiple Choice **Quiz**

1. A proxy is best described as
   a. your vote on company mergers.
   b. the vote of a mutual fund on behalf of its clients.
   c. the vote by managers of the firm.
   d. the form that must be returned to the SEC during a merger.

2. The P/E ratio is
   a. an absolute valuation method.
   b. a method that incorporates growth in the denominator.
   c. a ratio that tells how much investors will pay for $1 of earnings.
   d. a ratio that represents the market yield of the firm's stock.

3. The OTC market trades
   a. virtually over a network.
   b. only options and Treasury Bonds.
   c. in a physical location.
   d. only 3 percent of the largest of stocks.

4. The NYSE trades
   a. virtually over a network.
   b. only options and Treasury Bonds.
   c. in a physical location.
   d. only 3 percent of the largest of stocks.

5. The Nasdaq trades
   a. virtually over a network.
   b. only options and Treasury Bonds.
   c. in a physical location.
   d. only 3 percent of the largest of stocks.

6. Majority voting can best be described as
   a. the vote needed to overrule management.
   b. the vote of over half of the shareholders to sell the firm.
   c. the collective vote on the entire slate of proposals at an annual meeting.
   d. the individual vote on each proposal at an annual meeting.

7. Cumulative voting can best be described as
   a. the vote needed to overrule management.
   b. the vote of over half of the shareholders to sell the firm.
   c. the collective vote on the entire slate of proposals at an annual meeting.
   d. the individual vote on each proposal at an annual meeting.

8. Cumulative preferred stock is
   a. stock that earns larger dividends every year.
   b. stock that has the largest claim on assets.
   c. stock that must be paid first before any bonds are paid.
   d. stock that receives all the dividends owed to it before common is paid.

9. A block trade is
   a. a trade of 10,000 shares or more.
   b. a mistake by a trader that disrupts another trader's orders.
   c. a trade of a large number of bonds.
   d. a trade on the Nasdaq.

10. The three inputs to a constant growth dividend model are
    a. dividends, promised returns, and growth.
    b. dividends, expected returns, and growth.
    c. dividends, expected returns, and retained earnings.
    d. dividends, expected returns, and promised cash flows.

Answers to **Multiple Choice Questions**

1. B
2. C
3. A
4. C
5. A
6. D
7. C
8. D
9. A
10. B

Self Test with **Solutions**

Picture the Problem

Decide on Solution Strategy

Solve

Analyze

Self Test 1: Common Stock Valuation

You are valuing Cisco Systems and find that analysts have prepared the following data:

Reported earnings $1.20 Next Year's dividend .50

Trailing P/E 20 Forward P/E 18 Beta 1.2

Estimated earnings and dividend growth Rate 10 percent

Return on the market 10 percent

Risk-free return 5 percent

a. What is the constant dividend growth rate valuation for Cisco Systems using CAPM to find the required rate of return?
b. What is the value of Cisco using a forward P/E multiple?
c. What is your estimate for sustainable growth if Cisco has ROE of 15 percent and a dividend payout ratio of 40 percent? How would this affect firm value?

Step 1: Picture the Problem

The problem asks for the value of a common stock using the constant dividend growth equation and a P/E multiple approach.

Step 2: Decide on a Solution Strategy

To solve, we will use the constant dividend growth equation and a P/E multiple approach. To solve the sustainable growth problem we will use the sustainable rate of growth of dividends equation.

Step 3: Solve

a. To solve for the value of common using the constant dividend growth equation,

Equation:

$$V_{cs} = \frac{D_0(1+g)}{r_{cs} - g} = \frac{\text{Dividend in year 1}}{\text{Stockholder's Required Rate of Return} - \text{Growth Rate}} \tag{10–2}$$

Inputs: Next year's dividend .50

Growth rate 10 percent

Required rate of return ?

For required rate of return, use CAPM to solve for the appropriate expected return,

Equation:

$$\text{Expected Rate of Return} = \text{Risk Free Rate of Interest} + \text{Common Stock Beta Coefficient}\left(\text{Expected Rate of Return on the Market Portfolio} - \text{Risk Free Rate of Interest}\right) \tag{8-6}$$

Inputs: Risk-free rate 5 percent

Return on the market 10 percent

Beta 1.2

Solve for expected return,

$$\text{Expected Rate of Return} = 5\% + 1.20(.10 - .05) = 5\% + 6\% = 11\%$$

Then solve for the value of common stock,

$$V_{cs} = \frac{D_0(1+g)}{r_{cs} - g} = \frac{.50}{.11 - .10} = \$50$$

b. For the P/E Multiple valuation, use

Equation:

$$\text{Value of Common Stock, } V_{cs} = \left(\text{Approximate Price Earnings Ratio}\right) \times \left(\text{Estimated Earnings Per share for year 1}\right) = \frac{P}{E_1} \times E_1 \tag{10–4}$$

Inputs: Forward P/E 18

This year's earnings \$1.20

Estimated earnings Year 1 ?

Growth rate 10 percent

To find next year's earnings, grow this year's earnings forward one year

$1.20 × 1.10 = $1.32 Next Year's Earnings

Solve the equation for a forward multiple,

$$\text{Value of Common Stock, } V_{cs} = (18)\times(1.32) = \frac{P}{E_1}\times E_1 = \$23.76$$

c. For the sustainable growth rate, use

Equation:

$$\text{Rate of Growth in Dividends } (g) = \left(1 - \frac{\text{Dividend}}{\text{Payout Ratio}}\right) \times \text{Rate of Return on Equity } (ROE) \qquad (10\text{–}3)$$

Inputs:

Dividend Payout 40 percent

ROE 20 percent

Solve the equation,

$$\text{Rate of Growth in Dividends } (g) = (1-.40)\times.15 = 9\%$$

Step 4: Analyze

The value of the stock:

Constant Dividend Growth $50

Forward P/E Ratio $23.76

The two approaches give widely differing values. The growth model is very sensitive to small changes in the denominator ($r - g$) and 'blows up' as the denominator approaches 0. The forward multiple requires the next year's earnings which were found by growing this year's earnings at the growth rate which was given by analysts. When we calculate sustainable growth using the equation from dividend payout and ROE, we find 15 percent as the sustainable growth rate.

In either case, value will decline using a 9 percent growth rate. For the dividend growth model, value would fall from $50 to $25. For the forward P/E model, growing earnings at 9 percent rather than 10 percent would lower the forward value about 1 percent, to $23.54. Note that the P/E model is not as volatile when growth changes. The dividend growth model is a better representation of the volatility due to changes in growth based on what we have observed in the financial markets.

Self Test 2: Preferred Stock Valuation

You are looking at a new issue by a utility with 2 classes of preferred stock. What is the value of the new issue if the other two classes of preferred are similar?

Preferred A shares	Dividend $1	Price $22
Preferred B shares	Dividend $1.40	Price $$33
New issue preferred	Dividend $2	

Step 1: Picture the Problem

The problem asks for the value of a preferred stock.

Step 2: Decide on a Solution Strategy

To solve, we will use the market yield to discount the promised dividend of the new issue.

Step 3: Solve

To solve for the expected portfolio return, use the preferred stock equation. You will need to solve for the market yield of the two preferred classes at the utility.

Equation:

$$\text{Value of Common Stock} = \frac{\text{Annual Preferred Stock Dividend}}{\text{Market Yield on Preferred Stock}} \qquad (10\text{–}6)$$

Inputs:

Annual dividend $2

Market yield = ?

To solve for the market yield, rearrange the formula.

$$V_{ps} = \frac{D_{ps}}{r_{ps}}$$

$$r_{ps} = \frac{D_{ps}}{V_{ps}} = \frac{\$1}{\$22} = .0454 \text{ for Class A}$$

$$r_{ps} = \frac{D_{ps}}{V_{ps}} = \frac{\$1.4}{\$33} = .0424 \text{ for Class B}$$

Average of A and B, r = .044

To solve for the value of preferred,

$$\text{Value of Preferred Stock} = \frac{\text{Annual Preferred Stock Dividend}}{\text{Market Yield on Preferred Stock}} = \frac{\$2}{.044} = \$45.45$$

Step 4: Analyze

By using similar preferred stocks, we can determine the market yield as an average of the two classes, 4.4 percent and using this discount rate, we find the $2 dividend is worth $45.45 in the market.

CHAPTER 11

Investment Decision Criteria

Chapter **Orientation**

This chapter introduces the most important analysis method for capital budgeting and corporate investing: the net present value rule. This rule is one of many investment decision criteria that help corporations make wise choices when choosing from a number of alternatives. Other criteria include the profitability index, internal rate of return (IRR), and payback analysis. These criteria are universal and are applied in any industry, from real estate to technology.

Chapter Review: **Terms and Concepts**

11.1 An Overview of Capital Budgeting

Capital budgeting is the long-term, decision-making process of a firm with the goal of improving shareholder wealth. We know that common stock represents the ownership interest, a residual claim after debt is paid. Common shareholders elect a board of directors to represent their interests. The board hires and fires the management team. It is the management team's responsibility to allocate capital to the best alternatives of the firm.

Three important capital budgeting lessons from the Disney theme park story:

Lesson #1: Capital budgeting decisions are critical in defining a company's business.

Lesson #2: Very large investments are frequently the result of many smaller investment decisions that define a business strategy.

Lesson #3: Successful investment choices lead to the development of managerial expertise and capabilities that influence the firm's choice of future investments.

The Typical Capital Budgeting Process

The typical capital budgeting process at any firm has two basic phases:

Phase I: *The firm's management identifies promising investment opportunities.* These opportunities generally arise from ideas generated by the management and employees of the firm.

Phase II: Once an investment opportunity has been identified, its value-creating potential, what some refer to as its "value proposition," is thoroughly evaluated.

The logic of the two-phase process is very simple: identify promising investment opportunities and select those that offer an opportunity to create value for the firm's common stockholders.

What are the Sources of Good Investment Projects?

Good investment projects are those that give a competitive advantage to the firm in terms of unique products and lower costs. Projects must compete with internal firm offerings as well as the competitor's projects for scarce capital. The better opportunities come in the markets and areas with less competition that are difficult to enter.

Types of Capital Investment Projects (Three Types)

- Revenue enhancement investments
- Cost-reduction investments
- Mandatory investments that are a result of government requirements.

Revenue Enhancing Investments (Four Categories)

- Add a line of business to an existing one.
- Start a new line of business.
- Improve existing products.
- Create new products.

Cost-Reduction Investments

The majority of a firm's capital expenditure proposals are aimed at reducing the cost of doing business. Other types of cost-reducing investments arise when equipment either wears out or becomes obsolete due to the development of improved equipment.

Mandated Investments

Companies frequently find that they must make capital investments to meet safety and environmental regulations. These investments are not revenue producing or cost reducing but are required for the company to continue doing business. Not all investments have sufficient potential for value creation to be undertaken, and we need some analytical tools or criteria to help us ferret out the most promising investments.

The most commonly used criteria for determining the desirability of alternative investment proposals include: net present value (NPV), a closely related metric called the equivalent annual cost (EAC), the profitability index (PI), the internal rate of return (IRR), the modified internal rate of return (MIRR), the payback period, and the discounted payback period.

11.2 Net Present Value

The **net present value (NPV)** is the difference between the present value of the cash inflows and the cash outflows. As such, the NPV estimates the amount of wealth that the project creates. The NPV criterion simply states that investment projects should be accepted if the NPV of the project is positive and should be rejected if the NPV of the project is negative. Technically, zero NPV meets the required rate of return and should be accepted although the real world may opt for a cushion.

Why Is NPV the Right Criterion?

NPV of an investment is an estimate of the impact of the investment opportunity on the value of the firm. NPV is the holy grail of criteria for evaluating new investment opportunities. Other decision criteria may be relevant when choosing from a number of projects, but NPV is the predominant decision rule.

Calculating an Investment's NPV

The NPV of an investment is:

$$\text{Net Present Value or } NPV = \text{Cash Flow for Year 0 } (CF_0) + \frac{\text{Cash Flow for Year 1 } (CF_1)}{\left(1 + \text{Discount Rate } (k)\right)^1} + \frac{\text{Cash Flow for Year 2 } (CF_2)}{\left(1 + \text{Discount Rate } (k)\right)^2} + \cdots + \frac{\text{Cash Flow for Year } n \ (CF_n)}{\left(1 + \text{Discount Rate } (k)\right)^n} \quad (11\text{–}1)$$

Cost of making the investment = Initial cash flow, this is typically a cash outflow taking on a negative value.

Present value of the investment's cash inflows = Present value of the project's future cash inflows.

According to our three principles, NPV reflects cash flows as the source of value, discounting the time value of money, and the risk-return tradeoff.

NPV Decision Criteria: If the NPV is greater than zero, the project will add value and should be accepted, but if the NPV is negative, the project should be rejected. If the project's NPV is exactly zero, the project will neither create nor destroy value.

Independent versus Mutually Exclusive Investment Projects

An **independent investment project** is one that stands alone and can be undertaken without influencing the acceptance or rejection of any other project. A **mutually exclusive project** prevents another project from being accepted.

Evaluating an Independent Investment Opportunity

Project Long evaluated in Checkpoint 11.1 demonstrates the use of NPV to analyze an independent investment opportunity.

A Quick Reference Guide to Net Present Value

Net present value measures the value added to wealth from an investment project.

$$NPV = CF_0 + \frac{CF_1}{(1+k)^1} + \frac{CF_2}{(1+k)^2} + \cdots + \frac{CF_n}{(1+k)^n} \quad (11\text{–}1)$$

Important definitions and concepts:

- *NPV* is equal to the difference in the present value of the investment's future cash flows and the cost of making the investment (the initial cash outlay, CF_0).
- CF_0, is the initial cash flow which is typically a cash outflow which is represented by a negative number.

- CF_1 through CF_n represent the *expected* cash flows for periods 1 through n. Note that the expected cash flows can be either positive (inflows) or negative (outflows).
- k is the discount rate used to calculate the present value of the project's expected future cash flows. Projects with riskier cash flows should have higher discount rates than for projects with less risky cash flows.
- n is the number of periods of cash flows for the project being evaluated.

Evaluating Mutually Exclusive Investment Opportunities When Revenues Remain the Same

There are times when firms cannot undertake all positive NPV projects. When this happens the firm must choose the best project or set of projects from the set of positive mutually exclusive NPV investment opportunities it has before it. Two such circumstances in which the firm is faced with choosing from among a set of mutually exclusive projects:

1. Substitutes—When a firm is analyzing two or more alternative investments that each perform the same function, the mutually exclusive alternatives are substitutes.
2. Firm Constraints—The second reason for mutually exclusive investment opportunities arises when the firm faces:
   - Limited managerial time.
   - Limited financial capital. Capital rationing means that firms will need to choose between alternative investments that all have positive NPVs with the funds that they have available.

Choosing between Mutually Exclusive Investments

When comparing mutually exclusive investments that have the same useful life, we simply calculate the NPVs of the alternatives and choose the one with the higher NPV. For machines with different lives, consider the Equivalent Annual Cost (EAC) of the machine.

The EAC of the machine can be calculated as follows: First find the project's NPV, and next, convert this NPV into its annual equivalent by dividing by an annuity factor based on the useful life of the machine:

$$\text{Equivalent Annual Cost (EAC)} = \frac{\text{PV of Costs}}{\text{Annuity Present Value Interest Factor}} = \frac{CF_0 + \dfrac{CF_1}{(1+k)^1} + \dfrac{CF_2}{(1+k)^2} + \cdots + \dfrac{CF_n}{(1+k)^n}}{\left(\dfrac{1}{k} - \dfrac{1}{k(1+k)^n}\right)} = \frac{NPV}{\left(\dfrac{1}{k} - \dfrac{1}{k(1+k)^n}\right)} \tag{11–2}$$

Step 1: Calculate the net present value discounting the annual operating costs for the machine over one life cycle of the project and adding this sum to the initial cost of the machine. We discount the annual costs of operating the machine using the discount rate we used earlier to calculate NPV.

Step 2: Divide the NPV of the machine (calculated in Step 1) by the present value of an annuity discount factor defined above.

11.3 Other Investment Criteria

Criteria that we explore in this section include the profitability index, internal rate of return, modified internal rate of return, and payback period.

Profitability Index

The **profitability index (PI)** is a cost-benefit ratio equal to the present value of an investment's future cash flows divided by its initial cost:

$$\text{Profitability Index } (PI) = \left(\text{Present Value of Future Cash Flows}\right) \div \left(\text{Initial Cash Outlay}\right)$$

or

$$\text{Profitability Index } (PI) = \frac{\dfrac{\text{Cash Flow for Year 1 } (CF_1)}{\left(1+\text{Discount Rate } (k)\right)^1} + \dfrac{\text{Cash Flow for Year 2 } (CF_2)}{\left(1+\text{Discount Rate } (k)\right)^2} + \cdots + \dfrac{\text{Cash Flow for Year } n \ (CF_n)}{\left(1+\text{Discount Rate } (k)\right)^n}}{\text{Initial Cash Outlay } (CF_0)} \qquad (11\text{–}3)$$

A PI greater than 1 indicates that the present value of the investment's future cash flows exceeds the cost of making the investment and the investment should be accepted. So for the condo investment we introduced in the introduction, the PI is equal to 1.087 = \$100,000/\$92,000.

The PI is closely related to NPV since it uses the same inputs: the present value of the project's future cash flows and the initial cash outlay. The PI is a ratio, and NPV is the difference between these two quantities, i.e.,

$$\text{Profitability Index } (PI) = \text{Present Value of Future Cash Flows} \div \text{Initial Cash Outlay}$$

and

$$\text{Net Present Value} = \text{Present Value of Future Cash Flows} - \text{Initial Cash Outlay}$$

PI Decision Criteria: When the PI is greater than one, the NPV will be positive, so the project should be accepted. When PI is less than one, which indicates a bad investment, NPV will be negative and the project should be rejected.

Firms with easy access to capital prefer the NPV criterion, because it measures the amount of wealth created by the investment. However, if the firm's management is faced with a capital rationing situation, the PI offers a useful way to rank investment opportunities to determine which ones to accept. The PI is useful in this setting because it, unlike NPV, measures the amount of wealth created per dollar invested.

Internal Rate of Return

The **internal rate of return (IRR)** of an investment is analogous to the yield to maturity (YTM) on a bond. Specifically, the IRR is the discount rate that results in a zero NPV for the project. For example, if you invest $100 today in a project expected to return $120 in one year, the IRR for the investment is 20%.

$$\text{Net Present Value} = 0 = \text{Cash Flow for Year 0 } (CF_0) + \frac{\text{Cash flow for Year1 } (CF_1)}{\left(1+ \text{Internal Rate of Return } (IRR)\right)^1}$$

$$0 = -\$100 + \frac{\$120}{(1+IRR)}$$

For investments that offer more than one year of expected cash flows, the calculation is a bit more tedious. Mathematically, we solve for the internal rate of return for a multiple-period investment by solving for IRR, as shown in the following equation:

$$\text{Net Present Value} = \text{Cash Flow for Year 0 } (CF_0) + \frac{\text{Cash Flow for Year 1 } (CF_1)}{\left(1 + \text{Internal Rate of Return } (IRR)\right)^1} + \frac{\text{Cash Flow for Year 2 } (CF_2)}{\left(1 + \text{Internal Rate of Return } (IRR)\right)^2} + \cdots + \frac{\text{Cash Flow for Year } n \ (CF_n)}{\left(1 + \text{Internal Rate of Return } (IRR)\right)^n} = 0 \quad (11\text{–}4)$$

IRR Decision Criteria: Accept the project if the IRR is greater than the discount rate used to calculate the net present value of the project, and reject it otherwise.

Complications with IRR: Unconventional Cash Flows

For conventional cash flow patterns, an IRR greater than the discount rate used to value the project cash flows implies a positive NPV project; however, for unconventional cash flows the opposite is true. Note, however, that NPV gives the correct indication as to the value of the investment being considered. Therefore, the prudent thing to do is to use the NPV criteria.

Complications with IRR: Multiple Rates of Return

Although any project can have only one NPV, a single project can, under certain circumstances, have more than one IRR. We can trace the reasons for this to the calculations involved in determining the IRR as the discount rate that results in an NPV calculation of 0:

$$NPV = 0 = CF_0 + \frac{CF_1}{(1+IRR)^1} + \frac{CF_2}{(1+IRR)^2} + \frac{CF_3}{(1+IRR)^3} + \cdots + \frac{CF_n}{(1+IRR)^n} \quad (11\text{–}4)$$

When the first cash flow is negative (the initial investment) and the subsequent cash flows are positive, there is a unique IRR. However, there can be *N* values for IRR that solve Equation (11–4) when *N* of the later cash flows have a sign change.

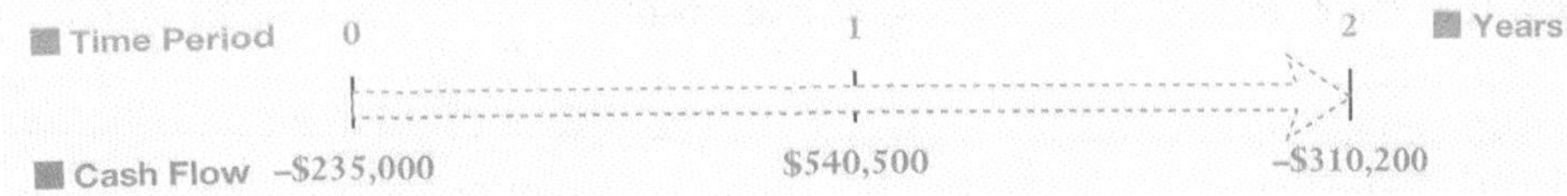

Where there are multiple IRRs, we should use NPV to solve this problem.

Using the IRR with Mutually Exclusive Investments

IRRs often are used by managers to select between mutually exclusive investments. A complication often arises because there can be ranking conflicts between the NPV and the IRR of the evaluated projects. Both mutually exclusive projects may have positive NPVs and IRRs greater than their required rates of return, one project may have a higher NPV while the other has a higher IRR. If the firm has access to external capital markets, the project with the higher NPV should be chosen.

Modified Internal Rate of Return

In order to eliminate the problem of multiple IRRs the **modified internal rate of return (MIRR)** was developed. The idea behind the MIRR is to rearrange the project cash flows such that there is only one change in the sign of the cash flows over the life of the project. This can be accomplished by discounting all the negative cash flows after the initial cash outflow back to year 0 using the process described below:

Step 1: Modify the project cash flow stream by discounting the negative future cash flows back to the present using the same discount rate that is used to calculate the project's NPV. The present value of these future negative cash flows is then added to the initial outlay to form a modified project cash flow stream.

Step 2: *Calculate the MIRR as the IRR of the modified cash flow stream*. We add the "Modified" to IRR since the MIRR is based on a *modified* set of cash flows.

To calculate the MIRR we must alter the amount and timing of the project cash flows and consequently the MIRR is not the same as the IRR.

Figure 11.1

Ranking Mutually Exclusive Investments—NPV vs. IRR

Apex Engineering is considering the purchase of an automated accounting system and is trying to decide between the AA+ and BBR systems. Both systems have the same cost, but because of functionality differences, the patterns of cash flows are quite different. Apex uses a 15 percent discount rate to evaluate its investments.

(Panel A) Expected Cash Flows

	Cash Flows	
Year	**AA+**	**BBR**
0	$(500,000)	$(500,000)
1	100,000	400,000
2	200,000	300,000
3	300,000	200,000
4	400,000	200,000
5	500,000	100,000
NPV	$412,730	$370,241
IRR	38%	52%

- Both alternatives have positive NPVs and IRRs that exceed Apex's 15% required rate of return.
- However, the projects are ranked differently using NPV or IRR: AA+ has the higher NPV while BBR has a higher IRR.
- The ranking difference is due to the effect of discounting and the difference in the patterns of the cash flows for the two projects.
- AA+ cash flows increase over time while BBR's decrease.
- Higher discount rates have a disproportionate effect on present values as we see in Panel B.

(Panel B) NPV Profiles

	NPV Profiles	
Discount Rate	**AA+**	**BBR**
0%	$1,000,000	$700,000
5%	$ 756,639	$568,722
10%	$ 565,259	$460,528
15%	$ 412,730	$370,241
20%	$ 289,673	$294,046
25%	$ 189,280	$229,088
30%	$ 106,532	$173,199
35%	$ 37,680	$124,709
40%	$ (20,111)	$ 82,317
45%	$ (69,011)	$ 44,998
50%	$ (110,700)	$ 11,934
55%	$ (146,489)	$ (17,531)
60%	$ (177,414)	$ (43,930)
65%	$ (204,298)	$ (67,701)

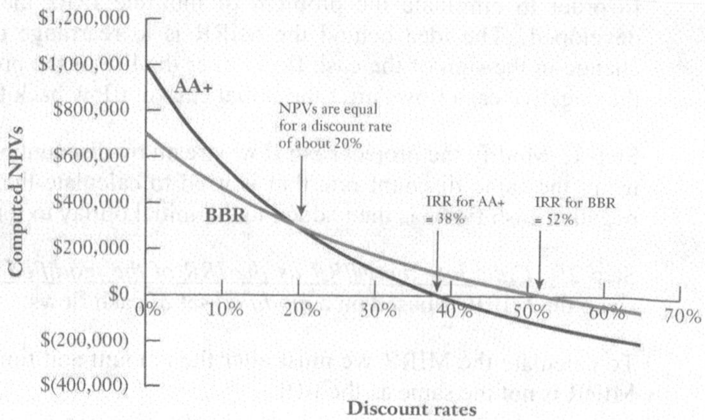

(Panel C) Estimating the Breakeven Discount Rate

	Cash Flows		Differential Cash Flows
Year	**AA+**	**BBR**	**BBR − AA+**
0	$(500,000)	$(500,000)	$ 0
1	100,000	400,000	$ 300,000
2	200,000	300,000	$ 100,000
3	300,000	200,000	$(100,000)
4	400,000	200,000	$(200,000)
5	500,000	100,000	$(400,000)

IRR of the Differential Cash Flows = 19.5%

- Using a 19.5% discount rate the two projects have exactly the same NPV.
- For discount rates lower than this break-even 19.5% rate, AA+ has the higher NPV whereas for higher discount rates BBR has the higher NPV.
- Trust NPV. Given the discount rate appropriate for valuing project cash flows, NPV gives the correct ranking of projects!

Investment in Education is a Positive NPV (Usually!)

Average Earnings by Education Level: 2012

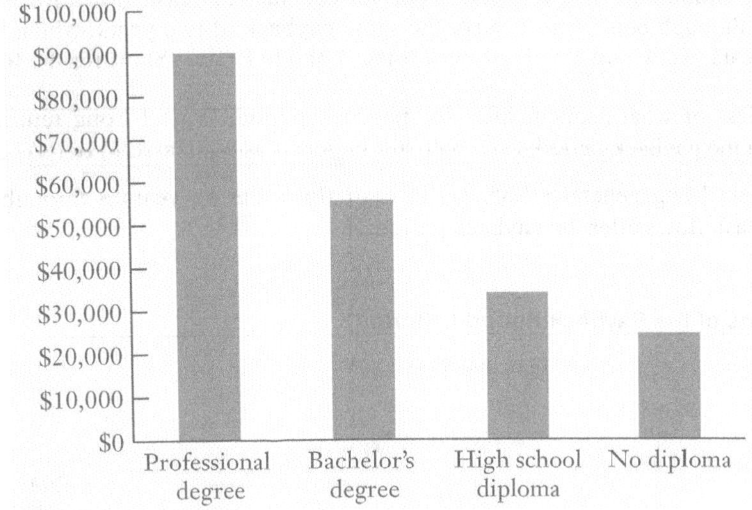

Source: U.S. Department of Labor, Bureau of Labor Statistics, Employment Projection (2012).

The salaries reported in the diagram are for all degrees and across the complete spectrum of years of experience (new hires to those close to retirement).

We can figure out that education pays. The average differential of $21,530 between the holder of a bachelor's degree and a high school diploma spread over a 45-year working life and discounted using a 5 percent discount rate produces a present value of $382,676. Looking at this as an NPV problem, if the cost of four years of college is $64,420 ($15,605 per year for four years beginning immediately and discounted at 5 percent), the NPV would be almost $260,000! Comparing this differential value of the extra income earned by having a bachelor's degree to the average cost of getting the education makes this decision look like a no-brainer!

*This is the average cost of attending a public four-year college. The average cost of attending a private university was $31,395 in 2010. Source: http://nces.ed.gov/fastfacts/display.asp?id=76 accessed 8th March 2013.

Payback Period

The **payback period** for an investment opportunity is the number of years needed to recover the initial cash outlay required to make the investment. For example, suppose Exec Corp. was deciding whether to spend $8 million for a new software system to monitor the daily production from its thousands of operating oil and gas wells. If the new automated system were to reduce the costs of monitoring production by $4 million a year, the payback period for the investment would be only two years.

Payback Decision Criteria: Accept the project if the payback period is less than a pre-specified maximum number of years.

Using the payback period as the sole criterion for evaluating whether to undertake an investment has three fundamental limitations.

Limitation #1: The payback period calculation ignores the time value of money, treating cash flows three years from now the same as cash flows in one year.

Limitation #2: The payback period ignores cash flows that are generated by the project beyond the end of the payback period.

Limitation #3: There is no clear-cut way to define the cutoff criterion for the payback period that is tied to the value creation potential of the investment.

To illustrate these limitations of the payback period, consider the cash flows for Project Long and Project Short. Note that although both projects have the same payback of two years, which is shorter than the cutoff criteria of three years, we would clearly prefer Project Long to Project Short for the following reasons.

- First, regardless of what happens after the payback period, Project Long returns the initial investment earlier within the payback period, (i.e., $70,000 in year 1 as compared to only $50,000 for Project Short).
- Second, Project Long generates $65,000 in cash flows during years 3 through 5, while Project Short provides no cash flows after the payback period.

Table 11.1 Limitations of the Payback Period Criterion

Limitations of the Payback Period as an investment criteria include:

a) Does not account for the time value of money.
b) Does not consider cash flows beyond the payback period.
c) Utilizes an arbitrary cutoff criterion.

	Project Long Cash Flows		Project Short Cash Flows	
	Annual	**Cumulative**	**Annual**	**Cumulative**
Initial cash outlay	($100,000)	($100,000)	($100,000)	($100,000)
Year 1	70,000	($30,000)	50,000	(50,000)
Year 2	**30,000**	**0**	**50,000**	**0**
Year 3	30,000	30,000	0	0
Year 4	25,000	55,000	0	0
Year 5	10,000	65,000	0	0

Payback equals two years for both projects since it takes two years to recover the cost of the initial outlay out of the cash inflows. However, Project Long looks a lot better!

Discounted Payback Period

To deal with the criticism that the payback period ignores the time value of money, some firms use the **discounted payback period** approach. The discounted payback period approach is similar to the traditional payback period except that it uses discounted cash flows.

Discounted Payback Decision Criteria: Accept the project if its discounted payback period is less that the pre-specified number of years.

The discounted payback is an improvement over the straight payback method.

Table 11.2 Discounted Payback Period Example (Discount Rate = 17 percent)

The standard Payback Period does not account for the time value of money, so the Discounted Payback Period discounts investment cash flows back to the present before cumulating them to calculate payback.

Project Long

	Annual Cash Flows	Cumulative Cash Flows	Discounted Cash Flows	Cumulative Discounted Cash Flows
Initial cash outlay	($100,000)	($100,000)	$(100,000)	($100,000)
Year 1	70,000	(30,000)	59,829	($40,171)
Year 2	**30,000**	**0**	**21,915**	**(18,256)**
Year 3	30,000	30,000	18,731	476
Year 4	25,000	55,000	13,341	13,817
Year 5	10,000	65,000	4,561	18,378

Discounted Payback equals 2.97 years for Project Long! Three years of discounted cash flows sum to a positive $476 and since we need to sum to 0 we do not need a full 3 years of discounted cash flows (we need $18,256/$18,731 = .97 of year three's cash inflow).

Project Short

	Annual Cash Flows	Cumulative Cash Flows	Discounted Cash Flows	Cumulative Discounted Cash Flows
Initial cash outlay	**($100,000)**	**($100,000)**	**$ (100,000)**	**($100,000)**
Year 1	50,000	(50,000)	42,735	(57,265)
Year 2	**50,000**	**0**	**36,526**	**(20,739)**
Year 3	-	-	-	(20,739)
Year 4	-	-	-	(20,739)
Year 5	-	-	-	(20,739)

Discounted Payback is never achieved for Project Short! The discounted cash flows never cumulate to equal zero.

Although the deficiencies of the payback criterion does limit the usefulness of the payback period and discounted payback period as tools for investment evaluation, these methods have several positive features.

- First, both payback and discounted payback are more intuitive and easier to understand than other decision criteria such as NPV.
- Second, the payback period often is used as a crude indicator of project risk since payback favors projects that produce significant cash flows in the early years of a project's life, which, in general, are less risky than more distant cash flows.
- Third, the discounted payback is used as a analytical tool in instances where obsolescence is a risk, to provide insight as to whether we get our money back in today's dollars before the market disappears or the product is obsolete.
- Fourth, managers often find payback useful when capital is being rationed and want to know how long the company's capital will be tied up in the project.

Summing Up the Alternative Decision Rules

We have reviewed seven different decision rules that are used by businesses to evaluate new investment alternatives. NPV reflects the expected impact of an investment alternative on shareholder value and for this reason; this technique is the preferred standard for making investment decisions. Table 11-3 summarizes each of the methods:

Table 11.3 Basic Capital Budgeting Techniques

There are the primary capital budgeting techniques or criteria that are used in industry practice. Of these techniques net present value or NPV offers the best single indicator of the investment alternative's potential contribution to the value of the firm.

Investment Criteria	Definition	Decision Rule	Advantages	Disadvantages
Net Present Value (NPV)	Present value of expected cash inflows minus the present value of cash outflows.	Accept investments that have a positive NPV.	Theoretically correct in that it measures the increase in value that the project is expected to produce. Measures the increase in shareholder wealth expected from the project being analyzed.	Somewhat complicated to compute (requires an understanding of the time value of money). Not familiar to managers without formal business education.
Equivalent Annual Cost (EAC) or Equivalent Annual Annuity (EAA)	The annual cost that is equivalent in present value to the initial cost and annual cash flows of an investment.	Select the investment alternative that has the lowest annual cost.	Provides a tool that can be used to account for differences in initial cost of purchase, different annual costs of operations, and different productive lives.	Should only be used where the investments being compared are expected to be used indefinitely. For single-use investments, NPV is appropriate.
Profitability Index (PI)	Present value of expected future cash flows divided by the initial cash investment.	When the PI is greater than 1, the NPV will be positive, so the project should be accepted. When PI is less than 1, which indicates a bad investment, the project should be rejected.	Theoretically correct in that it measures the increase in value that the project is expected to produce. Useful when rank ordering positive-NPV projects where capital is being rationed.	Not as familiar to managers as NPV and does not add any additional information.
Internal Rate of Return (IRR)	The discount rate that makes NPV equal to zero.	Accept the project if the IRR is greater than the discount rate used to calculate the net present value of the project, and reject it otherwise.	Provides a rate of return metric, which many managers prefer.	Cannot always be estimated. Sometimes provides multiple rates of return for projects with multiple changes in the sign of their cash flows over time. Can provide conflicting indications to NPV were mutually exclusive projects are compared.
Modified Internal Rate of Return (MIRR)	The discount rate that makes the NPV of the modified cash flow stream equal to zero.	Accept the project if the MIRR is greater than the discount rate used to calculate the net present value of the project.	Always produces a single rate of return estimate.	The rate of return produced by the MIRR is not unique to the project since it is influenced by the discount rate used to discount the negative cash flows.
Payback	Time until the initial cash outlay has been recovered.	If the project payback is less than the maximum the firm will accept, the project is acceptable.	Easy to understand and calculate. An indication of risk (how long it takes to recover the investment.)	Does not consider the time value of money. Ignores cash flows beyond the payback period. No rational way to determine the cutoff value for payback.
Discounted Payback	Years required to recover the initial investment out of project *discounted* future cash flows.	If the project payback is less than the maximum the firm will accept, the project is acceptable	Same as payback. By discounting the cash flows, this measure takes into account the time value of money.	Same as the last two items above. Since cash inflows must be discounted it is more complicated to compute than payback.

11.4 A Glance at Actual Capital Budgeting Practices

During the past 50 years, the popularity of each of the capital-budgeting methods we have discussed here has shifted from simple to more complex methods. In the 1950s and 1960s, the payback method dominated capital budgeting; however, in recent years the IRR and the NPV techniques have gained in popularity and are used by virtually all major corporations.

The results of a survey of the chief financial officers (CFOs) of large US firms, shows the popularity of the payback, discounted payback, NPV, PI, and IRR methods for evaluating capital investment opportunities. IRR and NPV are by far the most widely used methods, although more than half the firms surveyed used the payback method. The survey reported that larger firms tended to use NPV and IRR more frequently than their smaller counterparts which tended to rely more on payback.

Figure 11.2

Survey of the Popularity of Capital Budgeting Methods

These survey results are based on the survey responses of 392 chief financial officers of large US firms. The results below are the percentage of the CFOs who said they always or almost always used a particular method.

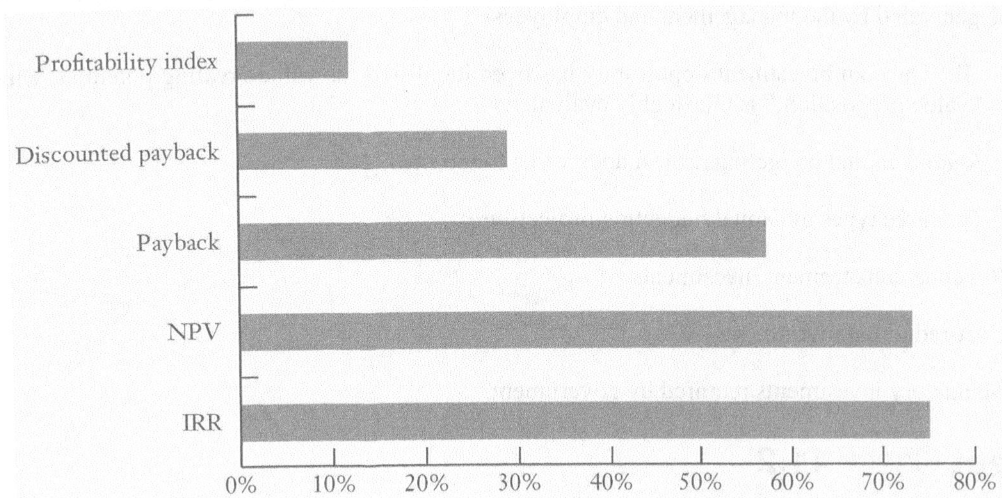

Source: John Graham and Campbell Harvey, "How do CFOs make capital budgeting and capital structure decisions?" Journal of Applied Corporate Finance, Volume 15, Number 1 (Spring 2002), 8 - 23.

Answers to **Concept Checks**

Concept Check **11.1**

1. What does the term *capital budgeting* mean?
2. Describe the two-phase process typically involved in carrying out a capital-budgeting analysis.
3. What makes a capital-budgeting project a good one?
4. What are the three basic types of capital investment projects?

Answer 1: Capital budgeting refers to the long-term investment evaluation process of a firm.

Answer 2: The two phases of capital budgeting are:

Phase I: *The firm's management identifies promising investment opportunities.* These opportunities arise from ideas generated by the management and employees.

Phase II: Once an investment opportunity has been identified, its value-creating potential, what some refer to as its "value proposition," is thoroughly evaluated.

Answer 3: A good capital budgeting project adds value to the firm.

Answer 4: The three types of capital budgeting projects are:

Revenue enhancement investments

Cost-reduction investments

Mandatory investments required by government.

Concept Check **11.2**

1. Describe what the NPV tells the analyst about a new investment opportunity.
2. What is the equivalent annual cost (EAC) measure, and when should it be used?
3. What is capital rationing?

Answer 1: NPV compares the present value of the cash outflows with the cash inflows and determines how much wealth is created.

Answer 2: The EAC is used to pick between two mutually exclusive projects with different useful lives, it is an annualized NPV in terms of present value.

Answer 3: Capital rationing occurs when a firm does not have all the money needed to fund all of the good projects it has available and must pick the best opportunities with the cash it has.

Concept Check **11.3**

1. Describe what the IRR metric tells the analyst about a new investment opportunity.
2. Describe the situations in which the NPV and IRR metrics can provide conflicting signals.
3. What is the modified internal rate of return metric, and why is it sometimes used?
4. What is the payback method, and what is the source of its appeal?
5. What is discounted payback, and how does it improve on the payback measure?

Answer 1: IRR gives the discount rate earned on the investment so that NPV = 0.

Answer 2: IRR gives contradictory signals compared to NPV when cash flows are irregular or when the signs on annual cash flows reverse. NPV and EAC are better for mutually exclusive choices.

Answer 3: MIRR is used when alternating signs cause the multiple IRR problem. It rearranges the negative cash flows in terms of either the present value or the future value of the project (by using the project's NPV discount rate) so that there is only one sign change before calculating the IRR.

Answer 4: Payback calculates the year that the original dollar is paid back by the project. It is simple and easy to understand. It is relevant for small business that has to reinvest its own capital to move on to the next project.

Answer 5: Discounted payback looks at the time value of money and repeats the payback calculation with present value dollars. It also is useful when considering obsolescence of a product.

Concept Check **11.4**

1. What is the most widely used measure of capital budgeting in business practice?
2. How does the payback method provide an indication of the risk of an investment proposal?

Answer 1: NPV and IRR are the most widely used capital budgeting measures with IRR edging out NPV slightly.

Answer 2: Payback is related to the risk of recovery as the most distant dollars in a project are the most risky in terms of interest rate, default risk, inflation risk, and other uncertainty.

Multiple Choice **Quiz**

1. Capital budgeting is
   a. the process of making a cash budget for the firm.
   b. the process of using limited cash to select among the investments available.
   c. the process of evaluating a firm's investment choices.
   d. the process of using decision rules for the firm's budget.

2. EAC is used when
   a. valuing a machine's cost.
   b. valuing the total shareholder wealth.
   c. valuing the discount rate that makes projects equal.
   d. valuing the project in terms of an annual NPV benefit.

3. Profitability Index is
   a. a ratio of profit to cost.
   b. a ratio of profit to assets.
   c. a ratio of net present value to investment cost.
   d. a ratio of IRR to NPV.

4. PI and EAC both use
   a. an annuity factor in the denominator.
   b. the shareholder wealth created in the numerator.
   c. annualized profits to determine the useful life of the investment.
   d. the value of the investment in the denominator.

5. Mutually exclusive investments with unequal useful lives are
   a. easily substituted by considering their NPV.
   b. investments the firm can take without choosing between them.
   c. investments the firm can take only if choosing both.
   d. investments the firm can take by choosing between them using EAC.

6. Discounted payback shows
   a. the wealth added by making an investment.
   b. the number of years in present value dollars to recover the investment.
   c. the discount rate that makes wealth added equal zero.
   d. the value of only mutually exclusive projects.

7. IRR shows
   a. the wealth added by making an investment.
   b. the number of years in present value dollars to recover the investment.
   c. the discount rate that makes wealth added equal zero.
   d. the value of only mutually exclusive projects.

8. MIRR is used when
   a. cash flows of a project change sign.
   b. projects have unequal costs.
   c. NPV is not zero.
   d. there is capital rationing.

9. NPV shows
   a. the wealth added by making an investment.
   b. the number of years in present value dollars to recover the investment.
   c. the discount rate that makes wealth added equal zero.
   d. the value of only mutually exclusive projects.

10. Capital rationing is
    a. the process of making a cash budget for the firm.
    b. the process of using limited cash to select among the investments available.
    c. the process of determining the present value of a firm's investment choices.
    d. the process of using decision rules for the firm's budget.

Answers to **Multiple Choice Questions**

1. C
2. D
3. C
4. B
5. D
6. B
7. C
8. A
9. A
10. B

Self Test with **Solutions**

Picture the Problem

Decide on Solution Strategy

Solve

Analyze

Self Test 1: Common Stock Valuation

You are valuing Cisco Systems and find that analysts have prepared the following data:

Reported earnings $1.20 Next Year's dividend 0.50

Trailing P/E 20 Forward P/E 18 Beta 1.2

Estimated earnings and dividend growth Rate 10%

Return on the market 10%

Risk-free return 5%

a. What is the constant dividend growth rate valuation for Cisco Systems using CAPM to find the required rate of return?

b. What is the value of Cisco using a forward P/E multiple?

c. What is your estimate for sustainable growth if Cisco has ROE of 15% and a dividend payout ratio of 40%? How would this affect firm value?

Step 1: Picture the Problem

The problem asks for the value of a common stock using the constant dividend growth equation and a P/E multiple approach.

Step 2: Decide on a Solution Strategy

To solve, we will use the constant dividend growth equation and a P/E multiple approach. To solve the sustainable growth problem we will use the sustainable rate of growth of dividends equation.

Step 3: Solve

a. To solve for the value of common using the constant dividend growth equation,

Equation:

$$V_{cs} = \frac{D_0(1+g)}{r_{cs}-g} = \frac{\text{Dividend in year 1}}{\text{Stockholders' Required Rate of Return} - \text{Growth Rate}} \qquad (10\text{–}2)$$

Inputs: Next year's dividend .50

Growth rate 10%

Required rate of return ?

For Required rate of return, use CAPM to solve for the appropriate expected return,

Equation:

$$\text{Expected Rate of Return} = \text{Risk Free Rate of Interest} + \text{Common Stock Beta Coefficient}\left(\text{Expected Rate of Return on the Market Portfolio} - \text{Risk Free Rate of Interest}\right) \qquad (8\text{–}6)$$

Inputs: Risk-free rate 5%

Return on the market 10%

Beta 1.2

Solve for expected return,

$$\text{Expected Rate of Return} = 5\% + 1.20(.10 - .05) = 5\% + 6\% = 11\%$$

Then solve for the value of common stock,

$$V_{cs} = \frac{D_0(1+g)}{r_{cs}-g} = \frac{0.50}{0.11-0.10} = \$50$$

b. For the P/E Multiple valuation, use

Equation:

$$\text{Value of Common Stock, } V_{cs} = \left(\text{Appropriate Price Earnings ratio}\right) \times \left(\text{Estimated Earnings per Share for year 1}\right) = \frac{P}{E_1} \times E_1 \qquad (10\text{–}4)$$

Inputs: Forward P/E 18

This year's earnings $1.20

Estimated earnings Year 1 ?

Growth rate 10%

To find next year's earnings, grow this year's earnings forward one year

$1.20 x 1.10 = $1.32 Next Year's Earnings

Solve the equation for a forward multiple,

$$\text{Value of Common Stock, } V_{cs} = (18)\times(1.32) = \frac{P}{E_1}\times E_1 = \$23.76$$

c. For the sustainable growth rate, use

Equation:

$$\text{Rate of Growth in Dividends } (g) = \left(1 - \text{Dividend Payout Ratio}\right) \times \text{Rate of Return on Equity } (ROE) \quad (10\text{–}3)$$

Inputs:

Dividend Payout 40%

ROE 20%

Solve the equation,

$$\text{Rate of Growth in Dividends } (g) = \left(1 - \text{Dividend Payout Ratio}\right) \times \text{Rate of Return on Equity } (ROE) \quad (10\text{–}3)$$

Step 4: Analyze

The value of the stock:

Constant Dividend Growth $50

Forward P/E Ratio $23.76

The two approaches give widely differing values. The growth model is very sensitive to small changes in the denominator ($r - g$) and "blows up" as the denominator approaches 0. The forward multiple requires the next year's earnings which were found by growing this year's earnings at the growth rate which was given by analysts. When we calculate sustainable growth using the equation from dividend payout and ROE, we find 15% as the sustainable growth rate.

In either case, value will decline using a 9% growth rate. For the dividend growth model, value would fall from $50 to $25. For the forward P/E model, growing earnings at 9% rather than 10% would lower the forward value about 1%, to $23.54. Note that the P/E model is not as volatile when growth changes. The dividend growth model is a better representation of the volatility due to changes in growth based on what we have observed in the financial markets.

Self Test 2: Preferred Stock Valuation

You are looking at a new issue by utility with two classes of preferred stock. What is the value of the new issue if the other two classes of preferred are similar?

Preferred A shares	Dividend \$1	Price \$22
Preferred B shares	Dividend \$1.40	Price \$\$33
New issue preferred	Dividend \$2	

Step 1: Picture the Problem

The problem asks for the value of a preferred stock.

Step 2: Decide on a Solution Strategy

To solve, we will use the market yield to discount the promised dividend of the new issue.

Step 3: Solve

To solve for the expected portfolio return, use the preferred stock equation. You will need to solve for the market yield of the two preferred classes at the utility.

Equation:

$$\text{Value of Preferred Stock} = \frac{\text{Annual Preferred Stock Dividend}}{\text{Market's Required Yield on Preferred Stock}} \qquad (10\text{–}6)$$

Inputs:

Annual dividend \$2

Market yield = ?

To solve for the market yield, rearrange the formula.

$$V_{ps} = \frac{D_{ps}}{r_{ps}}$$

$$r_{ps} = \frac{D_{ps}}{V_{ps}} = \frac{\$1}{\$22} = .0454 \text{ for Class A}$$

$$r_{ps} = \frac{D_{ps}}{V_{ps}} = \frac{\$1.4}{\$33} = .0424 \text{ for Class B}$$

Average of A and B, r = .044

To solve for the value of preferred,

$$\text{Value of Preferred Stock} = \frac{\text{Annual Preferred Stock Dividend}}{\text{Market's Required Yield on Preferred Stock}} = \frac{\$2}{.044} = \$45.45$$

Step 4: Analyze

By using similar preferred stocks, we can determine the market yield as an average of the two classes, 4.4% and using this discount rate, we find the $2 dividend is worth $45.45 in the market.

Self Test 3: Project Analysis and Decision Rules

You are valuing two projects with the following data:

Both projects cost $180,000 and provide the following cash flows over a period of 5 years:

Year	Project A	Project B
0	$ (180,000)	$ (180,000)
1	20,000	120,000
2	60,000	60,000
3	100,000	30,000
4	60,000	10,000
5	60,000	

a. Assuming that Robbins uses a 10% discount rate to evaluate its projects, calculate the following decision rules for each project:
NPV

IRR

Payback

Profitability Index

Discounted Payback

b. For a cash constrained firm which project(s) could it take if A and B are not mutually exclusive?
c. For a cash constrained firm which project could it take if A and B are mutually exclusive?

Step 1: Picture the Problem

The problem asks for the decision rules for two alternatives when the firm is cash constrained and when it is not constrained.

Step 2: Decide on a Solution Strategy

To solve, we will calculate the NPV, IRR, Payback, Profitability Index, and Discounted Payback for each project. This solution is easily done using a spreadsheet.

Step 3: Solve

To solve for the NPV of each project, using a discount rate of 10 percent

Equation:

$$NPV = CF_0 + \frac{CF_1}{(1+k)^1} + \frac{CF_2}{(1+k)^2} + \cdots + \frac{CF_n}{(1+k)^n}$$

Inputs:

$$\text{Project A } NPV = -180{,}000 + \frac{20000}{(1.1)^1} + \frac{60000_2}{(1.1)^2} + \frac{100000_3}{(1.1)^3} + \frac{60000_4}{(1.1)^4} + \frac{60000_5}{(1.1)^5} = \$41{,}136$$

$$\text{Project B } NPV = -180{,}000 + \frac{120000}{(1.1)^1} + \frac{60000_2}{(1.1)^2} + \frac{30000_3}{(1.1)^3} + \frac{10000_4}{(1.1)^4} = \$8{,}047$$

In a spreadsheet,

=*NPV*(rate, cells of the cash flows in Years 1 to 5) less the investment of 180,000

Project A =*NPV*(.1,B4:B8)+B3

Project B =*NPV*(.1,C4:C8)+C3

1	A	B	C
2	Year	Project A	Project B
3	0	($180,000)	($180,000)
4	1	20,000	120,000
5	2	60,000	60,000
6	3	100,000	30,000
7	4	60,000	10,000
8	5	60,000	

To solve for the IRR of each project, repeat the NPV calculation to find a discount rate for NPV = $0

Equation:

$$NPV = 0 = CF_0 + \frac{CF_1}{(1+k)^1} + \frac{CF_2}{(1+k)^2} + \ldots$$

In a spreadsheet,

=*IRR*(cells of the cash flows in Years 0 to 5, guess at rate so we'll use 10 percent)

Project A =*IRR*(B3:B8,.1) = 17.58%

Project B = *IRR*(C3:C8,.1) = 13.04%

To solve for the payback of each project, no formula is necessary, find the year that returns the cumulative dollar total equal to the investment of $180,000.

Equation:

Payback Year occurs when CF_0 = sum of *CFs* . . .

In a spreadsheet,

You could make a column summing each year with the previous years' cash flows so that they can be compared with the investment amount of $180,000.

Project A has the 180,000th dollar of cash flow in Year 3

Project B has the 180,000th dollar of cash flow in Year 2

To solve for the profitability index of each project, take the PV of project cash flows and divide by the investment.

Equation:

$$\text{Profitability Index} = \frac{PV \text{ of Cash flows after Investment}}{\text{Investment}}$$

In our spreadsheet,

Profitability Index = cell with *PV* amount of cash flows / cell with investment amount

(Note: Investment amount entered as a positive as it is a ratio of dollars in to dollars out)

Project A Profitability Index = *NPV*(.1,B4:B8)/180000 = 1.228 (could use –B3 for investment)

Project B Profitability Index = *NPV*(.1,C4:C7)/180000 = 1.045 (could use –C3 for investment)

To solve for the discounted payback of each project, find the year that returns the cumulative present value dollar total equal to the investment of $180,000.

Equation:

Payback Year occurs when CF_0 = sum of *CF* stated in PVs using the discount rate . . .

In our spreadsheet, find the PV of each year's cash flow by dividing by a present value factor of $1/(1+10\%)^{year}$ equals discounted cash flow for each year.

Project A Discounted Payback Year = 4

Project B Discounted Payback Year = 3

The spreadsheet with the running total of present value cash flows looks like this:

Present Value Each Year			Present Values Totalled	
Project A	Project B	Year	Project A	Project B
		0	($180,000)	($180,000)
18,182	109,091	1	18,182	109,091
49,587	49,587	2	67,769	158,678
75,131	22,539	3	142,900	181,217
40,981	6,830	4	183,881	188,047
37,255		5	221,136	

Step 4: Analyze

The results from our decision rules:

a.

	Project A	**Project B**
NPV	$41,136	$8,047
IRR	17.58%	13.04%
Payback	3 years	2 years
Profitability Index	1.23	1.04
Discounted Payback	4 years	3 years

If the firm is not capital constrained and the projects are not mutually exclusive, it would take both A & B as they have positive NPVs, IRRs greater than the discount rate of 12%, and profitability indexes greater than 1 which means the project's return more than the investment dollars in present value terms. The payback rules would not matter.

b. For a firm that has capital constraints, it will look at the best project in terms of return. The NPV decision rule suggests taking Project A and the Profitability Index agrees, as Project A offers more return per dollar invested. Some small businesses that are self-financing may be tempted to choose Project B based on the 2 year Payback but NPV and PI provide the better guidance. Since these are not mutually exclusive projects, the firm may take both as they have positive NPVs but may prefer in the real world to take Project A and look at other alternatives rather than invest in Project B.

c. For mutually exclusive projects, Project A is favored due to the Profitability Index being greater; it offers the better return per dollar invested and it has the larger NPV with the greater impact for owners' wealth.

Self Test 4: Equivalent Annual Costs

Your firm is considering two alternatives when replacing a computerized cutting machine. What is the EAC of each alternative using a discount rate of 10%? The cash flows including all costs and benefits are as follows:

Year	Project A	Project B
0	$ (180,000)	$ (180,000)
1	20,000	120,000
2	(60,000)	(60,000)
3	100,000	30,000
4	(60,000)	(10,000)
5	60,000	

Step 1: Picture the Problem

The problem asks for the EAC of each machine. To find EAC, find NPV and then the annualized cost of the machine.

Step 2: Decide on a Solution Strategy

To solve, we will calculate the NPV in terms of costs and benefits, then find the annualized cost by using the Present Value of an Annuity factor for the number of yearly cash flows in each project. This solution is easily done using a spreadsheet.

Step 3: Solve

To solve for the NPV of each project, using a discount rate of 10%

Equation:

$$NPV = CF_0 + \frac{CF_1}{(1+k)^1} + \frac{CF_2}{(1+k)^2} + \ldots$$

Inputs:

$$\begin{matrix}\text{Project A} \\ NPV\end{matrix} = -180,000 + \frac{20000}{(1.1)^1} + \frac{-60000_2}{(1.1)^2} + \frac{100000_3}{(1.1)^3} + \frac{-60000_4}{(1.1)^4} + \frac{60000_5}{(1.1)^5} = \$139,999$$

$$\begin{matrix}\text{Project B} \\ NPV\end{matrix} = -180,000 + \frac{120000}{(1.1)^1} + \frac{-60000_2}{(1.1)^2} + \frac{30000_3}{(1.1)^3} + \frac{10000_4}{(1.1)^4} = \$104,787$$

In a spreadsheet,

=*NPV*(rate, cells of the cash flows in Years 1 to 5) less the investment of 180,000

Project A =*NPV*(.1,B4:B8)+B3

Project B =*NPV*(.1,C4:C8)+C3

1	A	B	C
2	Year	Project A	Project B
3	0	($180,000)	($180,000)
4	1	20,000	120,000
5	2	-60,000	-60,000
6	3	100,000	30,000
7	4	-60,000	-10,000
8	5	60,000	
PV of Machines		$40,000.99	$75,213.44
	NPV	($139,999.01)	($104,786.56)
PV Annuity Factor		3.79	3.17
Annual Costs		$(36,931.39)	$ (33,057.10)

To solve for the EAC of each project, divide NPV calculation by the PV Annuity Factor for a five year annuity for Project A and a four year annuity for Project B (3.79 and 3.17).

Equation:

$$EAC = \frac{NPV}{PV \text{ Annuity Factor}}$$

In a spreadsheet, to find the PV Annuity Factor

=*PV*(rate,years, *PMT*, *FV*)

Project A =*PV*(.1,5,-1,0) = 3.79 (Note: *PMT* entered as -1 to make factor positive)

Project B = *PV*(.1,4,-1,0) = 3.17 (Note: *PMT* entered as -1 to make factor positive)

Step 4: Analyze

The results from our decision rule:

	Project A	**Project B**
EAC	– $36,931	– $33,057

Both machines are costly, but Project B has lower annualized costs and should be chosen. Project A, which had a much larger total negative NPV, was not as negative in comparison on an EAC basis. On an EAC basis, the two machines have similar costs. The firm might choose Project A if it had some other attributes that could overcome its $3,900 annual cost disadvantage, such as a cheaper upgrade to another function the firm isn't presently considering, but the firm should choose Project B given our decision rule.

CHAPTER 12

Analyzing Project Cash Flows

Chapter **Orientation**

This chapter discusses best practices in cash flow forecasting. Cash flow is the most significant factor in the valuation of business enterprises. Forecasting cash flows accurately will improve the valuation efforts of analysts, managers, and investors so that capital is allocated to the most successful opportunities. One issue for forecasters is to determine which cash flows in a forecast are relevant and which are not. By avoiding mistakes in the identification of relevant cash flows, forecasters will improve the accuracy of their valuation effort.

Managers, investors, and markets benefit from forecasting improvements and greater confidence in cash flow forecasts. Investors in an efficient market will be rewarded for better forecasts up to the point where the costs of improving a forecast exceed the gains from an improvement in the forecast. Managers are looking for reasonable estimates of value so that they can comfortably have confidence that their judgments and actions will be rewarded in the marketplace and in the financial markets.

Chapter Review: **Terms and Concepts**

12.1 Identifying Incremental Cash Flows

The important aspect of investing is to create incremental cash flows that results from a new project that adds to the value of the firm. Incremental cash flows consider both the positive and negative cash flows that result from a new investment

$$\begin{matrix}\text{Incremental Project} \\ \text{Cash Flows}\end{matrix} = \begin{pmatrix}\text{Firm Cash Flows} \\ \text{with the Project}\end{pmatrix} - \begin{pmatrix}\text{Firm Cash Flows} \\ \text{without the Project}\end{pmatrix} \quad (12\text{–}1)$$

To find the incremental cash flow for a project, we take the difference between the firm's cash flows if the new investment is, and is not, undertaken.

Guidelines for Forecasting Incremental Cash Flows

Sunk Costs Are <u>Not</u> Incremental Cash Flows

Sunk costs are costs that have already been incurred or are going to be incurred regardless of whether or not the investment is undertaken. The cost of the appraisal is a sunk cost since the money has already been spent and cannot be recovered whether you build the second convenience store or not.

Overhead Costs are Generally Not Incremental Cash Flows

Overhead expenses such as the cost of heat, light, and rent often occur regardless of whether we accept or reject a particular project. In these instances, overhead expenses are not a relevant consideration when evaluating project cash flows.

Look for Synergistic Effects

Oftentimes the acceptance of a new project will have an effect on the cash flows of the firm's other projects or investments. These effects can be either positive or negative, and if these synergistic effects can be anticipated, their costs and benefits are relevant.

- **Don't Overlook Positive Synergies**

  Harley-Davidson's introduction of lighter motorcycles targeted at younger riders and female riders was intended to expand its customer base into a new market made up of Generation X-ers and expand the market for existing products by introducing more people to motorcycling.

- **Beware of Cash Flows Diverted from Existing Products**

  An important type of negative synergistic effect comes in the form of revenue cannibalization.

Account for Opportunity Costs

In calculating the cash flows of an investment, it is important to account for what economists refer to as opportunity costs, the cost of passing up the next best choice when making a decision.

Work in Working Capital Requirements

Many times a new project involves an additional investment in working capital. Additional working capital arises out of the fact that cash inflows and outflows from the operations of an investment are often mismatched. As a result, the actual amount of new investment required by the project is determined by the difference in the sum of the increase in accounts receivables plus inventories less the increase in accounts payable. We will refer to this quantity as net operating working capital.

Ignore Interest Payments and Other Financing Costs

Although interest payments are incremental to the investments that are partly financed by borrowing, we do not include the interest payments in the computation of project cash flows. When we discount the incremental cash flows back to the present using the cost of capital, we are implicitly accounting for the cost of raising funds to finance the new project (including the after-tax interest expense). To include interest expense in the computation of the project's cash flows and in the discount rate would amount to counting interest twice.

12.2 Forecasting Project Cash Flows

To analyze an investment to determine whether it adds value to the firm, we use the project's free cash flow. In practice this cash flow information is compiled from pro forma financial statements. **Pro forma financial statements** are forecasts of future financial statements. We can calculate free cash flow using Equation (12–2) as follows:

$$\text{Free Cash Flow} = \overbrace{\underbrace{\text{Net Operating Income (Profit)} - \text{Taxes}}_{\text{Net Operating Profit after Taxes or NOPAT}} + \text{Depreciation Expense}}^{\text{Operating Cash Flow}} - \text{Increase in Capital Expenditures } (CAPEX) - \text{Increase in Net Operating Working Capital } (NOWC) \quad (12\text{–}2)$$

Dealing with Depreciation Expense, Taxes, and Cash Flow

Depreciation is a non–cash flow expense. As a result, the firm's net operating income understates cash flows by the amount of depreciation expense that is deducted for the period. Therefore, we'll want to compensate for this by adding depreciation back into net operating income when calculating cash flows.

Depreciation can be calculated using a version of the straight-line method. The modified accelerated cost recovery system (MACRS) is used for most tangible depreciable property. This method is typically used by firms to compute their tax liability but straight-line is used for financial reporting to the public.

Tools of Financial Analysis— Free Cash Flow

$$\text{Net Operating Income Profit} - \text{Taxes} + \text{Depreciation Expense} - \text{Capital Expenditures (CAPEX)} - \text{Change in Net Operating Working Capital (NOWC)} \quad \textit{Net Operating}$$

Net Operating Income is the profit after deducting the cost of goods sold and all operating expenses (including depreciation expense). Net operating income or net operating profit also is equal to earnings before interest and taxes (EBIT) for capital investment projects since projects do not have other (non-operating) sources of income or expense. For firms that have both operating and non-operating income and expenses, EBIT differs from net operating income by the amount of these non-operating sources of income and expense.

Net Operating Profit after Taxes (NOPAT) is equal to the firm's net operating profit times one minus the corporate tax rate. Note that we do not deduct interest expense before computing the corporate income taxes owed because the tax deductibility of interest is accounted for in the computation of the discount rate or the weighted average cost of capital which is discussed in detail in Chapter 14.

Depreciation Expense is allocation of the cost of fixed assets to the period when the assets are used.

Capital Expenditures (CAPEX) is the periodic expenditure of money for new capital equipment that generally occurs at the time the investment is undertaken (i.e. in year 0). However, many investments require periodic expenditures over the life of the investment to repair or replace worn out capital equipment. Finally, if the equipment has a salvage value then this becomes a cash inflow in the final year of the project's life.

Change in Net Operating Working Capital (NOWC) represents changes in the balance of accounts receivable plus inventories less accounts payable. Any changes in this quantity represent either the need to invest more cash or an opportunity to extract cash from the project.

Four-Step Procedure for Calculating Project Cash Flows

- Step 1: Estimating a Project's Operating Cash Flows
- Step 2: Calculating a Project's Working Capital Requirements
- Step 3: Calculating a Project's Capital Expenditure Requirements
- Step 4: Calculating a Project's Free Cash Flow

In the pages that follow we will discuss each of these steps in detail.

Step 1: Estimating a Project's Operating Cash Flows

Operating cash flow is simply the sum of the first three terms found in Equation 12-2. Specifically, operating cash flow for year *t* is defined in Equation 12-3:

$$\text{Operating Cash Flow}_t = \underbrace{\text{Net Operating Income (or Profit)}_t - \text{Taxes}_t}_{\text{NOPAT}_t} + \text{Depreciation Expense}_t \tag{12–3}$$

There are two observations regarding the computation of operating cash flow:

- First, our estimate of cash flows from operations begins with an estimate of net operating income. However, when calculating net operating income we subtract out depreciation expense since it is a tax deductible expense. Thus to estimate the cash flow the firm has earned from its operations we first calculate the firm's tax liability based on net operating income and then add back depreciation expense.
- Second, when we calculate the increase in taxes, we ignore interest expenses.

The format we use to calculate a project's operating cash flow looks a lot like a typical income statement. The left-hand column below depicts the calculation of operating cash flow whereas the right hand column depicts the calculation of net income using a traditional income statement:

Operating Cash Flow Calculation	Income Statement Calculation
Revenues	Revenues
Less: Cost of Goods Sold	Less: Cost of Goods Sold
Equals: Gross Profit	Equals: Gross Profit
Less: Operating Expenses	Less: Operating Expenses
Equals: Net Operating Income (Profit)	Equals: Net Operating Income (Profit)
Less: Taxes based on Net Operating Income	Less: Interest Expense
Equals: Net Operating Profit after Taxes (NOPAT)	Earnings before Taxes (EBT)
Plus: Depreciation Expense	Less: Taxes based on EBT
Operating Cash Flow	Net Income

Differences are here

To compute operating cash flow in the left-hand column above we begin with Revenues (just like the income statement). Next, we subtract Cost of Goods Sold and Operating Expenses to calculate Net Operating Income (Profit). To this point the calculation of operating cash flow looks just like the income statement in the right-hand column. From this point forward the calculation of operating cash flow deviates from the standard form of the income statement. Specifically, to calculate operating cash flow we estimate taxes based on the firm's net operating profit. Deducting taxes from net operating profit gives us an estimate of Net Operating Profit after Taxes, or NOPAT. Finally, since depreciation expense is a non-cash expense and so was subtracted before the tax calculation, we add back the annual depreciation expense to NOPAT to estimate Operating Cash Flow.

Step 2: Calculating a Project's Working Capital Requirements

When a firm invests in a new project, it often leads to an increase in sales that require the firm to extend credit, which means that the firm's accounts receivable balance will grow. In addition, new projects often lead to a need to increase the firm's investment in inventories. Both the increase in accounts receivable and in inventories mean that the firm must invest more cash in the business. This is a cash outflow. However, if the firm is able to finance some or all of its inventories using trade credit, this offsets the effects of the increased investment in receivables and inventories. The difference in the increased accounts receivable plus inventories, less the increase in accounts payable (trade credit), indicates just how much cash the firm must come up with to cover the project's additional working capital requirements.

To calculate the increase in net operating working capital we examine the levels of accounts receivable, inventory, and accounts payable with and without the project. For the Crockett Clothing Co., let's assume that the purchase of an automated sewing machine described in Checkpoint 12.1 would cause the following changes:

	Without the Project (A)	With the Project (B)	Difference (B – A)
Accounts receivable	$600,000	$660,000	$60,000
Inventory	390,000	426,000	36,000
Accounts payable	180,000	198,000	18,000

We can now use Equation (12–4) to calculate Crockett's additional investment in working capital as follows:

$$\text{Investment in Net Operating Working Capital} = \left(\begin{array}{c}\text{Increase in}\\ \text{Accounts Receivable}\end{array}\right) + \left(\begin{array}{c}\text{Increase in}\\ \text{Inventories}\end{array}\right) - \left(\begin{array}{c}\text{Increase in}\\ \text{Accounts Payable}\end{array}\right) \quad (12\text{–}4)$$

$$= \$60{,}000 + 36{,}000 - 18{,}000 = \$78{,}000$$

So to meet the needs of the firm for working capital in year 1 Crockett must invest $78,000. Although this investment will be made throughout the year, to be conservative we assume that the full $78,000 is invested immediately in year 0. Crockett expects to have a cash *outflow* of $78,000 for working capital in year 0 and receive a cash *inflow* of $78,000 in year 5 when the project is shut down.

Step 3: Calculating a Project's Capital Expenditure Requirements

Capital expenditures, or CAPEX, is the term we use to refer to the cash the firm spends to purchase fixed assets. As we discussed earlier, for accounting purposes, the cost of a firm's purchases of long-term assets is not recognized immediately, but is allocated or expensed over the life of the asset by depreciating the investment. Specifically, the difference between the purchase price and the expected salvage value of the investment is calculated as a depreciation expense over the life of the asset.

The effect of depreciation is simply to reduce the tax liability created by the investment. When the project life is over, the book value of the asset is expected to equal the salvage value. Since the book value and salvage value are equal, there is no taxable gain or loss on the sale, and we simply add the salvage value to the final year's free cash flow along with the recovery of any net operating working capital.

Step 4: Calculating a Project's Free Cash Flow

Using Equation (12–3), we calculate Crockett Clothing Company's free cash flows for the five-year life of its investment opportunity:

	Year 0	Year 1	Year 2	Year 3	Year 4	Year 5
Project Revenues **(growing at 0% per year)**		$ 360,000	$ 360,000	$ 360,000	$ 360,000	$ 360,000
− Cost of Goods Sold **(60% of revenues)**		(216,000)	(216,000)	(216,000)	(216,000)	(216,000)
= Gross Profit		$ 144,000	$ 144,000	$ 144,000	$ 144,000	$ 144,000
− Cash Operating Expenses **(fixed at $5,000 per year)**		(5,000)	(5,000)	(5,000)	(5,000)	(5,000)
− Depreciation **($200,000 / 5 years)**		(40,000)	(40,000)	(40,000)	(40,000)	(40,000)
= Net Operating Income		$ 99,000	$ 99,000	$ 99,000	$ 99,000	$ 99,000
− Taxes **(30%)**		(29,700)	(29,700)	(29,700)	(29,700)	(29,700)
= Net Operating Profit after Taxes (NOPAT)		$ 69,300	$ 69,300	$ 69,300	$ 69,300	$ 69,300
+ Depreciation		40,000	40,000	40,000	40,000	40,000
= Operating Cash Flow		$ 109,300	$ 109,300	$ 109,300	$ 109,300	$ 109,300
less: Increase in CAPEX	$(200,000)	—	—	—	—	—
less: Increase in net operating working capital	(78,000)	—	—	—	—	78,000
Free Cash Flow	**(278,000)**	**$ 109,300**	**$ 109,300**	**$ 109,300**	**$ 109,300**	**$ 187,300**

Note that in Year 0, the free cash flow is simply the sum of the capital expenditure of $200,000 and the investment in net operating working capital of $78,000. The operating cash flows for Years one through five are $109,300 and in Year 5 we add back the $78,000 investment in net operating working capital, which produces a total free cash flow in this year of $187,300. Finally, note that since the equipment is not expected to have a salvage value, none is added back in Year 5.

Computing Project NPV

If Crockett applies a 20 percent discount rate or required rate of return to evaluate the sewing machine investment, the net present value (NPV) of the investment follows:

$$NPV = CF_0 + \frac{CF_1}{(1+k)^1} + \frac{CF_2}{(1+k)^2} + \frac{CF_3}{(1+k)^3} + \frac{CF_4}{(1+k)^4} + \frac{CF_5}{(1+k)^5} \tag{11-1}$$

CF_0 is the -$278,000 initial cash outlay, r is the discount rate (20 percent) used by Crockett to discount the project's future cash flows, and CF_1 through CF_5 are the investment's free cash flows for Years 1 through 5. Substituting for each of these terms in the *NPV* equation above we get the following:

$$NPV = -\$278,000 + \frac{\$109,300}{(1+.20)^1} + \frac{\$109,300}{(1+.20)^2} + \frac{\$109,300}{(1+.20)^3} + \frac{\$109,300}{(1+.20)^4} + \frac{\$187,300}{(1+.20)^5}$$

$$NPV = \$80,220$$

Based on the investment's cash flows, Crockett should purchase the new automated machine since it offers an expected NPV of $80,220.

12.3 Inflation and Capital Budgeting

Since investments are expected to provide cash flows over many years, we cannot overlook the issue of price inflation. Cash flows that account for future inflation are generally referred to as **nominal cash flows**. **Real cash flows** are the cash flows that would occur in the absence of inflation.

When nominal cash flows are used, they should be discounted at the nominal interest rate and when firms calculate the real cash flows that are generated by a project, the cash flows should be discounted at the **real rate of interest**, which is the nominal rate adjusted for inflation. The typical practice is to base this estimate on nominal rates of interest.

Estimating Nominal Cash Flows

Example: Consider the situation faced by the Plantation Chemical Co. The firm purchases HDPE (High Density Polyethylene) pellets manufactured by oil refineries and uses them to manufacture the plastic containers used to package milk and fruit juice, and soft drinks. The firm is considering an expansion of one of its plants that makes milk bottles. The new plant will produce 5 million plastic bottles a year. The bottles currently sell for $0.20 each and cost $0.10 each to produce. The price of the bottles is expected to rise at a rate of 3 percent a year while the HDPE is expected to increase by 8 percent per year due to restrictions on world crude oil production. We can forecast the gross profit for the proposed investment for each of the next three years as follows:[1]

	1	2	3
Units Sold	5,000,000	5,000,000	5,000,000
Price per unit (inflation rate = 3%)	$0.2060	$0.2122	$0.2185
Cost per unit (inflation rate = 8%)	$0.1080	$0.1166	$0.1260
	1	2	3
Revenues	$1,030,000.00	$1,060,900.00	$1,092,727.00
Cost of Goods Sold	(540,000.00)	(583,200.00)	(629,856.00)
Gross Profit	$490,000.00	$477,700.00	$462,871.00

.2060 = .20(1.03)

.2165 = .2122(1.03)

.1260 = .1166(1.08)

.1080 = .10(1.08)

Note that Gross Profit actually declines over time as the cost of raw materials is inflating more rapidly than the price of the end product.

12.4 Replacement Project Cash Flows

An **expansion project** increases the scope of the firm's operations, but does not replace any existing assets or operations. A **replacement investment** is an acquisition of a new productive asset that replaces an older, less productive asset. A distinctive feature of many replacement investments is that the principal source of investment cash flows comes from cost savings, not new revenues.

---

[1] While the numbers listed for price and cost per unit have been rounded to four decimal places in this table, the calculations for revenue and cost of goods sold have been made without rounding.

Category 1: Initial Outlay, CF_0

For the replacement of an existing asset, the computation of the initial cash outlay is a bit more complicated because disposing of the existing asset can involve immediate expenses. If the old asset is sold for more than the book value of the asset, this gives rise to a taxable gain on the sale. On the other hand, if the old asset is sold for less than its book value then a tax deductible loss occurs.

When an existing asset is sold, there are three possible tax scenarios:

- The old asset is sold for a price above the depreciated value. Here the difference between the selling price of the old machine and its depreciated book value is a taxable gain, taxed at the marginal corporate tax rate and subtracted from the CAPEX. For example, assume the old machine was originally purchased for $350,000, had a depreciated book value of $100,000 today, and could be sold for $150,000, and the firm's marginal corporate tax rate is 30 percent. The taxes due from the gain would then be ($150,000 - $100,000) X (.30), or $15,000.

- The old asset is sold for its depreciated value. In this case, no taxes result, as there is neither a gain nor a loss from the asset's sale.

- The old asset is sold for less than its depreciated value. In this case, the difference between the depreciated book value and the salvage value of the asset is a taxable loss and may be used to offset capital gains. Thus, it results in tax savings and we add it to the CAPEX. For example, if the depreciated book value of the asset is $100,000 and it is sold for $70,000, we have a $30,000 loss. Assuming the firm's marginal corporate tax rate is 30 percent, the cash inflow from tax savings is ($100,000 - $70,000) X (.30), or $9,000.

Category 2: Annual cash flows

Annual cash flows for a replacement decision differ from a simple asset acquisition because we must now consider the differential operating cash flow of the new versus the old (replaced) asset.

Changes in Depreciation and Taxes. We are only interested in any change in taxes that the change in depreciation might bring about – after all, depreciation is not a cash flow expense, but since it is tax deductible it impacts taxes, which *are* a cash flow item. We want to look at the incremental change in taxes – that is, what the taxes would be if the asset were replaced versus what they would be if the asset were not replaced.

For a replacement project, the firm's depreciation expense increases by the depreciation on the new asset and decreases the depreciation on the replaced asset. Since our concern is with incremental changes, we take the new depreciation less the lost depreciation, and that difference would be our incremental change in depreciation. That is what we would use in our cash flow calculations to determine the change in taxes.

Changes in Working Capital. Many replacement projects require an increased investment in working capital. For example, if the new asset has greater capacity than the one it replaces and generates more sales, these new sales will result in an increased investment in accounts receivable, if they are credit sales. Also, in order to produce and sell the product, the firm may have to increase its investment in inventory, which also requires additional financing. On the other hand, some of this increased investment in inventory is financed by an increase in accounts payable, which offsets the outlay for new investment in inventories.

Changes in Capital Spending. The replacement asset will require an outlay at the time of its acquisition but also may require additional capital over its life. We must be careful, however, to net out any additional capital spending requirements of the older, replaced, asset when computing project free cash flows. Finally, at the end of the project's life, there will be a cash inflow equal to the after-tax salvage value of the new asset, if it is expected to have one. We need to net out any salvage value that the older asset might have.

Answers to **Concept Checks**

Concept Check **12.1**

1. What makes an investment cash flow relevant to the evaluation of an investment proposal?
2. What are sunk costs?
3. What are some examples of synergistic effects that affect a project's cash flows?
4. When borrowing the money needed to make an investment, is the interest expense incurred relevant to the analysis of the project? Explain.

Answer 1: The cash flow must be incremental (ie. result from the investment) to be relevant.

Answer 2: Sunk costs are not considered in an investment decision because they have been made in the past and are not a result of the impending decision to invest or not invest.

Answer 3: Synergistic effects of an investment include positive ones such as a new product drawing in customers for a firm's other product lines and negative ones such as cannibalization of existing sales by a new product.

Answer 4: Interest expense is not explicitly budgeted in cash flows because it is embedded in the discount rate of the project.

Concept Check **12.2**

1. What does the term *free cash flow* mean?
2. What are the four steps used to forecast a project's future cash flows?
3. What is net operating working capital, and how does it affect a project's cash flows?
4. What is CAPEX, and how does it affect a project's cash flows?

Answer 1: Free cash flow is the cash available to equity and debt investors after the costs of running and reinvesting in the business have been paid.

Answer 2: Forecasting cash flows require analysts to:

Estimate future operating cash flows

Estimate working capital requirements

Estimate capital spending requirements

Calculate the project's cash flow

Answer 3: Net working capital is the cash flow determined by INVENTORIES + AR - AP.

Answer 4: CAPEX is the capital spending of the firm in long-term or fixed assets and is the amount of investment a firm undertakes in order to grow the value of the firm.

Concept Check **12.3**

1. What is the distinction between nominal and real interest rates?

2. If you forecast nominal cash flows, should you use nominal or real discount rates? Why?

Answer 1: Nominal rates are the stated or observed rates and comprise a real rate plus the inflation rate. Real rates are the ex-inflation-adjusted (after inflation effects are removed) rate of return to cash flows and investors.

Answer 2: Nominal cash flows are discounted by nominal rates and real cash flows are discounted by real rates - any other combination will misstate the value of a project.

Concept Check **12.4**

1. What is a replacement investment?

2. What is the relevant depreciation expense when you are analyzing a replacement decision?

Answer 1: A replacement investment is not a new project per se, it is the replacement of existing equipment or process that removes an old asset and buys a new one to replace it. The benefit may be not higher positive cash flows but lower costs (or less negative cash flows).

Answer 2: The relevant depreciation expense is the net difference between the depreciation removed by the removal of the old equipment and the new depreciation from the replacement equipment.

Multiple Choice **Quiz**

1. An expansion project:
   a. replaces existing assets.
   b. substitutes for an existing investment.
   c. includes previously spent costs.
   d. invests to expand the scope of the firm's operations in a new way.

2. An incremental cash flow valuation considers
   a. project cash flows including cannibalization
   b. only the project cash flow and not cannibalization.
   c. previously spent costs.
   d. sunk costs.

3. A replacement investment is one that
   a. replaces existing assets.
   b. refinances an existing asset.
   c. includes previously spent costs.
   d. excludes relevant costs.

4. Nominal cash flows include
   a. inflation cash flows.
   b. real cash flows.
   c. real cash flows less inflation related cash flows.
   d. real cash flows less inflation.

5. Real cash flows are those that include
   a. inflation cash flows.
   b. nominal cash flows.
   c. both nominal and inflation cash flows.
   d. nominal cash flow less inflation.

6. Sunk costs are
   a. the losses on an investment.
   b. the negative cash flows of an investment.
   c. cash flows that include engineering reports from the project.
   d. previous cash outflows not relevant to the project decision.

7. Pro forma financial statements
   a. are future forecasts of firm expenses.
   b. are forecasts of the future financial statements.
   c. are forecasts of firm performance standardized by the SEC.
   d. are the reported earnings, balance sheet, and statement of cash flow of a firm.

8. Net working capital is
   a. the investment in inventory.
   b. the investment in the operating capital of the firm.
   c. the investment in CAPEX.
   d. the investment in long-term assets of the firm.

9. Salvage value is
   a. the value of operating the old project.
   b. the value from selling or disposing of the old asset.
   c. the value of the operating capital of the firm.
   d. the value of the long-term assets of the firm.

10. CAPEX is
    a. the investment in the operating capital of the firm.
    b. the discount rate used by analysts to present value cash flows.
    c. the investment in inventory by the firm.
    d. the investment in long-term assets of the firm.

Answers to **Multiple Choice Questions**

1. D
2. A
3. A
4. C
5. D
6. D
7. B
8. B
9. B
10. D

Self Test with **Solutions**

Picture the Problem

Decide on Solution Strategy

Solve

Analyze

Self Test 1: Calculating Free Cash Flow

Augusta Turf is looking to buy more farm equipment to expand its grass turf sales for the next four years to supply the Charleston market during a period of home sales growth. The farm equipment costs $1,900,000 and should generate pre-tax operating profits of $700,000 per year for four years. Depreciation expenses on the new equipment are expected to be $400,000 per year leaving a value of $300,000 for the equipment on the company's books.

To support the new sales, Augusta Turf will keep $100,000 more in inventory in Year 1, generate $50,000 more in accounts receivable in year 1, and incur $60,000 in accounts payable in Year 1. For Years 2 and 3, each item is expected to increase by $10,000. Also at the end of Year 4, net working capital will be reduced by $90,000. At the end of four years, the equipment will be sold for book value. Taxes are 35 percent.

a. What is the CAPEX of Augusta Turf's project?

b. What is the net working capital cash flow per year for Augusta Turf

c. What is the net operating income after tax (NOPAT) each year?

d. What is the free cash flow for years 1 to 4?

e. If Augusta uses a discount rate of 10 percent, should Augusta buy the equipment?

Step 1: Picture the Problem

The problem asks you to find the free cash flow of a project and value it with a discount rate of 10 percent. The initial investment amount was the total of capital spending. Find net operating cash flow, net working capital, and CAPEX to find the free cash flow. Then find the present value of the free cash flow using the 10 percent discount rate.

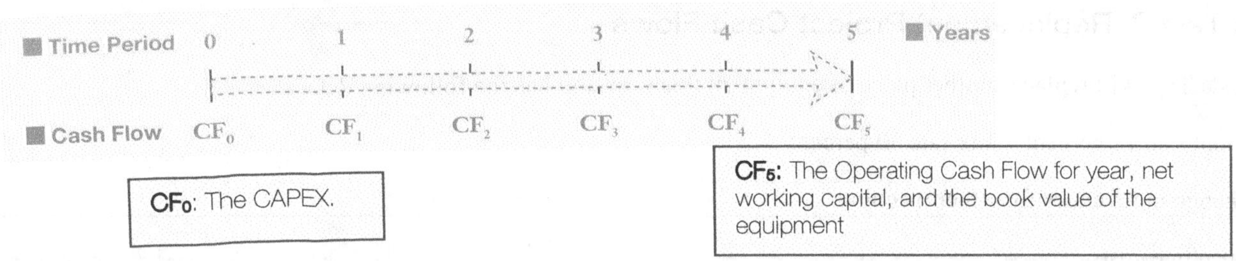

Step 2: Decide on a Solution Strategy

We can calculate the project's free cash flows each year using Equation (12–2):

$$\text{Free Cash Flow} = \underbrace{\text{Net Operating Income (Profit)} - \text{Taxes}}_{\text{Net Operating Profit after Taxes or NOPAT}} + \text{Depreciation Expense} - \text{Increase in Capital Expenditures } (CAPEX) - \text{Increase in Net Operating Working Capital } (NOWC) \quad (12–2)$$

Step 3: Solve

a. CAPEX is the investment amount of $1,900,00.

b. Net working capital equals Inventory + Accounts Receivable – Accounts Payable.

Year 1: 100,000 + 50,000 – 60,000 = $90,000

Year 2: 10,000 + 10,000 – 10,000 = 10,000

Year 3: 10,000 + 10,000 – 10,000 = 10,000

Year 4: -90,000

c. The after-tax NOPAT is the pre-tax amount x (1 – tax rate) or (1 – 35%).

After-tax NOPAT = 700,000 x (0.65) = $455,000

d. The free cash flow by year:

Year 0	**Year 1**	**Year 2**	**Year 3**	**Year 4**		
–1,900,000					CAPEX	-
	455,000	455,000	455,000	455,000	After-tax NOPAT	+
	400,000	400,000	400,000	400,000	Depreciation	+
	–90,000	-10,000	-10,000	+90,000	Net Working Capital	-
				+300,000	Salvage value	+
–1,900,000	765,000	845,000	845,000	1,245,000	Free Cash Flow	

e. Present value of free cash flow at 10 percent:

=*NPV*(.10,CF1:CF4) -1900000 equals $979,014

Step 4: Analyze

The farm equipment produces a positive *NPV* of $979,014. The project should be accepted.

Self Test 2: Replacement Project Cash Flows

Augusta Turf will replace another piece of equipment this year and has the following data:

Discount rate 12 percent Tax rate 30 percent

No change in revenues for either machine.

Old machine costs:

Remaining life 3 years	Depreciation $20,000 per year	Annual cost to run: $80,000
Book value $60,000	Salvage value today $40,000	Book and salvage in 3 years $0

New machine costs:

Life expected 3 years	Depreciation $40,000 per year	Annual cost to run: $40,000
Shipping $12,000	Book value $50,000 in 3 years	Salvage value $50,000 in 3 years
Purchase price $200,000		

a. Find the change in cash flows for years 0 to 3.

b. Should the firm replace the old machine?

c. If the new machine had a life of five years, how could you evaluate this replacement?

Step 1: Picture the Problem

An older machine with three years of useful life is being replaced with a new one with an expected life of three years. To calculate the change in cash flows we will take the cash flows from the new equipment and subtract out the cash flows from the old equipment:

0	1	2	3	Years
$CF(\text{New})_0$	$CF(\text{New})_1$	$CF(\text{New})_2$	$CF(\text{New})_3$	

Minus

$CF(\text{Old})_0$	$CF(\text{Old})_1$	$CF(\text{Old})_2$	$CF(\text{Old})_3$

Equals: Difference (New – Old)

Step 2: Decide on a Solution Strategy

This investment involves the replacement of an existing piece of equipment with newer equipment. The incremental cash flows uses equation (12–5) to represent the difference between those realized with and without the new equipment,

$$\begin{array}{c}\text{Replacement}\\ \text{Cash Flows } (\Delta CF)_{Year\ t}\end{array} = \begin{pmatrix}\text{Cash Flow for}\\ \text{the New Asset}\\ CF(\text{New})_{Year\ t}\end{pmatrix} - \begin{pmatrix}\text{Cash Flow for}\\ \text{the Old Asset}\\ CF(\text{Old})_{Year\ t}\end{pmatrix} \quad (12\text{–}5)$$

Step 3: Solve

a. The incremental cash flows from purchasing the new equipment in year 0 are the following:

Purchase new equipment	–200,000	
Ship and install new	–12,000	
Sale of the old	+40,000	
Tax benefit of loss on sale	+6,000	(20,000 loss to book value of $60,000, tax of 30 percent)
Cash flow in Year 0	–$166,000	

Years 1 and 2 are identical:

Cost savings of operating the new	40,000	($80,000 new less $40,000 old)
Higher depreciation of the new	20,000	($40,000 new less $20,000 old)
Pretax income change is	$20,000	
Taxes at 30 percent	$6,000	
After-tax net income change	$14,000	

To find free cash flow change,

Depreciation addback	$20,000
Cash flow change Year 1 and 2	$34,000

Year 3 is almost the same but has salvage value of the new machine.

Cash flow change Year 3	$34,000	
Sale of the new	$50,000	
Tax on sale	$0	(none since sold at book value)
Total cash flow change	$84,000	

Annual cash flows look like this:

CF0	CF1	CF2	CF3
–166,000	34,000	34,000	84,000

b. To find whether or not to replace with the new equipment, find the NPV at 12 percent:

NPV =$166,000+$34,000(1+.12)1+$34,000(1+.12)2+$84,000(1+.12)3=−$48,749

=*NPV*(.12,CF1-CF3)+CF0 equals -$48,749.

Reject the new equipment replacement decision this year.

c. If the new machine has a longer life than three years, one approach would be to forecast the old machine cash flows assuming the new machine was bought at the end of year 3 and compare those cash flows to replacing with the new machine bought today. Another approach would be to calculate the equivalent annual cost of both machines, the old with a three-year annuity factor and the new with a five-year annuity factor.

Step 4: Analyze

The replacement is not a good investment this year due to its negative NPV. Waiting a year may be the better option. If the new machine has a longer life, then the analysis will have to include EAC or some calculation for the costs of running the old machine or its replacement in the years after Year 3.

CHAPTER 13

Risk Analysis and Project Evaluation

Chapter Orientation

This chapter uses scenario analysis and other methods to estimate the riskiness of an investment. By understanding the nature of the risks faced, investors have a better idea of the returns needed to make the investment worthwhile. This chapter aims to improve our understanding and forecasts of cash flows.

13.1 The Importance of Risk Analysis

Since project cash flows may not have the same risk level and cost of capital as the firm, analysts should consider project specific risks in their forecasts.

Two Reasons to Perform Project Risk Analysis:

- Project cash flows are risky.
- Forecasts are subject to error.

Forecasts are too optimistic or too pessimistic, because analysts have bias. Shareholders want the managers to make investment decisions without bias.

13.2 Tools for Analyzing the Risk of Project Cash Flows

Sensitivity analysis is a primary means to assess the riskiness of cash flow forecasts. Rather than forecast one cash flow outcome, many possible outcomes and their associated probabilities are estimated. The analyst can improve the reliability of the NPV estimate and decision by improving cash flow estimates. Two other valuable tools used in addition to sensitivity analysis are scenario analysis and simulation, which compares a number of scenarios for their impact on cash flows.

Key Concepts: Expected Values and Value Drivers

Expected Values

The cash flows used are the **expected values** of the investment's risky cash flows. The expected value of a future cash flow is simply a probability weighted average of all the possible cash flows that might occur. If there are only two possible cash flows, \$0 and \$100, and the probability of each is 50 percent, then the expected cash flow is \$50 = .5 x \$0 + (1 – .5) x \$100.

It is customary to forecast cash flows for specific states of the economy—recession, normal, and expansion.

Consider the following hypothetical problem faced by the D. R. Horton Company. Horton is attempting to forecast the cash flows for a new subdivision in Kern County, California. Horton's management might estimate that if the homebuilding slump continues throughout 2011, cash flow will be –\$2 million; if a recovery begins during the year, cash flow will climb to \$1 million; and if the turn-around in the economy is dramatic and growth rates equal the high growth rates experienced before the recession began, cash flow will reach $6 million.

To complete this analysis of the expected cash flow, management must also make an estimate of the probabilities attached to each state of the home building economy. Suppose Horton's management estimates that there is a .50 probability of a continued housing slump that will result in the recession cash flow, a .40 probability of the beginning of a turnaround, and only a .10 probability of a return to the dramatic growth rate experienced before the onset of the recession. Given these estimates, the expected cash flow for 2014 is:

$$\begin{aligned}\text{Expected Cash Flow for 2014} &= (-\$2\text{ million}\times .50)+(\$1\text{ million}\times .40)+(\$6\text{ million}\times .10)\\ &= \$0\end{aligned}$$

In this example D. R. Horton estimates that in 2014, it will get a zero cash flow out of the Kern County development.

Value Drivers

Financial managers refer to the determinants of an investment's its performance using the term **value drivers**. A key value driver for a manufacturing firm would be its inventory turnover since high inventory turnover ratios indicate the efficient investment in inventories.

Identification of an investment's value drivers is crucial to the success of an investment project since they allow the financial manager to:

- Allocate more time and money toward refining their forecasts of these key variables.
- Monitor the key value drivers throughout the life of the project so that corrective action can be taken quickly in the event that the project does not function as planned.

Value drivers for investment cash flows consist of the fundamental determinants of project revenues (e.g., market size, market share, and unit price) and costs (e.g., variable and cash fixed costs, that is, fixed costs other than depreciation).

Sensitivity Analysis

Sensitivity analysis occurs when a financial manager evaluates the effect of each value driver on the investment's NPV. To illustrate the use of sensitivity analysis as a tool of risk analysis, consider the investment opportunity faced by Longhorn Enterprises, Inc. Longhorn has the opportunity to manufacture and sell a novelty third "brake light" for automobiles. Producing the light requires an initial investment of $500,000 in manufacturing equipment, which depreciates over a five-year time period toward a $50,000 salvage value, plus an investment of $20,000 in net operating working capital (increase in receivables and inventory less increase in accounts payable). The discount rate used to analyze the project cash flows is 10 percent. Other pertinent information describing the investment opportunity is summarized below:

Initial cost of equipment	$ (500,000)
Project and equipment life	5 years
Salvage value of equipment	$ 50,000
Working capital requirement	$ 20,000
Depreciation method	Straight-Line
Depreciation expense	$ (90,000)
Discount Rate	10%
Tax rate	30%

Longhorn's management estimates that it can sell 15,000 units per year for the next five years and expects to sell them for $200 each.

Longhorn's management team has identified four key value drivers for the project:

unit sales,

price per unit,

variable cost per unit,

and cash fixed costs (that is, fixed costs other than depreciation) per year.

The expected values for the value drivers, along with corresponding estimates for best and worst-case scenarios, are summarized below:

	Expected or Base-Case	Worst-Case	Best-Case
Unit sales	15,000	12,500	18,000
Price per unit	$ 200	190	220
Variable cost per unit	(150)	(160)	(130)
Fixed cash cost per year	(285,000)	(285,000)	(285,000)
Depreciation expense	$ (90,000)	$ (90,000)	$ (90,000)

Using the expected or base-case values for each of the value drivers, we calculate the investment cash flows for the expected or base-case as follows:

Calculating Net Operating Profit after Taxes (NOPAT).

Note: This calculation looks a lot like an income statement. But there is a subtle difference. We do not deduct interest expense when calculating the income tax liability.

Recapture of working capital in year 5.

Note: Because this is a recovery of the original investment in working capital, there is no profit; thus no taxes are owed on the $20,000.

Recovery of salvage value in year 5.

Note: Because the book value of the machinery and equipment is equal to the salvage value, there is no taxable gain or loss from the $50,000 salvage value received in Year 5.

	Year 0	Year 1	Year 2	Year 3	Year 4	Year 5
Revenues (15,000 units × $200)		$ 3,000,000	$ 3,000,000	$ 3,000,000	$ 3,000,000	$ 3,000,000
less: Variable cost ($150 per unit)		(2,250,000)	(2,250,000)	(2,250,000)	(2,250,000)	(2,250,000)
less: Depreciation expense		$ (90,000)	$ (90,000)	$ (90,000)	$ (90,000)	$ (90,000)
less: Fixed cash cost	NOPAT	(285,000)	(285,000)	(285,000)	(285,000)	(285,000)
Net operating income		375,000	375,000	375,000	375,000	375,000
less: Taxes		(112,500)	(112,500)	(112,500)	(112,500)	(112,500)
Net operating profit after tax (NOPAT)		$ 262,500	$ 262,500	$ 262,500	$ 262,500	$ 262,500
plus: Depreciation expense		90,000	90,000	90,000	90,000	90,000
less: Increase in CAPEX	$ (500,000)	—	—	—	—	50,000
less: Increase in working capital	(20,000)	—	—	—	—	20,000
Free cash flow (FCF)	$ (520,000)	$ 352,500	$ 352,500	$ 352,500	$ 352,500	$ 422,500

Note that the total initial cash outlay for Year 0 is –$520,000, which includes both the cost of acquiring machinery and equipment and the initial investment in net operating working capital required to get the business up and running.

Unit sales and price per unit are forecast to be the same for Years 1 through 5 so revenues are equal to \$3,000,000 per year = 15,000 units x \$200 per unit. Variable cost per unit of \$150 multiplied by 15,000 units produces a total annual variable cost of \$2,250,000. The firm has depreciation expense of \$90,000 plus cash fixed costs (such as salaries and utilities, which are cash expenses) of \$285,000 per year. Net operating income is estimated to be \$375,000 per year, and taxes are 30 percent of this total (\$112,500) such that net operating profit after tax (NOPAT) is \$262,500 = \$375,000 (1 − .30) per year. Adding back depreciation expense (which is not a cash expense) of \$90,000 produces a free cash flow estimate for Years 1 through 4 equal to \$352,500. In year 5 the company receives the salvage value of \$50,000 for the equipment (note that since this amount equals the book value of the equipment in that year, there are no taxable gains from the sale) plus the return of the \$20,000 investment in working capital to produce a free cash flow of \$422,500.

We calculate the expected NPV using the expected or base-case cash flows, which are the expected future cash flows, as \$859,717 as follows:

$$NPV = -\$520,000 + \frac{\$352,500}{(1+.10)^1} + \frac{352,500}{(1+.10)^2} + \frac{352,500}{(1+.10)^3} + \frac{352,500}{(1+.10)^4} + \frac{\$422,500}{(1+.10)^5}$$
$$NPV = -\$520,000 + \$1,379,717 = \$859,717$$

Therefore, the investment looks like a good one. Note that when we calculate NPV for a project, we do so using expected future cash flows, and hence, the NPV we estimate is the *expected* NPV.

Although the above analysis is based on expected values of the key value drivers, it is very likely that the actual realizations of these value drivers will turn out to be very different than our estimate. In this instance, the analyst can perform a sensitivity analysis to evaluate the project's risk. The analyst would do so by changing one variable at a time to determine its impact on the overall project NPV.

For example, consider the effect of a 10 percent decrease in unit sales on the project's NPV. In this case, unit sales would drop to 13,500 and the resulting NPV (holding everything else constant) would drop to \$660,700. This is a drop of 23 percent in NPV caused by a 10 percent drop in unit sales. Next, consider a 10 percent increase in variable cost per unit (\$165), which results in an NPV of \$262,668 or a drop of 69 percent. Finally, consider a 10 percent increase in annual cash fixed costs from (\$285,000) to (\$313,500). The resulting NPV is \$784,091, which is only 9 percent less than the base-case NPV.

Value Driver	Expected NPV	Revised NPV	% Change in NPV
Unit sales (−10%)	\$859,717	\$660,700	−23%
Variable cost per unit (+10%)	\$859,717	\$262,668	−69%
Cash fixed cost per year (+10%)	\$859,717	\$784,091	−9%

Clearly, the most critical value driver we have considered here is variable cost per unit. This tells the analyst that having a very good grasp on the variable cost per unit is absolutely critical to the project's success. This, in turn, might lead the analyst to go back to the engineering staff that provided the basis for the variable cost estimate to better understand their confidence in their estimate.

Scenario Analysis

Our sensitivity analysis of Longhorn Enterprises, Inc., involved changing only one value driver at a time and analyzing its effect on the investment NPV. This is very useful when attempting to determine the most critical value drivers, but it ignores the fact that some of the value drivers may move in unison or be correlated.

To consider the effects of multiple changes in value drivers, analysts often resort to something we will refer to as **scenario analysis**, which allows the financial manager to simultaneously consider the effects of changes in the estimates of multiple value drivers on the investment opportunity's NPV. Each scenario consists of a different set of estimates for the project value drivers. One possible scenario consists of value drivers all equal to Longhorn management's worst-case estimates presented earlier. To evaluate this possibility, we analyze the project cash flows and NPV using the worst-case estimates of the value drivers as follows:

	Year 0	Year 1	Year 2	Year 3	Year 4	Year 5
Revenues (12,500 units × $190 each)		$ 2,375,000	$ 2,375,000	$ 2,375,000	$ 2,375,000	$ 2,375,000
less: Variable cost ($160 per unit)		(2,000,000)	(2,000,000)	(2,000,000)	(2,000,000)	(2,000,000)
less: Depreciation expense		(90,000)	(90,000)	(90,000)	(90,000)	(90,000)
less: Fixed cash costs per year		(285,000)	(285,000)	(285,000)	(285,000)	(285,000)
Net Operating Income		$ —	$ —	$ —	$ —	$ —
less: Taxes (Tax rate = 30%)		—	—	—	—	—
Net Operating Profit after Tax (NOPAT)		$ —	$ —	$ —	$ —	$ —
plus: Depreciation expense		90,000	90,000	90,000	90,000	90,000
less: Increase in CAPEX	$(500,000)	—	—	—	—	50,000
less: Increase in working capital	(20,000)	—	—	—	—	20,000
Free Cash Flow (FCF)	$(520,000)	$ 90,000	$ 90,000	$ 90,000	$ 90,000	$ 160,000
NPV	$(135,365)					
IRR	0.00%					

Since the worst-case scenario has much lower estimates of revenues due to the lower selling price and number of units sold, the resulting cash flow estimates are much lower. Indeed, when we analyze the investment's NPV, we get a worst-case estimate of -$135,364, which means that in this case the project reduces shareholder wealth. But what is the likelihood that this worst-case scenario occurs? We will leave this question unanswered for the moment but will return to it shortly when we discuss the use of simulation analysis.

What about the best-case scenario? If this rosy outcome were to occur, then the following cash flows would result:

	Year 0	Year 1	Year 2	Year 3	Year 4	Year 5
Revenues (18,000 units × $220)		$ 3,960,000	$ 3,960,000	$ 3,960,000	$ 3,960,000	$ 3,960,000
less: Variable cost ($130 per unit)		(2,340,000)	(2,340,000)	(2,340,000)	(2,340,000)	(2,340,000)
less: Depreciation expense		$ (90,000)	(90,000)	(90,000)	(90,000)	(90,000)
less: Fixed cash cost		(285,000)	(285,000)	(285,000)	(285,000)	(285,000)
Net Operating Income		1,245,000	$ 1,245,000	$ 1,245,000	$ 1,245,000	$ 1,245,000
less: Taxes		(373,500)	(373,500)	(373,500)	(373,500)	(373,500)
Net Operating Profit after Tax (NOPAT)		$ 871,500	$ 871,500	$ 871,500	$ 871,500	$ 871,500
plus: Depreciation expense		90,000	90,000	90,000	90,000	90,000
less: Increase in CAPEX	$ (500,000)	—	—	—	—	50,000.00
less: Increase in working capital	(20,000)	—	—	—	—	20,000.00
Free Cash Flow (FCF)	$ (520,000)	$ 961,500	$ 961,500	$ 961,500	$ 961,500	$ 1,031,500
NPV	$3,168,306					
IRR	184.04%					

In this case the NPV of the project would be a whopping $3,168,306 and the IRR is 184.04 percent!

Combining our analysis of the expected or base-case, worst-case, and best-case scenarios indicates a wide range of possible NPVs for the project:

Scenario	NOPAT	Free Cash Flow (Years 1–4)	NPV
Expected or Base Case	$262,500	$352,500	$ 859,717
Worst Case	$ 0	$ 90,000	($135,365)
Best Case	$871,500	$961,500	$3,168,306

In fact, we have learned that the investment is expected to create value for Longhorn with an expected NPV equal to $859,717. However, this estimate is based on Longhorn's forecast of the expected values for the key value drivers but we also discovered a wide range of possible NPVs depending on what scenario happens. In the next section, simulation offers the analyst a useful tool for risk analysis that provides us with estimates of NPV for many scenarios and with probabilities for those scenarios.

Simulation Analysis

Scenario analysis provides the analyst with a discrete number of estimates of project NPVs for a limited number of cases or scenarios. **Simulation analysis**, on the other hand, provides the analyst with a very powerful tool for generating thousands of estimates of NPV that are built upon thousands of values for each of the investment's value drivers. These different values arise out of each value driver's individual probability distribution. This may sound confusing if you have not heard the term probability distribution in a while, so here is a simple example. Let's say that the unit selling price for Longhorn's third brake light product can be either $180 or $220 with equal probability of 50 percent. The expected price then is $200 = .50 x $180 + .50 x $220. The probability distribution for unit price in this instance is fully described by the two possible values for price and their corresponding probabilities.[1]

Let's consider how Longhorn might use simulation to evaluate the NPV of its proposed brake light project. The simulation process is summarized in the following five-step process:

Step 1: Estimate probability distributions for each of the investment's key value drivers

Step 2: Randomly select one value for each of the value drivers from their respective probability distributions.

Step 3: Combine the values selected for each of the value drivers to estimate project cash flows for each year of the project's life and calculate the project's NPV.

Step 4: Store or save the calculated value of the NPV and repeat Steps 2 and 3. Simulations are easily carried out using readily available computer software that allows one to easily repeat steps 2 and 3 thousands of times.

Step 5: Use the stored values of the project NPV to construct a histogram or probability distribution of NPV.

Once we have finished running the simulation, we can analyze the distribution of *possible* NPVs to determine the probability for a negative NPV. In Figure 13.1, we see a 15 percent probability that the project will produce a NPV that is less than zero. What simulation does is allow us to analyze all sources of uncertainty simultaneously and get some idea as to what might happen before we actually commit to the investment.

[1]The distribution of unit price in this example is discrete since price can only take on one of two discrete values. If the price could be anything between $180 and $200 then the distribution would be continuous. The bell-shaped normal distribution, for example, is an example of a continuous probability distribution.

Figure 13.1

Probability Distribution of NPVs for the Marketing Longhorn's Brake Lights

The final output of the simulation is a probability distribution of the project's NPVs. Having set up and run the simulation experiment, the analyst not only knows the expected NPV but can also make probability statements about the likelihood of achieving any particular value of NPV. For example, in the results that follow, the probability of achieving a positive NPV is 85 percent.

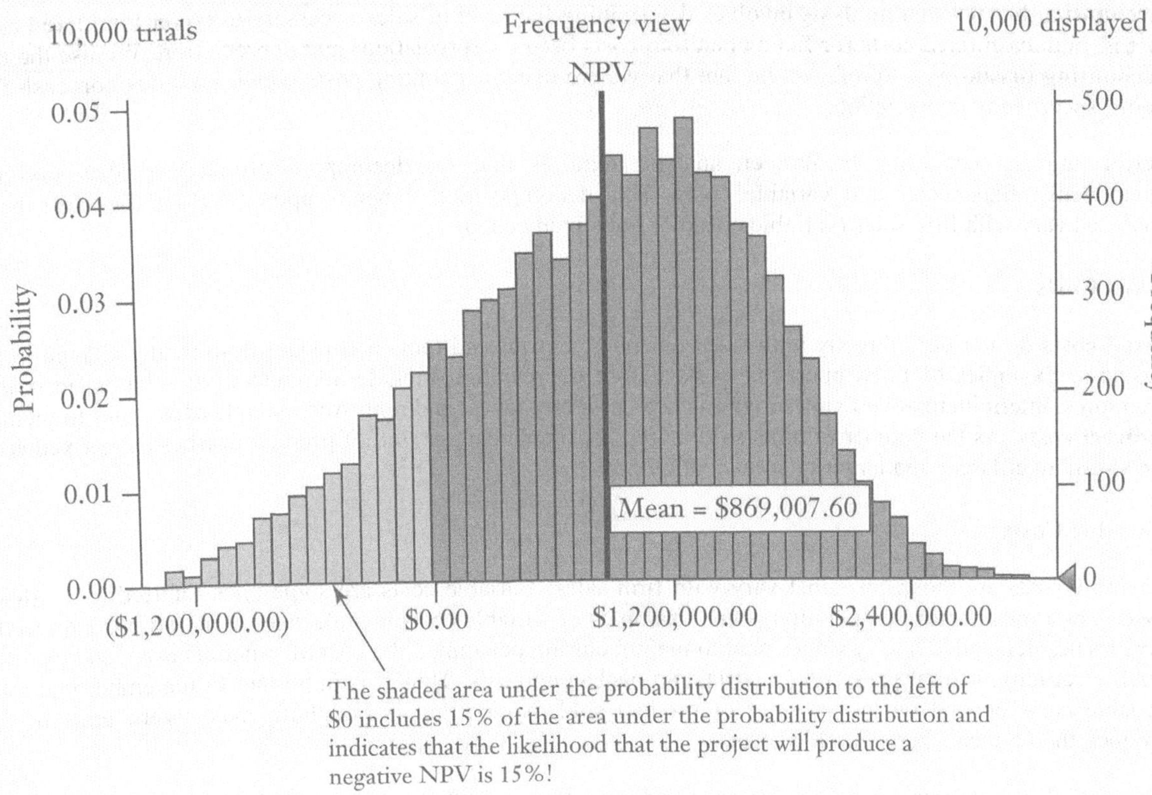

13.3 Break-Even Analysis

Managers typically do a **break-even analysis** to determine the minimum level of output or sales that the firm must achieve in order to avoid losing money—that is, to break even. In most cases, break-even sales estimate is defined as the level of sales for which net operating income equals zero. To illustrate break-even analysis, we refer back to the Longhorn Enterprises example introduced in the previous section. The worst-case scenario results are repeated below for the novelty brake light investment proposal:

	Year 0	Year 1	Year 2	Year 3	Year 4	Year 5
Revenues (12,500 units × $190 each)		$ 2,375,000	$ 2,375,000	$ 2,375,000	$ 2,375,000	$ 2,375,000
less: Variable cost ($160 per unit)		(2,000,000)	(2,000,000)	(2,000,000)	(2,000,000)	(2,000,000)
less: Depreciation expense		(90,000)	(90,000)	(90,000)	(90,000)	(90,000)
less: Fixed cash costs per year		(285,000)	(285,000)	(285,000)	(285,000)	(285,000)
Net Operating Income		$ —	$ —	$ —	$ —	$ —
less: Taxes (Tax rate = 30%)		—	—	—	—	—
Net Operating Profit after Tax (NOPAT)		$ —	$ —	$ —	$ —	$ —
plus: Depreciation expense		90,000	90,000	90,000	90,000	90,000
less: Increase in CAPEX	$(500,000)	—	—	—	—	50,000
less: Increase in working capital	(20,000)	—	—	—	—	20,000
Free Cash Flow (FCF)	$(520,000)	$ 90,000	$ 90,000	$ 90,000	$ 90,000	$ 160,000

Notice that Net Operating Income is equal to zero for a sales level of $2,375,000, which illustrates the sale of 12,500 units at a price of $190 per unit, with variable cost per unit equal to $160. Let's now consider how we could calculate the break-even level of sales.

Accounting Break-Even Analysis

Accounting break-even analysis involves determining the level of sales necessary to cover total fixed costs, that is, both cash fixed costs (or fixed operating costs before depreciation) and depreciation. We use the term **accounting break-even** to refer to the fact that we are using accounting costs which includes non-cash flow items, specifically depreciation.

Performing an accounting break-even analysis requires that we decompose production costs into two components: fixed costs and variable costs. This decomposition depends upon whether the costs being analyzed vary with firm sales (variable costs) or not (fixed costs).

Fixed Costs

Fixed costs do not vary directly with sales revenues, but instead remain constant despite any change to the business. Examples of fixed operating costs before depreciation include administrative salaries, insurance premiums, intermittent advertising program costs, property taxes, and rent. Accountants often refer to them as **indirect costs**. As the number of units sold increases, fixed cost *per unit* of product decreases, as fixed costs are spread over larger and larger quantities of output.

Variable Costs

Variable costs are those costs that vary with firm sales. Variable costs are sometimes referred to as **direct costs**. For a manufacturing operation, some examples of variable costs include sales commissions paid to the firm's sales personnel, hourly wages paid to manufacturing personnel, the cost of materials used, energy costs (fuel, electricity, natural gas), freight costs, and packaging costs. Thus it is important to remember that total variable costs depend on the quantity of product sold. Notice that if Longhorn makes zero units of the product, then it incurs zero variable costs.

Figure 13.2 depicts Longhorn Enterprises' fixed, variable, and total costs of producing novelty brake lights for output levels ranging from 0 to 20,000 units. Panel a. illustrates the behavior of fixed and variable costs as the number of units produced and sold increases. For example, at 20,000 units produced and sold, Longhorn will incur fixed costs of $375,000 plus $3,200,000 ($160 per unit x 20,000 units) of variable costs for a total cost of $3,575,000.

Figure 13.2

Accounting Break-Even Analysis

Longhorn Enterprises, Inc. is evaluating the accounting break-even level of sales units for its novelty brake light investment opportunity. The firm is using its worst-case scenario estimates of selling price ($190 per unit), variable cost ($160 per unit) and also its fixed cost estimate of $375,000 in its analysis. Variable costs include all the costs incurred in the manufacturing process that vary with the number of units produced. Fixed costs do not vary with the number of units produced.

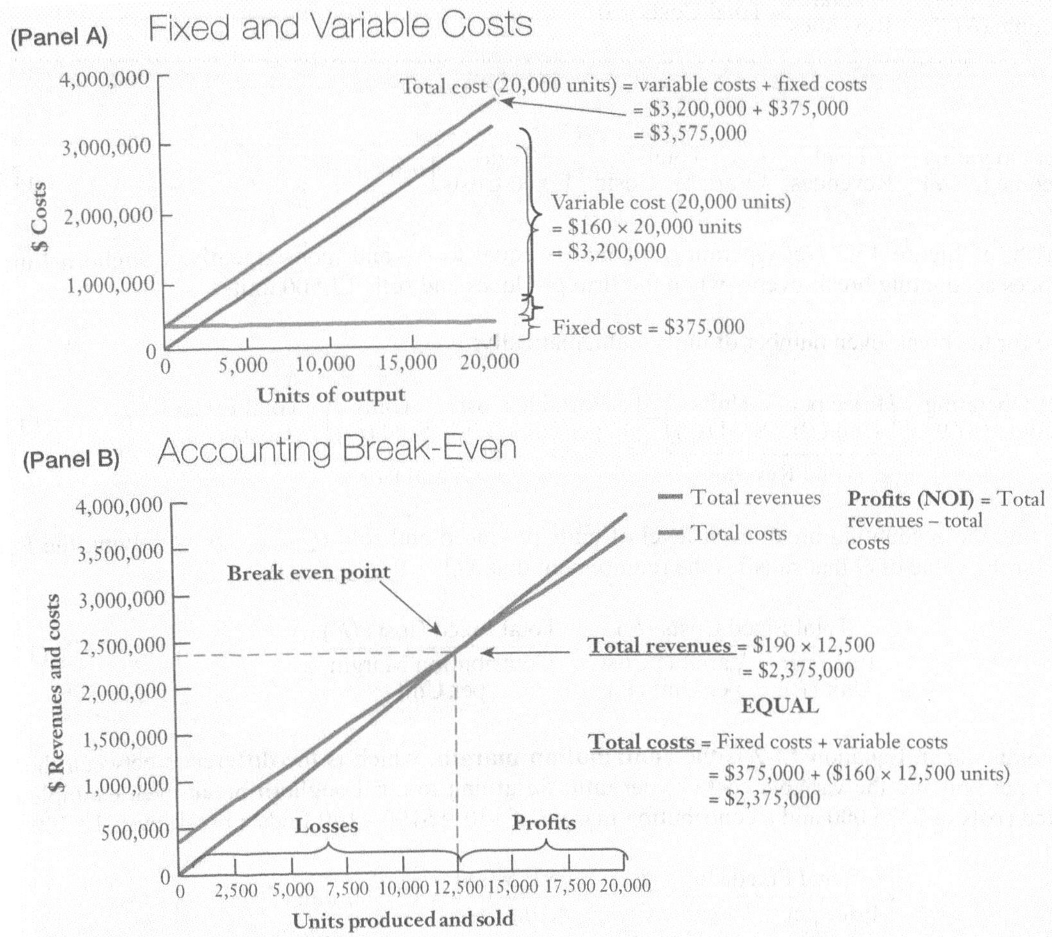

Total Revenue or Volume of Output

The last element used in accounting break-even analysis is total revenue. Total revenue is equal to the unit selling price multiplied by the number of units sold. Panel b. of Figure 13.2 contains a graphical depiction of the total revenues for Longhorn Enterprises' investment opportunity. Total revenues are equal to the product of the selling price of $190 per unit and the number of units produced and sold.

Calculating the Accounting Break-Even Point

The accounting break-even point is the level of sales or output that is necessary to cover both variable and total fixed costs, where total fixed costs equal cash fixed costs plus depreciation, such that the net operating income is equal to zero:

$$\text{Net Operating Income } (NOI) = \text{Total Revenues} - \text{Total Costs} = 0$$

or

$$\text{Net Operating Income } (NOI) = \text{Total Revenues} - \left(\text{Total Variable Costs} + \text{Total Fixed Costs}\right) = 0 \qquad (13\text{–}1)$$

In Panel b. of Figure 13.2 Net Operating Income is equal to 0—and, consequently, Longhorn Enterprises experiences accounting break-even—when the firm produces and sells 12,500 units.

To solve for the break-even number of units mathematically:

$$\text{Net Operating Income } (NOI) = \underbrace{\left(\text{Price per Unit } (P) \times \text{Units Sold } (Q)\right)}_{\text{Total Revenue}} - \underbrace{\left[\left(\text{Variable Cost per Unit } (V) \times \text{Units Sold } (Q)\right) + \text{Total Fixed Costs } (F)\right]}_{\text{Total Costs}} = 0 \qquad (13\text{–}1a)$$

We can find the accounting break-even level of units produced and sold ($Q_{\text{Break-even}}$) by solving the Equation (13-1a) for the value of Q that satisfies the requirement that $NOI = 0$ ($Q_{Break\text{-}even}$):

$$Q_{Accounting\ Break-even} = \frac{\text{Total Fixed Costs } (F)}{\text{Price per Unit } (P) - \text{Variable Cost per Unit } (V)} = \frac{\text{Total Fixed Costs } (F)}{\text{Contribution Margin per Unit}} \qquad (13\text{–}2)$$

The denominator in Equation 13-2 is the **contribution margin,** which is the difference between the selling price (P) per unit and the variable cost (V) per unit. Returning to our Longhorn break-even example we use total fixed costs of \$375,000 and a contribution margin of \$30 = \$190 - 160 finds a break-even 12,500 units:

$$Q_{Accounting\ Break-Even} = \frac{\text{Total Fixed Costs } (F)}{\text{Price per Unit } (P) - \text{Variable Cost per Unit } (V)} = \frac{\$375{,}000}{\$190 - 160} = 12{,}500 \text{ units}$$

Calculating the Cash Break-Even Point

In addition to calculating the accounting break-even point, it also is common to calculate the cash break-even point. This certainly makes sense when we think back to **Principle 3: Cash Flows Are the Source of Value.** The accounting break-even point tells us the level of sales necessary to cover our total fixed and variable operating costs where total fixed costs include both cash fixed costs and depreciation expense (which is not a cash expense for the period). The **cash break-even point** tells us the level of sales where we have covered our cash fixed costs (ignoring depreciation) and as a result our cash flow is zero. To calculate the cash break-even point, we consider only those fixed costs that entail a cash payment by the firm (specifically, we exclude depreciation expense):

$$\begin{aligned} Q_{Cash\ Break-even} &= \frac{\text{Fixed Operating Costs other than Depreciation per year}}{\text{Price per Unit } (P) - \text{Variable Cost per Unit } (V)} \\ &= \frac{\text{Total Fixed Costs } (F) - \text{Depreciation}}{\text{Contribution Margin per Unit}} \end{aligned} \qquad (13\text{–}2a)$$

Going back to the Longhorn example recall that the company had cash fixed costs of \$285,000 and depreciation expense of \$90,000 for a total of \$375,000 in total fixed costs. In calculating the cash break-even point, we are only interested in the fixed cash expenses, or fixed costs other than depreciation, of \$285,000. Longhorn's price per unit is \$190 and its variable costs per unit were \$160, the cash breakeven point can be calculated as

$$Q_{Cash\ Break-even} = \frac{\text{Fixed Operating Costs Other Than Depreciation per Year}}{\begin{matrix}\text{Price per} \\ \text{Unit } (P)\end{matrix} - \begin{matrix}\text{Variable Cost} \\ \text{per Unit } (V)\end{matrix}}$$

$$= \frac{\$375{,}000 - \$90{,}000}{\$190 - \$160} = 9{,}500 \text{ units}$$

NPV Break-Even Analysis

The **NPV break-even analysis** identifies the level of sales necessary to produce a zero level of NPV. It differs from accounting break-even analysis in that NPV break-even focuses on cash flows, not accounting profits. The worst-case cash flows are presented below, along with the estimated NPV and IRR for this scenario:

	Year 0	Year 1	Year 2	Year 3	Year 4	Year 5
Revenues (12,500 units × \$190 each)		\$ 2,375,000	\$ 2,375,000	\$ 2,375,000	\$ 2,375,000	\$ 2,375,000
less: Variable cost (\$160 per unit)		(2,000,000)	(2,000,000)	(2,000,000)	(2,000,000)	(2,000,000)
less: Depreciation expense		(90,000)	(90,000)	(90,000)	(90,000)	(90,000)
less: Fixed cash costs per year		(285,000)	(285,000)	(285,000)	(285,000)	(285,000)
Net Operating Income		\$ —	\$ —	\$ —	\$ —	\$ —
less: Taxes (Tax rate = 30%)		—	—	—	—	—
Net Operating Profit after Tax (NOPAT)		\$ —	\$ —	\$ —	\$ —	\$ —
plus: Depreciation expense		90,000	90,000	90,000	90,000	90,000
less: Increase in CAPEX	\$(500,000)	—	—	—	—	50,000
less: Increase in working capital	(20,000)	—	—	—	—	20,000
Free Cash Flow (FCF)	\$(520,000)	\$ 90,000	\$ 90,000	\$ 90,000	\$ 90,000	\$ 160,000
NPV	\$(135,365)					
IRR	0.00%					

Note that the Net Operating Income is zero, so this is the accounting break-even sales level. However, the annual free cash flows are equal to the depreciation expense, except for Year 5 when they also include the salvage value on the equipment plus the return of working capital. When we calculate the NPV for these cash flows, we find that it is negative and the IRR is equal to zero. If we require a rate of return greater than zero, the project does not produce enough cash flow to break even. This difference in results between break-even analysis and the NPV shouldn't come as much of a surprise; after all, break-even analysis does not look at cash flows and ignores the time value of money. Moreover, accounting break-even analysis only looks at one period, trying to determine the level of sales that will produce zero net operating income.

Solving for the break-even NPV is a bit more complicated than solving for accounting break-even and it is very helpful to have a spreadsheet model to do the calculations. However, you can also do it by trial and error by simply trying different output levels until the calculated NPV equals zero. In this example, the sales units that lead to a zero NPV are 14,200 as the following set of cash flows show:

	Year 0	Year 1	Year 2	Year 3	Year 4	Year 5
Revenues (14,200 units × $190 each)		$ 2,698,000	$ 2,698,000	$ 2,698,000	$ 2,698,000	$ 2,698,000
less: Variable cost ($160 per unit)		(2,272,000)	(2,272,000)	(2,272,000)	(2,272,000)	(2,272,000)
less: Depreciation expense		(90,000)	(90,000)	(90,000)	(90,000)	(90,000)
less: Fixed cash costs per year		(285,000)	(285,000)	(285,000)	(285,000)	(285,000)
Net Operating Income		$ 51,000	$ 51,000	$ 51,000	$ 51,000	$ 51,000
less: Taxes (Tax rate = 30%)		(15,300)	(15,300)	(15,300)	(15,300)	(15,300)
Net Operating Profit after Tax (NOPAT)		$ 35,700	$ 35,700	$ 35,700	$ 35,700	$ 35,700
plus: Depreciation expense		90,000	90,000	90,000	90,000	90,000
less: Increase in CAPEX	$(500,000)	—	—	—	—	50,000
less: Increase in working capital	(20,000)	—	—	—	—	20,000
Free Cash Flow (FCF)	$(520,000)	$ 125,700	$ 125,700	$ 125,700	$ 125,700	$ 195,700
NPV	$ 0					
IRR	10.00%					

Figure 13.3 contains NPV calculations for the break-even NPV of 14,200 units. This is much easier, of course, if you let the spreadsheet do the re-calculations of NPV. However, we leave this analysis to later finance classes since it is beyond the scope of this book.[2]

Figure 13.3

NPV Break-Even

Longhorn Enterprises is considering an investment that involves producing novelty brake lights for automobiles. The analysis of NPV break-even presented here corresponds to the assumptions underlying the worst-case scenario for the investment, that is,

	Worst-Case Scenario
Price per unit	$ 190
Variable cost per unit	(160)
Cash fixed costs per year	(285,000)

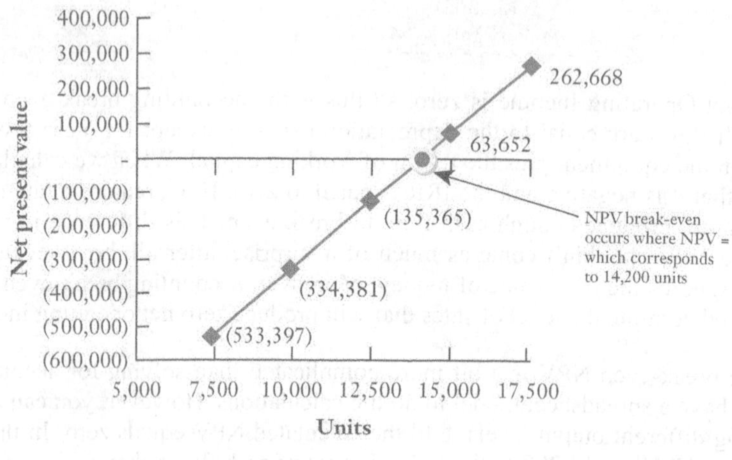

[2] For those who would like to do this analysis you will find the "Goal Seek" function in Excel very helpful.

Operating Leverage and the Volatility of Project Cash Flows

A project's break-even point is determined by the project's total fixed costs and the difference between the price per unit and the variable costs per unit. In general this mixture of fixed and variable operating costs is determined by the nature of the business. Most businesses have some flexibility in their cost structure and can substitute fixed costs for variable costs.

The mix of fixed and variable operating costs not only impacts the breakeven output but also determines something called operating leverage. **Operating leverage** results from the use of fixed costs in the operations of the firm and measures the sensitivity of changes in operating income to changes in sales. The greater the operating leverage, the greater the sensitivity of the firm's operating income is to changes in sales. We can measure the firm's operating leverage for a particular level of sales using the **degree of operating leverage (DOL),** the percent change in sales and how it is reflected in a percent change in NOI, as follows:

$$DOL = \frac{\%\text{ change in net operating profits } (NOI)}{\%\text{ change in sales}} \tag{13.3}$$

Thus, if the DOL is 4.0 and there is a 10 percent change in sales, NOI would increase by 40 percent, or 4.0 × 10 percent. To illustrate how this works, consider the Longhorn example found in Table 13.1. The firm's base case sales are $3,000,000 while the fixed costs are $375,000. To keep things simple, let's also assume that Longhorn's variable cost remain constant at $150 per unit. If Longhorn's sales increase 20 percent, up to $3,600,000 we calculate that the firm's NOI (or EBIT) will rise by 40 percent from $375,000 to $525,000. Note in the last column of Table 13.1 that we calculate the percent change in both sales and NOI. Therefore, the DOL for Longhorn can be calculated using Equation (13–4) to equal 2.0 = 40%/20%. The reason that NOI rose by 40 percent while sales rose by only 20 percent is that some of Longhorn's costs are fixed and consequently do not increase with sales. Clearly, a higher operating leverage means higher volatility in operating profit or NOI!

Table 13.1 How Operating Leverage Affects NOI for a 20% Increase in Longhorn's Sales

	Base Sales Level for year *t*	Forecast Sales Level for year *t* +1	Percentage Change in Sales and NOI
Unit Sales	15,000	18,000	
Sales	$3,000,000	$3,600,000	**+20%** = $3.6 million/$3.0 million – 1
Less: Total variable costs	2,250,000	2,700,000	
Revenue before fixed costs	$750,000	$900,000	
Less: Total fixed costs	375,000	375,000	
NOI (or EBIT)	$375,000	$525,000	**+40%** = $525,000/$375,000 – 1

Table 13.2 How Operating Leverage Affects NOI for a 20% Decrease in Longhorn's Sales

	Base Sales Level for year *t*	Forecast Sales Level for year *t* +1	Percentage Change in Sales and NOI
Unit Sales	15,000	12,000	
Sales	$3,000,000	$2,400,000	**–20%** = $2.4 million/$3.0 million – 1
Less: Total variable costs	2,250,000	1,800,000	
Revenue before fixed costs	$750,000	$600,000	
Less: Total fixed costs	375,000	375,000	
NOI (or EBIT)	$375,000	$225,000	**–40%** = $225,000/$375,000 – 1

Calculating the DOL using Equation (13–3) requires that we compute NOI for two sales levels. However there is a simpler way to do this calculation using Equation (13–4) as follows:

$$DOL_{Sales=\$3,000,000} = 1 + \frac{\text{Fixed Costs}}{NOI_{Sales=\$3\text{ million}}} = 1 + \frac{\$375,000}{\$375,000} = 1 + 1 = 2 \qquad (13\text{–}4)$$

Interestingly, a firm's DOL is not only a function of its mix of fixed and variable costs but also depends on the level of firm sales in relation to its breakeven sales level. Recall that the break-even sales level is where *NOI* equals 0. Thus, looking at equation (13–4) we can see that since *NOI* is in the denominator, as *NOI* approaches 0, $\frac{\text{Fixed Costs}}{NOI_{Sales}}$ becomes very large. As a result, the DOL is most negative for sales levels just below the break-even level and most positive for sales just over the break-even level. That only makes sense because DOL measures the *percent change* in NOI that results from a percent change in sales, and when NOI is near zero, a small dollar change in NOI will result in a large percent change in NOI.

We can summarize what have we learned about operating leverage as follows:

- Operating leverage results from the substitution of fixed operating costs for variable operating costs.
- The effect of operating leverage is to increase the effect of changes in sales on operating income.
- The degree of operating leverage (DOL) is an indication of the firm's use of operating leverage and can be calculated as the ratio of the percent change in NOI divided by the corresponding percent change in sales. The DOL is not a constant but decreases as the level of sales increases beyond the break-even point.
- Finally, operating leverage is a double-edged sword by magnifying both profits and losses, helping in the good times and causing pain in the bad times.

13.4 Real Options in Capital Budgeting

NPV provides the proper tool for evaluating whether a project is expected to add value to the firm. However, NPV is generally calculated using a static set of expected future cash flows that do not reflect the fact that managers are likely to make changes to the operation of the investment over its life. A project may be extended, scaled back, or shut down earlier than anticipated.

Having the flexibility to alter an investment's scale, scope, and timing enhances the value of an investment. All else equal, we would surely prefer an investment that allows managers substantial flexibility over an investment with no flexibility. However, traditional estimates of investment NPVs often ignore the implications of this flexibility, and so tend to understate project values.

Opportunities to alter the project's cash flow stream after the project has begun are commonly referred to as **real options**. The most common sources of flexibility or real options that can add value to an investment opportunity include:

(1) Timing options—the option to delay a project until estimated future cash flows are more favorable;

(2) Expansion options—the option to increase the scale and scope of an investment in response to realized demand; and

(3) Contract, Shut-down, and Abandonment options—the option to slow down production, halt production temporarily, or stop production permanently (abandonment).

The Option to Delay the Launch of a Project

There is no question that the estimated cash flows associated with a project can change over time. Let's consider Go-Power Batteries, a company that developed a high-voltage nickel-metal hydride battery that can be used to power a hybrid automobile. It is still relatively expensive to manufacture the nickel-metal hydride battery, and the market for a hybrid car is still relatively small. As a result, the option to delay manufacturing the hydride battery until a time when the profitability of the venture is more certain is extremely valuable.

Before leaving our discussion of the timing option, let's consider its source. Do all projects have this option? Not at all! In some cases the opportunity to make an investment is short-lived, and if one firm passes it up, another will take it.

The Option to Expand a Project

The estimated cash flows associated with a project can change over time, making it valuable to expand its scale and scope. Because this expansion option can have significant value, firms try to design their production facilities in ways that allow them to easily expand capacity in response to realized increases in demand.

The Option to Reduce the Scale and Scope of a Project

The option to reduce the scale and scope of an investment is the mirror image of the option to expand. In the face of worse-than-expected performance, it is very valuable to have the option to slow down or contract production, shut it down temporarily until prospects for the investment improve, or shut down the investment altogether.

The existence of this type of flexibility or optionality can greatly reduce the risks associated with the investment and thereby increases the project's value. A manufacturer may decide first to scale back production and, ultimately, to abandon the project and sell the technology, including all the patent rights it has developed. To the extent that the technology has value in applications other than hybrid automobiles and the manufacturer can realize value from the sale, the original investment risk is minimized.

Answers to **Concept Checks**

Concept Check **13.1**

1. What are the reasons for performing a project risk analysis?
2. How does the optimism or pessimism of the manager doing a cash flow forecast influence the cash flow estimates?

Answer 1: The two principal reasons are that cash flows are risky and that forecasts have bias.

Answer 2: Optimistic cash flow estimates are too high and would have the firm accept projects that are not good for the firm. Pessimistic forecasts would have the firm turning down good projects.

Concept Check **13.2**

1. What are value drivers, and how are they important in the analysis of project risk?
2. What is sensitivity analysis, and how is it used to evaluate the risk of project cash flows?
3. Describe scenario analysis, and contrast it with sensitivity analysis.
4. Describe the five-step process used to carry out simulation analysis. How is simulation analysis similar to scenario analysis?

Answer 1: Value drivers are the factors that determine corporate performance and they allow managers to focus efforts on refining forecasts and to monitor drivers to correct lagging performance.

Answer 2: Sensitivity analysis changes the variables identified as value drivers such as sales, profit margin, and fixed costs to determine the impact on profit and net present value. It helps to identify the items most critical to the success of the investment.

Answer 3: Scenario analysis looks at multiple changes in several variables at once that match an economic forecast (expected, best, worse). Sensitivity analysis only changes one variable at a time.

Answer 4: Simulation analysis considers the probabilities that accompany each scenario and use a probability distribution to generate several hundred of possibilities. The five steps are:

Step 1: Estimate probability distributions for each of the investment's key value drivers

Step 2: Randomly select one value for each of the value drivers from their respective probability distributions.

Step 3: Combine the values selected for each of the value drivers to estimate project cash flows for each year of the project's life and calculate the project's NPV.

Step 4: Store or save the calculated value of the NPV and repeat Steps 2 and 3. Simulations are easily carried out using readily available computer software that allows one to easily repeat steps 2 and 3 thousands of times.

Step 5: Use the stored values of the project NPV to construct a histogram or probability distribution of NPV.

Concept Check **13.3**

1. Explain the concepts of fixed and variable costs. Which is an indirect cost, and which is a direct cost?
2. What is accounting break-even analysis?
3. What is NPV break-even analysis, and why does it differ from accounting break-even analysis?
4. What is operating leverage?

Answer 1: Variable costs are direct costs and vary directly with sales. Fixed costs are indirect costs and do not change with the level of sales.

Answer 2: Accounting break-even analysis evaluates the level of sales that breaks-even on net operating income (profit equal zero on an accounting basis after considering depreciation).

Answer 3: NPV break-even analysis differs from accounting break-even analysis because it looks at the time value of cash flows, not accounting profits, by using an opportunity cost of capital over the life of the investment rather than a single year of accounting profits.

Answer 4: Operating leverage is the degree to which net operating profit increases with sales. This is influenced by the mix of fixed and variable costs. A firm with higher fixed costs relative to variable has high operating leverage.

Concept Check **13.4**

1. What are real options, and how do they relate to the notion of managerial flexibility?
2. Define timing options, and describe how they add value to investments.
3. What is an expansion option?
4. What is an option to contract an investment? When would you expect this type of option to be most valuable?

Answer 1: Real options consider the flexibility of management to change a project depending on the economic circumstances.

Answer 2: Timing options are the option to delay a project until circumstances improve.

Answer 3: An expansion option is the flexibility to expand the scale and scope of a project.

Answer 4: An option to contract allows managers to downsize, halt, or end a project when economic conditions are not favorable, as in a recession.

Multiple Choice **Quiz**

1. Accounting break-even analysis examines
   a. profits before depreciation and sales required to break even.
   b. profits after depreciation and sales required to break even.
   c. net income and sales required to break even.
   d. gross profit and sales required to break even.

2. NPV break-even analysis examines
   a. net profits before depreciation and sales required to break even.
   b. net profits after depreciation and sales required to break even.
   c. cash flows and the sales required to break even.
   d. the present value of cash flows and sales required to break even.

3. Contribution margin is
   a. a ratio of profit to cost.
   b. the difference between variable and fixed costs.
   c. a ratio of fixed to variable costs.
   d. the difference between price and variable costs per unit.

4. Direct cost
   a. does not change with sales.
   b. is a fixed cost.
   c. varies with sales.
   d. varies with assets.

5. Indirect cost is
   a. is a variable cost.
   b. is a fixed cost.
   c. varies with assets.
   d. is part of inventory.

6. Value drivers are
   a. the determinants of costs.
   b. the ratios used to value the firm.
   c. the factors that affect revenue.
   d. the determinants critical to the success of the investment.

7. Real options represent
   a. the compensation of the firm's managers.
   b. the flexibility to choose different investments.
   c. the flexibility to alter a project after making the investment.
   d. the flexibility to choose different managers.

8. Simulation analysis uses
   a. different values of a variable to determine its impact on NPV.
   b. different values of a number of variables to determine their impact on NPV.
   c. different values and probabilities of variables to determine their impact.
   d. different probabilities on many scenarios to determine the distribution of NPV.

9. Scenario analysis uses
   a. different values of a variable to determine its impact on NPV.
   b. different values of a number of variables to determine their impact on NPV.
   c. different values and probabilities of variables to determine their impact.
   d. different probabilities on many scenarios to determine the distribution of NPV.

10. Sensitivity analysis uses
    a. different values of a variable to determine its impact on NPV.
    b. different values of a number of variables to determine their impact on NPV.
    c. different values and probabilities of variables to determine their impact.
    d. different probabilities on many scenarios to determine the distribution of NPV.

Answers to **Multiple Choice Questions**

1. B
2. D
3. D
4. C
5. B
6. D
7. C
8. D
9. B
10. A

Self Test **with Solutions**

Picture the Problem

Decide on Solution Strategy

Solve

Analyze

Self Test 1: Expected Cash Flows

As a financial analyst for a furniture maker, you have found sales to vary with the business cycle. You have the firm's estimates of recession, normal, and expansion business probabilities to be 10 percent, 60 percent, and 30 percent respectively. You believe the firm will have cash flows of $1,000,000 in a recession; $6,000,000 in normal conditions; and, $10,000,000 in an expansion. What is the firm's expectation for cash flows?

Step 1: Picture the Problem

The problem asks for the expected value of cash flows using the weighted probability of the three economic phases.

Step 2: Decide on a Solution Strategy

To solve, we will use the expected value formula to find the weighted probability of cash flows.

Step 3: Solve

Equation: Expected Cash Flow = sum of probabilities × cash flows

$$= .10 \times 1M + .60 \times \$6M + .30 \times \$10M = \$6.7M$$

Step 4: Analyze

The expected value of cash flow is $6,700,000.

Self Test 2: Accounting Break-even and Cash Break-even

Pinkie's Choppers builds custom bikes for high net worth clients. You've been provided the following data:

Units sold	500
Sales	$14,000,000
Cost of goods sold	$10,000,000
Fixed costs	$900,000 (includes $100,000 of depreciation)

a. What is Pinkie's contribution margin?

b. What is Pinkie's accounting break-even?

c. What is Pinkie's cash break-even?

Step 1: Picture the Problem

The problem asks for accounting and cash break-even which require knowing the contribution margin.

Step 2: Decide on a Solution Strategy

a. To solve for contribution margin, we need to know the per unit sales price and cost per unit.

b. To solve for accounting break-even, we use total fixed costs and contribution margin.

c. To solve for cash break-even, we use fixed costs less depreciation and contribution margin.

Step 3: Solve

a. Contribution margin

Equation:

$$\text{Contribution Margin} = \text{Per unit sales price less per unit cost}$$

$$= \frac{14,000}{500} - \frac{10,000,000}{500} = \$8,000$$

b. Accounting Break-even

Equation:

$$Q_{Accounting\ Break-even} = \frac{\text{Fixed Costs } (F)}{\text{Price per Unit } (P) - \text{Variable Cost per Unit } (V)}$$

$$= \frac{900,000}{8,000} = 112.5$$

c. Cash Break-even

Equation:

$$Q_{Accounting\ Break-even} = \frac{\text{Fixed Costs }(F) - \text{Depreciation}}{\begin{matrix}\text{Price per} \\ \text{Unit }(P)\end{matrix} - \begin{matrix}\text{Variable Cost} \\ \text{per Unit }(V)\end{matrix}}$$

$$= \frac{(900{,}000 - 100{,}000)}{8{,}000} = 100$$

Step 4: Analyze

The contribution margin of $8,000 per bike requires that Pinkie's sells 113 bikes to break even on an accounting basis and 100 bikes on a cash basis, which excludes the non-cash charge of depreciation.

Self Test 3: Real Options Analysis

Your boss has asked if you could put a real options framework into the firm's employment decision process. Give some examples of using a real options analysis in the firm's hiring and layoff decisions.

Step 1: Picture the Problem

The problem asks for the real options view of risk management.

Step 2: Decide on a Solution Strategy

To solve, we first should examine the three types of real options. Then we should see how employment levels can match those types and what conditions may create those situations.

Step 3: Solve

To solve, we list the three types of real options: timing, expansion, and contraction.

Timing options usually involve delaying investment. In the case of staffing levels, it may be better to not hire immediately as business picks up and instead pay overtime. Some firms may choose to contract out services and functions rather than staff for varying workloads during the year or the business cycle. Firms entering a new market seeking first-mover advantage may see the need to do the opposite, put the people in place ahead of the demand in order to capture a greater percentage of the market. These decisions on timing require a cost-benefit analysis.

The option to expand may cover the simple decision to add a salesperson to a business line that is doing well to adding an entire plant to meet demand. In either case, the firm will choose to maximize NPV based upon improving opportunities.

The option to contract covers small layoffs to align with current demand and profitability to large employment reductions when exiting an entire line of business. If the demand is expected to lag for only a short time, then it may be better to keep staff and delay any layoffs until more information on the market conditions can be collected. The goal in any contraction is to improve the profitability (and perhaps the survivability) of the firm.

Step 4: Analyze

The real options approach can be extended to employee staffing. The options to delay or expand employment are regular features of a firm's operations.

$$= \frac{(\$900{,}000 - 100{,}000)}{8{,}000} = 100$$

Step 4: Analyze

The contribution margin of $8,000 per bike requires that Pinkie's sells [illegible] bikes to break even on an accounting basis, and 100 bikes on a cash basis, which excludes the non-cash charge of depreciation.

CHAPTER 14

The Cost of Capital

Chapter **Orientation**

The cost of capital is the appropriate discount rate for a firm's or an investment's cash flows. Using the appropriate cost of capital allows analysts to determine the proper value of alternatives facing the firm. NPV decisions are greatly impacted by the cost of capital. This chapter presents the methods used to calculate an appropriate cost of capital.

Chapter Review: Terms and Concepts

14.1 The Cost of Capital: An Overview

The cost of capital for a firm is the weighted average of the required returns of the securities that are used to finance the firm. We refer to this as the firm's **Weighted Average Cost of Capital**, or **WACC**. WACC not only incorporates the required rates of return of the firm's lenders and investors but also reflects the financing sources that the firm uses.

Risk affects the firm's WACC two ways: return required on debt and equity will be higher and the amount of debt a firm uses will be affected by the risk level of the firm.

WACC is used to:

Value the firm,

Value projects, and

Evaluate performance.

Investor's Required Return and the Firm's Cost of Capital

For debt costs, the firm can deduct interest payments from taxable income. As a result, the firm's after-tax cost of capital is less than the required return of investors who lend to the firm. The firm's after-tax cost of debt capital is the taxable required return X (1 – tax rate).

WACC Equation

$$\begin{array}{c}\text{Weighted}\\ \text{Average Cost}\\ \text{of Capital } (WACC)\end{array} = \left[\left(\begin{array}{c}\text{After-tax Cost}\\ \text{of Debt } (k_d)\end{array}\right) \times \left(\begin{array}{c}\text{Proportion of}\\ \text{Capital Raised}\\ \text{by Debt } (w_d)\end{array}\right)\right] + \left[\left(\begin{array}{c}\text{Cost of Common}\\ \text{Stock } (k_{cs})\end{array}\right) \times \left(\begin{array}{c}\text{Proportion of}\\ \text{Capital Raised}\\ \text{by Common Stock } (w_{cs})\end{array}\right)\right] \quad (14\text{–}1)$$

Three-Step Procedure for Estimating Firm WACC

Step 1: Define the firm's capital structure. Evaluate the firm's mix of debt and equity financing (commonly referred to as its capital structure) and determine the relative importance of each component in the mix, which is based on the current market value of each source of capital.

Step 2: Estimate the opportunity cost of each of the sources of financing. These costs are equal to the investor's required rates of return after adjusting the cost of debt for the effects of taxes. To estimate these costs, we'll use the current market value of each source of capital based on its current, not historical, costs.

Step 3: Calculate a weighted average of the costs of each source of financing. Finally, we calculate the product of the after-tax costs of each capital source used by the firm and the weights associated with each source. The firm's WACC is a weighted average of the costs of each source of capital used by the firm where the weights capture the relative importance by market value and market rate of each source of capital to the firm's capital structure.

WACC of the Firm:

$$WACC = \underbrace{\left(k_d \times (1-T) \times w_d\right)}_{\text{Weighted After-tax Cost of Debt}} + \underbrace{\left(k_{ps} \times w_{ps}\right)}_{\text{Weighted Cost of Preferred Stock}} + \underbrace{\left(k_{cs} \times w_{cs}\right)}_{\text{Weighted Cost of Common Stock}} \qquad (14\text{–}1)$$

Definitions

- k_d = the *required rate of return on the firm's debt*. Correspondingly, the after-tax cost of debt to the firm is $k_d(1 - T)$.
- T is the firm's marginal tax rate on the firm's taxable income.
- k_{ps} = the *required rate of return of the firm's preferred stockholders* and the cost of preferred equity capital to the firm.
- k_{cs} = the *required rate of return of the firm's common stockholders* and the cost of common equity capital to the firm.
- w_d = the fraction of the firm's total financing that is comprised of debt financing.
- w_{ps} = the proportion of the firm's total financing that is comprised of preferred stock.
- w_{cs} = the proportion of the firm's total financing that is comprised of common stock.

Key Assumptions

- The required rates of return used to estimate the cost of capital to the firm should reflect current market rates of return.
- The firm WACC is assumed to remain constant in the future so that the firm's current capital structure and the costs of each source of capital do not change over time.

The weights used to determine the importance of the firm's sources of capital should reflect the current market value (not historical book value) of each source of capital.

14.2 Determining the Firm's Capital Structure Weights

To assess the firm's capital structure for finding the cost of capital, a manager must know the market value weights of short-term debt, long-term debt, preferred stock, and common stock. As a practical matter, analysts will use the book values for debt since traded prices of debt are rarely found and most debt trades near its accounting value.

Once the weight or percentage of each financing source relative to the total sources is known, then that weight is used with the required rates of return to find the WACC.

$$WACC = \underbrace{\left(k_d \times (1-T) \times w_d\right)}_{\text{Weighted After-tax Cost of Debt}} + \underbrace{\left(k_{ps} \times w_{ps}\right)}_{\text{Weighted Cost of Preferred Stock}} + \underbrace{\left(k_{cs} \times w_{cs}\right)}_{\text{Weighted Cost of Common Stock}}$$

14.3 Estimating the Cost of Individual Sources of Capital

Step two is to estimate the cost of each capital source, debt and equity.

The Cost of Debt

The **cost of debt** is the rate of return the firm's lenders demand when they loan money to the firm. We base our estimate of this rate on the current market value of the firm's debt, which can change over time because of changes in the level of interest rates in the economy as well as changes in the creditworthiness of the firm. This cost is the YTM of newly issued debt not the coupon rate of previously issued debt.

If we cannot solve for a firm's YTM, we can look up the firm's credit rating and see what yields similar firms have to pay on their debt. A sample table:

Three firms are the primary sources of default ratings on corporate debt: Moody's, S&P, and Fitch. Investment grade debt is rated Baa3 and BB- or higher.

Figure 14.2

A Guide to Corporate Bond Ratings

Three firms are the primary sources of default ratings on corporate debt: Moody's, S&P, and Fitch. Investment grade debt is rated Baa3 and BBB– or higher.

Moody's	S&P	Fitch	Definitions
Aaa	AAA	AAA	Prime. Maximum Safety
Aa1	AA+	AA+	High Grade High Quality
Aa2	AA	AA	
Aa3	AA–	AA–	
A1	A+	A+	Upper Medium Grade
A2	A	A	
A3	A–	A–	
Baa1	BBB+	BBB+	Lower Medium Grade
Baa2	BBB	BBB	
Baa3	BBB–	BBB–	
Ba1	BB+	BB+	Non Investment Grade
Ba2	BB	BB	Speculative
Ba3	BB–	BB–	
B1	B+	B+	Highly Speculative
B2	B	B	
B3	B–	B–	
Caa1	CCC+	CCC	Substantial Risk
Caa2	CCC	–	In Poor Standing
Caa3	CCC-	–	
Ca	–	–	Extremely Speculative
C	–	–	May be in Default
–	–	DDD	Default
–	–	DD	
–	D	D	

A sample of yields and credit ratings:

Figure 14.3

Corporate Bond Yields—Default Ratings and Term to Maturity

Yield to maturity for corporate bonds, arrayed by default rating and term to maturity. These data are representative of first quarter 2013, and are typical for this time period. However, you would want to use the most recent data available when analyzing the cost of debt financing. Note that as the credit rating falls, the yield to maturity rises. Also, the yield to maturity typically increases for longer-maturity bonds.

Rating	1 yr	2 yr	3 yr	5 yr	7 yr	10 yr	30 yr
Aaa/AAA	0.22	0.31	0.42	0.76	1.26	2.00	3.41
Aa1/AA+	0.26	0.43	0.58	0.96	1.46	2.17	3.62
Aa2/AA	0.29	0.55	0.74	1.16	1.66	2.35	3.83
Aa3/AA−	0.31	0.58	0.77	1.20	1.70	2.39	3.88
A1/A+	0.32	0.60	0.80	1.23	1.73	2.43	3.93
A2/A	0.55	0.80	0.98	1.40	1.89	2.57	4.03
A3/A−	0.62	0.95	1.18	1.66	2.19	2.92	4.51
Baa1/BBB+	0.83	1.19	1.42	1.91	2.45	3.18	4.80
Baa2/BBB	1.00	1.39	1.65	2.17	2.73	3.48	5.17
Baa3/BBB−	1.49	1.87	2.11	2.62	3.16	3.91	5.56
Ba1/BB+	2.27	2.64	2.90	3.41	3.98	4.75	6.37
Ba2/BB	3.04	3.41	3.68	4.21	4.79	5.58	7.19
Ba3/BB−	3.82	4.18	4.47	5.00	5.61	6.42	8.00
B1/B+	4.60	4.95	5.25	5.79	6.42	7.26	8.82
B2/B	5.38	5.72	6.04	6.59	7.24	8.10	9.63
B3/B−	6.15	6.49	6.82	7.38	8.06	8.93	10.45
Caa/CCC+	6.93	7.26	7.61	8.17	8.87	9.77	11.26
U.S. Treasury Yield	0.18	0.25	0.32	0.60	1.00	1.59	2.76

Legend:

These data are actually reported as "spread to Treasury yields," so for a 30-year Baa1/BBB+ corporate bond the yield would be reported as 204 basis points over the 30-year Treasury yield of 2.76%. A basis point is 1/100th of a percent, so 204 basis points correspond to 2.04%.

The Cost of Preferred Equity

To find the cost of capital on preferred, solve this for k:

$$\text{Preferred Stock Price } (P_{ps}) = \frac{\text{Preferred Dividend } (Div_{ps})}{\text{Preferred Stockholder's Required Rate of Return } (k_{ps})} \quad (14\text{–}2)$$

Or

$$k_{ps} = \frac{Div_{ps}}{P_{ps}} \quad (14\text{–}2a)$$

The Cost of Common Equity

To estimate the cost of capital on common, use either the dividend discount model or the CAPM model:

$$\text{Market Price of Common Stock } (P_{cs}) = \frac{\text{Common Stock Dividend for Year 1 } (D_1)}{\begin{pmatrix}\text{Common Equity Required} \\ \text{Rate of Return } (k_{cs})\end{pmatrix} - \begin{pmatrix}\text{Growth Rate in} \\ \text{Dividends } (g)\end{pmatrix}} \quad (14\text{–}3)$$

The dividend growth model for valuing common stock that was first discussed in Chapter 10 provides a popular basis for estimating the cost of new equity financing (k_{cs}). Solving the valuation equation found in (14–3) produces the cost of common equity equation as follows:

$$k_{cs} = \frac{D_1}{P_{cs}} + g \quad (14\text{–}3\text{a})$$

Definitions:

- $D_1 = D_0(1 + g)$ = the dividend expected to be received by the firm's common shareholders one year in the future. That is, the most recent dividend paid to the common shareholders, D_0, multiplied by one plus the expected rate of growth in dividends, g.
- g = the expected rate of growth in dividends each year forever. This growth rate is expected to be constant for all future years such that the expected dividend in year 1 is equal to the most recent dividend paid (D_0) multiplied by 1 plus the annual rate of growth in dividends (i.e., $D_1 = D_0(1 + g)$. Similarly, the expected dividend in year 2 is equal to $D_2 = D_0(1 + g)^2$.
- k_{cs} = the investor's required rate of return for investing in the firm's shares of common stock.

Key Assumptions:

- The first is that the rate of growth in common stock dividends, g, is the same for all future years.
- Second, this rate of growth in dividends must be less than the rate of return the stockholder requires to invest in the firm's shares. The latter assumption may seem a bit odd, but it is critical and very reasonable once you think about it. For example, how much would you be willing to pay for an investment where the rate of increase in the cash flow you receive each year is greater than the rate of return you want, given the risk of the investment? The answer is that the price could not be high enough. This would be a "money machine"!

Estimating the Growth Rate

The dividend discount model method requires an estimate of the future growth rate in dividends which is usually collected from the market's estimates of future growth, from historical growth rates, or from the analyst's own guess as to the future growth rate.

Pros and Cons of the Dividend Growth Model Approach

The primary appeal of the dividend growth model is its simplicity. To estimate an investor's required rate of return, the analyst needs only to observe the current dividend and stock price and to estimate the rate of growth in future dividends.

Of course, forecasting the growth rate of a firm's dividends is likely to be difficult and subject to errors. Indeed, the examples we have presented here assume that dividends are expected to grow at a constant rate g forever, which is clearly an oversimplification.

The Capital Asset Pricing Model

We determine the risk premium for a particular firm's common equity, by its systematic risk or beta and the market risk premium.

$$\underbrace{\text{Cost of Common Equity } (k_{cs})}_{} = \text{Risk-Free Rate } (r_f) + \overbrace{\text{Equity Beta Coefficient } (\beta_{cs}) \underbrace{\left(\text{Expected Return on the Market Portfolio } (r_m) - \text{Risk Free Rate } (r_f)\right)}_{\text{Market Risk Premium}}}^{\text{Risk Premium for Common Equity } (=\text{ Equity Beta} \times \text{Market Risk Premium})} \tag{14–4}$$

Definitions and important concepts:

- Risk-free rate (r_f) . The rate of return an investor could expect to earn where there is no risk that the return on the investment or the money invested will not be received. Typically, the rate of return on U.S. Treasury securities is used as an estimate of this rate.
- Common stock beta coefficient (β_{cs}). Beta, as we learned in Chapter 8, is a measure of the systematic risk of the common stock's returns. Systematic risk reflects how the returns earned by a risky investment co-vary with the returns earned by the market portfolio of all risky investments.
- Market risk premium ($r_m - r_f$). The difference in the rate of return that an investor expects to earn from investing in the market portfolio comprised of all risky investments and the risk-free rate.

Advantages of the CAPM Approach

The CAPM approach has two important advantages over the dividend growth rate model approach:

- First, the model is simple and easy to understand and calculate since it is simply the sum of two components: the risk-free rate of interest and the firm's risk premium.
- Second, because the model does not rely on dividends or any assumption about the growth rate in dividends, it can be applied to companies that do not currently pay dividends or are not expected to experience a constant rate of growth in dividends.

Disadvantages of the CAPM Approach

The CAPM approach suffers from some important disadvantages that arise because of difficulties in estimating the three variables that determine the cost of common equity (the risk-free rate, the beta coefficient, and the market risk premium).

- Specifying the risk-free rate—The analyst has a wide range of US government securities that can be used as the risk-free rate. It is now customary to use the 10-year Treasury bond rate as the measure of the risk-free rate of return.
- Estimating beta—Analysts can obtain estimates of beta coefficients from a wide variety of investment advisory services, such as Merrill Lynch and Value Line. Alternatively, they can use historical stock market returns for the company of interest and a general market index (such as the Standard and Poor's 500) and estimate the stock's beta. There are slight differences in the methodologies and time periods used to estimate beta, which is why beta estimates from various sources generally differ.
- Estimating the market's risk premium—Finally, the analyst can estimate the market risk premium by looking at the history of stock returns and the premium earned over the risk-free rate of interest. Since 1926, common stocks have earned an average annual return of 12.3 percent, a premium of roughly 6.5 percent over long-term government bonds and 8.6 percent over short-term Treasury Bills. Estimates of the market's risk premium vary widely and have drifted down in recent years. For our purposes we will use an estimate of 5 percent for the market's risk premium.

14.4 Summing Up: Calculating the Firm's WACC

Use Market-Based Weights

Use Market-Based Opportunity Costs

Use Forward-Looking Weights and Opportunity Costs

14.5 Estimating Project Costs of Capital

Firms often use the firm-wide cost of capital to discount investment projects.

The Rationale for Using Multiple Discount Rates

Using a single rate could have the firm accepting too many risky projects and rejecting many safer projects by using a rate that underestimates the former's risk and overestimates the latter's risk.

Why Don't Firms Typically Use Project Costs of Capital?

There are at least two important reasons for sticking with a single discount rate. First, there are technical issues that can potentially make the use of multiple discount rates more trouble than it is worth. For example, individual investment projects, unless they are very large ones, do not have their own capital structure, nor are the sources of capital for the project easily identified or their market prices easily observed.

The second issue that arises with the use of project costs of capital is more subtle and relates to something we will refer to as *influence costs*. These added costs arise as a result of the extra time and effort someone in charge of trying to get a project approved for funding by the firm's upper management spends trying to justify a lower discount rate, as well as the time spent by the firm's managers charged with evaluating the project.

Estimating Divisional WACCs

The approach taken by most firms that undertake investments with very different risk characteristics is to try and isolate their costs of capital for each of their business units or divisions by estimating **divisional WACCs**.

The advantages of using a divisional WACC include the following:

- It provides different discount rates that reflect differences in the systematic risk of the projects evaluated by the different divisions.
- It entails only one cost of capital estimate per division (as opposed to unique discount rates for each project), thereby minimizing the time and effort of estimating the cost of capital.

The use of a common discount rate throughout the division limits managerial latitude and the attendant influence costs.

Using Pure Play Firms to Estimate Divisional WACCs

One approach that can be taken to deal with differences in the costs of capital for each of the firm's business units involves identifying what we will call "pure play" comparison firms (or comps) that operate in only one of the individual business areas (where possible). For example, ExxonMobil (XOM) is a fully integrated oil company that engages in everything from the exploration and production of oil to its refining and sale. Specifically, the firm has three different business units:

- Upstream—the unit that is involved in searching for oil and gas, drilling exploratory wells, operating wells and recovering the oil and gas deposits.

- Downstream—Refining of crude oil into a variety of products including such things as gasoline, jet fuel, and diesel fuel.
- Chemicals—the conversion of petroleum into plastics, fertilizers, pesticides, pharmaceuticals and other byproducts.

To estimate the cost of capital for each of these different types of activities we use the WACCs for these comparison firms that are not fully integrated and operate in only one of ExxonMobil's business segments.

Divisional WACC—Estimation Issues and Limitations

Although the divisional WACC is generally a significant improvement over the single, company-wide WACC, the way that it is often implemented using industry-based comparison firms has a number of potential shortcomings:

- The sample of firms in a given industry may include firms that are not good matches for the firm or one of its divisions. The firm's management can easily address this problem by selecting appropriate comparison firms with similar risk profiles from among the many included in these industries.
- The division being analyzed may not have a capital structure that is similar to the sample of firms in the industry data.
- The firms in the chosen industry that are used to proxy for divisional risk may not be good reflections of project risk.
- Good comparison firms for a particular division may be difficult to find. Most publicly traded firms report multiple lines of business.

The preceding discussion suggests that although the use of divisional WACCs to determine project discount rates may represent an improvement over the use of a company-wide WACC, this methodology is far from perfect. However, if the firm has investment opportunities with risks that vary principally with industry-risk characteristics, the use of a divisional WACC has clear advantages over the use of the firm's WACC.

14.6 Floatation Costs and Project NPV

Firms should consider the cost of raising capital, the floatation costs.

The floatation cost as a percentage:

$$\begin{matrix}\text{Weighted Average}\\ \text{Flotation Cost}\end{matrix} = \left(w_d \times \begin{matrix}\text{Flotation Cost}\\ \text{of Debt as a percent}\end{matrix}\right) + \left(w_{cs} \times \begin{matrix}\text{Flotation Cost}\\ \text{of Equity as a percent}\end{matrix}\right) \tag{14–5}$$

The total amount of capital needed including floatation costs:

$$\begin{matrix}\text{Flotation Cost Adjusted}\\ \text{Initial Outlay}\end{matrix} = \frac{\begin{matrix}\text{Financing}\\ \text{Needed}\end{matrix}}{\left(1 - \begin{matrix}\text{Flotation Cost}\\ \text{as a percent}\end{matrix}\right)} \tag{14–6}$$

NPV should be adjusted for the costs of floating new securities.

Answers to **Concept Checks**

Concept Check **14.1**

1. How is an investor's required rate of return related to the firm's cost of capital?
2. Why is the firm's cost of capital calculated as a weighted average?
3. List the three-step procedure used to estimate a firm's weighted average cost of capital.

Answer 1: An investor's cost of capital matches the firm's cost of capital for equity risk but the firm's after-tax cost of capital is lower than the investor's by (1 – tax rate).

Answer 2: The firm's cost of capital is a blend of its sources of financing by their market weight times the cost for each source, a weighted average.

Answer 3: The three steps to estimate the firm's weighted average cost of capital are

Define the firm's Capital Structure

Estimate the Opportunity Cost of Capital for each and

Calculate the weighted average cost of capital.

Concept Check **14.2**

1. Should book or market values be used to determine the weights used in calculating the WACC? Explain.
2. Why are accounts payable not included in the capital structure used to estimate a firm's WACC?

Answer 1: Market values are used to find the appropriate weight on financing structure since market value represents the current importance of each financing choice at the time of the analysis.

Answer 2: Accounts payable arise out of the operations of the firm and are already embedded in those costs so counting them would be double-counting.

Concept Check **14.3**

1. How can we estimate the cost of new debt financing?
2. How is the cost of new preferred stock estimated?
3. Describe the two approaches that can be taken to estimate the cost of common equity.

Answer 1: Find the YTM of currently traded debt or find the firm's credit rating and the corresponding credit spread over treasuries.

Answer 2: Preferred stock dividend divided by the market price of preferred.

Answer 3: The first approach uses the Dividend Discount Model and the second uses the CAPM model to estimate the cost of capital for common equity.

Concept Check **14.4**

1. Why do we use market values as the basis for calculating the weights used in calculating WACC?

2. Why are current costs and required rates of return used when estimating a firm's WACC instead of historical costs?

Answer 1: Market values are used to find the appropriate weight on financing structure since market value represents the current importance of each financing choice at the time of the analysis.

Answer 2: Current costs of debt and equity give the best representation of what a project will cost at the time of the analysis.

Concept Check **14.5**

1. What is the main problem that firms encounter when using the firm's WACC as the cost of capital for all their investment analyses?

2. What are divisional WACCs and how do they address the problems encountered in using a single company-wide WACC?

Answer 1: A single WACC can be lower than the appropriate discount rate, accepting too many bad projects or it can be higher than the appropriate discount rate, rejecting too many good projects.

Answer 2: Divisional WACCs help the firm use a more appropriate discount rate for different operations of the firm with differing risk levels.

Concept Check **14.6**

1. What are flotation costs and how do they affect a firm's cost of raising capital?
2. How can flotation costs be incorporated into project analysis?

Answer 1: Floatation costs are the costs associated with issuing debt and equity to make an investment. Floatation costs increase the costs of capital and lower NPV.

Answer 2: Floatation costs are calculated based on the weighted average of debt and equity costs in percentage and the total financing is increased by dividing by (1 – floating %).

Multiple Choice **Quiz**

1. The cost of capital represents
   a. the firm's discount rate.
   b. a weighted average cost of capital.
   c. the opportunity cost to common shareholders.
   d. the required rate on preferred stock.

2. The WACC represents
   a. the firm's discount rate.
   b. a weighted average cost of capital.
   c. the opportunity cost to common shareholders.
   d. the required rate on preferred stock.

3. The cost of debt represents
   a. the firm's discount rate.
   b. a required rate of return on fixed income financing.
   c. the opportunity cost to common shareholders.
   d. the required rate on preferred stock.

4. The cost of equity capital represents
   a. the firm's discount rate.
   b. a required rate of return on fixed income financing.
   c. the opportunity cost to common shareholders.
   d. the required rate on preferred stock.

5. The cost of preferred equity is typically
   a. the firm's discount rate.
   b. a required rate of return on fixed income financing.
   c. the opportunity cost to common shareholders.
   d. the required rate on preferred stock.

6. The divisional cost of capital represents
   a. the firm's discount rate.
   b. a required rate of return on a project.
   c. the opportunity cost to shareholders.
   d. the required rate on a specific unit of the firm.

7. Floatation cost represents
   a. payments for interest.
   b. payments incurred when issuing securities for financing.
   c. payments for dividends.
   d. payments to preferred holders.

8. The proper weights to use in a WACC calculation are
   a. historical values.
   b. accounting values.
   c. the greater of historical or accounting values.
   d. market values.

9. The proper capital costs to use in a WACC calculation are
   a. historical interest rates.
   b. short-term rates today.
   c. forward-looking opportunity costs of capital over the life of the project.
   d. the real return rates without inflation adjustment for the project.

10. Which is not a challenge or problem for the CAPM approach:
   a. does not use dividends.
   b. specifying the risk-free rate.
   c. estimating beta.
   d. estimating the market's risk premium.

Answers to **Multiple Choice Questions**

1. A
2. B
3. B
4. C
5. D
6. D
7. B
8. D
9. C
10. A

Self Test **with Solutions**

Picture the Problem

Decide on Solution Strategy

Solve

Analyze

Self Test 1: Weighted Average Cost of Capital

Bobby Jones Golf Apparel wished to determine its cost of capital and provided you with several items of data. What is the WACC for the firm?

Bobby Jones Accounting Data:

Sales:	$40,000,000	Net Income:	$10,000,000
Assets:	$20,000,000	Long-term Debt	$10,000,000
Equity	$10,000,000	Outstanding shares	1,000,000

Bobby Jones Market Data:

Risk-free rate	4%	Beta of equity:	1.20
Return on market	10%	Share Price	$30
Rate on firm's debt	6%	Tax rate	35%

Step 1: Picture the Problem

The problem calculates asks for the weighted average cost of capital using data provided by the firm. The weighted average cost of capital combines the after-tax cost of financing for each of the firm's sources of capital in a weighted average where the weights are proportionate to the relative importance of each source of financing in the firm's capital structure (by using market—not book—values).

Step 2: Decide on a Solution Strategy

To calculate the weighted average, we sum the products of the after-tax cost of each source of financing multiplied by its corresponding capital structure weight:

$$WACC = \left(k_d \times (1-T) \times w_d\right) + \left(k_{ps} \times w_{ps}\right) + \left(k_{cs} \times w_{cs}\right)$$

where k_d is the required rate of return on the firm's debt; k_{ps} is the rate of return required by the firm's preferred stockholders; k_{cs} is the rate of return required by the firm's common stockholders; T is the firm's marginal tax rate on corporate income; w_d is the fraction of the firm's total financing that has been raised by borrowing; w_{ps} is the proportion of the firm's total financing consisting of preferred stock; and w_{cs} is the proportion of the firm's total financing consisting of common stock.

Step 3: Solve

$$WACC = \left(k_d \times (1-T) \times w_d\right) + \left(k_{ps} \times w_{ps}\right) + \left(k_{cs} \times w_{cs}\right)$$

To find the weights or fraction of debt, preferred and common, use the market values of each if available. Debt value is \$10,000,000 (no market value available). Preferred equity is \$0. Common equity is market price X shares outstanding or \$30,000,000.

So the weight of debt equals \$10,000,000 / \$40,000,000 or ¼ and the equity weight is 3/4s.

Next we need to find the cost of capital for each source of financing.

Rate on debt 6% Cost of preferred N/A Rate on common?

To find the cost of common equity, use the CAPM formula for cost of equity. To use CAPM, use the risk free rate, the return on the market, and the firm's beta:

Cost of common equity:

$$(k_{cs}) = r_f + \beta_{cs}(r_m - r_f) = 4\% + 1.20\ (10\% - 4\%) = 11.20\%$$

Plugging into our WACC formula:

$$WACC = \left(.06 \times (1-.35) \times .25\right) + \left(.112 \times .75\right) = 9.375\%$$

Step 4: Analyze

Debt lowers the weighted average cost of capital of the firm to 9.375 percent using market weights and rates where possible.

Self Test 2: Flotation Costs

Bobby Jones has looked into raising \$10,000,000 in capital with 25 percent debt and 75 percent equity. The estimated floatation costs of debt run 3 percent and for equity they are 8 percent. How much should Bobby Jones raise if the firm wants to have \$10,000,000 in net proceeds after costs?

Step 1: Picture the Problem

The problem requires the analyst to find the average floatation cost prior to finding the gross proceeds needed to solve the problem.

Step 2: Decide on a Solution Strategy

To solve the problem, use the two floatation cost formulas: one for average costs and one for floatation proceeds. The firm will need to raise more than $10,000,000 depending on the mix of financing and the cost of floatation.

Step 3: Solve

To solve for the future weighted average cost of floatation,

$$\text{Weighted Average Flotation Cost} = w_d \times \begin{matrix}\text{Flotation Cost}\\ \text{of Debt as a percent}\end{matrix} + w_{cs} \times \begin{matrix}\text{Flotation Cost}\\ \text{of Equity as a percent}\end{matrix}$$
$$= .25 \times .03 + .75 \times .08 = .0675 \text{ or } 6.75\%$$

To solve for the gross proceeds,

$$\begin{matrix}\text{Flotation Cost}\\ \text{Adjusted Initial Outlay}\end{matrix} = \frac{\text{Financing Needed}}{\left(1 - \begin{matrix}\text{Flotation Cost}\\ \text{as a percent}\end{matrix}\right)}$$
$$= \frac{10{,}000{,}000}{(1 - .0675)} = \$10{,}723{,}861$$

Step 4: Analyze

By raising $10.723 million, Bobby Jones can pay for the floatation costs and have $10 million left for investment. Any new project requiring $10 million in funds also needs to produce an NPV that covers the $723,861 in floatation costs. Note that 6.75 percent of $10 million is not enough to cover the floatation as the extra funds raised also must pay floatation costs: $2.5M X 3% + $7.5M X 8% = $6.75M.

Self Test 3: Cost of Capital by Security

Bobby Jones Golf Apparel's CFO examines the following market conditions when analyzing the cost of capital on debt, preferred, and common stock.

a. Find the cost of its debt after raising capital.

b. Find the cost of preferred after raising capital.

c. Find the cost of common equity after raising capital.

Market data:

Long-term Treasury YTM	5.2%
Long-term Market Return	11%
Bobby Jones credit rating before issue	AA
Bobby Jones credit rating after issue	A
Bobby Jones tax rate	35%
Preferred stock of AA rated firms had a median dividend of $4 and a price of $60	
Preferred stock of A rated firms had a median dividend of $5 and a price of $65	
Beta common equity	1.5
Credit spread AA	30bp
Credit spread A	50bp

Step 1: Picture the Problem

The problem asks for the cost of debt capital, preferred stock, and common equity after the rating change created by the capital issue.

Step 2: Decide on a Solution Strategy

The cost of any source of capital should reflect the risk of the firm, the tax treatment of the security, and the priority of that security in case of financial distress. The cost of capital also should be forward-looking.

Step 3: Solve

a. To solve for the cost of debt, the corporate yield will be a Treasury yield plus a spread and adjusted for tax benefits:

$$\text{Corporate debt YTM} = (\text{Treasury YTM} + \text{credit spread}) \text{ X } (1 - \text{tax rate})$$

$$\text{Corporate debt YTM} = (.052 + .005) \text{ X } (1 - .35) = 3.705\%$$

b. To solve for the cost of preferred stock, compare to similar preferred from firms with a similar credit rating. Note that preferred dividends are not tax preferred.

Preferred credit rating A

$$\text{Cost of preferred stock } (k_{ps}) = \frac{\text{Preferred stock dividend}}{\text{Price per preferred share}}$$

$$\text{Cost of preferred stock } (k_{ps}) = \frac{\$5}{\$65} = .077 = 7.7\%$$

c. To solve for the cost of common equity which has no tax preference, use CAPM:

$$\text{Cost of common equity } (k_{cs}) = r_f + \beta_{cs}(r_m - r_f) = 5.2\% + 1.5\,(.11 - .052) = 13.90\%$$

Step 4: Analyze

The capital issue results in a A-rating and the costs of debt are 3.705 percent, the costs of preferred are 7.7 percent, and the costs of common equity are 13.90 percent. When each security goes lower in the priority of claims due to financial distress, the cost of capital rises.

CHAPTER 15

Capital Structure Policy

Chapter **Orientation**

A firm's choice of capital structure, the mix of debt and equity, may influence cash flows. If so, then capital structure policy affects valuation. There are some cases when the choice of capital structure may be irrelevant. This chapter covers the policy choices and effects.

Chapter Review: **Terms and Concepts**

15.1 A Glance at Capital Structure Choices in Practice

The primary goal of capital structure choice is to maximize firm value and the value of shareholder's equity. The mix that increases shareholder's value the most is known as the optimal capital structure.

Defining a Firm's Capital Structure

Capital structure is a subset of the firm's financial structure, which includes accounts payable and accrued expenses in addition to the capital structure securities used to finance the firm.

The debt ratio describes this financial structure: Debt ratio = Total Liabilities / Total Assets (15–1)

The debt-to-enterprise-value ratio describes the capital structure:

$$\text{Debt-to-Enterprise Value} = \frac{\begin{matrix}\text{Book Value of}\\\text{Interest-Bearing Debt}\end{matrix} - \text{Excess Cash}}{\left(\begin{matrix}\text{Book Value of}\\\text{Interest-Bearing Debt}\end{matrix} - \begin{matrix}\text{Excess}\\\text{Cash}\end{matrix}\right) + \begin{matrix}\text{Market Value}\\\text{of Equity}\end{matrix}} = \frac{\text{Net Debt}}{\text{Enterprise Value}} \quad (15\text{–}3)$$

Since market value of debt is not usually observable, the book value is used in the denominator.

The Times Interest Earned Ratio measures the ability to pay debt:

$$\text{Times Interest Earned Ratio} = \frac{\text{Net Operating Income or EBIT}}{\text{Interest Expense}} \quad (15\text{–}4)$$

Financial Leverage

Debt that is fixed enhances returns to equity when returns are good (favorable) and magnifies losses to equity when returns are bad (unfavorable). Financial leverage increases volatility.

How Do Firms in Different Industries Finance Their Assets?

It is normal for firms to choose different levels of debt:

Figure 15.1

Debt-to-Enterprise-Value Ratios for Selected Industries

Average debt-to-enterprise-value ratios for firms in selected industries. Net debt includes only the book value of interest-bearing short- and long-term debt of the firm less excess cash. Note that we have assumed excess cash to be zero. We measure the enterprise value of the firm as the sum of the book value of the firm's interest-bearing debt less excess cash plus the market value of its equity.*

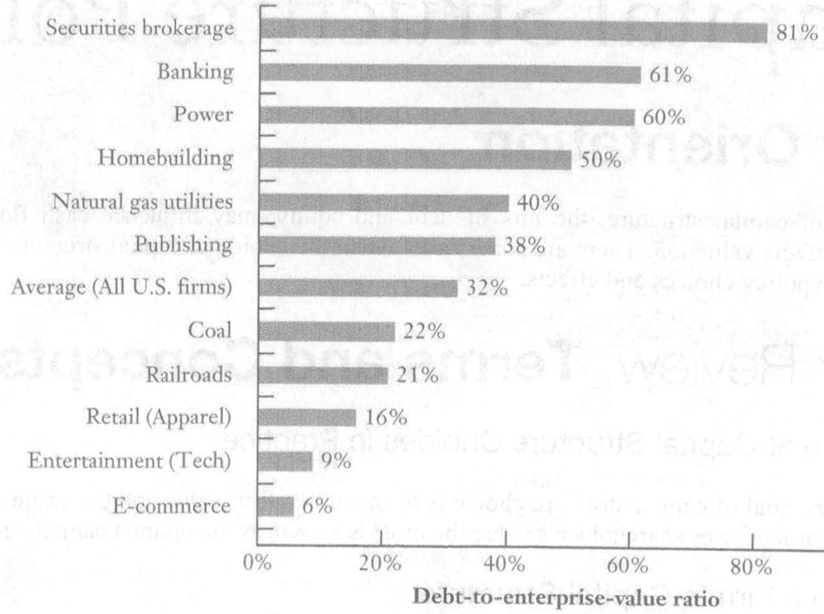

*Because of the difficulty in calculating excess cash, we have assumed excess cash to be zero in these calculations.

15.2 Capital Structure Theory

A First Look at the Modigliani and Miller Capital Structure Theorem

Franco Modigliani and Merton Miller's (M&M) analysis of the capital structure choice, which contributed to the Nobel Prizes for each of the authors, provides us with the conditions under which the capital structure decision has no influence on a firm's value. This result is so important to the study of finance that it bears repeating: *M&M showed that under some idealistic conditions that it does not matter whether a firm uses no debt, a little debt, or a lot of debt in its capital structure.*

M&M's capital structure theory relies upon two basic assumptions:

- Cash flows are not affected by the choice of financing.
- Financial markets are perfect.

If cash flows do not change and it is costless to switch between equity and debt, then the capital structure choice doesn't matter: firm value is independent of the choice.

Capital Structure, Cost of Equity, and the Weighted Average Cost of Capital

Cost of Equity:

$$\text{Cost of Equity (or } k_e) = k_{\text{unlevered}} + (k_{\text{unlevered}} - k_d)\left(\frac{D}{E}\right) = .10 + (.10 - .08) \times 1.0 = .12 \text{ or } 12\%$$

Cost of equity increases proportionately with debt while overall WACC stays the same.

Why Capital Structure Matters in Reality

Capital structure matters to financial managers because poor structure choices do harm shareholders. Since transaction costs are not zero (imperfect markets), the choice of financing does matter. Cash flows also change because interest payments by the firm are tax deductible while dividend payments are not. Also, cash flows can change in the case of bankruptcy due to the costs of bankruptcy. The threat of bankruptcy can lower cash flows from clients and suppliers.

Corporate Taxes and Corporate Structure. Debt interest payments create interest tax savings for the firm in the form of lower corporate income taxes.

$$\begin{bmatrix}\text{Cash flow to}\\ \text{a firm with}\\ \text{financial leverage}\end{bmatrix} = \begin{bmatrix}\text{Cash flow to}\\ \text{the firm without}\\ \text{leverage}\end{bmatrix} + \begin{bmatrix}\text{Interest}\\ \text{tax}\\ \text{savings}\end{bmatrix} \quad (15\text{–}7)$$

This increases the preference for debt.

Corporate Taxes and the WACC. The interest tax savings lowers the WACC of the firm. Firms prefer to use debt.

$$k_{wacc} = \left[\begin{matrix}\text{Cost of}\\ \text{Debt } (k_d)\end{matrix}\left(1 - \begin{matrix}\text{Tax}\\ \text{Rate}\end{matrix}\right) \times \begin{matrix}\text{Debt to}\\ \text{Value } (D/V)\end{matrix}\right] + \left[\begin{matrix}\text{Cost of}\\ \text{Equity } (k_e)\end{matrix} \times \begin{matrix}\text{Equity to}\\ \text{Value } (E/V)\end{matrix}\right]$$

$$\text{Cost of Equity (or } k_e) = k_{\text{Unlevered Equity}} + (k_{\text{Unlevered Equity}} - k_d)\left(\frac{D}{E}\right)$$

Bankruptcy and Financial Distress Costs. Failure to meet debt obligations is financial distress that is very costly to investors, suppliers, creditors, and the firm. Debt and especially high levels of debt can limit financial flexibility.

Tradeoff Theory and the Optimal Capital Structure

Two key items that affect firm value and capital structure:

- Interest expense is tax deductible.
- Debt increases the likelihood of financial distress and its costs.

As a result, there should be an optimal tradeoff of benefits and costs.

Capital Structure Decisions and Agency Costs

Debt can limit a manager's ability to make poor decisions with the firm's cash flow and so it is a tool to lower agency costs.

Making Financing Choices When Managers are Better Informed than Shareholders

Myers states that firms rely on

- Internally generated funds first
- Available cash
- Issue debt and then hybrid debts such as convertible bonds
- Issue equity as a last resort.

Managerial Implications

Higher levels of debt benefit firms due to the tax deductibility of interest and by aligning managers with shareholders.

Higher levels of debt increase the probability of financial distress and its costs.

15.3 Why Do Capital Structures Differ Across Industries?

The benefits of debt differ across industries. Some industries, such as technology, would be greatly impacted by financial distress costs through the loss of customers and suppliers. More profitable, stable industries receive the greatest benefit from interest tax savings.

15.4 Making Financing Decisions

Managers usually compare the firm with the industry debt average, consider the impact on earnings and earnings volatility, the risk of default, the tax savings, and the costs of any increased probability of default.

Benchmarking the Firm's Capital Structure

Benchmarking is a starting point for analysis after comparing the firm to its industry.

Firms can be compared using the debt ratio, the interest bearing debt ratio, the **EBITDA coverage ratio**, and other ratios linked to capital structure. Benchmarking is a tool to compare the firm's ratios before a change in financing and after an increase in either debt and/or equity financing, and with the industry average.

Evaluating the Effect of Financial Leverage on Firm Earnings Per Share

The increased volatility of earnings is the financial leverage effect.

Financial Leverage and the Level of EPS

The key for financial leverage to benefit favorably is that the firm has to earn at a higher rate than the cost of financing for shareholder's to benefit with a higher level of EPS. If the firm earns a lower rate than the cost of financing, earnings will be worse.

Financial Leverage and the Volatility of EPS

Since leverage can create earners that are greater or less than the non-levered earnings, the volatility of the firm's earnings increases with debt.

Using the EBIT-EPS Chart to Analyze the Effect of Capital Structure on EPS

The EBIT-EPS Chart is a tool to compare the EPS (earnings) under different financing plans (leverage effect) for different levels of EBIT (operating performance).

Figure 15.7

EBIT-EPS chart for the House of Toast, Inc.: Under New Financing

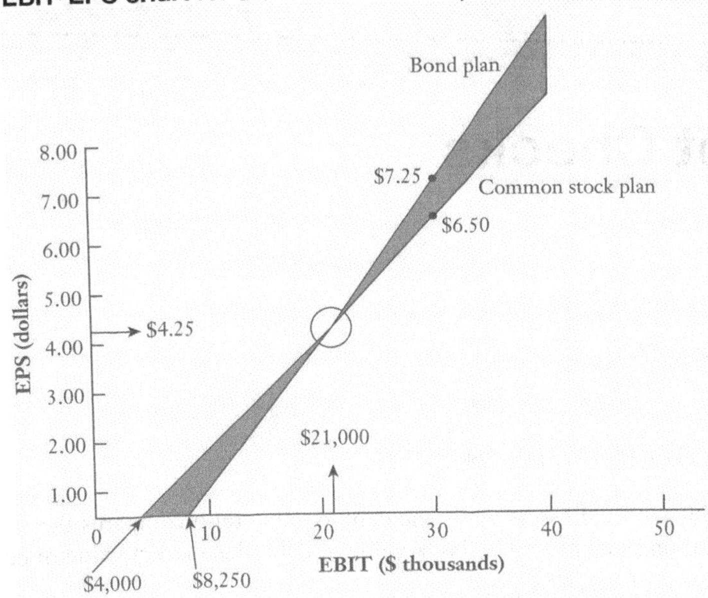

	Earnings per Share	
EBIT	Common Stock Financing	Debt Financing
$ 4,000	0	(1.42)
8,250	1.06	0
20,000	**4.00**	**3.92**
21,000	4.25	4.25
30,000	6.50	7.25
40,000	**9.00**	**10.58**

Computing the EPS Indifference Points for Capital Structure Alternatives

The EBIT level that has the two financing alternatives that deliver the same EPS is called the EPS-EBIT indifference point. The firm can choose either financing plan at that point.

The formula to find the EPS-EBIT indifference point:

$$\underbrace{\frac{(\text{EBIT} - \text{Interest Expense}_{\text{Stock Plan}})(1 - \text{Tax Rate})}{\text{Shares Outstanding (Stock Plan)}}}_{\text{EPS for the Stock Plan}} = \underbrace{\frac{(\text{EBIT} - \text{Interest Expense}_{\text{Bond Plan}})(1 - \text{Tax Rate})}{\text{Shares Outstanding (Bond Plan)}}}_{\text{EPS for the Bond Plan}} \quad (15\text{–}11)$$

Note that EPS should not be the determinant of the appropriate capital structure choice.

Can the Firm Afford More Debt?

Financing ratios tell managers how much debt is appropriate.

$$\text{Times Interest Earned} = \frac{\text{Operating Income or EBIT}}{\text{Interest Expense}}$$

$$\text{EBITDA Coverage Ratio} = \frac{\begin{matrix}\text{Earnings before} \\ \text{Interest and Taxes}\end{matrix} + \begin{matrix}\text{Depreciation} \\ \text{Expense}\end{matrix}}{\text{Interest Expense} + \text{Principal Payments}}$$

$$= \frac{\text{EBITDA}}{\text{Interest Expense} + \text{Principal Payments}}$$

Survey Evidence: Factors that Influence CFO Debt Policy

In order of importance, the following factors mattered to managers:

- Financial flexibility
- Credit rating
- Cash flow and earnings volatility
- Tax deductibility of interest expense

Answers to **Concept Checks**

Concept Check **15.1**

1. How does the debt ratio differ from the debt to value ratio?
2. What does the times interest earned ratio measure?
3. What is financial leverage?
4. What determines whether financial leverage is favorable or unfavorable?

Answer 1: The debt ratio compares total liabilities to total assets while the debt to value ratio compares the value of interest bearing liabilities to total firm capitalization as measured by book value of debt plus market value of equity.

Answer 2: The times interest earned ratio measures the firm's ability to make interest payments by comparing EBIT to interest expense.

Answer 3: Financial leverage is the firm's capital structure or mix of debt and equity financing. By increasing the percentage of debt in the firm's mix of financing, the firm can lever its rate of return above the return earned using only equity financing so long as the firm earns more than the cost of debt financing.

Answer 4: If the firm's return exceeds the cost of debt, then financial leverage is favorable and if the firm earns less than the cost of debt, financial leverage is unfavorable.

Concept Check **15.2**

1. Who were the financial economists that in 1958 challenged the importance of capital structure management? What is the essence of their theory of capital structure?
2. Discuss the role of the following factors on the firm's capital structure decision: taxes, bankruptcy costs, managerial incentives, and how well-informed managers are compared to stockholders.

Answer 1: Modigliani and Miller identified the assumptions necessary to make the choice of financing irrelevant as well as the factors that influence the value of the firm when the capital structure of the firm is altered. If cash flows are not altered by the choice of capital structure and if markets are perfect, then the firm's capital structure is irrelevant to firm value.

Answer 2: Taxes lower the cost of debt financing relative to equity financing and increase firm value. Bankruptcy costs lower the value of debt financing and firm value. Managerial incentives align managers with shareholders by reducing agency costs and increase firm value. Investors believe managers are better informed on valuation and prospects and so they are skeptical when equity is issued, so firms prefer to issue debt in this case.

Concept Check 15.3

1. What are some reasons for firms in different industries to have different capital structures?

Answer 1: The benefits of debt differ across industries. Some industries, such as technology, would be greatly impacted by financial distress costs through the loss of customers and suppliers. More profitable, stable industries receive the greatest benefit from interest tax savings. Industries also differ in the ability of lenders to attach liens to property owned by the firm to secure debts.

Concept Check 15.4

1. In what ways does the firm's capital structure affect its earnings per share?
2. What is the EBIT-EPS indifference point, and how is this concept useful in analyzing a capital structure decision?
3. How are various leverage ratios and industry norms used in capital structure management?

Answer 1: Capital structure or leverage can increase earnings if the firm performs well and substantially decrease earnings if the firm does not exceed its cost of debt capital. Leverage increases earnings and cash flow volatility.

Answer 2: The EBIT-EPS indifference point shows the level of EBIT (operating performance) that generates the same EPS under either financing structure choice. At EBIT above the indifference point, more leverage will generate higher earnings and below the point, less leverage is better.

Answer 3: The times interest earned ratio shows the firm's ability to pay interest expense and is a measure of accounting earnings available to pay interest. The EBITDA Coverage ratio shows the cash flow available to pay interest by adding back depreciation. By benchmarking the ratios those of industry peers, a firm's managers can evaluate the firm's financial position and identify areas that might require additional analysis.

Multiple Choice Quiz

1. Agency costs are
   a. borne by shareholders.
   b. borne by managers.
   c. borne by debt owners.
   d. borne by government regulators.

2. Benchmarking of capital structure choices
   a. compares a firm to its history.
   b. compares a firm to its peers.
   c. compares a firm to the market.
   d. compares a firm to a random sort of firms.

3. The primary difference between the interest coverage and the EBITDA ratio is
   a. only interest coverage considers debt.
   b. only EBITDA considers debt.
   c. EBITDA resembles cash flow flexibility.
   d. interest coverage resembles cash flow flexibility.

4. Financial distress costs
   a. occur when a firm lends to risky borrowers.
   b. occur only when accounts receivable are not collected.
   c. occur only when accounts payable are not collected.
   d. occur when a firm is unable to meet debt obligations.

5. Internal sources of financing are
   a. raised by issuing debt.
   b. raised from cash flow and cash on hand.
   c. raised by issuing equity.
   d. raised from cash dividends.

6. Unfavorable financial leverage effect occurs when
   a. the firm earns more than its cost of debt capital.
   b. the firm earns only its weighted average cost of capital.
   c. the firm earns a debt rate of return.
   d. the firm earns less than its cost of debt capital.

7. Financial leverage effect
   a. increases earnings and cash flow volatility.
   b. decreases earnings.
   c. increases cash flow.
   d. increases earnings while decreasing cash flow.

8. The interest bearing debt ratio measures a firm's financing mix and is the ratio of
   a. total liabilities to cash flow.
   b. interest bearing debt to cash flow.
   c. interest bearing debt to total assets.
   d. total liabilities to total fixed assets.

9. Optimal capital structure
   a. provides the greatest value to shareholders.
   b. provides the highest EPS.
   c. reduces the value of equity.
   d. reduces the value of debt.

10. An EBIT-EPS chart shows the EBIT levels,
    a. that if higher than the indifference point will benefit from less firm leverage.
    b. that if lower than the indifference point will benefit from more firm leverage.
    c. that if higher than the indifference point will benefit from more firm leverage.
    d. that if lower than the indifference point will have the same firm EPS.

Answers to **Multiple Choice Questions**

1. A
2. B
3. C
4. D
5. B
6. D
7. A
8. C
9. A
10. C

Self Test **with Solutions**

Picture the Problem

Decide on Solution Strategy

Solve

Analyze

Self Test 1: Interest Coverage and EBITDA Coverage Ratios

You are trying to determine the financial position of Trick Knee, Inc, a medical device company in Las Vegas. Describe their financial flexibility using the ratios and information below.

a. interest coverage,

b. the debt to value, and

c. the debt ratio.

Medical Equipment Industry			
Debt Ratio	0.50	EBITDA Interest Coverage Ratio	6.00
Debt to Value	0.40	Interest Coverage	7.50
Trick Knee Financial Data:			
Cash	1,000,000	Accounts Payable	3,000,000
Accounts Receivable	5,000,000	Accrued Expenses	1,000,000
Inventory	4,000,000	Short-term Notes	4,000,000
PPE	9,000,000	Long-term Debt	7,000,000
		Common Equity	4,000,000
Total Assets	19,000,000	Total Liabilities and Equity	19,000,000
Revenues	30,000,000		
EBIT	15,000,000		
EBITDA	12,000,000		
Interest Expense	1,000,000		
Principal Payment	500,000		

Step 1: Picture the Problem

The problem calculates debt and interest coverage ratios to determine the financial position of the firm.

Step 2: Decide on a Solution Strategy

To solve the first part, use the two interest coverage ratios. To solve the second part, use the debt to value ratio. To solve the last part, use the debt ratio.

Step 3: Solve

The times interest earned ratio:

$$\text{Times Interest Earned Ratio} = \frac{\text{Operating Income or EBIT}}{\text{Interest Expense}}$$
$$= \frac{15,000,000}{1,000,000} = 15$$

The EBITDA interest coverage ratio:

$$\text{EBITDA Coverage Ratio} = \frac{\begin{matrix}\text{Earnings before} \\ \text{Interest and Taxes}\end{matrix} + \begin{matrix}\text{Depreciation} \\ \text{Expense}\end{matrix}}{\text{Interest Expense} + \text{Principal Payments}}$$
$$= \frac{12,000,000}{1,500,000} = 8.0$$

The Debt ratio:

$$\text{Debt Ratio} = \frac{\text{Total Liabilities}}{\text{Total Assets}}$$
$$= \frac{15,000,000}{19,000,000} = .789$$

The Debt to Value ratio:

$$\text{Debt to Value Ratio} = \frac{\text{Total Book Value of Interest Bearing Debt}}{\text{Book Value of Interest Bearing Debt} + \text{Market Value of Equity}}$$
$$= \frac{11,000,000}{15,000,000} = .733$$

(Accrued Expenses and A/P are not interest bearing debts, so $4 million is subtracted.)

Step 4: Analyze

Trick Knee has excellent coverage ratios. The interest coverage ratio is 15X compared to the industry ratio of 7.5X and the EBITDA coverage ratio is 8X, compared to 6X for the industry. The debt ratio is .79 and the debt to value ratio is .73 compared to .50 and .40 for the industry. The firm relies on more interesting bearing debt than the industry but is more profitable and perhaps financed with a different maturity and rate than the typical industry firm so its coverage ratios compare favorably.

Self Test 2: EBIT-EPS and Indifference Point Analysis

You are tasked with analyzing two capital structure scenarios for your business. You would like to determine whether you should increase leverage to continue investment in your business or decrease leverage by using equity or internal funds.

a. Looking at the data below, should you increase leverage?

b. What is the EBIT indifference point for this firm?

	Firm Scenario 1	**Firm Scenario 2**
EBIT	\$10,000,000	\$10,000,000
Interest Expense	\$1,000,000	\$2,000,000
EBT	\$9,000,000	\$8,000,000
Tax 40%	\$3,600,000	\$3,200,000
Net Income	\$5,400,000	\$4,800,000
Shares	100,000	80,000

Step 1: Picture the Problem

The problem examines the impact of additional debt and interest expense on earnings. EBIT-EPS analysis will provide answers to these types of decisions.

Step 2: Decide on a Solution Strategy

To solve the first part, we should examine how earnings per share changed after the firm issued more debt and bought back shares. To solve the second part, use the EBIT-EPS indifference point formula.

Step 3: Solve

a. To find EPS, divide net income by outstanding shares:

Scenario 1	Scenario 2
EPS = \$5,400,000 / 100,000 = \$54	EPS = \$4,800,000 / 80,000 = \$60

b. To find the indifference point, use the EBIT-EPS indifference formula:

$$\underset{\text{Scenario 1}}{\frac{(\text{EBIT} - \text{Interest Expense}_{\text{Stock Plan}})(1 - \text{Tax Rate})}{\text{Shares Outstanding (Stock Plan)}}} = \underset{\text{Scenario 2}}{\frac{(\text{EBIT} - \text{Interest Expense}_{\text{Bond Plan}})(1 - \text{Tax Rate})}{\text{Shares Outstanding (Bond Plan)}}}$$

$$\frac{(EBIT - \$1,000,000)(1 - .40)}{100,000} = \frac{(EBIT - \$2,000,000)(1 - .40)}{80,000}$$

$$= \frac{(.6EBIT - \$600,000)}{100,000} = \frac{(.6EBIT - \$1,200,000)}{80,000}$$

$$= (.6EBIT \text{ - } \$600,000) = 1.25(.6EBIT\text{-}\$1,200,000)$$

$$= .6EBIT \text{ - } \$600,000 = .75EBIT \text{ - } \$1,500,000$$

$$= .15EBIT = \$900,000$$

$$EBIT = \$6,000,000$$

The indifference point is an EBIT of \$6,000,000.

Step 4: Analyze

By increasing leverage to buy back stock, EPS climbs to \$60 per share. As long as the firm can maintain financial flexibility, more leverage increases earnings of shareholders. The firm would usually choose more leverage when EBIT exceeds \$6,000,000 as that is the EBIT-EPS indifference point.

CHAPTER 16

Dividend Policy

Chapter **Orientation**

This chapter focuses on the firm's dividend policy, when it is important and when it is not important to the firm's valuation. Share repurchases are another form of repayment to stock owners. One of the important aspects of dividend policy is the information that changes in policy convey to markets. This chapter also covers the tax treatment of dividends, repurchases, and stock splits.

Chapter Review: **Terms and Concepts**

16.1 Do Firms Distribute Cash to Their Shareholders?

Firms may use a cash dividend distribution or a share's repurchase to return cash to their owners. A share repurchase reduces the number of outstanding shares. Share repurchases have become more popular since 1972.

Cash Dividends

The two attributes of dividend policy:

1. The fraction of earnings paid in dividends, the payout ratio.
2. The pattern of payments over time, the stability of dividends.

Dividend Payment Procedures

Dividends are usually paid quarterly.

The declaration date is the date the board of directors formally declares a dividend.

The ex-dividend date is two days before the date of record and during those two days the stock trades without the dividend payment to allow for stock trades to process.

The date of record is the date that determines who owns the dividend payment.

The dividend payment date is the day the dividend is paid.

Figure 16.1

Historical Distributions to Shareholders through Dividends and Share Repurchases

Cash distributions to a firm's shareholders take one of two principal forms: cash dividends and share repurchases. In recent years two important trends have been observed. First, share repurchases have grown to the point where they are equal to cash distributions through dividends. Second, the proportion of firm earnings distributed through both approaches has grown from about 40 percent in the 1970s to near 80 percent by 2000.

(Panel A) Cash Distributions to Shareholders: Dividends and Repurchases

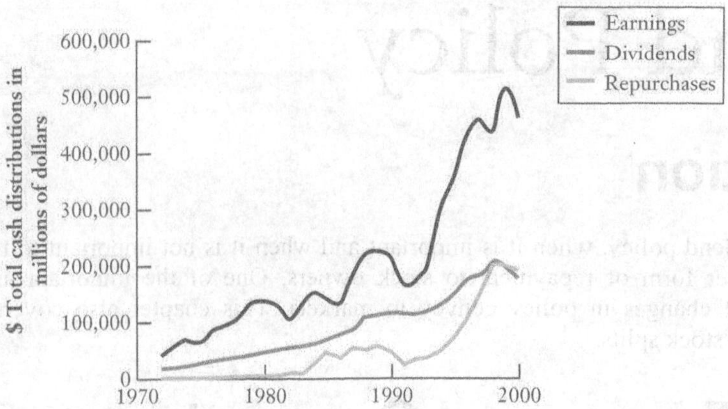

(Panel B) Relative Importance of Dividends and Share Repurchases

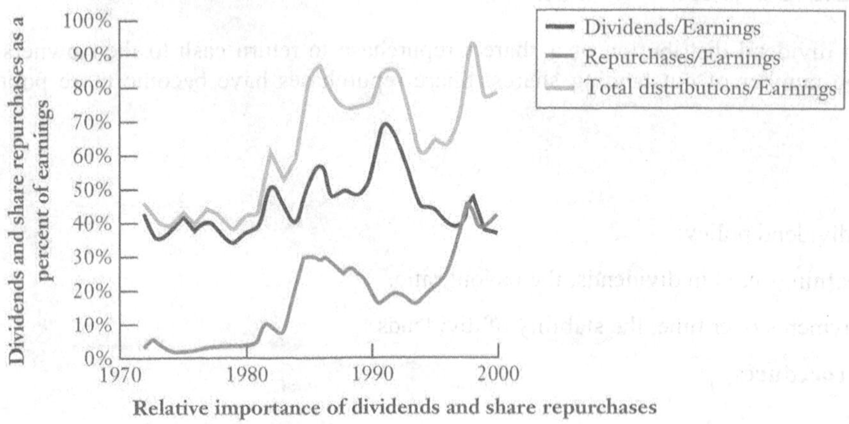

Source: Gustavo Grullon and Roni Michaely, "Dividends, Share Repurchases, and the Substitution Hypothesis," *Journal of Finance* 57, 4 (August 2002), 1649–1684.

Stock Repurchases

A company engages in a share or stock repurchase (stock buyback) when it uses the firm's cash to repurchase some of its own stock. This results in a reduction in the firm's cash balance as well as the number of shares of stock outstanding.

How Do Firms Repurchase Their Shares?

Firms use one of three methods to repurchase their firm's shares:

- Open market repurchase—buy shares in the market at traded prices (popular)
- Tender offer—the firm offers to buy a specific number of shares at a stated price
- Private negotiated repurchase—buy shares from a major shareholder

Personal Tax Considerations—Dividend versus Capital Gains Income

After the 2006 tax act, long-term owners of dividends and capital gains pay 15 percent federal income tax. To pay the 15 percent tax rate, shareholders must own the stock 60 days before the dividend date. If they do not hold the stock long enough, the dividends will be taxed at the personal income tax rate which is higher.

Non-Cash Distributions: Stock Dividends and Stock Splits

A **stock dividend** is a pro-rata distribution of additional shares of stock to the firm's current stockholders. A stock dividend only increases the number of shares of stock outstanding such that the total value of the firm's common shares is unchanged.

A **stock split** is essentially a very large stock dividend. For example, a 2-for-1 split would entail issuing two new shares of stock to each shareholder in exchange for each old share they currently hold. The 2-for-1 stock split is equivalent to a 100 percent stock dividend since both will result in the number of shares outstanding doubling while the share price drops in half.

Rationale for a Stock Dividend or Split

A rationale for splits and stock dividends is the belief that there is an optimal price range for the firm's stock. Within this range, the total market value of the common stockholders is thought to be maximized. As the price exceeds this range, fewer investors will want to purchase the firm's stock because of the high cost of purchasing a round lot (100 shares), thereby restraining the demand for the firm's shares.

16.2 Does Dividend Policy Matter?

Modigliani and Miller find that with no transaction costs and no taxes, the timing of dividend payments is irrelevant to firm value, if operating and investment policies are fixed.

The Irrelevance of the Dividend Choice

Dividend choice is irrelevant if:

- There are no taxes.
- There are no transactions.
- The firm's investment and operating policies are fixed.

If these hold, then the timing of a dividend payment does not affect value and a dividend payment is the same as a share repurchase. If there are taxes, then shareholders will prefer a repurchase over a dividend payment.

The Timing of Dividends Is Irrelevant

If the firm tries to pay out cash and raises funds by selling shares when cash payments exceed cash on hand, the value of the firm will be the same as new shareholders will receive a portion of the firm's equity. The total value of the firm is the same, as the firm earns the same cash flow amounts no matter the dividend policy.

The Form of Payment (Cash Dividends versus Share Repurchases) Is Irrelevant

A firm can pay a cash dividend or repurchase shares with cash if investors have the same tax exposure and preferences.

Individual Investor Wealth Effects: No Personal Taxes

Table 16.1 contains the details of GoFast's situation and an analysis of the investor wealth effects of the two alternatives for distributing the firm's $1,000,000 in cash flow:

Alternative 1: A $1,000,000 cash dividend.

Alternative 2: A $1,000,000 stock repurchase.

In either case, the wealth of investors remains the same.

Individual Wealth Effects: Personal Taxes

We have just demonstrated that in the absence of transaction costs and personal taxes, investors would be indifferent between the alternative of receiving a cash dividend payment or having the opportunity to sell shares to the firm in a share repurchase. However, this result can change if the tax consequences of the alternatives differ.

Some tax facts concerning dividends and stock repurchase:

Fact #1: 100 percent of the cash dividends received by individuals is taxable in the year in which they are received.

Fact #2: When an individual sells shares of stock, the only part of the cash payment that is taxable is the gain in price over the original price that was paid for the shares (i.e., the tax basis used to determine whether there has been a gain or loss).

Fact #3: If an individual investor decides not to sell his or her shares back to the company making the stock repurchase, they will not incur a taxable gain from the transaction since they did not sell.

Table 16.1 Wealth Effects of Cash Distributions: Dividends and Share Repurchases

The following example illustrates that the common stockholder will not care whether the firm pays cash dividends or repurchases shares of stock because the economic consequences of the two cash distribution methods is the same for the stockholder.

Alternative I: A $1,000,000 cash dividend.

Alternative II-a: A $1,000,000 stock repurchase, where the Petty family maintains their percentage ownership of the firm by selling 10 percent of their shares.

Alternative II-b: A $1,000,000 stock repurchase, resulting in the Petty family holdings climbing from 10 percent to 11.11 percent of the shares outstanding.

(Panel A) Firm Setting

			Share Repurchase	
	Current Situation	Alternative I—Pay Dividend	Alternative II-a—Sell Shares	Alternative II-b—Retain Shares
Earnings	$1,000,000			
Shares	500,000	500,000	450,000	450,000
Earnings per Share	$ 2.00	$ 2.00	$ 2.22	$ 2.22
Cost of Equity	11.11%			
Share Price (Pre-distribution)	$ 18.00	$ 20.00	$ 20.00	$ 20.00
Share Price (Post-distribution)		$ 18.00	$ 20.00	$ 20.00
Equity Value (Market Cap)	$9,000,000	$9,000,000	$9,000,000	$9,000,000

(Panel B) Wealth Effects on the Petty Family's 10% Holdings: No Taxes

Cash Distribution Proceeds		$ 100,000	$ 100,000	$ –
% Share Ownership of Petty Family	10%	10%	10.00%	11.11%
Shares Held by the Petty Family	50,000	50,000	45,000	50,000
Value of Equity Holdings	$ 900,000	$ 900,000	$ 900,000	$1,000,000

			Share Repurchase	
Wealth Effects of the Alternatives		Alternative I—100% Dividend	Alternative II-a—Sell Shares	Alternative II-b—Retain Shares
Cash Distribution (Dividends or sale of shares)		$ 100,000	$ 100,000	$ —
Total Value of Shares Held by the Petty Family		$ 900,000	$ 900,000	$1,000,000
Total Cash plus Value of Shares		$1,000,000	$1,000,000	$1,000,000

Post-2003 Tax Treatment: Dividends and Capital Gains Taxed at 15 Percent

To illustrate the effect of differences in tax treatments of dividends and share repurchases, Table 16.2 contains the after-tax cash flow consequences of the alternative methods for distributing cash to shareholders.

Investors prefer the repurchase plan, regardless of whether they sell the shares (II-a) or retain them (II-b), because they do not incur any taxes, whereas if they received dividends they would have to pay taxes on them.

Table 16.2 Dividends versus Share Repurchases with Personal Taxes

This example continues the analysis begun in Table 16.1 and considers the effect of personal taxes on the Petty family shares in the GoFast Corporation. We use a 15 percent personal tax rate for both dividend income and capital gains resulting from the sale of shares for more than the amount originally paid for them (the tax basis). For the share repurchase alternative where the Petty family decides not to sell their shares, we assume they intend to hold them for a period of five years, at which time they will be sold and the taxes on the gain paid.

Alternative I: A $1,000,000 cash dividend.

Alternative II-a: A $1,000,000 stock repurchase, where the Petty family maintains their number of shares by selling 10 percent of their shares.

Alternative II-b: A $1,000,000 stock repurchase, resulting in the Petty family holdings climbing from 10 percent to 11.11 percent of the shares outstanding.

(Panel A) Tax Rates Equal 15% for Dividends and Capital Gains: Basis in Shares Sold Is $0

Tax Basis in Shares	$ 0			
Tax Rate on Dividends and Capital Gains	15%		Share Repurchase	
After-Tax Wealth Effects of the Alternatives		Alternative I—100% Dividend	Alternative II-a—Repurchase/Sell Shares	Alternative II-b—Repurchase/Retain Shares
Cash Distribution (Dividends or Sale of Shares)		$100,000	$ 100,000	$ —
Less: Taxes		(15,000)	(15,000)	—
Equals: After-Tax Cash Distribution		$ 85,000	$ 85,000	$ —
Total Value of Shares Held by the Petty Family		900,000	900,000	1,000,000
Total Cash plus Value of Shares		$985,000	$ 985,000	$1,000,000

(Panel B) Tax Rates Equal 15% for Dividends and Capital Gains: Basis in Shares Sold Is $20

Tax Basis in Shares	$ 20.00			
Tax Rate on Dividends and Capital Gains	15%		Share Repurchase	
After-Tax Wealth Effects of the Alternatives		Alternative I—100% Dividend	Alternative II-a—Repurchase/Sell Shares	Alternative II-b—Repurchase/Retain Shares
Cash Distribution		$100,000	$ 100,000	$ —
Less: Taxes		(15,000)	—	—
Equals: After-Tax Cash Distribution		$ 85,000	$ 100,000	$ —
Total Value of Shares Held by the Petty Family		900,000	900,000	1,000,000
Total Cash plus Value of Shares		$985,000	$1,000,000	$1,000,000

Pre-2003 Tax Treatment: Dividends Taxed at Higher Rate than Capital Gains

Prior to the passage of the 2003 tax law, dividends were taxed as ordinary income while capital gains were taxed at the capital gains tax rate. In addition, the capital gains tax rate was lower than the ordinary income tax rate for long-term capital gains (gains from the sale of securities held for more than one year). Under this tax scenario, investors preferred share repurchases over dividends.

Why Dividend Policy Is Important

We have just demonstrated that tax policy can influence an investor's preference for capital gains income that results from a share repurchase versus cash dividends. However, there are other reasons why a firm might want to continue paying a cash dividend. We review a few of the more important ones below.

Transactions Are Costly

Some investors may create their own dividend policy by reinvesting cash dividends if they do not want current income, or selling some of the shares they own to create cash income if the firm's dividend payout is less than they prefer.

If there were no taxes and investors did not incur transaction costs when they bought and sold shares, they could simply satisfy their personal income preferences by purchasing or selling securities when the dividends received did not satisfy their current needs. However, if taxes are incurred when dividends are paid and if there are costs to buying and selling shares, it is easier for investors to simply select companies to invest in that pay dividends that match up with their particular preferences.

Because firms with different dividends attract different **dividend clienteles**, groups of investors who prefer the firm's cash distribution policy, it is important that dividend policy is stable.

The Information Conveyed by Dividend and Share Repurchase Announcements

Investors and stock market analysts are constantly trying to decipher the information released by firms to better understand what they imply about firm values. Firms tend to increase their dividends only when they believe the higher dividend can be sustained in the future. If this is the case, then a dividend increase is clearly good news. Share repurchases also are viewed very favorably because it shows investors that the firm has generated more money than it currently needs. Since accounting statements can be misleading, a cash payout is much easier to interpret.

The timing of large share repurchases also conveys information to shareholders. A share repurchase announcement implies that the firm has plenty of cash and, in addition, it is a good time to repurchase equity.

The empirical evidence indicates that dividends and share repurchases do in fact convey favorable information to investors. When firms announce that they will increase their dividends, their stock prices do tend to increase. Similarly, when firms announce that they are initiating a repurchase program, their stock prices also tend to rise. In contrast, stock prices tend to decline when firms cut or eliminate their dividends.

The Information Conveyed by Stock Dividends and Stock Splits

The announcements of stock dividends and splits also tend to generate positive stock returns. The fact that these announcements convey information to investors is somewhat more difficult to explain because stock dividends and splits have no effect on the firm's cash flows, and as we have discussed, it is the cash flows that ultimately determine a firm's value.

There are two theories that explain why stock prices tend to respond favorably:

1. Firms have a preferred trading range. There is some empirical support for the idea of a preferred trading range that we can glean from the number of stock splits used by very successful high growth firms. Walmart (WMT), has split 2 for 1 on 11 different occasions since going public in 1970 and Dell Computer (DELL) has split 3 for 2 once and 2 for 1 on six occasions since going public in 1988.
2. Splits and stock dividends attract attention. This suggests that any corporate action that attracts attention, even one with no direct effect on cash flows, is likely to convey favorable information.

16.3 Cash Distribution Policies in Practice

Stable Payout

Managers are primarily concerned with a stable dividend payout pattern. The size of dividend changes is smaller than the change in earnings as managers do not want to reduce dividends. For repurchase decisions, they are more concerned with undervaluation of their stock and lack of alternative opportunities in their business.

Figure 16.3

Survey of CFO Opinions Regarding Dividend Policy Issues

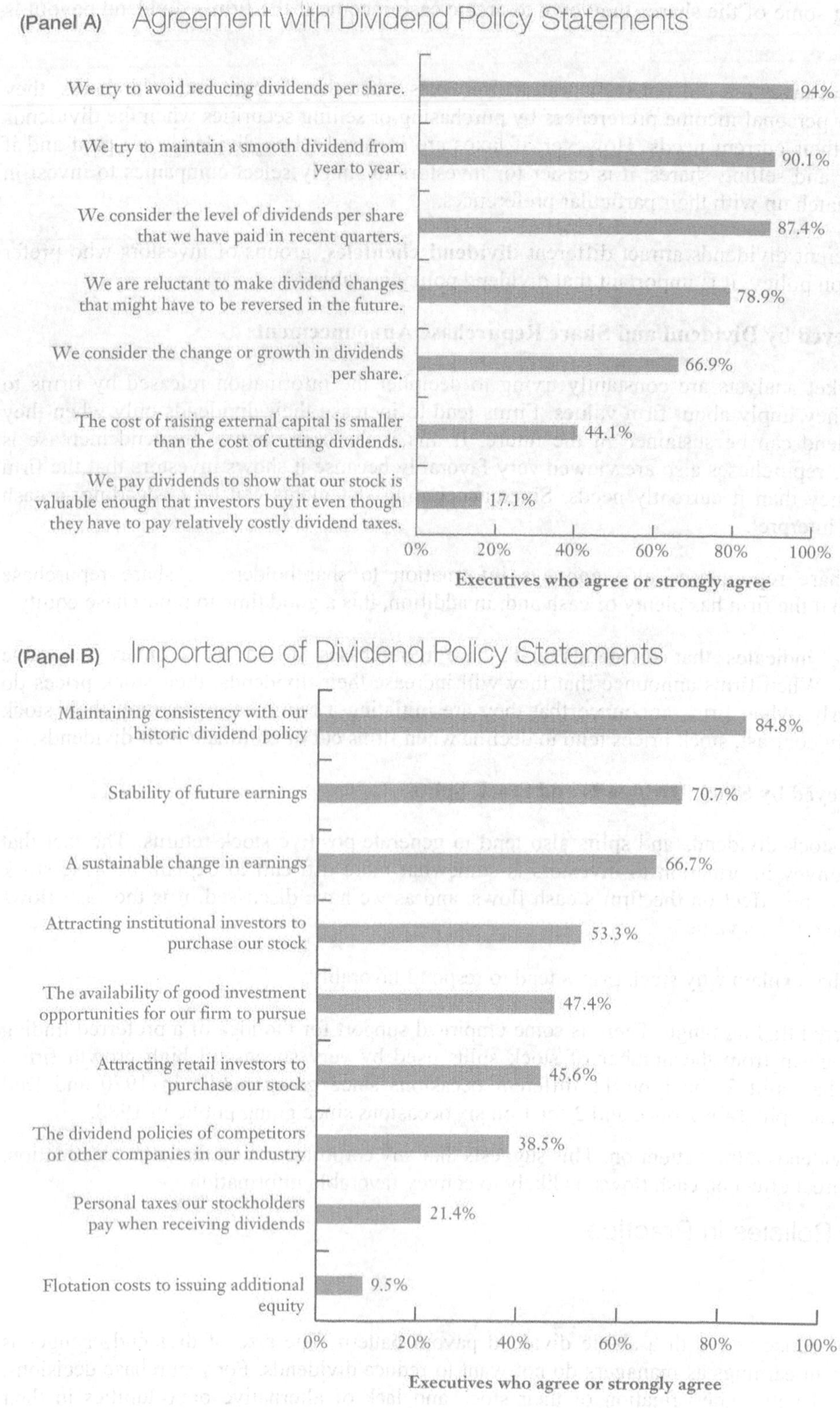

Source: A. Brav, J. R. Graham, C. R. Harvey, and R. Michaely, "Payout Policy in the 21st Century," NBER working paper series, Working paper #9657, April 2003.

Figure 16.4

Factors important to your company's repurchase decision

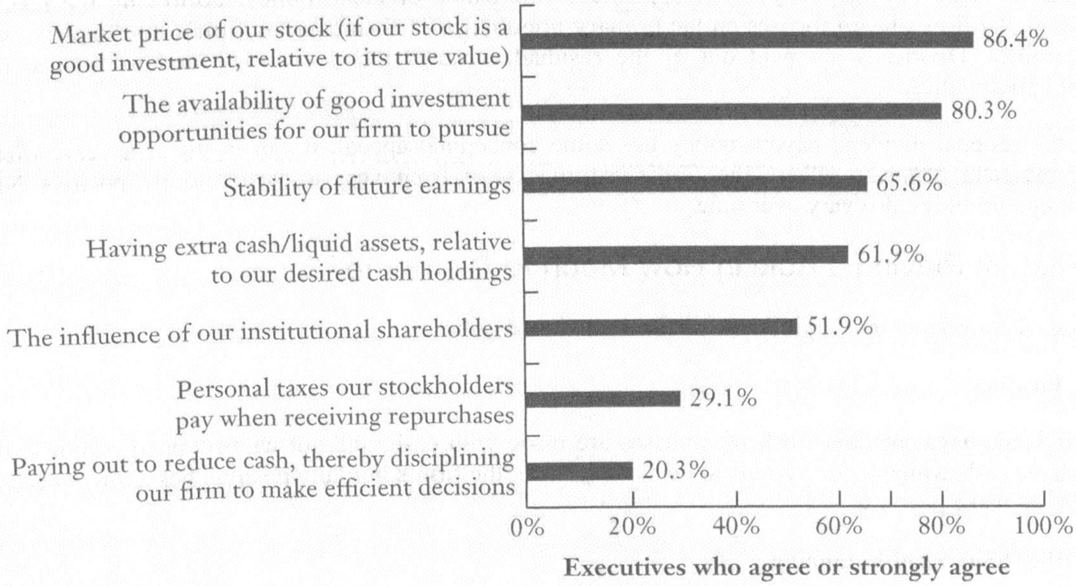

Source: A. Brav, J. R. Graham, C. R. Harvey, and R. Michaely, Payout Policy in the 21st Century, *Journal of Financial Economics,* 77 (September 2005), pp. 483–527.

Table 16.3 **Summary of Financial Executives' Views about Payout Policy**

DIVIDENDS		REPURCHASES
Very Important. Do not cut dividends except in extreme circumstances.	**Historical Level**	Historic level is not important.
Sticky. Inflexible. Smooth through time.	**Flexibility**	Very Flexible. No need to smooth. out
Little reward for increasing.	**Consequence If Increased**	Stock price increase when repurchase plan announced.
Big market penalty for reducing or omitting.	**Consequence If Reduced**	Little consequence to reducing from one year to the next, though firms try to complete plans.
Most common target is the level of dividend, followed by payout ratio and growth in dividends. Target is viewed as rather flexible.	**Target**	Most common target is dollar amount of repurchases, a very flexible target.
External funds would be raised before cutting dividends.	**Relation to External Funds**	Repurchases would be reduced before raising external funds.
First maintain historic dividend level; then make incremental investment decisions.	**Relation to Investment**	First investment decisions, then make repurchase decisions.
Dividend increases tied to permanent, stable earnings.	**Earnings Quality**	Repurchase increase with permanent earnings but also with temporary earnings.

Source: A. Brav, J. R. Graham, C. R. Harvey, and R. Michaely, "Payout Policy in the 21st Century," *Journal of Financial Economics,* 77 (September 2005), pp. 483–527

Residual Dividend Payout Policy

The residual dividend payout policy is the opposite of the stable dividend policy. Following the residual payout policy, the firm's board focuses on the primary importance of financing the firm's investments using its own earnings. Dividends are paid out of the residual earnings that are not needed to finance new investment opportunities.

Although the residual dividend payout policy has some conceptual appeal, it can result in a very volatile stream of dividend payments where the firm's earnings vary from year to year and its positive NPV investment opportunities also vary over time.

Other Factors Playing a Role in How Much to Distribute

Some practical considerations that influence a firm's dividend policy:

Liquidity Position

Because dividend payments and stock repurchases are made with cash, and not with retained earnings, the firm must have cash available for payouts to be made. Hence, the firm's liquidity position has a direct bearing on its ability to make payouts.

Lack of Other Sources of Financing

Many small or new companies do not have access to the capital markets, and as a result they must rely upon internally generated funds to fund their investment opportunities. As a consequence, the payout ratio is generally much lower for a small or newly established firm than for a large, publicly owned corporation.

Earnings Predictability

A company's payout ratio depends to some extent on the predictability of a firm's profits over time. If earnings fluctuate significantly, management cannot rely on internally generated funds to meet future needs. When profits are realized, the firm may retain larger amounts to ensure that money is available when needed. Conversely, firms with stable earnings will typically pay out a larger portion of its earnings. These companies have less concern about the availability of profits to meet future capital requirements.

Answers to **Concept Checks**

Concept Check **16.1**

1. What are the two forms of cash distributions that firms typically use?
2. What is the frequency with which cash dividends are typically paid to investors?
3. Identify three motives that might encourage a firm to buy back its common stock shares.
4. What are the three different methods that firms use to repurchase their shares?
5. How is a stock dividend like a stock split and why do financial managers sometimes use one or the other?

Answer 1: The two forms of cash distributions are dividends and share repurchases.

Answer 2: Cash dividends are usually paid quarterly.

Answer 3: The three motives that might encourage a firm to buy back shares are: different tax rates on dividends and capital gains, reduce shares to increase EPS, and to signal to investors its future prospects (undervalued stock).

Answer 4: The three methods to buy back shares are: open market purchase, tender offer, and negotiated purchase with a specific holder of shares.

Answer 5: A stock dividend is a distribution of shares, pro-rata, which increases outstanding shares by less than 25 percent, otherwise it is called a stock split.

Concept Check **16.2**

1. What are the fundamental conditions or assumptions used by M&M to demonstrate the irrelevance of dividend policy?
2. Describe in simple terms why the timing of a firm's dividend payments that result from its dividend policy should not impact the value of its shares.
3. What is the tax treatment of the investor's dividend income and the income resulting from the firm's stock repurchases?
4. How is it that share repurchases are *tax favored* when compared to a cash dividend, even though the rate of tax paid on dividend income and capital gains income is the same?

Answer 1: Modigliani and Miller identified that if cash flows are not altered by the choice of dividend policy and if markets are perfect, then the firm's dividend policy is irrelevant to firm value. This requires no taxes, no transaction costs, and that investment and operating policies of the firm are fixed.

Answer 2: Firm value depends on the value of cash flows generated by the firm and not the timing of cash distributions. Investors can create their own dividends by selling shares if the firm retains cash.

Answer 3: Dividends are taxed as ordinary income at a rate of 15 percent if the shares were held for a year and higher rates for short-term holdings. Taxes on shares after a share repurchase are due only if the shares are sold and calculated only on the gain over the owner's cost basis.

Answer 4: Share repurchases are tax favored since the investor can defer taxes indefinitely if the shares are not sold.

Concept Checks **16.3**

1. Why is a stable payout policy for cash dividends preferred by so many firms?
2. What are the key factors considered by firms when determining their dividend payout policies?

Answer 1: A stable payout policy attracts clienteles of investors who are risk-averse and reward firms with stable dividends with higher valuations.

Answer 2: The factors considered by firms when setting payout policy are liquidity, earnings and cash flow stability, and financial flexibility since raising capital is costly.

Multiple Choice **Quiz**

1. The date of record is
   a. when the stock trades without a dividend.
   b. when the board sets the dividend.
   c. when the dividend is paid.
   d. when the owner of the dividend is determined.

2. The declaration date is
   a. when the stock trades without a dividend.
   b. when the board sets the dividend.
   c. when the dividend is paid.
   d. when the owner of the dividend is determined.

3. Dividend clienteles are
   a. levels of dividend payments.
   b. groups of investors seeking similar dividend policies.
   c. investors trading low paying firms for higher.
   d. dividends backed by assets.

4. The primary dividend policy used by most firms is
   a. a dividend clientele.
   b. a residual payout.
   c. a stable payout.
   d. a flexible payout.

5. The dividend payout ratio is set
   a. by managers.
   b. automatically depending on the share price.
   c. by the level of earnings.
   d. by the board.

6. A tender offer repurchase occurs when the firm
   a. offers to buy a fixed number of shares from the public.
   b. offers to buy a fixed number of shares from one holder.
   c. trades in the market for shares at anytime after a filing with the SEC.
   d. trades in the market after a public announcement.

7. Open market repurchases occur when the firm
   a. offers to buy a fixed number of shares from the public.
   b. offers to buy a fixed number of shares from one holder.
   c. trades in the market for shares at any time after a filing with the SEC.
   d. trades in the market after a public announcement.

8. A form of a non-cash dividend is a(n)
   a. stock split.
   b. irregular dividend.
   c. open market repurchase.
   d. tender offer.

9. A stock dividend requires less than
   a. 5 percent of shares to be issued.
   b. 10 percent of shares to be issued.
   c. 25 percent of shares to be issued.
   d. 50 percent of shares to be issued.

10. A stock split
    a. does not convey information as the firm is doubling shares and halving the price.
    b. does not convey information since the market is efficient.
    c. conveys misinformation and distracts investors from fundamentals.
    d. conveys information about the future prospects of the firm's stock trading range.

Answers to **Multiple Choice Questions**

1. D
2. B
3. B
4. C
5. D
6. A
7. C
8. A
9. C
10. D

Self Test **with Solutions**

Picture the Problem

Decide on Solution Strategy

Solve

Analyze

Self Test 1: Dividend Irrelevance

Show that owners of Tim-Tam can pay themselves by creating a dividend though stock sales even though the firm has no cash on hand. In one year the firm will liquidate like a chocolate wafer in coffee. Tim-Tam will pay out $11,200,000 in cash at liquidation and has 1,000 owners each with 1,000 shares who require a 12 percent annual return. Assume Tim-Tam has no debt and there are no taxes and no transaction costs.

a. What is today's value to each owner if they intend to hold all shares until liquidation?

b. What is the value to an owner if they wish to pay themselves a dividend by selling 100 shares immediately to create a dividend?

c. What is the value to an owner if Tim-Tam sells stock to pay a $1,000 dividend to each owner ($1,000,000 total)?

Step 1: Picture the Problem

You can think of the dividend policy as a set of possible outcomes:

1. Tim-Tam does nothing; owners do nothing and wait for liquidation.
2. Tim-Tam does nothing; an owner creates a dividend by selling 1/10th shares.
3. Tim-Tam creates a dividend by selling stock; owners collect cash now and at liquidation.

Step 2: Decide on a Solution Strategy

We will compare the present values of the firm under the dividend payment policies under each plan. Since the firm will be liquidated at the end of one year, we do a one period present value.

Step 3: Solve

a. The value of the firm's equity can be calculated using the present value of the liquidation.

$$\text{Value of Tim-Tam's Equity} = \text{Dividend}_{\text{Year 0}} + \frac{\text{Dividend}_{\text{Year 1}}}{(1+K_{equity})}$$

$$= \$0 \text{ million} + \frac{\$11.2 \text{ million}}{(1+.12)} = \$10 \text{ million total equity}$$

Tim-Tam has 1 million shares of stock, so the value per share of the firm's stock will be $10.

b. In this case, the firm does nothing different but the owner creates a dividend by selling 1/10th of their holdings. The value of the firm's equity can be calculated using the present value of the liquidation.

$$\text{Value of Tim-Tam's Equity} = \text{Dividend}_{\text{Year 0}} + \frac{\text{Dividend}_{\text{Year 1}}}{(1+K_{equity})}$$

$$= \$0 \text{ million} + \frac{\$11.2 \text{ million}}{(1+.12)} = \$10 \text{ million total equity}$$

For the owner, today's value of Tim-Tam shares is $10 per share found in part A.* Selling 100 shares raises $1,000 today. The owner now owns 900 shares of the 1 million shares that will split the $11,200,000 liquidation or $10,080 in one year. The present value of $10,080 in one year is $9,000. Thus the owner still has $10,000 in value ($1,000 in an immediate dividend and a present value of $9,000 in liquidation).

c. In this case, the firm creates a dividend by issuing shares to raise the funds needed for the dividend. If the current shareholders wish to have $1,000 dividend each, the firm will need to raise $1,000,000 in funds. The new shareholders also have a required rate of return of 12 percent. So at liquidation, the new shareholders receive $1,120,000 of the liquidating dividend payment. This leaves $10,080,000 for the old shareholders or $10,080 per owner in one year. The value of the firm's equity can be calculated using the present value of the liquidation plus the immediate dividend payment.

$$\text{Value of Tim-Tam's Equity} = \text{Dividend}_{\text{Year 0}} + \frac{\text{Dividend}_{\text{Year 1}}}{(1+K_{equity})}$$

$$= \$1 \text{ million} + \frac{\$10.08 \text{ million}}{(1+.12)} = \$1\text{m} + \$9\text{m} = \$10 \text{ million total equity}$$

Tim-Tam pays each old owner an immediate dividend of $1,000 and then a liquidating dividend of worth $9,000 today. Shares are worth $9 each today due to the dilution of issuing shares to pay a dividend. Dividing the $1,000,000 dividend raised by a share price of $9, Tim-Tam issues approximately 111,111 new shares.

Step 4: Analyze

The value of equity is the same under any of the payout policies. So long as there are no taxes, the firm's cash flows are not altered due to any change in the investment and operating policy of the firm, and no transaction costs, the investor will see the same value no matter the timing or means to create a dividend. So long as invested funds by the firm, the old, and any new investors earn the same rate of 12 percent, the ultimate value of the firm remains the same.

CHAPTER 17

Financial Forecasting and Planning

Chapter Orientation

Forecasting is a means to plan for future investments and capital raising needs. Planning helps firms reduce risk, take opportunities that arise in the market, and improve operations. Effective planning should improve shareholder value. The three types of planning are strategic, long-term, and short-term planning.

Chapter Review: Terms and Concepts

17.1 An Overview of Financial Planning

The firm's financial plan has two components: a short-term plan up to one year and a long-term plan that is usually for a period of five years. Both plans attempt to estimate the future financing needs of the firm.

The primary objective of financial planning by firms is to estimate financing needs before they are needed. This permits the firm to seek out the best terms available. Another reason for planning is to make managers focus on the future in a systematic process and develop contingency plans for several likely scenarios that the business may face.

The firm's strategic plan defines how the firm intends to make money and asks:

- Who are we and what do we do?
- Who are our customers?
- Who are our competitors and how do we compete?

The strategic plan serves as a guideline for both short- and long-term financial plans.

The long-term financial plan usually plans for the next three to five years and includes balance sheets and income statements for each year, known as pro formas.

The short-term financial plan usually plans for one year and is focused on the firm's cash flows. The cash budget is the typical planning format and contains detailed revenue and cost data.

Two benefits of financial planning:

- Firm has a base plan consistent with goals and strategy.
- The process of planning prepares managers for future contingencies.

17.2 Developing a Long-Term Financial Plan

The long-term plan of three to five years serves as a basis for short-term plans. The format of long-term financial plans consists of pro forma income statements and pro forma balance sheets for the entire firm's operation rather than detailed business segment data. The process starts with a sales forecast. Sometimes expenses are estimated as a percentage of sales rather than estimating them directly.

Steps in a Long-Term Financial Forecast:

Step 1: Construct a sales forecast.

Step 2: Prepare pro forma financial forecasts.

Step 3: Estimate the future financing need.

Sales forecasts use reliable past trends and adjust for any new event that affects the trend.

Pro formas often use the percent of sales method. The percentages used in the forecast can come from the most recent financial statements, from an average computed over several years, from the judgment of the analyst, or from some combination of these methods.

Estimating the future financing need requires the firm to extract the cash and financing needs from the pro forma forecasts.

Example Financial Forecasting for Ziegen, Inc.

Ziegen uses the percent of sales method. Table 17.1 shows this method.

Sources of Spontaneous Financing: Accounts Payable and Accrued Expenses

These liabilities vary directly with sales and are considered spontaneous sources of financing.

Sources of Discretionary Financing

Raising financing with notes payable, long-term debt, and common stock requires a managerial decision or exercise of managerial discretion; thus, these are discretionary sources. Another source is the retention of earnings.

Table 17.1 Using the Percent of Sales Method to Forecast Ziegen, Inc.'s Financing Requirements for 2014

Preparation of Ziegen's financial forecast for 2014 begins with a forecast of firm sales for the year. This forecast is followed by a projection of assets required to support the projected level of sales. Offsetting the firm's need for discretionary financing is the financing that the firm receives from accounts payable and accrued expenses, which arise automatically (or spontaneously) as a result of the firm's having made a sale. Ziegen's financial analysts forecast $12 million in sales for 2014, which will require that the firm invest a total of $7.2 million in assets. The $1.2 million increase in assets will be financed partially by the $400,000 increase in the levels of accounts payable and accrued expenses (equal to $2.4 million **2** $2.0 million). In addition, the analysts expect the firm to generate another $300,000 from the firm's retention of one-half the firm's 2014 net income. The firm's discretionary financing need of $500,000 is calculated by subtracting the $400,000 in accounts payable and accrued expenses and the $300,000 increase in retained earnings from the total increase in financing needs of $1.2 million.

Ziegen, Inc. Income Statement for 2013		Calculation	% of 2013 Sales	Ziegen, Inc. Pro Forma Income Statement for 2014	Calculation	
				Sales growth rate =	20%	
Sales	$10,000,000			Sales	$10m × (1 + .20) =	$12,000,000
Net Income	$ 500,000	$.5m/$10m =	5.0%	Net Income	$12m × (.05) =	$ 600,000
Ziegen, Inc. Balance Sheet for 2013		**Calculation**	**% of 2013 Sales**	**Ziegen, Inc. Pro Forma Balance Sheet for 2014**	**Calculation**	
Current assets	$ 2,000,000	$2m/$10m =	20.0%	Current assets	.20 × 12m =	$ 2,400,000
Net fixed assets	4,000,000	$4m/$10m =	40.0%	Net fixed assets	.40 × 12m =	$ 4,800,000
Total	$ 6,000,000			Total		$ 7,200,000
Accounts payable	$ 1,000,000	$1m/$10m =	10.0%	Accounts payable	.10 × 12m =	$ 1,200,000
Accrued expenses	1,000,000	$1m/$10m =	10.0%	Accrued expenses	.10 × 12m =	1,200,000
Notes payable	500,000		NA[a]	Notes payable	No change	500,000
Current liabilities	$ 2,500,000			Current liabilities		$ 2,900,000
Long-term debt	2,000,000		NA[a]	Long-term debt	No change	$ 2,000,000
Total liabilities	$ 4,500,000			Total liabilities		$ 4,900,000
Common stock (par)	100,000		NA[a]	Common stock (par)	No change	100,000
Paid-in capital	200,000		NA[a]	Paid-in capital	No change	200,000
Retained earnings	1,200,000			Retained earnings	Calculation[b]	1,500,000
Common equity	$ 1,500,000			Common equity		1,800,000
Total	$ 6,000,000			Projected sources of financing		$ 6,700,000
				Discretionary financing needs (Plug figure)[c]		$ 500,000
				Total financing needs = Total assets		$ 7,200,000

[a] Not applicable. These account balances do not vary with sales.

[b] Projected retained earnings for 2014 equals $1,500,000, which is equal to the 2013 level of retained earnings of $1,200,000 plus net income of $600,000 less common dividends equal to 50% of projected net income, or $300,000.

[c] Discretionary financing needs (DFN) for 2014 is a "plug figure" that equals the difference in the firm's projected total financing requirements or total assets equal to $7,200,000 and projected sources of financing, which is $6,700,000. In this scenario DFN is $500,000.

Summarizing Ziegen's Financial Forecast

Ziegen will need $500,000 in additional financing using either debt or stock issues. This is known as the firm's discretionary financing needs and follows the process below:

Discretionary Financing Needs (*DFN*) = Pro Forma Total Assets − Accounts Payable − Accrued Expenses − Notes Payable − Long-term Debt − Common Equity

(Accounts Payable + Accrued Expenses: Projected spontaneous sources of financing; Notes Payable + Long-term Debt + Common Equity: Existing discretionary sources of financing)

Total Financing Needs less Projected Sources of Financing

= Discretionary Financing Needs (*DFN*) (17–1)

Substituting for the Ziegen, Inc. example we get

Discretionary Financing Needs = $7.2 million − $1.2 million − $1.2 million − .5 million − 2.0 million − $1.8 million

(Projected spontaneous sources of financing = $2.4 million; Existing discretionary sources of financing = $4.3 million)

Total Financing Needs = $7.2 million less Projected Sources of Financing = $6.7 million

Discretionary Financing Needs = $500,000

Analyzing the Effects of Profitability and Dividend Policy on the Firm's DFN

By changing assumptions, we can evaluate the sensitivity of the firm's Discretionary Financing Needs (DFN) to the changes. The chart below examines profitability and dividend policy:

- More profitability—less DFN
- Higher dividends—more DFN

Discretionary Financing Needs (DFN) for Various Net Profit Margins and Dividend Payout Ratios

Using the information from the Zeigen example, we can evaluate the effect of net profit margins (NPMs), which is net income/sales, equal to 1 percent, 5 percent, and 10 percent in combination with dividend payout ratios of 30 percent, 50 percent, and 70 percent, as follows:

	Dividend Payout ratios = Dividends ÷ Net Income		
Net Profit Margin	**30%**	**50%**	**70%**
1%	$716,000	$740,000	$764,000
5%	380,000	500,000	620,000
10%	(40,000)	200,000	440,000

Analyzing the Effect of Sales Growth on DFN

- Higher sales growth —more DFN

Figure 17.1

Sales Growth and the Discretionary Financing Needs of the Firm

The more rapidly the firm's revenues (and corresponding needs for assets) are expected to grow, the greater will be its needs for sources of financing above and beyond the profits it retains from its operations. In this example, the firm will have sufficient sources of funds from the retention of 50 percent of its earnings to finance growth rates in sales up to 6.667 percent. However, once the rate of growth in sales exceeds this threshold, the firm will find itself needing to seek out other sources of financing.

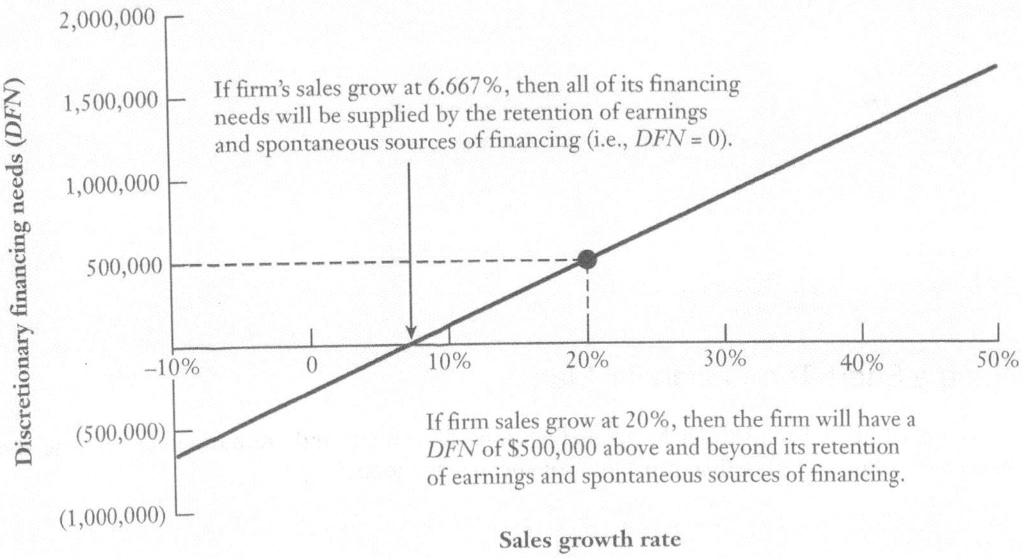

Table 17.2 Discretionary Financing Needed (DFN) and the Growth Rate in Sales

Ziegen, Inc. forecasts its financing requirements for 2014 using two different rates of growth in sales: 0 percent and 20 percent. The firm's discretionary financing needs vary dramatically with each of these growth rates, indicating the sensitivity of a firm's financing requirements to the firm's rate of growth in revenues.

Ziegen, Inc. Income Statement for 2013			% of 2013 Sales	Ziegen, Inc. Pro Forma Income Statement for 2014			
					Growth Rates in Sales	0%	20%
Sales	$10,000,000			Sales		$10,000,000	$12,000,000
Net Income	$ 500,000		5.0%	Net Income		$ 500,000	$ 600,000
Ziegen, Inc. Balance Sheet for 2013		**Calculation**	**% of 2013 Sales**	**Ziegen, Inc. Pro Forma Balance Sheet for 2014**	**Calculation**		
Current assets	$ 2,000,000	$2m/$10m =	20.0%	Current assets	.20 × Sales =	$ 2,000,000	$ 2,400,000
Net fixed assets	4,000,000	$4m/$10m =	40.0%	Net fixed assets	.40 × Sales =	$ 4,000,000	$ 4,800,000
Total	$ 6,000,000			Total		$ 6,000,000	$ 7,200,000
Accounts payable	$ 1,000,000	$1m/$10m =	10.0%	Accounts payable	.10 × Sales =	$ 1,000,000	$ 1,200,000
Accrued expenses	1,000,000	$1m/$10m =	10.0%	Accrued expenses	.10 × Sales =	1,000,000	1,200,000
Notes payable	500,000		NA[a]	Notes payable	No change	500,000	500,000
Current liabilities	$ 2,500,000			Current liabilities		$ 2,500,000	$ 2,900,000
Long-term debt	2,000,000		NA[a]	Long-term debt	No change	$ 2,000,000	2,000,000
Total liabilities	$ 4,500,000			Total liabilities		$ 4,500,000	$ 4,900,000
Common stock (par)	100,000		NA[a]	Common stock (par)	No change	$ 100,000	$ 100,000
Paid-in capital	200,000		NA[a]	Paid-in capital	No change	200,000	200,000
Retained earnings	1,200,000			Retained earnings	Calculation	1,450,000	1,500,000
Common equity	$ 1,500,000			Common equity		$ 1,750,000	$ 1,800,000
Total	$ 6,000,000			Projected sources of financing		$ 6,250,000	$ 6,700,000
				Discretionary financing needs (Plug figure)		$ (250,000)	$ 500,000
				Total financing needs = Total assets		$ 6,000,000	$ 7,200,000

[a]Not applicable. These account balances do not vary with sales.

17.3 Developing a Short-Term Financial Plan

Short-term financial plans have shorter horizons than long-term plans and are more detailed. The short-term plan includes a cash budget rather than pro forma financial statements.

Example Cash Budget: Melco Furniture, Inc.

Table 17.3 presents the cash budget details of Melco.

Table 17.3 Melco Furniture, Inc. Cash Budget for the Six Months Ended June 30, 2014

The cash budget for Melco Furniture, Inc. consists of four components or sections: (1) cash receipts, including cash received from sales made during the month of the budget as well as from sales made in previous months; (2) cash disbursements made during the month for various categories of expenses, such as labor (wages and salaries), rent, and interest and principal on the firm's debt; (3) the calculated change in cash for the month, which is simply cash receipts less cash disbursements; and finally (4) the computation of new financing needed to maintain the firm's desired cash balance.

	October	November	December	January	February	March	April	May	June	July	August
Worksheet											
Sales (forecasted)	55,000	62,000	50,000	60,000	75,000	88,000	100,000	110,000	100,000	80,000	75,000
Purchases (75% of sales in 2 months)			56,250	66,000	75,000	82,500	75,000	60,000	56,250		
Cash receipts											
Collections:											
First month after sale (30%)				15,000	18,000	22,500	26,400	30,000	33,000		
Second month after sale (50%)				31,000	25,000	30,000	37,500	44,000	50,000		
Third month after sale (20%)				11,000	12,400	10,000	12,000	15,000	17,600		
Total cash receipts				57,000	55,400	62,500	75,900	89,000	100,600		
Cash disbursements											
Payments (one-month lag of purchases made the previous month)				56,250	66,000	75,000	82,500	75,000	60,000		
Wages and salaries				3,000	10,000	7,000	8,000	6,000	4,000		
Rent				4,000	4,000	4,000	4,000	4,000	4,000		
Other expenses				1,000	500	1,200	1,500	1,500	1,200		
Interest expense on existing debt[a]								600	7,500		
Taxes						4,460			5,200		
Purchase and equipment					14,000						
Loan repayment[b]								12,000			
Total cash disbursements				64,250	94,500	91,660	96,000	99,100	81,900		
Net change in cash for the period				(7,250)	(39,100)	(29,160)	(20,100)	(10,100)	18,700		
Plus: Beginning cash balance				20,000	12,750	10,000	10,000	10,000	10,000		
Less: Interest on short-term borrowing				0	0	(364)	(659)	(866)	(976)		
Equals: Ending cash balance before short-term borrowing				12,750	(26,350)	(19,524)	(10,759)	(966)	27,724		
New financing needed[c]				0	36,350	29,524	20,759	10,966	(17,724)[d]		
Ending cash balance				12,750	10,000	10,000	10,000	10,000	10,000		
Cumulative borrowing				0	36,350	65,874	86,633	97,599	79,875		

[a] An interest payment of $600 on the $12,000 loan is due in May, and an interest payment of $7,500 on the $150,000 long-term debt is due in June.
[b] The principal amount of the $12,000 loan is also due in May.
[c] The amount of financing that is required to raise the firm's ending cash balance up to its $10,000 desired cash balance.
[d] Negative financing needed simply means the firm has excess cash that can be used to retire a part of its short-term borrowing from prior months.

Uses of the Cash Budget

Two important roles of the cash budget:

- Tool for predicting the amount and timing of future financing needs.
- Tool to monitor and control the firm's operations.

The cash budget is a useful benchmark for the firm's operations over time.

Answers to **Concept Checks**

Concept Check **17.1**

1. What are the fundamental benefits of financial planning?
2. Distinguish between a firm's short-term financial plan, long-term financial plan, and strategic plan.

Answer 1: The plan aligns the firm's operations with its strategic goals and the process of planning prepares it for the unexpected event.

Answer 2: The strategic plan describes how the firm will make money. The long-term financial plan looks out three to five years and develops pro forma financial statements to forecast investment and capital needs. The short-term plan develops cash budgets for the year ahead and focuses on liquidity.

Concept Check **17.2**

1. Why are sales forecasts so important to developing a firm's financial forecast?
2. What is the percent-of-sales method of financial forecasting?
3. Give some examples of spontaneous and discretionary sources of financing.

Answer 1: Forecasts using percent of sales method starts with a sales forecast.

Answer 2: The percent of sales method uses the ratio of each accounting item to total revenue as a means to predict each future year's values based on future revenues.

Answer 3: Spontaneous sources of financing arise from the operations of the firm such as accounts payable and accrued expenses that can vary with sales. Discretionary sources result from managerial decisions to issue notes payable, long-term debt or equity.

Concept Check **17.3**

1. What are the basic elements of a cash budget?
2. How is a cash budget used in financial planning?

Answer 1: A cash budget has four elements: cash receipts, cash disbursements, net change in cash for the period, and new financing needed.

Answer 2: The cash budget is used as a tool for predicting the amount and timing of the firm's future financing requirements and as a tool to monitor and control the firm's operations.

Multiple Choice **Quiz**

1. Discretionary financing needs are
   a. set by management.
   b. set by investors.
   c. arise due to the difference between capital sources and uses.
   d. set by financial markets.

2. Discretionary financing sources are
   a. accrued expenses and accounts payable.
   b. prepaid expenses and accounts receivable.
   c. notes payable and stock issues.
   d. bonds and stocks repurchases.

3. A cash budget is useful for
   a. strategic planning.
   b. long-term financial planning.
   c. pro forma financials.
   d. short-term financial planning.

4. A long-term financial plan forecasts the firm's
   a. liquidity.
   b. credit rating.
   c. investment requirements and capital needs.
   d. cash revenue.

5. The firm's strategic plan is
   a. set by managers and sales staff.
   b. set automatically depending on the firm's performance.
   c. set by investors with large holdings.
   d. set by the board.

6. The short-term financial plan forecasts the firm's
   a. liquidity.
   b. credit rating.
   c. investment requirements and capital needs.
   d. cash revenue.

7. Pro forma financial statements are used in the
   a. strategic plan.
   b. long-term plan.
   c. short-term budget.
   d. cash budget.

8. Sources of spontaneous financing are
   a. accrued expenses and accounts payable.
   b. prepaid expenses and accounts receivable.
   c. notes payable and stock issues.
   d. bond and stock repurchases.

9. Percent of sales forecasts are used to prepare
   a. cash budgets.
   b. strategic forecasts.
   c. short-term and long-term forecasts.
   d. operating forecasts.

10. Which serves as a tool for monitoring the operations of a firm?
    a. Cash budgets
    b. Strategic forecasts
    c. Short-term forecasts
    d. Long-term forecasts

Answers to **Multiple Choice Questions**

1. A
2. C
3. D
4. C
5. D
6. A
7. B
8. A
9. C
10. A

Self Test **with Solutions**

Picture the Problem

Decide on Solution Strategy

Solve

Analyze

Self Test 1: Pro Forma Financial Statements

Rickenbacker, the oldest maker of electric guitars, expects sales to rise to $8,000,000 next year. Construct a balance sheet and income statement for next year using the percent of sales method. Assume that depreciation, long-term debt, and interest expense remain the same and that taxes are 30 percent. Increase retained earnings by the net income amount found for next year. To make next year's liabilities and equity equal total assets, decide if the firm needs to declare dividends or issue short-term notes.

Rickenbacker Inc. Income Statement

	This Year	Next Year
Revenues	6,000,000	8,000,000
CGS	1,500,000	
Gross Profit	4,500,000	
Interest Expense	1,000,000	
Depreciation	2,000,000	
EBT	1,500,000	
Tax 30%	450,000	
Net Income	1,050,000	

Rickenbacker Inc. Balance Sheet

Cash	200,000	
Accounts Receivable	1,500,000	
Inventory	1,200,000	
PPE	2,100,000	
Total Assets	5,000,000	
Accounts Payable	20,000	
Short-term Notes	-0-	
Long-term Debt	4,900,000	
Equity & Retained Earnings	80,000	
Total Liabilities and Equity	5,000,000	

Step 1: Picture the Problem

Create a pro forma statement by forecasting the future income statement and balance sheet for Rickenbacker. Pro forma financials follow the same format as the firm's financial statements.

Step 2: Decide on a Solution Strategy

Produce values in each account based on its ratio to total revenue or an assumed value given.

Step 3: Solve

The income statement for Rickenbacker:

	This Year	% sales	Next Year	
Revenues	6,000,000	100%	8,000,000	
CGS	1,500,000	25%	2,000,000	
Gross Profit	4,500,000	75%	6,000,000	
Interest Expense	1,000,000	16.7%	1,000,000	assume same
Depreciation	2,000,000	33.3%	2,000,000	assume same
EBT	1,500,000	25%	3,000,000	
Taxes 30%	450,000	7.5%	900,000	
Net Income	1,050,000	17.5%	2,100,000	

The balance sheet for Rickenbacker:

	This Year	% sales	Next Year	
Cash	200,000	3.3%	266,667	
Accounts Receivable	1,500,000	25%	2,000,000	
Inventory	1,200,000	20%	1,600,000	
PPE	2,100,000	35%	2,800,000	
Total Assets	5,000,000	83.3%	6,666,667	
Accounts Payable	20,000	0.3%	26,667	
Short-term Notes	None	0%		plug to increase liabilities
Long-term Debt	4,900,000	81.7%	4,900,000	assume same
Equity & R.E.	80,000	1.3%	2,180,000	add net income less dividend
Total L&E	5,000,000	83.3%	7,106.667	too high, declare dividend
Dividend = Total Assets less Total Liabilities and Equity				
Dividend = 6,666,667 – 7,106,667 = -440,000				to balance pay a dividend
Correct Equity next year = 2,180,000 – 440,000 = 1,740,000				
Corrected Liabilities				
Accounts Payable	20,000	0.3%	26,667	
Short-term Notes	None	0%	0	
Long-term Debt	4,900,000	81.7%	4,900,000	assume same
Equity & R.E.	80,000	1.3%	1,740,000	
Total L&E	5,000,000	83.3%	6,666.667	now equals total assets

Step 4: Analyze

Due to Rickenbacker's high financial leverage and high profitability, the firm will pay a dividend next year of $440,000. Another option would be to pay a small dividend and pay down long-term debt.

Self Test 2: Discretionary Financing Needed

The Island Tourism Board of Vanuatu produced the following financial table based on three scenarios, normal economy, recession, and high growth. Determine the board's DFN.

Vanuatu Financial Position

	Recession	Normal	High Growth
Total Assets	5,000,000	8,000,000	10,000,000
Accounts Payable	1,000,000	1,500,000	2,000,000
Accrued Expenses	100,000	100,000	500,000
Notes Payable	1,000,000	1,400,000	1,500,000
Long-term Debt	3,000,000	3,000,000	3,000,000
Total Liabilities	5,100,000	6,000,000	7,000,000
Common Stock	100,000	100,000	100,000
Retained Earnings	20,000	1,200,000	2,000,000
Total L, E, and R.E.	5,220,000	7,300,000	9,100,000

Step 1: Picture the Problem

Discretionary financial needs arise when the growth in liabilities and equity lags the growth in assets.

Step 2: Decide on a Solution Strategy

Produce values in each account based on its ratio to total revenue or an assumed value given.

Step 3: Solve

To solve for DFN, use the following relationship:

$$\text{Discretionary Financing Needs (DFN)} = \text{Pro forma Total Assets} - \text{Accounts Payable} - \text{Accrued Expenses} - \text{Notes Payable} - \text{Long-term Debt} - \text{Common Equity}$$

This relationship can be shortened in a simple financial statement to total assets less total liabilities and equity.

	Recession	Normal	High Growth
Vanuatu Total Assets:			
	5,000,000	8,000,000	10,000,000
Less Vanuatu Total Sources:			
	5,220,000	7,300,000	9.100,000
Equals Discretionary Financing Needed:			
	–220,000	700,000 900,000	

Step 4: Analyze

The tourism board has financing in place to sustain it during a recession with $220,000 in surplus funding. However, if the tourism business grows with the economy, the board will need to seek an additional $700,000 if growth is normal and $900,000 if growth is high. This funding can come from issues of long-term or short-term debt or from stock issuances.

Self Test 3: Cash Budgeting

Spudnuts, a donut shop in Charlottesville, Virginia, is preparing their cash budget for the second quarter (April, May, and June) and they've asked you for help.

Spudnuts sells 75 percent of their donuts for cash and 25 percent on corporate account. The corporate accounts pay 50 percent of the month's balance in the month following the sale and the remaining 50 percent in the month following that payment.

Spudnuts pays for its supplies partially on account, paying 20 percent one month prior to the sale, 60 percent in the sales month, and the last 20 percent in the following month. Labor costs are paid in the month earned and total $8,000 a month and utilities are $1,000 paid monthly. Determine the cash impact on Spudnuts given the information below:

Spudnut Cash Uses and Sources

	Feb	Mar	Apr	May	June	July
Sales	$30,000	$24,000	$22,000	$20,000	$18,000	$16,000
CGS	$6,000	$4,800	$4,400	$4,000	$3,600	$3,200

Step 1: Picture the Problem

Cash budgets place the cash uses and sources according to the actual time of payment or receipt.

Step 2: Decide on a Solution Strategy

Cash budgeting is similar to placing cash uses and sources on a timeline in a spreadsheet.

Step 3: Solve

To solve, put down a timeline of the months (or quarters) you are studying and place the cash receipts followed by the cash payments in the appropriate time period.

List out the cash receipts by month and then do the same for the cash payments.

	Feb	Mar	Apr	May	June	July
Sales	$30,000	$24,000	$22,000	$20,000	$18,000	$16,000
Cash	$22,500	$18,000	$16,500	$15,000	$13,500	$12,000
Credit Feb	$3,750	$3,750				
Credit March		$3,000	$3,000			
Credit April			$2,750	$2,750		
Credit May				$2,500	$2,500	
Credit June					$2,250	
Revenue Sources		$23,250	$20,750	$18,750		

	Feb	Mar	Apr	May	June	July
CGS	$6,000	$4,800	$4,400	$4,000	$3,600	$3,200
Cash	$960	$880	$800	$720	$640	
Payable March		$2,880	$960			
Payable April			$2,640	$880		
Payable May				$2,400	$800	
Payable June					$2,160	$720
Payable July						$1,920
CGS Total Payables	$4,400	$4,000	$3,600			

	Feb	Mar	Apr	May	June	July
Labor	$8,000	$8,000	$8,000	$8,000	$8,000	$8,000
Utilities $1000	$1,000	$1,000	$1,000	$1,000	$1,000	

Total cash receipts and payments for the second quarter:

	Apr	May	June
Cash In	$23,250	$20,750	$18,750
Cash Out	$13,400	$13,000	$12,600
Change Cash	$9,850	$7,750	$6,150

Step 4: Analyze

Spudnuts' high profit margins and predominantly cash sales allow it to operate during the slower summer months without the need for short-term borrowing as long as no other payments are necessary. Businesses with low margins or long lag times between the sale and the collection of revenue or poor credit that requires the advance purchase of inventory and materials with cash would have great difficulty running their normal operations. When credit is scarce, many manufacturers and retailers find that long cash conversion cycles can threaten the financial stability and viability of many firms in those industries.

CHAPTER 18

Working Capital Management

Chapter **Orientation**

Working capital management encompasses managing the composition of short-term assets and liabilities to give the firm the financial flexibility to purse its day-to-day operating requirements. Working capital management is a part of the firm's short-term liquidity alternatives and improvements in the amount of the firm's assets tied to working capital can dramatically improve the cash needs and liquidity of a firm. There are tradeoffs between carrying inventory and assets to avoid losing a sale and the cost of tying up corporate resources in those assets to make sales. This chapter presents accepted practices in working capital management that are common to most industries.

Chapter Review: **Terms and Concepts**

18.1 Working Capital Management and the Risk–Return Tradeoff

Working capital management manages the day-to-day liquidity of the firm. Firm operations impact cash position and managers must manage the changes in short-term liquidity.

Measuring Firm Liquidity

The current ratio is one of the most popular ratios for measuring liquidity. Since current assets are converted to cash within a year, they can be used to pay off current liabilities. If the current ratio is greater than 1, then working capital is positive.

Managing Firm Liquidity

Management needs to keep a balance between assets and liabilities typically looking for favorable terms for payables and minimizing the use of current assets. Retailers usually keep a large investment in inventories and larger holdings of cash and marketable securities. Using long-term debt or equity to reduce short-term borrowings will increase the firm's liquidity.

Risk–Return Tradeoff

Managing working capital involves a risk-return tradeoff. Increasing profitability may reduce flexibility to respond to unexpected events.

18.2 Working Capital Policy

Managing working capital requires the adoption of a strategy for financing assets and liabilities.

The Principle of Self-Liquidating Debt

This principle matches the maturity of the debt with the length of time that the business activity exists. Seasonal demands for capital are financed with short-term capital that is repaid with proceeds from running the business. Excess liquidity often has firms investing excess capital in safe, low-yield, marketable securities.

Permanent and Temporary Asset Investments

Temporary investments in assets will be liquidated and not replaced within the current year. Examples are cash, marketable securities, accounts receivable, and seasonal fluctuation in inventories.

Permanent investments will not be liquidated within the year. Minimum desired balances of accounts receivable, inventories, and fixed assets are examples.

Spontaneous, Temporary, and Permanent Sources of Financing

Spontaneous sources of financing arise out of the day-to-day operations of the firm. Trade credit is an example as are wages, taxes, and interest.

Temporary sources of financing develop from discretionary actions of the firm. These include unsecured bank loans, commercial paper, and short-term loans.

Permanent sources of financing are intermediate-term loans, long-term debt, preferred stock, and common stock.

Figure 18.1 lists the terminology underlying the principle of self-liquidating debt.

Figure 18.1

Terminology Underlying the Principle of Self-Liquidating Debt

(Panel A) Classification of Types of Investments in Assets

Types of Investments in Assets	Definition and Examples
Temporary	Definition—assets that will be liquidated and not replaced within the current year. Examples—typically current assets such as inventories and accounts receivable.
Permanent	Definition—assets that the firm expects to hold for a period longer than one year. Examples—typically fixed assets such as plant and equipment, although the minimum level of investment in current assets is considered a permanent asset investment as well.

(Panel B) Classification of Types of Sources of Financing

Types of Sources of Financing	Definition and Examples
Spontaneous	Definition—financing sources that arise naturally or spontaneously out of the day-to-day operations of the business. Examples—trade credit or accounts payable, accrued expenses related to wages and salaries, as well as interest and taxes.
Temporary	Definition—current liabilities the firm incurs on a discretionary basis. Unlike spontaneous sources of financing, the firm's management must make an overt decision to use one of the various sources of temporary financing. Examples—unsecured bank loans and commercial paper, as well as loans secured by the firm's inventories or accounts receivable.
Permanent	Definition—long-term sources of discretionary financing used by the firm. Examples—intermediate-term loans, long-term debt (e.g., installment loans and bonds), preferred stock, and common equity.

Figure 18.2 illustrates the principle of self-liquidating debt.

Figure 18.2

Working Capital Policy: The Principle of Self-Liquidating Debt

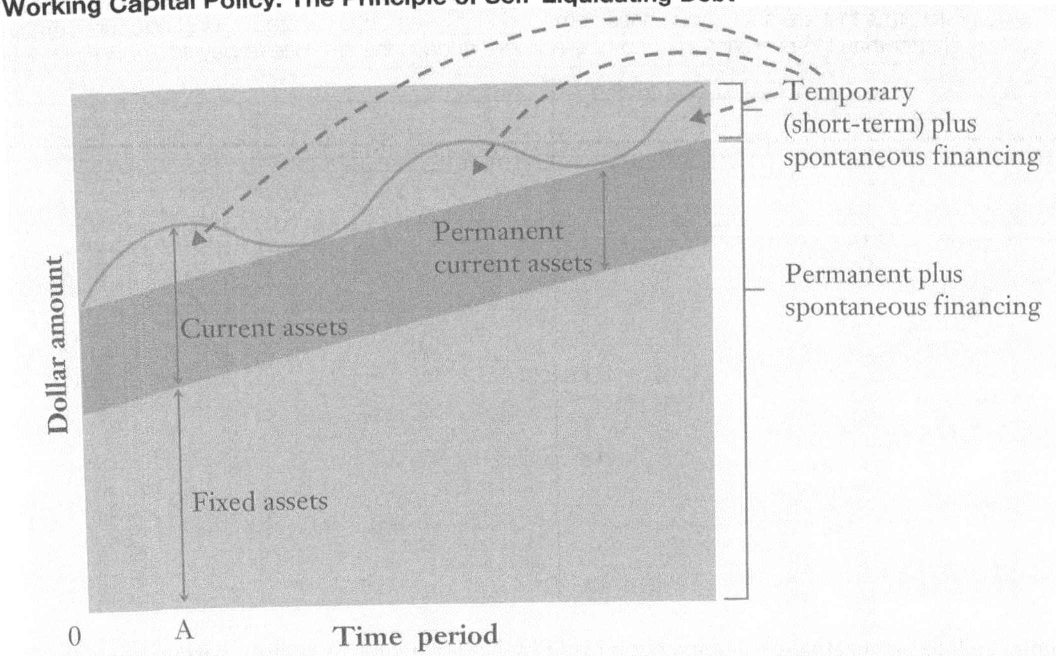

The key observation we make from Figure 18.2 is that the firm's temporary or short-term debt rises and falls with the rise and fall in the firm's temporary investments in current assets.

18.3 Operating and Cash Conversion Cycles

The firm's operating and cash conversion cycle are two popular measures of working capital management. If these cycles are short, then the firm usually has an efficient working capital management system.

Measuring Working Capital Efficiency

The operating cycle measures the time from when inventory is purchased until when the firm collects the cash from its sale. It is the sum of the inventory conversion period plus the days it takes to collect accounts receivable.

$$\text{Operating Cycle} = \text{Inventory Conversion Period} + \text{Average Collection Period} \tag{18–1}$$

The accounts payable deferral period represents the number of days it takes to pay suppliers.

$$\begin{matrix}\text{Accounts Payable}\\ \text{Deferral Period}\end{matrix} = \frac{365}{\left(\begin{matrix}\text{Cost of}\\ \text{Goods Sold}\end{matrix} \div \begin{matrix}\text{Accounts}\\ \text{Payable}\end{matrix}\right)} \tag{18–2}$$

The cash conversion cycle is shorter than the operating cycle due to trade credit.

$$\text{Cash Conversion Cycle} = \text{Operating Cycle} - \text{Accounts Payable Deferral Period} \tag{18–3}$$

Figure 18.3

The Cash Conversion Cycle

A firm's operations typically follow a sequence of milestones: the purchase of items for inventories, the sale of items from inventory for credit, and the collection of accounts receivable. The period of time required for this entire process is called the operating cycle. However, for firms that are able to purchase items for their inventories on credit using accounts payable, the cash conversion cycle is shorter than the operating cycle by the number of days the firm has to pay its accounts payable.

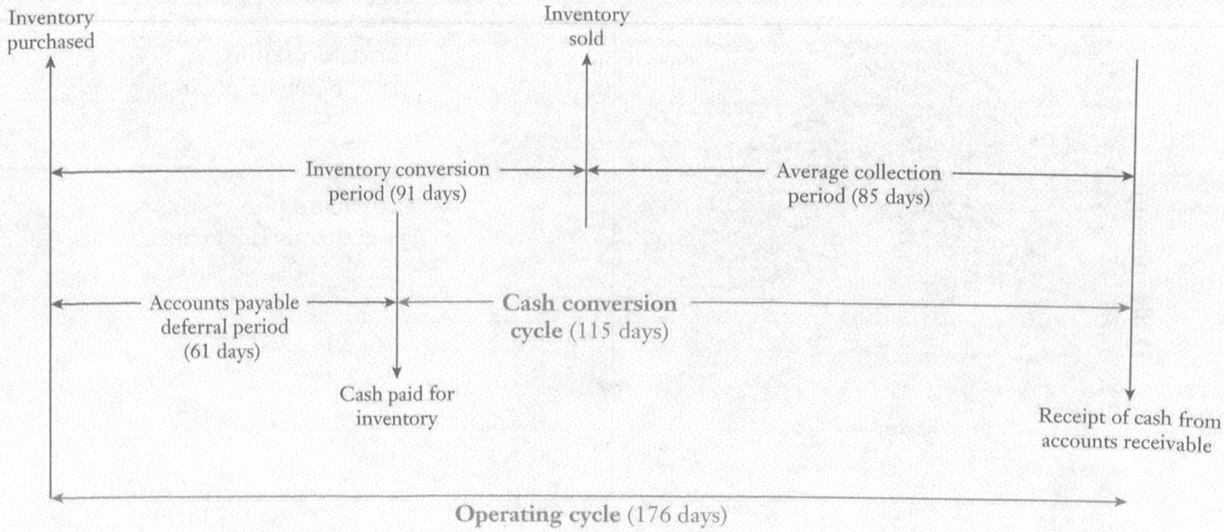

For example, Dell has a negative cash conversion cycle by having a short inventory period, a quick collection period, and a long accounts payable defferal period. In this case, cash flow grows with sales growth, which is unusual for many firms.

Formulas:

$$\text{Operating Cycle} = \text{Inventory Conversion Period} + \text{Average Collection Period} \quad (18\text{–}1)$$

$$\text{Accounts Payable Deferral Period} = \frac{365}{\left(\text{Cost of Goods Sold} \div \text{Accounts Payable}\right)} \quad (18\text{–}2)$$

$$\text{Cash Conversion Cycle} = \text{Operating Cycle} - \text{Accounts Payable Deferral Period} \quad (18\text{–}3)$$

$$\text{Inventory Conversion Period} = \frac{365}{\text{Inventory Turnover Ratio}} \quad (18\text{–}4)$$

$$\text{Inventory Turnover Ratio} = \frac{\text{Cost of Goods Sold}}{\text{Inventory}} \quad (18\text{–}5)$$

$$\text{Average Collection Period} = \frac{\text{Accounts Receivable}}{\text{Daily Credit Sales}} = \frac{\text{Accounts Receivable}}{\left(\text{Annual Credit Sales} \div 365\right)} \quad (18\text{–}6)$$

Calculating the Operating and Cash Conversion Cycle

An example of the calculation:

The example firm has \$15 million in annual credit sales and \$12 million in cost of goods sold. In addition the firm maintains an inventory balance of \$3 million, \$3.5 million in accounts receivable, and has \$2 million in accounts payable outstanding.

To calculate the operating cycle, we need only the inventory conversion period and the accounts receivable collection period.

$$\text{Inventory Turnover Ratio} = \frac{\text{Cost of Goods Sold}}{\text{Inventory}} = \frac{\$12{,}000{,}000}{\$3{,}000{,}000} = 4.0 \qquad (18\text{–}5)$$

This tells us that we run through our average inventory 4.0 times a year, which translates into an inventory conversion period of 91 days,

$$\text{Inventory Conversion Period} = \frac{365}{\text{Inventory Turnover Ratio}} = \frac{365}{4.0} = 91 \text{ days} \qquad (18\text{–}4)$$

The inventory conversion period is simply the number of days it takes for the firm to convert its inventory to credit sales.

The second half of the operating cycle is the average number of days it takes to convert accounts receivable to cash or the average collection period. If credit sales are \$15 million per year and average accounts receivable is \$3.5 million, then,

$$\text{Average Collection Period} = \frac{\text{Accounts Receivable}}{\text{Daily Credit Sales}} = \frac{\$3{,}500{,}000}{\$15{,}000{,}000 / 365} = 85 \text{ days} \qquad (18\text{–}6)$$

We calculate the operating cycle using Equation (18–1) as the sum of the inventory conversion period (91 days) and the average collection period (85 days), is 176 days.

We can calculate the cash conversion cycle using Equation (18–3), but first we need to calculate the accounts payable deferral period.

$$\text{Accounts Payable Deferral Period} = \frac{365}{\left(\text{Cost of Goods Sold} \div \text{Accounts Payable}\right)} \qquad (18\text{–}2)$$

$$\text{Accounts Payable Deferral Period} = \frac{365}{\$12{,}000{,}000 \div 2{,}000{,}000} = 61 \text{ days}$$

$$\text{Cash Conversion Cycle} = \text{Operating Cycle} - \text{Accounts Payable Deferral Period} \qquad (18\text{–}3)$$

$$\text{Cash Conversion Cycle} = 176 \text{ days} - 61 \text{ days} = 115 \text{ days}$$

18.4 Managing Current Liabilities

Current liabilities include unsecured (trade credit, bank loans, and CF) and secured (collateralized loans) of credit. Secured lending based on accounts receivable is known as factoring and the financial institution making the loan is called a factor.

Table 18.1 Sources of Short-Term Credit

(Panel A) Unsecured Sources of Credit:

Trade Credit

Accounts payable arises out of the normal course of business when the firm purchases from its suppliers who allow the firm to make payment after the delivery of the merchandise or services.

Line of Credit

A **line of credit** is generally an informal agreement or understanding between the borrower and the bank about the maximum amount of credit that the bank will provide the borrower at any one time. Under this type of agreement there is no legal commitment on the part of the bank to provide the stated credit. In a revolving credit agreement, which is a variant of this form of financing, a legal obligation is involved. The line of credit agreement generally covers a period of one year corresponding to the borrower's fiscal year.

Bank Transaction Loans

Bank transaction loans are a form of unsecured short-term bank credit made for a specific purpose. This is the type of loan commonly associated with bank credit and is obtained by signing a promissory note.

Commercial Paper

Commercial paper is a short-term debt obligation that is issued by the most creditworthy firms and are bought and sold in the capital markets. One of the advantages of commercial paper rates is that it generally carries a lower rate than do bank loans and comparable sources of short-term financing.

(Panel B) Secured Sources of Credit:

Pledging Accounts Receivable (or Inventories)

Under the pledging accounts receivable (or inventories) arrangement, the borrower simply pledges accounts receivable (inventory) as collateral for a loan obtained from either a commercial bank or a finance company. The amount of the loan is stated as a percentage of the face value of the receivables (inventory) pledged. If the firm provides the lender with a general line on its receivables (inventory), then all of the borrower's accounts (inventories) are pledged as security for the loan.

(Panel C) Raising Cash by Selling Accounts Receivables:

Factoring Accounts Receivable

Factoring accounts receivable involves the outright sale of a firm's accounts to a financial institution called a factor. A **factor** is a firm that acquires the receivables of other firms. The factoring institution may be a commercial finance company that engages solely in the factoring of receivables (known as an old-line factor) or it may be a commercial bank. The factor, in turn, bears the risk of collection and, for a fee, services the accounts. The fee is stated as a percentage of the face value of all receivables factored (usually 1 to 3 percent).

Calculating the Cost of Short-Term Financing

The basic interest equation:

$$\text{Interest} = \text{Principal} \times \text{Rate} \times \text{Time} \quad (18\text{–}7)$$

The cost of short-term financing as an annual percentage rate (APR):

$$\text{Annual Percentage Rate } (APR) = \frac{\text{Interest}}{\text{Principal} \times \text{Time}}$$

or

$$\text{Annual Percentage Rate } (APR) = \frac{\text{Interest}}{\text{Principal}} \times \frac{1}{\text{Time}} \tag{18–8}$$

Evaluating the Cost of Trade Credit

Firm suppliers provide credit at a cost.

Credit Terms and Cash Discounts

A supplier that offers 2/10 net 30 offers a 2 percent discount if paid within 10 days and the full amount is due within 30 days. A firm that doesn't take the 2 percent discount and pays in full 20 days later pays 37 percent interest.

$$APR = \frac{\$.02}{\$.98} \times \frac{1}{20/365} = .3724 \text{ or } 37.24\%$$

Table 18.2 lists the annualized cost of alternative credit terms.

Table 18.2 Annualized Rates of Interest on Selected Trade Credit Terms

Credit Terms	Annualized Rate
2/10, net 60	14.90%
2/10, net 90	9.31
3/20, net 60	28.22
6/10, net 90	29.12

Evaluating the Cost of Bank Loans

Borrowing from a bank requires a firm to set up a line of credit with its lender by keeping a minimum amount on deposit called a compensating balance which increases the rate of interest on borrowings.

18.5 Managing the Firm's Investment in Current Assets

The primary current assets of a firm are cash and marketable securities, accounts receivable, and inventories.

Cash and Marketable Securities

Cash and marketable securities are used to pay bills on a timely basis. Firms hold higher cash balances to avoid defaulting on financial obligations but they earn low rates of return. Table 18.3 summarizes various features.

Costs of Managing Cash and Marketable Securities

Firms accept a lower rate of return to hold highly liquid assets.

Two fundamental problems of cash management:

1. Keeping enough cash on hand to meet obligations on a timely basis.
2. Managing the composition of the firm's marketable securities portfolio.

Problem #1: Maintaining a Sufficient Cash Balance

The cash budget is the principal tool to meet the cash needs of the firm. Firms may try to reduce cash needs by speeding up cash collections and slowing down payments. Some firms try to manage their float, the difference between the firm's records and the bank's records while a check clears by trying to speed (slow) collection (payment). Payers wish to extend float and payees wish to shorten float. Today this is not as large as issue as in the past when checks took a week to clear the banking system.

Problem #2: Managing the Composition of the Firm's Securities Portfolio.

Most firms hold money market securities which mature in less than a year.

Managing Accounts Receivable

Credit sales increase accounts receivable balance and are usually 25 percent of assets. Efficient collection policies will increase profitability and liquidity.

Determinants of the Size of a Firm's Investment in Accounts Receivable

Factors affecting accounts receivable are credit sales as a percentage of sales, the level of sales, and the credit/collection policies of the firm. Figure 18.4 lists these factors.

Figure 18.3 **Features of Selected Money-Market Instruments**

Instruments	Denominations	Maturities	Basis	Liquidity	Taxability
U.S. Treasury bills—direct obligations of the U.S. government	$1,000 and increments of $1,000	28 days, 91 days, and 182 days	Discount	Excellent secondary market	Exempt from state and local income taxes
Federal agency securities—obligations of corporations and agencies created to effect the federal government's lending programs	Wide variation; from $1,000 to $1 million	5 days to more than 10 years	Discount or coupon; usually on coupon	Good for issues of "largest federal" agencies	Generally exempt at local level
Bankers' acceptances—drafts accepted for future payment by commercial banks	No set size; typically range from $25,000 to $1 million	Predominantly from 30 to 180 days	Discount	Good for acceptances of large "money market" banks	Taxed at all levels of government
Negotiable certificates of deposit—marketable receipts for funds deposited in a bank for a fixed time period	$25,000 to $10 million	1 to 18 months	Accrued interest	Fair to good	Taxed at all levels of government
Commercial paper—short-term unsecured promissory notes	$5,000 to $5 million; $1,000 and $5,000 multiples above the initial offering size are sometimes available	3 to 270 days	Discount	Poor; no active secondary market in usual sense	Taxed at all levels of government
Repurchase agreements—legal contracts between a borrower (security seller) and lender (security buyer). The borrower will repurchase at the contract price plus an interest charge	Typical sizes are $500,000 or more	According to terms of contract	Not applicable	Fixed by the agreement; that is, borrower will repurchase	Taxed at all levels of government
Money market mutual funds—holders of diversified portfolios of short-term, high-grade debt instruments	Some require an initial investment as small as $1,000	Shares can be sold at any time	Net asset value	Good; provided by the fund itself	Taxed at all levels of government

Figure 18.4

Determinants of Investment in Accounts Receivable

A firm's accounts receivable balance is a arises out of its sales on credit. Therefore, the level of accounts receivable the firm has outstanding at any point in time depends on the terms of sale offered to customers (i.e., how long they have to repay the firm), the quality of the customers to whom credit is offered (i.e., the likelihood they will repay in a timely manner), and the amount of effort the firm puts into collecting past-due accounts.

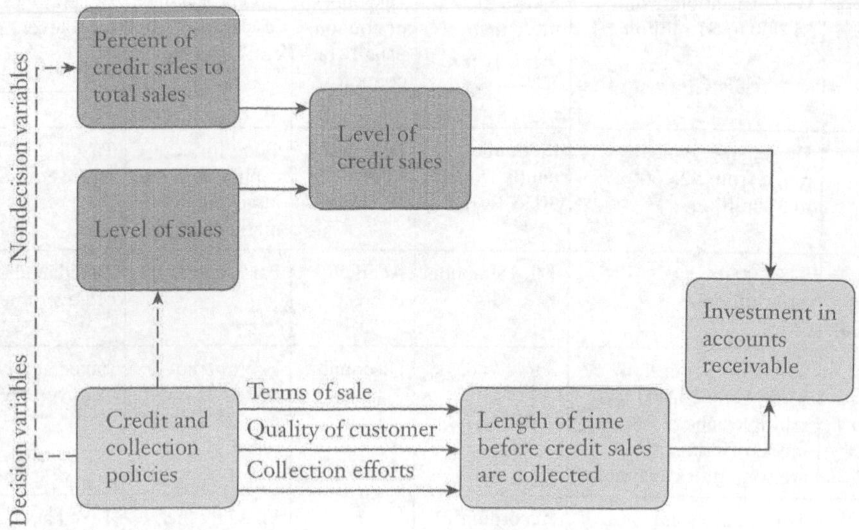

Terms of Sale

The terms of sales list possible discounts, the discount period, and the total credit period.

To calculate the annual opportunity cost:

a: percent discount

b: discount period

c: credit period

Example 2/10 net 30

$$\text{Annualized Opportunity Cost of forgoing the Discount} = \frac{a}{1-a} \times \frac{365}{c-b} \quad (18\text{–}9)$$

Substituting the values from the example, we get

$$\frac{.02}{1-.02} \times \frac{365}{30-10} = 37.24\%$$

The terms of credit vary, but they tend to remain relatively uniform within a given industry.

Customer Quality

As firms extend credit to riskier customers, they have to spend money to identify credit risks. Default and collection costs increase as customer credit quality declines. Credit decisions usually focus on the liquidity of the customer. Credit scores provide an efficient, inexpensive, and uniform method of evaluating credit quality numerically. Customers with good credit quality have a high credit score (more than 700) and borrow at lower rates.

Table 18.4 Representative Rates and Monthly Payments for Different FICO Scores on a $25,000, Three-Year Auto Loan in Mid-2009

FICO Score	Interest Rate	Monthly Payment
760–850	6.000%	$761
700–759	7.150%	$774
660–699	9.000%	$795
620–659	11.534%	$825
580–619	15.275%	$870
500–579	15.761%	$876

Now let's look at the five factors that determine your credit score, with Figure 18.6 illustrating this breakdown.

1. **Your Payment History (35 percent of your score).** Since a lender is considering extending credit to you, it only makes sense that they want to know how you've handled your credit payments in the past.
2. **The Amount You Owe and Your Available Credit (30 percent of your score).** The amount you owe on your credit cards, your mortgage, your car loans, and any other outstanding debt, along with whether you are close to or at your credit limit also is factored in.
3. **Length of Credit History (15 percent of your score).** The longer your credit accounts have been open and the longer you have had accounts with the same creditors, the higher your credit score will be.
4. **Types of Credit Used (10 percent of your score).** If you have several different types of credit outstanding (for example, credit cards, retail accounts, installment loans, auto loans, and a mortgage loan), that is taken as an indicator that you know how to handle your money.
5. **New Credit (10 percent of your score).** Applying for lots of new credit is generally a bad sign. This is because individuals who are moving toward bankruptcy generally take one last grasp at credit, hoping it will keep them afloat. This will lower your score.

Figure 18.6

Factors That Determine Your Credit Score

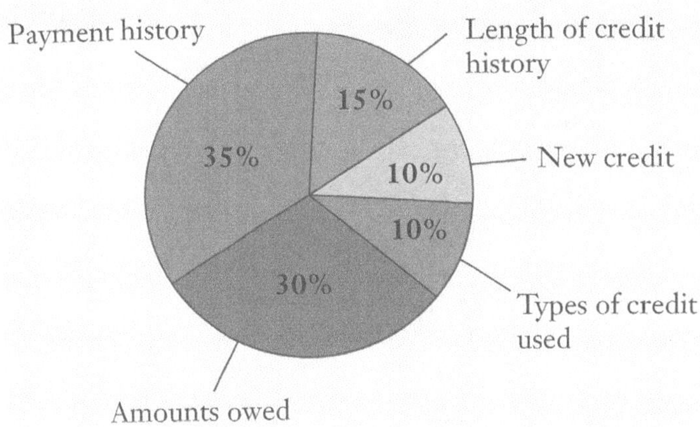

Collection Efforts

Control of accounts receivable focuses on the elimination of past-due receivables by using ratio analysis, aging schedules for receivables, and average collection period analysis. The aging schedule shows how long the firm has been waiting for repayment of receivables.

Table 18.5 Aging Accounts Receivable

Age of Accounts Receivable (Days)	Dollar Value (00)	Percent of Total
0–30	$2,340	39%
31–60	1,500	25
61–90	1,020	17
91–120	720	12
Over 120	420	7
Total	$6,000	100%

Managing Inventories

Inventory management involves the control of assets sold in the normal course of the firm's operations. How much inventory depends on the sales target and the importance of inventory to the sales effort.

Answers to **Concept Checks**

Concept Check **18.1**

1. How does investing more heavily in current assets, other things remaining the same, increase firm liquidity?

2. How does the use of short-term as opposed to long-term liabilities affect firm liquidity?

Answer 1: Investing in current assets increases cash and marketable securities relative to the cash needs of the firm and increase firm liquidity.

Answer 2: Short-term liabilities decrease liquidity as the cash needs are more immediate than those under long-term financing alternatives.

Concept Check **18.2**

1. What is the principle of self-liquidating debt and how can it be used to help the firm manage its liquidity?

2. What are some examples of permanent and temporary investments in current assets?

3. What makes trade credit a source of spontaneous financing?

Answer 1: The principle of self-liquidating debt suggests matching the maturity of debt with the life of the investment. Short-term needs to increase inventories will use short-term debt and long-term assets will use debt with longer maturities.

Answer 2: Temporary investments in current assets are cash, accounts receivable, marketable securities, and seasonal increases in inventories. Permanent assets are fixed assets and minimum levels of inventory and accounts receivables that the firm intends to keep longer than a year.

Answer 3: Spontaneous financing using trade credit arises as the firm's business with its suppliers expands and will decline as business contracts.

Concept Check **18.3**

1. What is a firm's operating cycle?

2. What is the firm's cash conversion cycle and how does it differ from the operating cycle?

Answer 1: The operating cycle measures the time from the purchase of an item for inventory until the time the cash is collected from its sale.

Answer 2: The cash conversion cycle is shorter than the operating cycle by subtracting accounts payable to show cash purchases in the inventory cycle. By making the inventory cycle shorter and stretching out payables, firms can increase profitability and financial flexibility.

Concept Check **18.4**

1. Give some examples of unsecured and secured forms of current liabilities.

2. What does a factor do?

3. What is a bank line of credit?

4. What is the APR equation, and how is it used?

Answer 1: Unsecured liabilities are trade credit, some bank loans, and short-term notes. Secured liabilities are collateralized loans and mortgages.

Answer 2: A factor lends to the firm and is secured by the accounts receivable of the firm.

Answer 3: A bank will extend a line of credit, allowing a firm to borrow up to a limit as needed, in exchange for the firm keeping a minimum level of deposits with the bank.

Answer 4: The APR equation is used to find the annual rate of interest paid on short-term borrowings and is given in the following equation:

$$\text{Annual Percentage Rate (APR)} = \frac{\text{Interest}}{\text{Principal}} \times \frac{1}{\text{Time}} \tag{18–8}$$

Concept Check **18.5**

1. Describe the relationship between the firm's cash management program and the firm's risk of not being able to pay its bills on time.
2. What are the fundamental decisions that the financial manager must make with respect to cash management?

Answer 1: Carrying a high cash balance reduces the risk that a firm will be unable to meet its obligations. An efficient cash management program increases firm profitability and liquidity.

Answer 2: The cash management fundamentals are keeping enough cash on hand to meet the firm's cash disbursal requirements on a timely basis and managing the composition of the firm's marketable securities portfolio.

Multiple Choice **Quiz**

1. The cash conversion cycle is
   a. longer than the operating cycle due to the impact of accounts payable.
   b. equal to the inventory cycle.
   c. shorter than the operating cycle due to the impact of accounts payable.
   d. longer than the inventory cycle due to the impact of accounts payable.

2. A factor lends to firms that have
   a. fixed assets to pledge against the loan.
   b. accounts receivable to pledge against the loan.
   c. real estate to mortgage against the loan.
   d. retained earnings to pledge against the debt.

3. Credit scoring looks at
   a. the interest rate on a firm's debt.
   b. the probability of repayment based on demographic factors.
   c. the probability of repayment based on history of repayment and ability to pay.
   d. the amount of income a borrower earns.

4. Float refers to
   a. the amount of bank debt held by the firm.
   b. the amount of corporate debt by investors.
   c. the credit balance at suppliers.
   d. the difference between the firm's books and the bank's records for the balance available in checking.

5. Money market securities are
   a. loans from banks.
   b. factored accounts receivable resold as debt.
   c. short-term secured borrowings of firms.
   d. short-term unsecured borrowings of firms.

6. Permanent sources of financing are
   a. liabilities that arise out of the operations of the firm's business.
   b. liabilities that will be in place for an extended period of time.
   c. current liabilities that require the firm's discretion to establish.
   d. current assets that will not be replaced within the current year.

7. Temporary sources of financing are
   a. liabilities that arise out of the operations of the firm's business.
   b. liabilities that will be in place for an extended period of time.
   c. current liabilities that require the firm's discretion to establish.
   d. current assets that will not be replaced within the current year.

8. Spontaneous sources of financing are
   a. liabilities that arise out of the operations of the firm's business.
   b. liabilities that will be in place for an extended period of time.
   c. current liabilities that require the firm's discretion to establish.
   d. current assets that will not be replaced within the current year.

9. A line of credit is given
   a. by a bank to a firm to meet short-term cash needs.
   b. by a credit scoring agency to a firm for investors to evaluate.
   c. by a supplier to the firm.
   d. to a customer of the firm.

10. Trade credit is given by a
    a. bank to a firm to meet short-term cash needs.
    b. credit scoring agency to a firm for investors to evaluate.
    c. supplier to the firm.
    d. customer of the firm.

Answers to **Multiple Choice Questions**

1. C
2. B
3. C
4. D
5. D
6. B
7. C
8. A
9. A
10. C

Self Test **with Solutions**

Picture the Problem

Decide on Solution Strategy

Solve

Analyze

Self Test 1: Measuring Firm Liquidity

Comment on the liquidity position of the two firms below as measured by net working capital, the quick ratio, and the current ratio.

	Firm 1	Firm 2
Cash	5,000	25,000
Accounts Receivable	5,000	100,000
Inventory	5,000	25,000
Fixed Assets	20,000	50,000
Accounts Payable	20,000	200,000
Long-term Debt	9,000	80,000
Equity & Retained Earnings	8,000	90,000

Step 1: Picture the Problem

Liquidity analysis often involves a ratio analysis in order to compare large to small firms.

Step 2: Decide on a Solution Strategy

The formulas for the three ratios are:

Net Working Capital = CA – CL

Current ratio = CA / CL

Quick ratio = (Cash + Marketable Securities + Accounts Receivable) / CL

Step 3: Solve

Using the formulas:	**Firm 1**	**Firm 2**
Net Wk'g Cap:	-5,000	-50,000
Current ratio:	.75	.75
Quick ratio:	.50	.625

Step 4: Analyze

Net working capital of Firm 2 is -$50,000 but that should not be compared directly with Firm 1's value of -$5,000. Comparing the current ratio, both firms have the same value of .75. Firm 2 has a better quick ratio due to having less illiquid inventory per dollar of liabilities on hand.

Self Test 2: Analyzing the Conversion Cycle

You and your boss are looking for a business opportunity as a factor that requires you find a firm that can repay you within 90 days. Your boss suggests that you calculate the operating cycle and the cash conversion cycle for Deck Everything and make a recommendation.

Deck Everything, Inc.	
Sales	2,000,000 ($1,600,000 were credit sales)
CGS	1,000,000
Gross Profit	1,000,000
Net Profit	500,000
Accounts Receivable	750,000
Inventory	250,000
Accounts Payable	100,000

Step 1: Picture the Problem

We can use the operating cycle and the shorter cash conversion cycle to determine whether or not Deck Everything has the ability to generate funds to repay your firm within 90 days.

Step 2: Decide on a Solution Strategy

To solve use the formulas for operating cycle and cash conversion cycle:

Operating Cycle = Inventory Conversion Period + Average Collection Period

Cash Conversion Cycle = Operating Cycle – Accounts Payable Deferral Period

Step 3: Solve

To solve for Operating Cycle:

$$\text{Inventory Conversion Period} = \frac{365}{\text{Inventory Turnover Ratio}} = \frac{365}{4.0} = 91 \text{ days}$$

$$\text{Inventory Turnover Ratio} = \frac{\text{Cost of Goods Sold}}{\text{Inventory}} = \frac{\$1,000,000}{\$250,000} = 4.0$$

To solve for the Average Collection Period:

$$\text{Average Collection Period} = \frac{\text{Accounts Receivable}}{\text{Daily Credit Sales}} = \frac{\text{Accounts Receivable}}{\text{Annual Credit Sales} \div 365} = \frac{\$750,000}{\$1,600,000/365} = 171 \text{ days}$$

Operating Cycle = Inventory Conversion Period + Average Collection Period = 91 + 171 = 262 days

To solve for the Cash Conversion Cycle, use the Accounts Payable Deferral Period:

$$\text{Accounts Payable Deferral Period} = \frac{365}{\text{Cost of Goods Sold} \div \text{Accounts Payable}} = \frac{365}{\$1,000,000 \div \$100,000} = 36.5$$

Cash Conversion Cycle = Operating Cycle – Accounts Payable Deferral Period = 262 – 36 = 226 days

Step 4: Analyze

Deck Everything is not a good candidate for factoring unless your firm can accelerate the collections process of 171 days down to 35 days. At the present time the operating cycle is 262 days, and the cash conversion cycle is 226 days. It is unlikely that Deck Everything has any power over its trade creditors and will not be able to expand the payables deferral period. You and your boss will have to find another firm as a factoring candidate.

Self Test 3: Analyzing the Cost of Short-term Credit

Ducati Motorcycles of Medina Lake is evaluating several credit options from local banks. It plans to borrow \$100,000 seasonally for six months to finance its "floor plan," which is used to carry its inventory of Italian motorcycles. Evaluate the four options and recommend one to the dealer.

Option 1. A 15 percent rate of interest, payable at the end of six months with no compensating balance requirement.

Option 2. A 12 percent rate of interest, payable at the end of six months with a 20 percent compensating balance requirement.

Option 3. A 12 percent rate of interest, discounted loan payable at the end of six months with no compensating balance requirement.

Option 4. A 10 percent rate of interest, discounted loan payable at the end of six months with a 20 percent compensating balance requirement.

Step 1: Picture the Problem

The true cost of interest is a function of interest paid, time to repayment, and the money available for the firm's needs less any discount or compensating balances.

Step 2: Decide on a Solution Strategy

The cost of short-term credit can be estimated using the annual percentage rate (APR) equation found in Equation (18–7) as follows:

$$\begin{array}{c}\text{Annual Percentage}\\ \text{Rate } (APR)\end{array} = \frac{\text{Interest}}{\text{Principal}} \times \frac{1}{\text{Time}}$$

Step 3: Solve

Option 1. $$APR = \frac{.15 \times \$100,000}{\$100,000} \times \frac{1}{1/2} = .30 \text{ or } 30\%$$

Option 2. $$APR = \frac{.12 \times \$100,000}{\$100,000 - (.20 \times \$100,000)} \times \frac{1}{1/2} = .30 \text{ or } 30\%$$

Option 3. $$APR = \frac{.12 \times \$100,000}{\$100,000 - \ (.12 \times \$100,000)} \times \frac{1}{1/2} = .273 \text{ or } 27.3\%$$

Option 4. $$APR = \frac{.10 \times \$100,000}{\$100,000 - \ (.10 \times \$100,000) - (.2 \times \$100,000)} \times \frac{1}{1/2} = .286 \text{ or } 28.6\%$$

Step 4: Analyze

The cheapest source of capital is Option 3, the discounted loan without a compensating balance and an interest rate of 12 percent. The first two options have the same *APR* of 30 percent. The last option has the lowest rate, only 10 percent, but the discounted loan structure and the compensating balance makes the *APR* equal to 28.6 percent.

CHAPTER 19

International Business Finance

Chapter Orientation

Expanding internationally brings the opportunity to increase earnings with the risk of currency and economic fluctuations. This chapter focuses on the effect an expansion from domestic to an international business has on a firm's cash flows as well as the risk-return tradeoffs faced by firms that have global operations. Even with the great economic disruptions of the past, firms still see great value in expanding abroad.

Chapter Review: Terms and Concepts

19.1 Foreign Exchange Markets and Currency Exchange Rates

The foreign exchange market is the largest financial market with daily trading volumes of more than $4 trillion. The four major currencies traded are the U.S. dollar, the British pound, the Japanese yen, and the Euro. This market is an over-the-counter market between major banks and financial institutions. Figure 19.1 lists the top 10 currencies and market participants which include:

- Importers and exporters of goods and services,
- Investors and portfolio managers, and
- Currency traders who make markets in currencies.

Foreign Exchange Rates

An exchange rate is the price of one currency stated in terms of another. Quotes can be direct or indirect in terms of the domestic currency. An indirect quote is the reciprocal of the direct quote.

Reading Exchange Rate Quotes

Direct quotes are exchange quotes that list other currencies in terms of the domestic currency. For U.S. firms, a direct quote gives other currencies in terms of the dollar (how many dollars to buy a currency).

An indirect quote lists the domestic currency in terms of other currency (how much is needed to buy one dollar for the United States).

Figure 19.1

The Market for Foreign Exchange

Most Traded Currencies

Currency	% Daily Share of Total Volume	Rank
United States dollar (USD $)	84.9%	1
Euro EUR (EUR €)	39.1%	2
Japanese yen (JPY ¥)	19.0%	3
Pound sterling (GBP £)	12.9%	4
Swiss franc (CHF Fr)	6.4%	5
Australian dollar (AUD $)	7.6%	6
Canadian dollar (CAD $)	5.3%	7
Hong Kong dollar (HKD $)	2.4%	8
Swedish krona (SEK kr)	2.2%	9–10
Norwegian krone (NOK kr)	2.2%	9–10
New Zealand dollar (NZD $)	1.6%	11
Mexican peso (MXN $)	1.3%	12
Other	18.6%	
Total[a]	200.0%	

[a]The total is 200% because trading volume includes one trade for buying and one for selling on each transaction, such that volume is double counted.

Source: *Triennial Central Bank Survey* (December 2011), Bank for International Settlements.

Table 19.1 Foreign Exchange Rates (January 26, 2012)

Country/Currency	in US$	Per US$	Country/Currency	in US$	Per US$
Americas			**Europe**		
Brazil real	0.4791	2.0875	**Euro area euro**	1.3183	0.7585
Canada dollar	1.0074	0.9927	**Norway krone**	0.1784	5.6045
Chile peso	0.002086	479.35	**Russia ruble**	0.03269	30.588
Colombia peso	0.0005629	1776.50	**Sweden krona**	0.1527	6.5483
Mexico peso	0.0770	12.9923	**Switzerland franc**	1.0917	0.9160
Asia-Pacific			1-mos forward	1.0928	0.9151
Australian dollar	1.0362	0.9650	3-mos forward	1.0939	0.9141
1-mos forward	1.0338	0.9673	6-mos forward	1.0961	0.9123
3-mos forward	1.0293	0.9715	**Turkey lira**	0.5574	1.7940
6-mos forward	1.0228	0.9777	**UK pound**	1.6133	0.6198
China yuan	0.1604	6.2352	1-mos forward	1.6133	0.6198
Hong Kong dollar	0.1290	7.7507	3-mos forward	1.6130	0.6200
India rupee	0.01818	55.01545	6-mos forward	1.6128	0.6200
Japan yen	0.01179	84.81	**Middle East/Africa**		
1-mos forward	0.01180	84.78	**Egypt pound**	0.1620	6.1716
3-mos forward	0.01180	84.74	**Israel shekel**	0.2667	3.7492
6-mos forward	0.01181	84.67	**Saudi Arabia riyal**	0.2666	3.7504
New Zealand dollar	0.8215	1.2172	**South Africa rand**	0.1166	8.5791
Pakistan rupee	0.01023	97.720	**UAE dirham**	0.2723	3.6730
South Korea won	0.0009314	1073.70			

Source: Reuters, *The Wall Street Journal Online*, imf.org, Bloomberg.com, ft.com, finance.yahoo.com, fxstreet.com, and cnn.money.com, December 27, 2012.

Example: Direct and Indirect Quotes

From column 1 of Table 19.1, the direct quote for the British pound is \$1.6133. The related indirect quotes is:

$$\text{Indirect quote} = \frac{1}{\text{Direct Quote}} \tag{19–1}$$

Thus,

$$\frac{1}{1.6133} = £.6198$$

Exchange Rates and Arbitrage

An arbitrage in currency exists when two countries have differences in their quoted exchange rates for a currency. The arbitrageur would buy the currency in the cheaper market while selling it at the same time in the more expensive market to lock in a profit on the difference. The differences do not exist for very long as trading will move the two market quotes together as buyers push up prices and sellers push down prices.

Simple arbitrage is trading to lock in a profit on one currency that is quoted differently in two different markets. For example if the pound were quoted with a difference of .0121 pounds between New York and London, an arbitrageur could sell the overpriced pounds in London at .6360 and buy in New York at .6239 to lock in a riskless arbitrage profit. This difference disappears as traders move the quotes together based on the changing demand and supply for currencies.

Asked and Bid Rates

Dealers quote an asked rate and a bid rate on each currency. The asked rate is what the dealer is willing to sell at and the bid rate is the currency quote the dealer is willing to pay for a currency. The difference in the two quotes is the bid-ask spread and is usually very small. It compensates banks for providing liquidity and currency services to customers.

Cross Rates

Finding the quote for a currency by using two exchange rates from different countries is a cross rate. A table of currencies quoted against each other in direct and indirect quotes is a cross rate table. Table 19.2 is a cross rate table.

Example: Finding a Cross Rate between Euro and Pounds

We can take the dollar/pound and the euro/dollar rates from Table 19.2 to find the euro/pound and pound/euro exchange rates. Multiplying the dollar/pound and the euro/dollar exchange rates together, the dollar will cancel out leaving the euro/pound exchange rate,

$$(\$/£)\times(€/\$) = (€/£) \qquad (19–2)$$

Or $1.6133 \times 0.7585 = €1.2237/£$

Thus, the pound/euro exchange rate is $1/1.2237 = £.8172/€$

These rates are the same as those given in the top portion of Table 19.2.

Cross-rate computations make it possible to use quotations in New York to compute the exchange rate between pounds, dollars, and euros. Arbitrage conditions hold in cross rates, too. For example, the pound exchange rate in London (the direct quote euros/pound) must be 1.2237 as shown in the example. The euro exchange rate in London must be £.8172/€.

Table 19.2 Key Currency Cross Rates (December 26, 2012)

The New York foreign exchange selling rates below apply to trading among banks in amounts of $1 million and more, as quoted at 4 p.m. eastern time by Dow Jones and other sources. Retail transactions provide fewer units of foreign currency per dollar.

	Dollar	Euro	Pound	SFranc	Peso	Yen	CanadnDlr
Canada	0.9927	1.3087	1.6015	1.0837	0.0764	0.0117	....
Japan	84.8066	111.8026	136.8181	92.5856	6.5274	....	85.4312
Mexico	12.9923	17.1281	20.9604	14.1841	....	0.1532	13.0880
Switzerland	0.9160	1.2076	1.4777	....	0.0705	0.0108	0.9227
U.K.	0.6198	0.8172	....	0.6767	0.0477	0.0073	0.6244
Euro	0.7585	....	1.2237	0.8281	0.0584	0.0089	0.7641
U.S.	....	1.3183	1.6133	1.0917	0.0770	0.0118	1.0074

Source: Available from Thomson Reuters, wsj.com, and Bloomberg.com/markets/currencies.

Types of Foreign Exchange Transactions

Exchange quotes for immediate action or delivery are spot exchange rates. However, firms may wish to contract now for a transaction at a later date and those exchange rates are forward rates. The actual payment date is known as the delivery date. The terms of an exchange are detailed in a futures or forward exchange contract. Since the actual rates that exist at a later date can vary from the rates that exist today, firms use the contracts to manage exchange rate risk.

Forward rates can be quoted at a premium or discount to the spot rate, known as the forward-spot differential.

Notationally, the relationship may be written:

F – S = premium (F > S) or discount (S > F)

$$F - S = \begin{cases} \text{Premium if } F > S \\ \text{Discount if } F < S \end{cases} \qquad (19\text{–}3)$$

where F = the forward rate, direct quote

S = the spot rate, direct quote

The premium or discount can also be expressed as an annual percentage rate:

$$\frac{F - S}{S} \times \frac{12}{n} \times 100 = \text{annualized percentage} \qquad (19\text{–}4)$$

Premium ($F > S$) or Discount ($S > F$)

where n = the number of months of the forward contract

For example, if you wanted to compute the percent-per-annum discount or premium on the 30-day pound using the information in Table 19.1 you would use Equation (19–4) as follows,

Step 1: Identify F, S, and n.

$F = 1.6130$, $S = 1.6133$, $n = 3$ month

Step 2: Because F is less than S, we compute the annualized percentage discount as follows:

$$= \frac{1.6130 - 1.6133}{1.6133} \times \frac{12 \text{ months}}{3 \text{ months}} \times 100$$

$$= -0.00019 \times 4 \times 100 = -0.0744\%$$

The percent-per-annum discount (that's why the answer takes on a negative value) on the 30-day pound is –0.0744 percent.

19.2 Interest Rate and Purchasing-Power Parity

Interest Rate Parity

Interest rates between countries are linked by their exchange rates. Specifically, the interest parity condition can be stated as follows:

$$\text{Difference in interest rates} = \text{Ratio of the forward and spot rates}$$

$$\frac{\left(1 + \text{Domestic Rate of Interest}\right)}{\left(1 + \text{Foreign Rate of Interest}\right)} = \left(\frac{\text{Forward Exchange Rate}}{\text{Spot Exchange Rate}}\right) \tag{19–5}$$

This equation can be rearranged such that,

$$\left(1+\text{Domestic Rate of Interest}\right) = \left(\frac{\text{Forward Exchange Rate}}{\text{Spot Exchange Rate}}\right)\left(1+\text{Foreign Rate of Interest}\right) \tag{19–5a}$$

Example: Dollar and Yen Interest Rate Parity

The six-month risk-free rate of interest in the United States was 2 percent on January 26, 2012. The U.S. dollar and the Japanese yen spot exchange rate on this date was .01179 and the forward exchange rate for six months hence was .01181. According to interest rate parity, what is the six-month risk-free rate of interest to be in Japan? Substituting into Equation (19–5a) we calculate the following:

$$\left(1+\text{U.S. Six-Month Risk-Free Rate of Interest}\right) = \left(\frac{\text{Forward Exchange Rate}}{\text{Spot Exchange Rate}}\right)\left(1+\text{Japanese Six-Month Risk-Free Rate of Interest}\right)$$

$$(1+.02) = \left(\frac{.01181}{.01179}\right)\left(1+\text{Japanese Six-Month Risk-Free Rate of Interest}\right)$$

$$(1+.02) = 1.001696\left(1+\text{Japanese Six-Month Risk-Free Rate of Interest}\right)$$

Thus, the Japanese six-month risk-free rate of interest =.018273 or 1.8273%

Your return is the same whether you stay in dollars or exchange to yen, invest abroad, and convert back to dollars. The yen appreciation plus interest on the debt equals 2 percent.

Purchasing-Power Parity and the Law of One Price

Purchasing power parity (PPP) finds that exchange rates adjust so that the cost of goods and services have roughly the same value in different economies and countries. The spot rate of exchange should be identical to the ratio of the price of goods between the home and foreign country.

$$\text{Spot Exchange Rate for Euros} \times \text{U.S. Price of an iPod} = \text{French Price of an iPod} \tag{19–6}$$

More generally, the spot exchange rate for the foreign country (in this case the spot exchange rate for euros) should be equal to the ratio of the price of the good in the home country (P_h) to the price of the same good in the foreign country (P_f), i.e. for an iPod priced at $350 in the United States and €250 in Europe,

$$\text{Spot Exchange Rate } = \frac{P_h}{P_f}$$

Thus, as we just showed, the spot exchange rate of $/€ should be the following:

$$\text{Spot Exchange Rate } = \frac{P_h}{P_f} = \frac{\$350}{€250} = \$1.40 / €$$

Therefore, PPP implies that if a new Callaway FT-i golf club cost €300 in France, it should cost €300 × 1.4 = $420 in the United States where the $/€ exchange rate is 1.4.

This makes economic sense due to the Law of One Price. In international trade, the worth (or value) of a good should not depend on where it is sold since exchange rates can adjust prices for the differences in currency values. Taxes, regulations, land costs, and labor costs may cause the law of one price to hold approximately rather than exactly.

Figure 19.2 presents the Big Mac index compiled by the *Economist* magazine.

The International Fisher Effect

The domestic Fisher effect (FE) finds that nominal rates reflect expected inflation and the real rate of return. The international Fisher effect (IFE) assumes that real returns are the same worldwide and exchange rates vary due to differences in expected rates of inflation between economies.

The Domestic Fisher Effect:

$$\begin{matrix}\text{Nominal Rate}\\ \text{of Interest}\end{matrix} = \begin{matrix}\text{Expected Rate}\\ \text{of Inflation}\end{matrix} + \begin{matrix}\text{Real Rate}\\ \text{of Interest}\end{matrix} + \begin{bmatrix}\text{Expected Rate}\\ \text{of Inflation}\end{bmatrix}\begin{bmatrix}\text{Real Rate}\\ \text{of Interest}\end{bmatrix} \qquad (19\text{–}7)$$

The International Fisher Effect:

$$\begin{matrix}\text{Nominal Rate}\\ \text{of Interest in Country A}\end{matrix} \approx \begin{matrix}\text{Expected Rate}\\ \text{of Inflation in Country A}\end{matrix} + \begin{matrix}\text{Real Rate}\\ \text{of Interest}\end{matrix} \qquad (19\text{–}8)$$

As a result,

$$\begin{matrix}\text{Real Rate}\\ \text{of Interest}\end{matrix} \approx \begin{matrix}\text{Nominal Rate}\\ \text{of Interest in Country A}\end{matrix} - \begin{matrix}\text{Expected Rate}\\ \text{of Inflation in Country A}\end{matrix} \qquad (19\text{–}9)$$

Figure 19.2

Purchasing-Power Parity and the Price of a Big Mac

The relative prices of Big Macs are used in a light-hearted attempt to determine the percentage of overvaluation of a currency relative to the U.S. dollar.

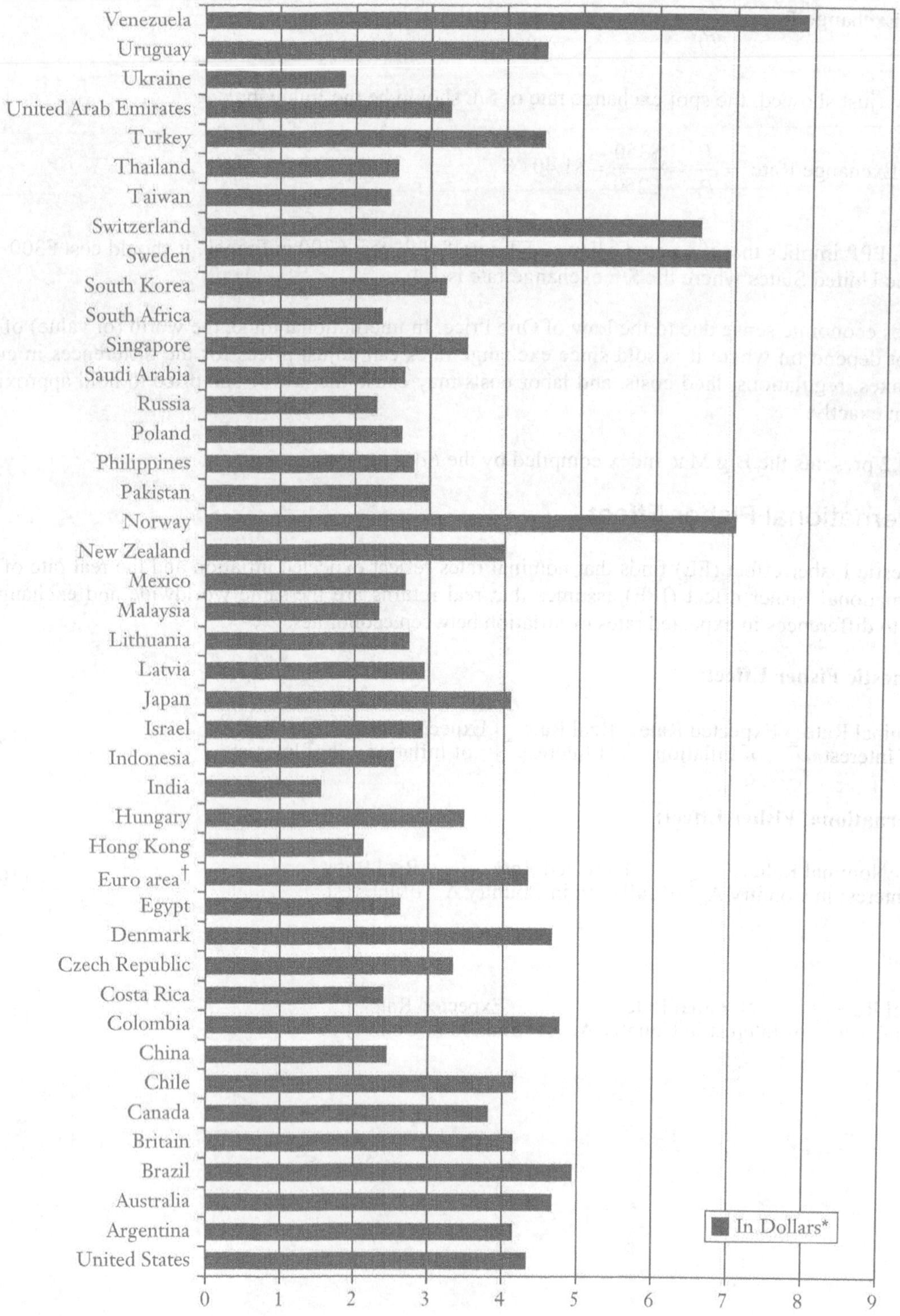

*At current exchange rates (July 25, 2012).

†Average of four cities.

Example: International Fisher effect for U.K. and Japan

Assume that the real rate of interest is 3 percent in all countries. This means that if the expected inflation rate in Great Britain is 10 percent, and the expected inflation rate in Japan is 6 percent, interest rates in Great Britain and Japan will be (.10 + .03 + .003) or 13.3 percent and (.06 + .03 + .0018) or 9.18 percent, respectively.

The IFE is an approximation but suggests that high nominal rates are created by high levels of expected inflation and that high nominal earnings will be offset by inflation's impact on the value of currency.

Note that the United States represents about one-half of the world's equity markets and divisification into other assets should consider currency effects.

19.3 Capital Budgeting for Direct Foreign Investment

Direct foreign investment occurs when a firm in one country makes a physical investment in another country. Multinational corporations (MNCs) operate across international borders.

The prime reason for international investment is the prospect of earning higher rates of return even though they may have higher risk. Projects in foreign countries may not be able to return 100 percent of their cash flows to the parent company, so project analysis should only include cash flows that the parent firm expects to receive from its foreign subsidiary.

If the firm uses a discount rate based on dollar interest rates, then the cash flows also must be measured in dollars.

Example: American Firm Invests in Brazil

An American firm is considering investing in a new project that will produce the following cash flows measured in Brazilian Reals (BRL) that are expected to be repatriated to the parent company,

Year:	Cash Flow (in million of BRL) :
0	–8
1	3
2	4
3	5
4	6

The first task at is to determine the appropriate discount rate. Given the combination of currency risk and other risks associated with doing business in Brazil, the firm has determined that it should require a 10 percent premium over the 4 percent risk-free rate. Thus, the appropriate discount rate for this project is 14 percent.

Next, the cash flows have to be converted from Brazilian reals into U.S. dollars. The problem we run into is that futures markets (the Chicago Mercantile Exchange) only provide exchange rates for the BRL for about a year forward. However, from equation (19–5), we know that forward rates reflect the interest rate differential in the two countries, implying that we can determine forward exchange rates we the following formula,

$$n\text{-Year Forward Exchange Rate} = \left(\frac{\left(1+\begin{array}{c}\text{Domestic}\\\text{Rate of Interest}\end{array}\right)}{\left(1+\begin{array}{c}\text{Foreign}\\\text{Rate of Interest}\end{array}\right)}\right)^{n} \times (\text{Spot Exchange Rate}) \qquad (19\text{–}10)$$

Let's assume n is 1, and let's solve for the interest rate differential,

1 year forward exchange rate = (interest rate differential)^1 × (Spot Exchange Rate)

Let's assume the one year forward exchange rate is 0.41BRL/$ and the spot exchange rate is 0.45BRL/$, from that we can determine the interest rate differential to be 0.9111. Thus, we can determine the implied forward exchange rates as follows,

Year	Spot Exchange Rate	×	(interest rate differential)^n	=	Forward Exchange Rate for year n
0	spot rate			=	0.45BRL/$
1	0.45BRL/$	×	0.9111	=	0.41BRL/$
2	0.45BRL/$	×	$(0.9111)^2$	=	0.3735BRL/$
3	0.45BRL/$	×	$(0.9111)^3$	=	0.3403BRL/$
4	0.45BRL/$	×	$(0.9111)^4$	=	0.3101BRL/$

We can now use these forward exchange rates to convert the cash flows measured in Brazilian reals to US$ as follows,

Year:	Cash Flow (in million of BRL)	×	Conversion factor	=	Cash Flow (in millions of $)
0	–8	×	$2.222/BRL/	=	–$17.78
1	3	×	$2.439/BRL	=	7.317
2	4	×	$2/677/BRL	=	10.708
3	5	×	$2.939/BRL	=	14.691
4	6	×	$3.225/BRL	=	19.350

Using Equation 11–1 and discounting these cash flows back to the present at the required rate of return of 14 percent we get a net present value of $878,620,

$$NPV(\$\text{ millions}) = -\$17.78 + \frac{\$7.317}{(1+.14)^1} + \frac{\$10.708}{(1+.14)^2} + \frac{\$14.691}{(1+.14)^3} + \frac{\$19.350}{(1+.14)^4}$$

$$= \$18.25 \text{ million}$$

Thus, the project should be accepted.

Foreign Investment Risks

Two sources of risk in domestic capital budgeting are: business risk related to the product or project, and financial risk based on the capital structure of the firm. Foreign capital budgeting risk also includes political risk and exchange rate risk.

Political Risk

Political risk may arise from operating in a politically unstable part of the world. Nationalization is an extreme outcome. Some examples of political risk that may change the cash flow paid to the parent firm are:

1. Expropriation of plants and equipment without compensation.
2. Expropriation with minimal compensation that is below actual market value.
3. Nonconvertibility of the subsidiary's foreign earnings into the parent's currency—the problem of blocked funds.
4. Substantial changes in tax rates.

5. Governmental controls in the foreign country regarding the sale price of certain products, wages and compensation paid to personnel, the hiring of personnel, transfer payments made to the parent, and local borrowing.
6. Requirements regarding the local ownership of the business.

All of these controls and governmental actions put the cash flows of the investment to the parent company at risk. Thus, these risks must be considered before making the foreign investment decision. For example, the MNC might decide against investing in countries with risks of types 1 and 2 as mentioned above, whereas other risks can be borne—provided that the returns from the foreign investments are high enough to compensate for them. In fact, insurance against some types of political risks can be purchased from private insurance companies or from the U.S. government's Overseas Private Investment Corp. It should be noted that although an MNC cannot protect itself against all foreign political risks, political risks also are present in domestic business.

Exchange Rate Risk

Exchange rate risk is that the value of a firm's operations and investments will be adversely affected by chagnes in exchange rates.

Answers to **Concept Checks**

Concept Check 19.1

1. What is a spot transaction? What is a direct quote? An indirect quote?
2. What is a forward exchange rate? Why would a company be interested in it?
3. What is the forward spot differential and how is it calculated? Why would a company be interested in it?

Answer 1: A spot transaction is one that immediately delivers the good or service that is purchased. A direct quote is the amount of domestic currency it takes to buy one unit of foreign currency, i.e., how many dollars does it take to buy one euro? An indirect quote is the reciprocal, how much does foreign currency buy of our currency, i.e., euro per dollar.

Answer 2: A forward exchange rate is the quoted price of two currencies for a transaction at a later date. Firms are interested in forward exchange rates so that they can lock in the value of their transaction now rather than face the uncertainty later.

Answer 3: The forward spot differential shows the difference between spot exchange rates and those exchange rates for transactions at later times. Firms are interested in the differential when managing their exchange rate risk. The calculations for the differential are:

Notationally, the relationship may be written:

F – S = premium (F > S) or discount (S > F)

$$F - S = \begin{cases} \text{Premium if } F > S \\ \text{Discount if } F < S \end{cases} \qquad (19\text{–}3)$$

where F = the forward rate, direct quote

S = the spot rate, direct quote

The premium or discount can also be expressed as an annual percentage rate, computed as follows:

$$\frac{F-S}{S} \times \frac{12}{n} \times 100 = \text{annualized percentage} \qquad (19\text{–}4)$$

Premium (F > S) or Discount (S > F)

where n = the number of months of the forward contract

Concept Check **19.2**

1. What does the term *interest rate parity* mean?

2. What is the law of one price? Give a simple example.

3. What is the International Fisher Effect?

Answer 1: Interest-rate parity finds that interest rates between countries are directly linked to the ratio of their currency exchange rates.

Answer 2: The law of one price finds that goods should have the same value in the world no matter what country sells the good. For example, gold should be worth about the same amount regardless of the country where it trades.

Answer 3: The International Fisher Effect finds that the difference in interest rates between countries is related to differences in expected inflation (assumes that the real rate is the same globally).

Concept Check **19.3**

1. Define the types of risk that are commonly referred to as political risk, and give some examples of them.

2. What is exchange rate risk? Why would a multinational firm be concerned about it?

Answer 1: Political risk represents risk due to changes in governmental policy toward business. Political risk can be changes in regulation, legislation, taxation, and even nationalization of assets.

Answer 2: Exchange rate risk to an MNC is the risk that values of projects and investments change unexpectedly and adversely from the conditions present when the investment was made. Firms operating globally can increase value to shareholders by managing their exchange rate risk and lowering overall firm risk levels.

Multiple Choice **Quiz**

1. The buying rate for a currency dealer is the same as the
   a. bid-ask spread.
   b. ask rate.
   c. bid rate.
   d. real rate.

2. A cross rate is found by
   a. adding inflation to the real rate.
   b. solving for the value of a third currency from two exchange rates.
   c. averaging the bid and ask rates.
   d. finding the rate quotes of several banks and averaging.

3. A direct currency quote is
   a. the amount of domestic currency needed to buy one unit of a foreign currency.
   b. the real-time differences from currency dealers seeking to buy currency.
   c. the difference between buying and selling a currency.
   d. the amount of foreign currency needed to buy one unit of a domestic currency.

4. The bid-ask spread is
   a. the amount of domestic currency needed to buy one unit of a foreign currency.
   b. the real-time differences from currency dealers seeking to buy currency.
   c. the difference between buying and selling a currency.
   d. the amount of foreign currency needed to buy one unit of a domestic currency.

5. An indirect quote is
   a. the amount of domestic currency needed to buy one unit of a foreign currency.
   b. the real-time differences from currency dealers seeking to buy currency.
   c. the difference between buying and selling a currency.
   d. the amount of foreign currency needed to buy one unit of a domestic currency.

6. The forward exchange rate is
   a. the ratio of domestic to foreign currency for immediate delivery.
   b. the exchange quote for a specific country.
   c. the ratio of domestic to foreign currency for later delivery.
   d. the value of a currency priced in gold.

7. The spot exchange rate is
   a. the ratio of domestic to foreign currency for immediate delivery.
   b. the exchange quote for a specific country.
   c. the ratio of domestic to foreign currency for later delivery.
   d. the value of a currency priced in gold.

8. The International Fisher Effect states:
   a. Global inflation is the same across countries.
   b. The value of goods and services are the same across countries.
   c. The expectation of inflation is the same, but real rates differ across countries.
   d. The expectation of inflation differs, but real rates are the same across countries.

9. Purchasing Power Parity relies upon
   a. the domestic Fisher effect to price goods.
   b. the Law of One Price to price goods.
   c. the International Fisher Effect to price goods.
   d. the forward premium relationship to price goods.

10. Interest rate parity states:
    a. Rates differ between countries due to the cost of goods.
    b. Rates differ between countries due to the differences in exchange rates.
    c. Rates differ between countries due to unexpected inflation.
    d. Rates differ between countries due to the cross rate.

Answers to **Multiple Choice Questions**

1. C
2. B
3. A
4. C
5. D
6. C
7. A
8. D
9. B
10. B

Self Test **with Solutions**

Picture the Problem

Decide on Solution Strategy

Solve

Analyze

Self Test 1: Currency Arbitrage

As a trader for JP Morgan, you trade dollars against euros to find small mispricings of 5 to 20bp on most trades. You prefer to trade mispricings greater than 10bp. Look at the euro quoted in New York and London and find the arbitrage profit in dollars and percent on a trade of 100M euros.

New York Currency Euro	London Contract	$ / Euro	$ / Euro
	Spot	1.1942	1.1955
	30 Day	1.1967	1.1967
	90 Day	1.1977	1.19775

Step 1: Picture the Problem

In this problem you will be buying the cheap currency market and selling in the expensive currency market, trading dollars for euros in one and euros for dollars in the other.

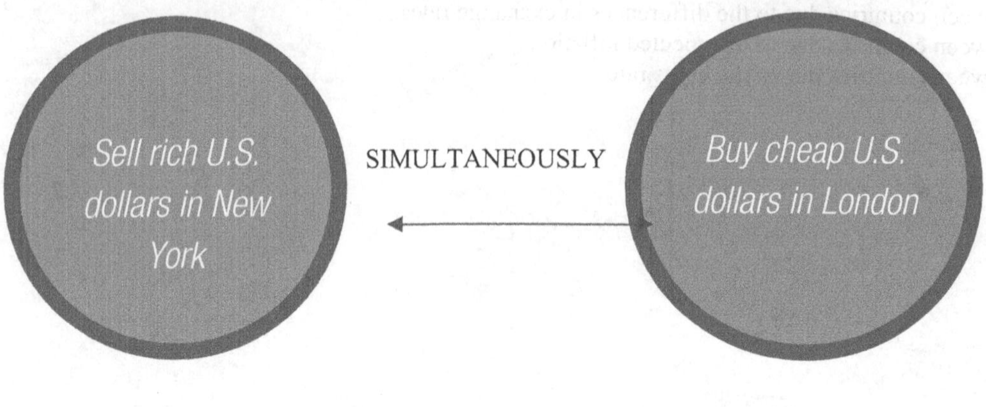

Step 2: Decide on a Solution Strategy

The spot quote in New York for euros is 1.1942 dollars and in London the quote is 1.1955 dollars, a difference of 13bp. The euro buys more in London than it does in New York (or the dollar has a lower value in London than New York). To buy the dollar low, buy it in London (sell euros) and sell it (buy euros) in New York.

Step 3: Solve

Step 1. Because the dollar is cheaper in London, buy €100,000,000 worth of dollars in London. The number of dollars purchased would be $\$100,000,000 \times 1.1955 = 119,550,000$ dollars.

Step 2. Simultaneously sell the dollars in New York at the prevailing rate of 1.1942. The amount received in euros upon the sale of the dollars would be:

$$119,550,000 \,/\, \$1.1942/\text{euro} = €100,108,859$$

The net gain is $100,108,859 – €100,000,000 = €108,859 profit or about 10.8bp, 1/10 of 1 percent, on the trade.

Step 4: Analyze

Assuming no transaction costs, arbitrage profits are possible. In this example, there was no risk at all in your transactions. Transactions costs, trading delays, and trading pressure by other traders will make this more difficult to do in the real world. As traders move prices , the arbitrage disappears. Had the trader started with US $100M, the trader would start with a buy of euros in New York and sell them in London to convert back to dollars for a $108,859 profit.

Self Test 2: Interest Rate Parity

You have to determine the nine-month rate for a U.K. bond that is priced in pounds. Your boss suggests that you look at exchange rates and make an educated guess. On your Bloomberg terminal, you find the following information:

	U.S.	U.K.
Risk free 6 mo	1.2%	1.0%
Risk free 9 mo	1.5%	?
Risk free 12 mo	2.0%	2.2%
USD per UK £		
Spot		1.4421
6 mo		1.4446
9 mo		1.4430
12 mo		1.4440

Step 1: Picture the Problem

In this problem we are determining what the nine-month rate of interest will be in the United Kingdom. To do this, use the interest rate parity equation.

The difference in interest rates is related to the difference in spot and forward exchange ratios.

Step 2: Decide on a Solution Strategy

This problem can be easily solved using the inteest rate parity equation. In this case we know everything except the foreign interest rate.

Step 3: Solve

Substituting into Equation (19–5a) we calculate the following:

$$\left(1+\frac{\text{U.S. nine-month risk-free}}{\text{Rate of Interest}}\right)=\left(\frac{\text{Forward Exchange Rate}}{\text{Spot Exchange Rate}}\right)\left(1+\frac{\text{UK nine-month risk-free}}{\text{Rate of Interest}}\right)$$

$$(1+.015)=\left(\frac{1.4430}{1.4421}\right)\left(1+\frac{\text{Foreign}}{\text{Rate of Interest}}\right)=1.014367$$

Thus, $\frac{\text{Foreign}}{\text{Rate of Interest}}=.014367$ or 1.4367%.

Step 4: Analyze

Since the value of the pound is appreciating against the dollar, the rate paid by U.K. bonds is a little less than the comparable U.S. rate for nine months. Interest rate parity is based upon the idea that you get the same total return whether you change your dollars to pounds, and invest in the risk-free rate in London and then convert them back to dollars, or simply invest your dollars in the U.S. risk-free rate of interest. In effect, interest rate differentials are considered when spot and forward exchange rates are determined in the market.

CHAPTER 20

Corporate Risk Management

Chapter Orientation

Risk management is the process of analyzing a firm's risk exposure and developing alternatives to manage firm risk. Firms actively manage their risk exposure by operational changes, long-term contracts to control costs, and by the use of insurance and financial derivatives. Firms can manage the risk of natural events (hurricanes, floods), product prices, currency prices, and interest rate changes. The chapter covers a five-step process to setting a risk management strategy and details some common approaches to controlling risk.

Chapter Review: Terms and Concepts

20.1 Five-Step Corporate Risk Management Process

Step 1: Identify and Understand the Firm's Major Risks

Most common sources of risks are:

1. Demand risk—changes in product or service demand driven by competitive forces and economic growth.
2. Commodity risk—changes in commodity prices.
3. Country or political risk—changes in corporate wealth due to government policy and political unrest.
4. Operational risk—cost overruns and poor execution of business plans creates volatility in cash flow.
5. Foreign exchange risk—changes in exchange rates alter cash flows and the value of projects.

Four of the five sources are external to the firm.

Step 2: Decide Which Sources of Risk to Keep and Which to Transfer

This is the heart of risk management: keeping and transferring risks.

Step 3: Decide How Much Risk to Assume

Determine the firm's risk profile, its appetite for risk. Factors such as management preferences for risk, access to capital, industry practice, and capital structure will influence this profile.

Step 4: Incorporate Risk into All the Firm's Decisions and Processes

Develop a systematic means to control the firm's risk exposures. Every important decision should be made with the firm's overall risk profile in mind. To transfer risk, the firm has to decide on the means to remove risk such as insurance, derivatives, contracts, and/or operational changes.

Step 5: Monitor and Manage the Risks the Firm Assumes

To assure the firm's actions are consistent, firms will centralize monitoring of the firm's risk exposure with a chief risk officer who reports to the CEO and presents to the board.

All five steps are essential.

20.2 Managing Risk with Insurance Contracts

Insurance exchanges a payment for the transfer of a risk of loss.

Types of Insurance Contracts

There are five types of insurance commonly found in business: property insurance, business interruption insurance, key person insurance, directors' and officers' insurance, and workers' compensation.

Type of Risk	Type of Insurance Contract Used to Hedge
Property damage to company facilities due to fire, storm, or vandalism	Property insurance
Loss of business resulting from a temporary shutdown because of fire or other insured peril.	Business interruption insurance
Loss of income resulting from the disability or death of an employee in a key position	Key person life insurance
Losses suffered by the officers and directors of the firm due to alleged errors in judgment, breaches of duty, and wrongful acts related to their organizational activities	Directors and officers insurance
Losses due to on-the-job injuries suffered by employees	Workers' compensation insurance

Why Purchase Insurance?

Usually the benefit of insurance outweighs the costs of retaining the risk over the long term. Companies choose to self-insure those risks that the firm is willing to take. Self-insurance usually entails setting aside funds in case of a loss.

20.3 Managing Risk by Hedging with Forward Contracts

The term hedging refers to taking a strategy or action to offset price risk. A forward contract allows a firm to set a price on a later transaction, removing uncertainty. A spot contract transacts without delay while forward and futures contracts are settled at future dates using prices agreed to today.

Hedging Commodity Price Risk Using Forward Contracts

By entering a forward contract for fuel at $100 per barrel, both airlines and refineries lock in a price of $100, no matter what the actual price of the fuel is on the settlement date when the actual transaction occurs. Both sides agreed to the contract knowing that one may benefit on the price change and the other will lose on the price change. By knowing the exact price of the transaction occurring at a later date, firms can plan more effectively. One side is protecting against the risk of buying at higher prices later and the other is protecting against the risk of selling at a lower price later.

Figure 20.2

Delivery Date Profits or Losses (Payoffs) from a Forward Contract

The term **long position** often is used to refer to the ownership of a security, contract, or commodity. That is, if you purchase a share of stock you are said to be "long" the stock. Correspondingly, a **short position** is the opposite of a long position and involves the sale of a security, contract, or commodity. This means that the payoff to a short position is simply minus the payoff to a long position. If you would make money with a long position this means you would lose money with a short position, and vice versa.

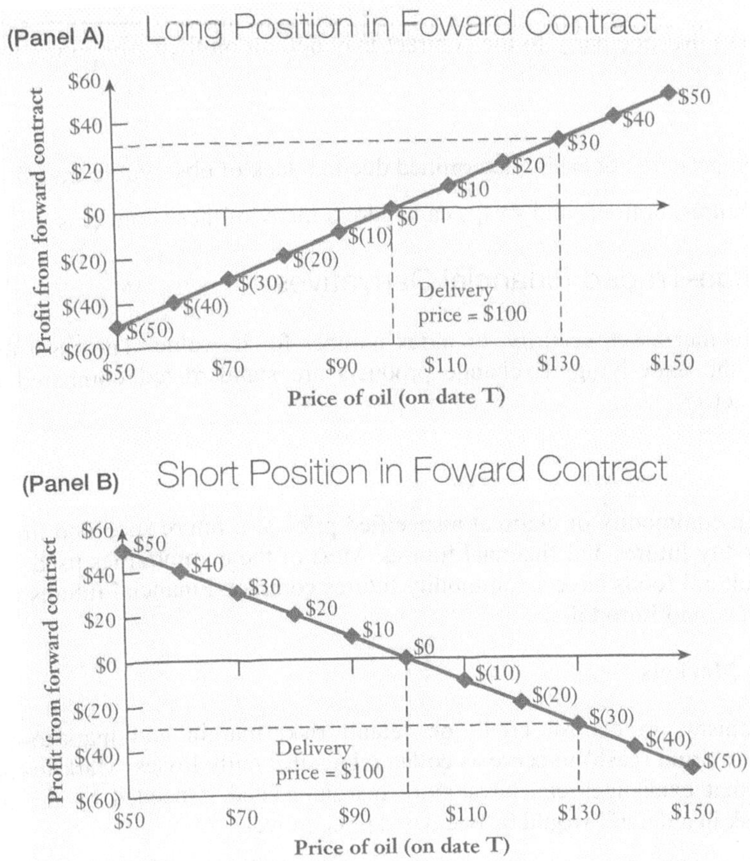

Hedging Currency Risk Using Forward Contracts

Firms operating globally will have to convert currencies to their home currency. Firms expecting cash flows in later months can use forward currency contracts to lock in the value of the transaction.

Example: Disney and Yen Risk

Disney expects 500M yen in three months and again in six months which it will convert to dollars by buying USD in the currency market.

Step 1: To hedge the first cash flow, Disney enters a three-month currency forward, quoted at .009123 and sells 500M yen at the forward price. In three months, Disney will have the 500M to deliver at the settlement date per the forward contract.

Step 2: To complete the transaction at the settlement date in three months, Disney will take the $4,561,500 USD it receives via the futures contract from its 500M yen using the forward contract price of .009123.

To hedge the second cash flow, Disney would repeat the steps with a six-month forward, quoted at .009178.

The mirror opposite of this trade would be Toyota receiving dollars periodically and using a forward to lock in the value in terms of yen by buying the yen contract that Disney sells. It also is possible for these firms to swap values directly rather than go through the exchange is there is a cost advantage to the swap.

Limitations of Forward Contracts

Forwards are negotiated long-term contracts that can be tailored to the needs of the firm. Some limitations are:

1. Credit risk exposure (default risk) that one party to the contract may default on their obligation to pay at the settlement date.
2. Sharing of strategic information.
3. Market values of negotiated contracts are not easily determined due to a lack of observable traded prices.

Exchange-traded contracts such as futures, options, and swaps can address many of these concerns.

20.4 Managing Risk with Exchange-Traded Financial Derivatives

A derivative contract depends on another asset, security, or index number for its value. The asset that the derivative depends upon is called the underlying. Exchange products are standardized compared to the customized terms of a forward contract.

Futures Contracts

A future is a contract to buy or sell a commodity or claim at a specified price at a future specified time. The two categories of futures are commodity futures and financial futures. Most of the commodities used in large scale manufacturing and most agricultural foods have a commodity futures contract. Financial futures include bonds, equity indexes, currencies, CDs, and Eurodollars.

Managing Default Risk in Futures Markets

Futures exchanges use two mechanisms to control credit or default risk: margin and mark-to-market accounting. Participants have to post margin (cash) to serve as collateral against daily losses. Mark-to-market updates losses and gains daily so that exchanges can have more margin posted if needed by the losing counterparty. Thus, the maximum risk in a default would be one day's price move.

Figure 20.4

Marking to Market on Futures Contracts

Upon initiating a futures contract the exchange will require the parties to the contract to post an initial margin. In this example the margin is roughly 16 percent of the $25,780 (= $2,578 x 10 contracts) value of the 10 contracts. In addition, the exchange requires that the firm not allow the margin account to drop below a maintenance margin level such that the margin account never goes to zero.

Date	Margin Account Balance on 10 Contracts	Value of 1 Futures Contract	Change in 1 Futures Price	Change in Value of 10 Contracts
1-Oct-12	$4,000	$2,578		
2-Oct-12	3,180	2,496	$(82)	$(820)
3-Oct-12	3,250	2,503	7	70
4-Oct-12	3,880	2,566	63	630

Hedging with Futures

Futures hedges are very similar to forward hedges. A firm will sell a future to protect against a selling price going lower and will buy a future to protect it from a buying price going higher. Selling a future is a short hedge, and buying a future is a long hedge. Futures contracts are standardized and may not be a perfect hedge given the firm's needs.

Some practical problems are:

1. No contract or a dissimilar contract is available for hedges.
2. The hedging firm may not know the exact date of the transaction.
3. The settlement dates of the futures contracts do not match the firm's needs exactly.

All of these issues result in basis risk, which means the price of the hedge contract doesn't follow the actual prices the firm is trying to offset. Firms will choose a similar contract with high correlation to their price risk when an identical contract is not available. Firms often hold hedges to a settlement date beyond when they intend to transact to avoid having to deliver on the terms of the future before the risk is resolved by transacting.

Options Contracts

If a firm would like a chance at an upside while hedging against a downside, it may use option contracts. A call option gives its owner the right, but not the obligation, to buy at a price over a given time period. A put option gives the right, but not the obligation, to sell at a price over a time period. Owners of the options pay for their rights and will use them only when it is valuable to do so. The process of selling options is known as option writing.

The exercise or strike price is the contract price for the transaction. The option premium is the price paid for the option. The option expiration date is the date the contract expires along with all the rights in the contract. An American option can be exercised at any time up to the expiry while a European option contract can only be exercised on the expiry date.

A Graphical Look at Option Pricing Relationships

In Figure 20.5 and all other profit and loss graphs, the vertical axis represents the profits or losses realized *on* the option's expiration date, and the horizontal axis represents the corresponding stock price *on* the expiration date. To keep things simple, we ignore any transaction costs.

Figure 20.5

Expiration Date Profit or Loss from Purchasing a Call Option

Suppose you purchase a call on Ford Motor Company (F) stock with an exercise price of $20 for a premium of $4. As long as the expiration date price of Ford's common stock is less than the $20 exercise price, the call option will expire worthless. It is said to be "out of the money." If the price of Ford's stock on the expiration date is equal to $20 it is "at the money," and if it is higher than $20 then the call option is "in the money" with a profit equal to the difference between the stock price and the exercise price.

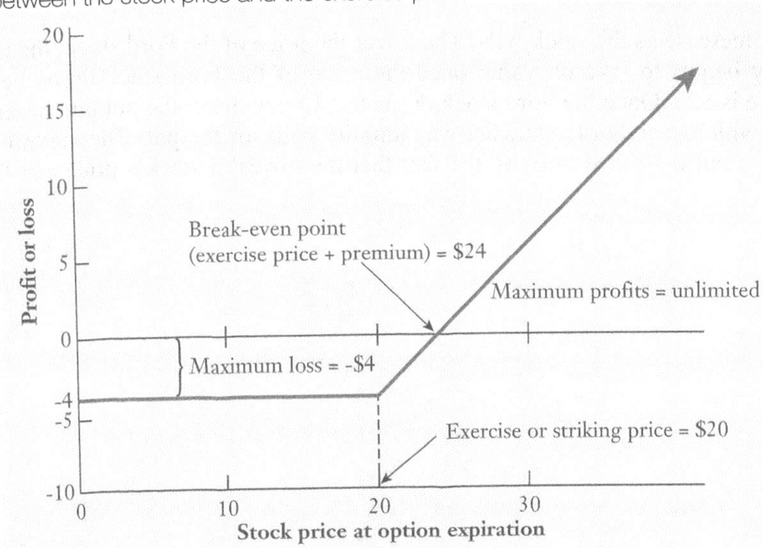

For the Ford 20 call, the call will be worthless at expiration if the value of the stock is less than the exercise or striking price. Although the option will be worthless at expiration, if the stock price is below the exercise price, the most that an investor can lose is the option premium—that is, how much he or she paid for the option, which in this case was $4. Once the stock price climbs above the exercise price, the call option takes on a positive value and increases in a linear one-to-one basis as the stock price increases. Once the price hits $24 the investor breaks even since the investor has earned enough profits to cover the $4 premium he or she paid for the option in the first place.

To the call writer, the profit and loss graph is the mirror image of the call purchaser's graph. Figure 20.6 shows the profits and losses at expiration associated with writing a call option. Once again, we will look at the profits and losses at expiration. The maximum profit to the call writer is the premium, or how much the writer received when the option was sold, whereas the maximum loss is unlimited.

Figure 20.6

Expiration Date Profit or Loss from Selling (Writing) a Call Option

In this example we assume that you sell or "write" a call option on Ford Motor Company (F) stock with an exercise price of $20 for which you are paid a premium of $4. If the price of Ford's shares ends up below $20 per share, then the call option will expire worthless and the option writer (seller) will not face any financial obligation. However, if the price of Ford's shares rises above $20, the owner of the option gets the difference in the stock price and the exercise price (a profit—see Figure 20.5) and the option writer faces a loss equal to this same difference.

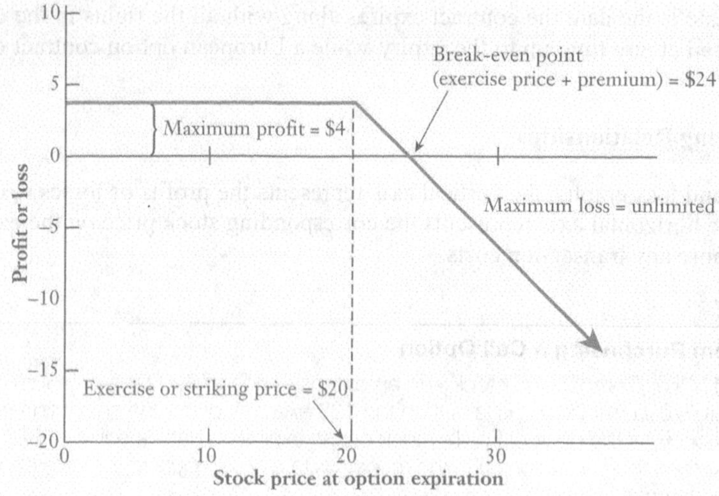

For owners of puts, their profits increase as the stock falls. The lower the price of the Ford stock, the more the put is worth. Here the put only begins to take on value once the price of the Ford stock drops below the exercise price, which in this case is $20. Once the Ford stock drops to $17 per share, the put purchaser breaks even by making $3 on the put, which exactly offsets what was initially paid for the put. The maximum gain associated with the purchase of a put is limited only by the fact that the lowest a stock's price can fall to is zero.

Figure 20.7

Expiration Date Profit or Loss on Holding a Put Option

Suppose you purchase a put option on Ford Motor Company (F) stock with an exercise price of $20 and for a premium of $3. As long as the expiration date price of Ford's shares remains above the $20 exercise price, the put is worthless or "out of the money." Should the price of Ford's shares fall below $20 per share on the expiration date, then the put option holder will receive $1 for every dollar the price falls below $20, and once the price falls below $17, he or she will make a profit.

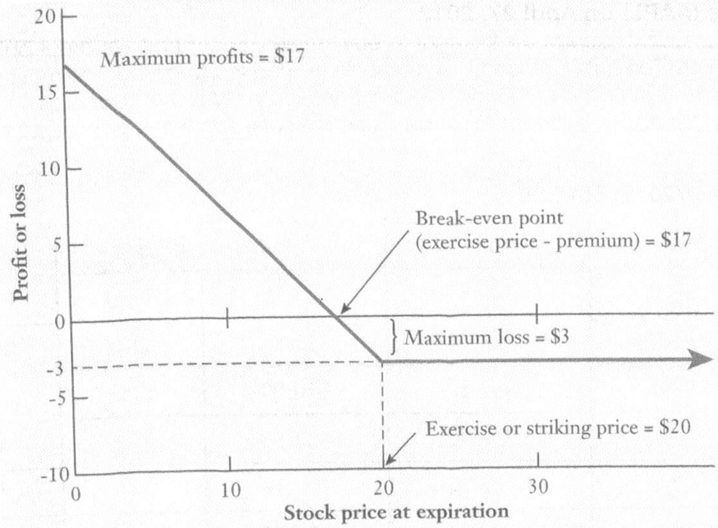

To a put writer, the profit-and-loss graph is the mirror image of the put purchaser's graph. Here the most a put writer can earn is the premium, or the amount for which the put was sold. The potential losses for the put writer are limited only by the fact that the stock price cannot fall below zero.

Although the stock price may fluctuate, the possible losses to the purchaser of an option are limited, whereas the possible gains are almost unlimited. That is, the most you can ever lose when you purchase a put or call option is the premium you pay for the contract. Owners of options have limited downside while writers of options have limited upside: that limited amount is the option premium.

Figure 20.8

Expiration Date Profit or Loss from Selling (Writing) a Put Option

Suppose you write or sell a put option on Ford Motor Company (F) stock with an exercise price of $20 for a premium of $3. Should the price of Ford's shares drop below the $20 exercise price on the put option you have sold, you will then be obligated to pay the difference in the $20 exercise price and the stock price to the holder of the option (see Figure 20.7).

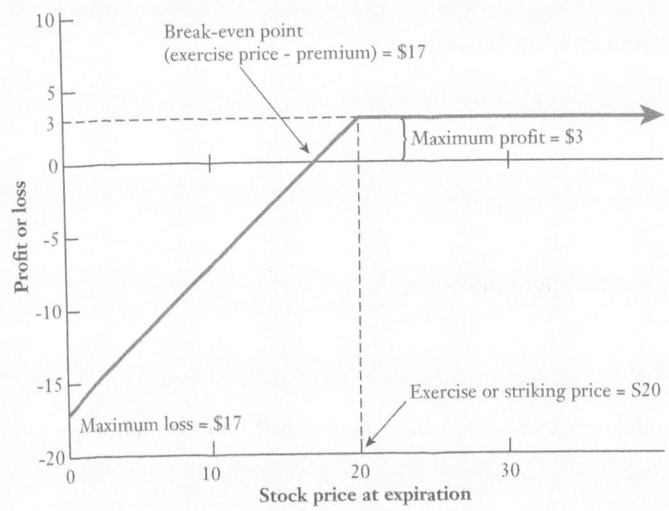

Reading Option Price Quotes

Option prices are per share and the option contract usually covers 100 shares. The contracts give the month of expiration and the day is usually the third Friday of the month. Various contract prices known as strike or exercise prices are listed for each month.

Figure 20.9

Option Price Quotes for Apple Computers (AAPL) on April 27, 2012

Pricing information is provided for both call options, which represent the right to buy the shares of Apple, and put options, which carry with them the right to sell Apple shares. The data included in the graphic include the following: the most recent price of Apple's common stock, "Last Sale" identifies the price of the most recent transaction, "Volume" represents the number of option contracts traded that day, and "Open Int" is the total number of option contracts that have not yet been exercised, expired, or fulfilled by delivery.

AAPL (APPLE INC) Closing price as of 12/27/2012: $515.06

Calls	Last Sale	Vol	Open Int	Puts	Last Sale	Vol	Open Int
13 Jan 510	$20.55	3740	5462	13 Jan 510	$15.45	4034	9364
13 Jan 515	$17.80	3431	3667	13 Jan 515	$17.85	2954	7759
13 Jan 520	$15.50	5714	8395	13 Jan 520	$20.00	2552	16866
13 Jan 525	$13.67	2582	7229	13 Jan 525	$22.55	739	14957
13 Feb 510	$32.20	1326	2737	13 Feb 510	$27.34	646	2832
13 Feb 515	$29.65	829	1485	13 Feb 515	$30.35	543	2681
13 Feb 520	$26.80	1752	3359	13 Feb 520	$32.30	541	2862
13 Feb 525	$24.75	722	2905	13 Feb 525	$35.25	309	3903

Sources: www.cboe.com, www.quote.com, Wall Street Journal online, www.fidelity.com, and OptionsHouse.com

20.5 Valuing Options and Swaps

Option prices at expiration are the difference between the underlying asset price and the option strike price. This section covers how to value options before the expiration date.

The Black-Scholes Option Pricing Model

The BSOPM is the most popular option pricing model. The value of an option depends on the probability of it having value at expiration.

Key Variables in the Black-Scholes Option Pricing Equation

The six key inputs to BSOPM:

1. Price of the underlying asset
2. The option's exercise or strike price
3. The length of time left until expiration
4. The expected stock price volatility over the life of the option
5. The risk-free rate of interest
6. The underlying stock's dividend yield

The Price of the Underlying Stock. Higher prices increase the value of call options and decrease the value of puts.

The Option's Exercise or Strike Price. Higher strike prices decrease the value of call options and increase the value of put options.

The Length of Time Left Until Expiration. More time increases the probability of the underlying moving beyond the strikes for both calls and puts. As time decreases, both call and put options waste away and decrease in value.

The Expected Stock Price Volatility over the Life of the Option. More volatility increases the probability that prices move beyond the strike prices and increases the value of both calls and puts.

The Risk-Free Rate of Interest. Higher risk-free rates represent a higher opportunity cost to cash that is used to buy stock, so higher rates increase call values which save cash by not owning the underlying. Higher rates decrease put values.

The Underlying Stock's Dividend Yield. When dividends are paid, stock prices drop. Higher dividends will reduce the value of call options and increase the value of put options.

The Black-Scholes Option Pricing Equation

The Black-Scholes option pricing model for call options can be stated as follows:

$$\begin{matrix}\text{Call Option}\\ \text{Value } (Call)\end{matrix} = \begin{pmatrix}\text{Stock Price}\\ \text{Today } (P_0)\end{pmatrix} N(d_1) - \begin{pmatrix}\text{Strike}\\ \text{Price } (X)\end{pmatrix}\left[e^{-(\text{risk-freerate})\times(\text{time to expiration})}\right] N(d_2) \quad (20\text{–}1)$$

In this formula, the value of the call option is a function of the current stock price (P_0), the strike price of the option (X), the risk-free rate of interest, time to expiration of the option, plus two remaining terms that need some additional explanation, $N(d_1)$ and $N(d_2)$.

The bracketed term $\left[e^{-(\text{risk-freerate})\times(\text{time to expiration})}\right]$ is simply a discount factor where continuous discounting is used and "e" is the base of natural logarithms (approximately 2.7183).

The two remaining terms in Equation (20–1) are $N(d_1)$ and $N(d_2)$ where $N(d_i)$ is the probability of drawing a value less than d_i from the standard normal distribution. To calculate the Black-Scholes option price, we calculate this probability for two different values, d_1 and d_2, that are defined as follows:

$$d_1 = \frac{ln\left(\dfrac{\begin{matrix}\text{Stock Price}\\ \text{Today}\end{matrix}}{\begin{matrix}\text{Strike}\\ \text{Price}\end{matrix}}\right) + \left(\begin{matrix}\text{Risk-free}\\ \text{Rate}\end{matrix} + \dfrac{\begin{matrix}\text{Variance in}\\ \text{Stock Returns}\end{matrix}}{2}\right) \times \begin{matrix}\text{Time to}\\ \text{Expiration}\end{matrix}}{\sqrt{\begin{matrix}\text{Variance in}\\ \text{Stock Returns}\end{matrix}} \times \sqrt{\begin{matrix}\text{Time to}\\ \text{Expiration}\end{matrix}}} \quad (20\text{–}2)$$

and

$$d_2 = d_1 - \sqrt{\begin{matrix}\text{Variance in}\\ \text{Stock Returns}\end{matrix}} \times \sqrt{\begin{matrix}\text{Time to}\\ \text{Expiration}\end{matrix}} \quad (20\text{–}3)$$

Of the six variables, the variance must be estimated, but the other variables are directly observable.

Checkpoint 20.3 provides an example that illustrates how the Black-Scholes formula is used to value a call option. Note that you will need to refer to your statistics book to estimate $N(d_1)$ and $N(d_2)$ or use the Normdist function for a mean of 0 and a standard deviation of 1 or the Normsdist function in Excel.

Swap Contracts

A swap contract allows firms to trade a set of payments tied to an interest rate or a currency with another firm's payments tied to an alternate set of payments tied to a different rate or currency. Interest rate sways trade interest payments and currency swaps trade currency payments. The amount of the payments is tied to the swap's baseline value known as notional principal. Notional principal doesn't change hands, only the payments in interest or currency that are based on it.

An example of a Libor for fixed 9.75 percent rate swap on a $250 million notional principal follows:

Figure 20.10

Fixed Rate for Floating Interest Rate Swap

The notional principal of the swap is $250 million with coupon interest payments made semiannually. The variable (floating) rate is equal to the six-month LIBOR rate observed at the beginning of each six-month interest period, and the fixed rate is 9.75%.

$\frac{9.75\%}{2} \times \$250 \text{ million}$ (Fixed Rate Coupon, C)

$\frac{8.5\%}{2} \times \$250 \text{ million}$ (Floating Rate Coupon, D)

Year (A)	6-Month LIBOR Rate (B)	Fixed Rate Coupon (C)	Floating Rate Coupon (D)	Net Swap Cash Flow Fixed for Floating (E)
0.00	8.5%			
0.50	7.2%	12,187,500	$10,625,000	$(1,562,500)
1.00	10.0%	12,187,500	$ 9,000,000	$(3,187,500)
1.50	9.3%	12,187,500	$12,500,000	$ 312,500
2.00	9.8%	12,187,500	$11,625,000	$ (562,500)
2.50	10.8%	12,187,500	$12,250,000	$ 62,500
3.00	11.3%	12,187,500	$13,500,000	$ 1,312,500
3.50	11.5%	12,187,500	$14,125,000	$ 1,937,500
4.00	10.5%	12,187,500	$14,375,000	$ 2,187,500
4.50	9.5%	12,187,500	$13,125,000	$ 937,500
5.00		12,187,500	$11,875,000	$ (312,500)

In this illustration, the firm that initiates the swap contract has a floating rate obligation, so it must pay floating rate payments found in column (D) of Figure 20.10. However, after entering into the swap the firm now pays the swap counterparty the fixed coupon payments found in column (C) and receives a set of payments equal to the floating rate payments found in column (D). The floating rate payments that the firm receives as part of the swap are exactly equal to its floating rate obligations under the terms of its floating rate loan. Thus, the firm pays the floating rate interest using the proceeds of the swap agreement and then is left with the set of fixed rate coupon payments. Consequently, the firm has converted its floating rate loan into a fixed rate loan.

A swap contract is typically structured as a "zero cost" security. That is, the fixed rate in the swap contract is set based on the current market conditions and the credit worthiness of the borrower.

An American firm that has a substantial amount of its income generated from sales made in England might enter in a currency swap with an English firm. If the value of the British pound depreciated from 1.90 dollars to the pound to 1.70 dollars to the pound, each sale made in England would bring fewer dollars back to the parent company in the United States. This could be offset by the effects of the currency swap because it costs the U.S. firm fewer dollars to fulfill the English firm's interest obligations. The nice thing about a currency swap is that it allows the firm to engage in long-term exchange rate risk hedging because the debt obligation covers a relatively long time period.

These look like great ideas—enter into a contract that reduces risk—but just as with the other derivative securities, they are dangerous if used by those who don't understand their risks. For example, in 1994 Procter & Gamble Corp. lost $157 million on swaps that involved interest rate payments made in German marks and U.S. dollars. How did this happen? Exchange rates and interest rates did not go the way Procter & Gamble had anticipated and the costs were greater than the company expected.

Answers to **Concept Checks**

Concept Check 20.1

1. What are the five steps in the risk management process?

2. Describe the primary types of risk that a firm might face.

Answer 1: The five steps of the risk management process are:

1. Identify and understand the firm's major risks.
2. Decide which types of risks to transfer.
3. Decide how much risk to assume.
4. Incorporate risk into all the firm's decisions.
5. Monitor and manage the risks the firm assumes.

Answer 2: The primary types of risk faced by the firm are demand, commodity, political, operational, and foreign-exchange risks.

Concept Check **20.2**

1. What is insurance, and how is it used to manage risk?

2. What are some common risks that are transferred through the use of insurance?

Answer 1: Insurance is a contract to transfer risk of loss from one entity to another for a premium. Insurance allows firms to transfer large unwanted risks to an insurer in exchange for a small premium.

Answer 2: Insurance can be used to insure property from loss, directors and officers from liability, firms from loss of a key manager or a loss of business, and employees from losses due to job injuries.

Concept Check **20.3**

1. What is a forward contract? Contrast a forward contract with a spot contract.

2. What are the limitations of forward contracts as tools for managing risk?

Answer 1: A forward contract sets the terms of a transaction to occur at a later date. A forward contract covers a transaction at a later date and a spot contract is for a transaction occurring that day.

Answer 2: The limitations of forward contracts are that they are illiquid, custom contracts between two counterparties and are subject to default risk. Forwards require firms to share strategic information. Another limitation is that the value of the forward is not easily observable.

Concept Check **20.4**

1. What is meant by the term *financial derivative* contract?
2. Define and contrast the following types of financial derivatives: options, futures, and forwards.

Answer 1: A financial derivatives contract determines its value based on the price of another asset or index (the underlying asset determines the value of the derivative). Standardized contracts are traded on public exchanges.

Answer 2: An option gives the owner the right, but not the obligation, to buy or sell an asset. A future is similar to a forward but it is an exchange-traded standardized contract that obligates a buyer or seller to a transaction at a specific time period at a specific price. A forward is an illiquid, custom contract that requires both parties to trade at a later date and can be for a longer period of time than is possible using futures. All of these allow firms to transfer unwanted risks.

Concept Check **20.5**

1. What are the six factors that determine the value of an option contract?
2. Define a swap contract and describe how it can be used to manage risk.

Answer 1: The six factors that determine the value of an option are time, risk-free rate, dividends, asset price, strike price, and volatility.

Answer 2: Swaps allow large firms to exchange payments based on one rate or currency for another over longer periods than a typical standardized contract. This allows firms to transfer interest rate, currency, and credit risk subject to the credit quality of their counterparties.

Multiple Choice **Quiz**

1. Basis risk from derivatives exists because
   a. counterparties may be unable to pay for their transaction.
   b. claims may be held with the same time period as the derivative.
   c. there are mismatches between the firm's actual risk and hedge contract terms.
   d. the risk-free rate is used to price the derivative.

2. Credit risk from derivatives is greater in
   a. options.
   b. exchange-traded futures.
   c. exchange-traded swaps.
   d. forwards.

3. A European option requires
   a. the writer to use the option anytime after the expiry.
   b. the owner to use the option only on the expiration date.
   c. the owner to use the option anytime before the expiry.
   d. the writer to use the option only on the expiration date.

4. A futures contract is
   a. an exchange-traded derivative that give the owner a right to trade.
   b. a derivative that does not have easily observable prices.
   c. a legal contract that outlines the terms of a transaction.
   d. a custom contract between two parties.

5. Marking to market is
   a. a daily posting to futures accounts to reflect market values of positions.
   b. the trading of futures contracts between funds.
   c. the accounting audit of a futures trader.
   d. the written order to close out a futures trade.

6. Notional principal is
   a. the amount exchanged in a swap.
   b. the amount that determines the value of payments exchanged on a swap.
   c. the face value of a bond.
   d. the face value of an option contract.

7. An option writer has
   a. the right to sell an asset.
   b. the right to buy an asset.
   c. the obligation to perform according to the terms of the contract.
   d. no obligation to perform according to the terms of the contract.

8. Margin is used to
   a. reduce counterparty risk in futures.
   b. protect borrowers from investment banks.
   c. protect lenders to the exchange.
   d. reduce risk of option premiums.

9. A put option gives
   a. the owner the obligation to buy an asset.
   b. the seller the obligation to buy an asset.
   c. the owner the right to sell an asset.
   d. the seller the right to sell an asset.

10. An oil refinery setting a direct, simple hedge for its purchases of crude would
    a. buy a put option.
    b. sell a forward.
    c. buy a future.
    d. sell a call option.

Answers to **Multiple Choice Questions**

1. C
2. D
3. B
4. C
5. A
6. B
7. C
8. A
9. C
10. C

Self Test **with Solutions**

Picture the Problem

Decide on Solution Strategy

Solve

Analyze

Self Test 1: Hedging Commodity Price Risk

You run the risk management operation for a large manufacturer that buys steel as a material for its products. The head of production has forecasted that they will need approximately 1,000,000 tons of steel next quarter. Your boss, the CEO, has asked for two alternatives to lower the price risk of steel in three months.

Steel sells for $600 per ton today. There's an 80 percent chance that steel prices do not move substantially in three months, but a 10 percent chance that steel can move higher by 30 percent and a 10 percent chance of moving lower by 30 percent. You look at two derivatives: a steel future and an OTC call option. The three-month futures contract has a contract price of $610 per ton. The option has an exercise price of $600 and a premium of $20 per ton.

What would be your trading position in the future: long or short?

What would be your trading position in the call option: long or short?

With the three scenarios below, give the outcomes of the futures and options positions as well as an unhedged position from the firm's perspective.

	Price in 3 mo
Scenario 1	Steel $690
Scenario 2	Steel $600
Scenario 3	Steel $510

Which would you recommend and why?

Step 1: Picture the Problem

This problem involves buying a future or buying the call option to offset price increases in steel.

Step 2: Decide on a Solution Strategy

The futures contract will lock in a price of $610 per ton no matter where prices go. The options contract cost $20 per ton and will only be profitable if prices move above $620. The number of option or futures contracts to use could be as simple as taking the 1 million tons and dividing by the contract size or taking the dollar value of the transaction and dividing by the dollar value of the derivatives. To simplify, assume the 1 million tons is hedged by 1 million tons in derivatives.

Step 3: Solve

Find the payoffs at the expiration date for the derivatives less any costs of ownership and compare to the unhedged costs of acquiring steel.

Steel	Unhedged Costs	Futures Costs	Call Option Costs
$690	$690,000,000	$690M less $80M profit	$690M less $90M profit plus $20M cost
$600	$600,000,000	$600M plus $10M loss	$600M less $0 profit plus $20M cost
$510	$510,000,000	$510M plus $100M loss	$510M less $0 profit plus $20M cost

The future locks in the contract price of $610 as gains or reductions in cost in the market are offset directly by the moves in the futures. The call option costs $620M, $620M, and $530M depending on the outcome due to the asymmetric nature of option payoffs.

If you consider the 10% / 80% / 10% probabilities:

	Unhedged	Futures	Call Option
Expected Values:	$600M	$610M	$611M

Step 4: Analyze

To hedge, the future offers a lower cost compared to the option. Also, the option requires the upfront payment of $20M in premium which is worthless 90 percent of the time. The future is a better hedge in this case however the firm will not benefit the 10 percent of the time when prices move down significantly. Businesses would prefer price certainty over speculation.

Self Test 2: Valuing a Call Option with BSOPM

Consider British Petroleum in the summer of 2010; it was selling for $32 a share and had lost 50 percent of its value in a few months due to the oil spill. You have decided that you wish to speculate that BP returns to $50 per share in 10 months. You also assume that BP cancels all dividends for the next year.

Since there are no 10 month options available on the options exchange, your hedge fund is getting quotes from several bankers willing to sell you an OTC option with a strike price of $35. What is the value of a 10 month option on BP using the following date?

On your Bloomberg terminal, you find the following information on the \$35 strike call closest to 10 months expiry:

British Petroleum

Stock Price	\$32	
Strike Price	\$35	
Risk-free rate	1.2% annual	
Time to expiry	10 months or .8333 of a year	
Volatility	.6 = sd, .36 = variance	high due to spill uncertainty
Dividend	NA, assumed to be \$0	

Step 1: Picture the Problem

Thus, if the option were expiring today it would be not be worth anything. That's because this call option allows you to purchase a share of stock that is selling for \$32 per share for \$35 per share. Use the BSOPM to find the value of the option with 10 months until expiration.

Step 2: Decide on a Solution Strategy

The Black-Scholes option pricing model found in Equation (20–1) provides us with a means of estimating the value of the call option.

Step 3: Solve

To estimate the value of the call option using Equation (20–1) we must first solve for d_1 and d_2 as follows:

$$d_1 = \frac{\ln\left(\frac{\$32.00}{\$35.00}\right) + \left(.012 + \frac{.36}{2}\right) \times \frac{10}{12}}{\sqrt{.36} \times \sqrt{\frac{10}{12}}} = .1285 \qquad N(.1285) = .5511$$

and

$$d_2 = .1285 - \sqrt{.36} \times \sqrt{\frac{10}{12}} = .4192 \qquad N(-.4192) = .3375$$

Now, using Equation (20–1) and the table of areas under the standard normal distribution to calculate the $N(di)$ that can be found in any standard statistics book, we calculate the value of the option as follows:[1]

$$\begin{array}{c}\text{Call Option}\\ \text{Value (Call)}\end{array} = \$32\ (.5511) - \$35\ e^{-.012 \times .833}\ (.3375) = \$5.94$$

[1] We can use the Normdist(*d*) as Normdist(x,0,1,1) or Normsdist(*x*) function in Excel to calculate N(*d*) directly.

Step 4: Analyze

The quotes from your bankers should be a little under $6 per share optioned, around $600 a contract. So a million share bet would be approximately $6,000,000 in option premium. The option's value is $5.94 even though the current stock price is $3.00 less than the strike price. The reason for this is that the stock has the potential for higher value over the next 10 months due to the high volatility which could move it above the strike price of $35.